APPROACHES TO LEGAL ONTOLOGIES

Law, Governance and Technology Series

VOLUME 1

For further volumes:
http://www.springer.com/series/8808

APPROACHES TO LEGAL ONTOLOGIES

Theories, Domains, Methodologies

Edited by

Giovanni Sartor
European University Institute, Florence, Italy

Pompeu Casanovas
UAB Institute of Law and Technology, Bellaterra, Barcelona, Spain

Maria Angela Biasiotti
Ittig-CNR, Florence, Italy

and

Meritxell Fernández-Barrera
European University Institute, Florence, Italy

 Springer

Editors
Giovanni Sartor
European University Institute
Via Boccaccio, Villa Schifanoia 121
50133 Florence
Italy
giovanni.sartor@gmail.com

Maria Angela Biasiotti
Ittig- CNR
Via dei Barucci 20
50127 Firenze
Italy
mariangela.biasiotti@ittig.cnr.it

Pompeu Casanovas
Universitat Autònoma de Barcelona
Institut de Dret i Tecnologia
Facultat de Dret
Campus UAB, Edifici B
08193 Barcelona - Bellaterra
Spain
pompeu.casanovas@uab.es

Meritxell Fernández-Barrera
Universitat Autònoma de Barcelona
Institut de Dret i Tecnologia
Facultat de Dret
Campus UAB, Edifici B
08193 Barcelona - Bellaterra
Spain
Meritxell.Fernandez@EUI.eu

ISBN 978-94-007-0119-9   e-ISBN 978-94-007-0120-5
DOI 10.1007/978-94-007-0120-5
Springer Dordrecht Heidelberg London New York

Printed on acid-free paper

Springer is part of Springer Science+Business Media (www.springer.com)

Foreword: What LGTS Intends to Be

Law is becoming one of the most suitable application domains for technology developments. Annual technology surveys are part of the legal marketplace, and law firms spend a substantial part of their budget specifically for technology, according to the American Bar Association Tech reports. The average law firm spends 6–7% of gross revenue on technology-related expenses. This is correlated with firm size (from 2 to 7%). Small firms (fewer than 200 attorneys) have higher implementation expenses for case management, courtroom technology, docketing software, imaging/scanning/OCR, patch and records management software, while large law firms are more interested in for remote access technology, voicemail upgrades, wireless connections and workflow automation. Over 40% of the firms indicated an average $ 8,000–$ 17,000 spending per attorney. Seventy-two percent of respondents report that the firm files court documents electronically, up from 55% in the 2007 survey. Moreover, according to the 2008 and 2009 ABA Legal Technology Survey Reports, over 97% of lawyers are using mobile technologies.

Usually, researchers split up the IT and Law field into two different domains: (i) *IT law* (Data protection, Copyright, Security, Domain names...), (ii) and *IT for lawyers* (e-Government, e-Court, Online Dispute Resolution, Multi-Agent Systems...). The first area covers regulations and protocols. The second one refers to all the languages, tools, software... that bring support to legal activities at the workplace. This seems quite reasonable.

However, recent developments in semantic technologies, Natural Language Processing (NLP), ontologies, Information retrieval technologies (IR) and the Web 2.0 and 3.0 contribute to the convergence of the two approaches into a single techno-legal one. A lawyer seriously interested in tags and semantic conflicts cannot ignore OWL. A computer scientist developing legal ontologies for procedural legal knowledge must have a clear picture of the court proceedings.

We may distinguish the following scenarios within the general landscape of AI and IT law: (i) Legal Information Retrieval (LIR), (ii) Electronic Data Discovery (E-Discovery), (iii) Collaborative Tools (e.g. Online Dispute Resolution platforms), (iv) Metadata and XML Technologies (for Semantic Web Services), (v) Technologies in Courtrooms and Judicial Offices (E-Court), (vi) Technologies for Governments and Administrations (E-Government), (vii) Legal Multimedia,

(viii) Legal Electronic Institutions (Multi-Agent Systems and Artificial Societies), (ix) The Socio-legal Web (*Blawgs*) and the Web of Data (3.0).

We think that this fast development may be followed up and monitored by research focused on regulations, regulative devices and behavioral patterns. The law field is not only covered by legal drafting, sentencing and contracting as it used to be in the recent past. Technological applications open wide the regulatory field, and new markets—as in the NBIC[1] domain—are just emerging adding complexity to the use of technological solutions.

This is why a new convergence is required: legal norms and principles, governance protocols, social patterns and applied technologies may represent a crossroad. In our global world, legal, ethical and regulatory issues through the Internet and Web Services constitute an interdisciplinary field in which multiple actors are involved: not only lawyers and judges, not only philosophers and legal theorists, but entrepreneurs, businessmen, politicians, policy makers, end-users, customers, consumers and citizens (lay people).

Those are the fundamentals for the *Law, Governance and Technology Series* that the present volume is starting up. LGTS intends to bridge the gap between political and ethical philosophy, legal theory, AI proposals, professional and business applications, and citizens' needs and requirements. This is close to say that LGTS tries to overcome the traditional and old divide between legal research and empirical political science.

Summer 2010   Pompeu Casanovas and Giovanni Sartor
                                                                                    (LGTS Editors)

---

[1] NBIC stands for the convergence between science and technology. Nano-Bio-Cogno-Info: NBIC.

Preface

The ontological approach to information organization is becoming increasingly important in all areas of science, in industry, in government (including defense and intelligence), and now also in the law. Ontologies are (very roughly) standardized terminologies for describing the types of entities that exist in given domains of reality and the relations between them. They provide the basis for a strategy to counteract the silo effects which come into effect wherever data needs to be assembled from multiple different sources, by providing for this data a common mode of description, focusing on the common reality which serves as benchmark for the different providers of data. Through the use of well-structured ontologies heterogeneous data can become more easily integrated, more easily queried, and in principle more easily subjected to domain-transcendent modes of computational reasoning.

The term "ontology" (or "*ontologia*") is of course derived from philosophy, where it seems to have been first used in 1606 in the book *Ogdoas Scholastica* by the German Protestant scholastic Jacob Lorhard. For Lorhard, as for many subsequent philosophers, "ontology" is a synonym of "metaphysics" (a label meaning literally: "what comes after the *Physics*"), conceived as something like the science of being.

The term first began to play a role in the field of computer and information science through the influence of Quine, whose work on the use of first-order logic in the representation of the ontological commitments of, for example, different scientific theories, attracted the attentions of researchers in artificial intelligence such as John McCarthy and Patrick Hayes, who applied Quine's method to the representation of the "naïve physics" that would be needed to guide the actions of a robot. The influence of this work continues today in computational fields such as Knowledge Representation and Conceptual Modeling.

In 1999 there was initiated a second wave of computationally oriented work on ontology, this time in the arena of bioinformatics through the creation of the Gene Ontology (GO). The GO addresses the task of solving the problem of data comparability for biologists working with the results of experiments on mice or fish, who need to draw from these data consequences relevant to the understanding of human health and disease. The problem faced by the GO's biologist authors turned on the fact that each group of model organism researchers had developed its own idiosyncratic vocabularies for describing the phenomena revealed in their respective bodies of data. Most importantly, these vocabularies were inconsistent with the vocabularies used to describe the corresponding phenomena in humans. By providing a solution to these problems in the form of a common, species-neutral, controlled vocabulary covering the entire spectrum of biological processes, the GO has proved tremendously successful, and is almost certainly the first real demonstration case of the advantages brought by ontological technology in supporting the integration of data for scientific purposes.

In a third development, initiated in around 2000 in part as an effect of US Defense Department sponsored research, the term "ontology" began to play a role in what later came to be called the "Semantic Web". This occurred through the medium of the DAML-OIL (DARPA Agent Markup Language—Ontology Inference Layer/Ontology Interchange Language) framework, which served as the basis for the current Web Ontology Language (OWL), a World Wide Web Consortium standard language for ontology representation.

One result of these developments is the growth of a new multidisciplinary field of research on ontology and its applications. It is an interesting historico-cultural phenomenon that Italy has proven to be a world leader in this field. What is almost certainly the world's first ontology research group, on "Conceptual Modeling and Knowledge Engineering" was founded by Nicola Guarino already in 1991 in the LADSEB Institute for Systems Science and Biomedical Engineering in Padua. In 1999 Maurizio Ferraris founded Labont, the Laboratory for Theoretical and Applied Ontology, in the University of Turin. In 2003, Guarino's Padua group merged with the Ontology and Conceptual Modelling Group of the Rome Institute of Biomedical Technologies to form the Laboratory for Applied Ontology with locations in Trento and Rome. One expression of this activity was the establishment of the International Association for Ontology and Its Applications, with Nicola Guarino as initial President.

It is thus fitting that this volume should appear, documenting a seminal meeting on the topic of legal ontology that was held in Fiesole and Florence in December 2008. The volume includes contributions not only from some of the leading practitioners of applied ontology in the legal domain, but also from leading representatives of the science of ontology itself.

Buffalo, NY   Barry Smith

Contents

Contributors

Kevin D. Ashley Learning Research and Development Center, Intelligent Systems Program, and School of Law, University of Pittsburgh, Pittsburgh, PA, USA, Ashley@pitt.edu

Maria Angela Biasiotti Ittig, CNR, Florence, Italy, mariangela.biasiotti@ittig.cnr.it

Eva Blomqvist Semantic Technology Lab, ISTC-CNR, Roma, Italy, eva.blomqvist@istc.cnr.it

Guido Boella Dipartimento di Informatica, Università di Torino, Torino, Italy, guido@di.unito.it

Romain Boulet Université de Toulouse, UPS (OMP) CNRS IRD, Toulouse, France; LMTG, Toulouse, France, romain.boulet@lmtg.obs-mip.fr

Danièle Bourcier CERSA-CNRS, Université de Paris 2, Paris, France, daniele.bourcier@cersa.cnrs.fr

Paul Bourgine CREA-Ecole Polytechnique & Réseau national des systèmes complexes, RNSC, Paris, France, bourgine@poly.polytechnique.fr

Joost Breuker Leibniz Center for Law, University of Amsterdam, Amsterdam, The Netherlands, breuker@science.uva.nl

Pompeu Casanovas Department of Political Science and Public Law, Institute of Law and Technology, Autonomous University of Barcelona, Faculty of Law, Barcelona, Spain, pompeu.casanovas@uab.cat

Núria Casellas Department of Political Science and Public Law, Institute of Law and Technology, Autonomous University of Barcelona, Faculty of Law, Barcelona, Spain, nuria.casellas@uab.es

Luca Cervone CIRSFID, University of Bologna, Bologna, Italy, luca.cervone@unibo.it

Meritxell Fernández-Barrera Law Department, European University Institute, Florence, Italy; Institute of Law and Technology, Autonomous University of Barcelona, Barcelona, Spain, Meritxell.Fernandez@EUI.eu

Carlos Fernández Hernández Research and Development Department, Wolters Kluwer Spain, Madrid, Spain, cafernandez@wke.es

Roberta Ferrario Laboratory for Applied Ontology, ISTC-CNR, Trento, Italy, ferrario@loa-cnr.it

Maurizio Ferraris Department of Philosophy, University of Torino, Turin, Italy, maurizio.ferraris@labont.it

Enrico Francesconi ITTIG-CNR, Institute of Legal Information Theory and Techniques, Italian National Research Council, Florence, Italy, francesconi@ittig.cnr.it

Aldo Gangemi Semantic Technology Lab, ISTC-CNR, Roma, Italy, aldo.gangemi@istc.cnr.it

Jorge González-Conejero UAB Institute of Law and Technology, Autonomous University of Barcelona, Barcelona, Spain, jorge.gonzalez.conejero@uab.es

Nicola Guarino Laboratory for Applied Ontology, ISTC-CNR, Trento, Italy, guarino@loa-cnr.it

Rinke Hoekstra Leibniz Center for Law, University of Amsterdam, Amsterdam, The Netherlands; AI Department, VU University, Amsterdam, The Netherlands, hoekstra@uva.nl

José Manuel Mateo Rivero Research and Development Department, Wolters Kluwer Spain, Madrid, Spain, jmmateo@wke.es

Pierre Mazzega Université de Toulouse, UPS (OMP) CNRS IRD, Toulouse, France; LMTG, Toulouse, France, mazzega@lmtg.obs-mip.fr

Nadia Nadah CNRS UMR 6599 UTC, Cedex, France, nadia.nadah@spim.jussieu.fr

Monica Palmirani CIRSFID, University of Bologna, Bologna, Italy, Monica.Palmirani@unibo.it

Valentina Presutti Semantic Technology Lab, ISTC-CNR, Roma, Italy, valentina.presutti@istc.cnr.it

PierCarlo Rossi Dipartimento di Studi per l'Impresa e il Territorio, Università del Piemonte Orientale, Torino, Italy, piercarlo.rossi@unito.it

Ángel Sancho Ferrer Research and Development Department, Wolters Kluwer Spain, Madrid, Spain, asancho@wke.es

Giovanni Sartor Law Department, European University Institute, Florence, Italy; CIRSFID, Università di Bologna, Bologna, Italy, Giovanni.Sartor@EUI.eu

Barry Smith Department of Philosophy, University of Buffalo, Buffalo, NY, USA, phismith@buffalo.edu

Daniela Tiscornia Ittig, CNR, Florence, Italy, daniela.tiscornia@ittig.cnr.it

Joan-Josep Vallbé Department of Political Science and Public Law, Institute of Law and Technology, Autonomous University of Barcelona, Faculty of Law, Barcelona, Spain, pep.vallbe@uab.es

Fabio Vitali Department of Computer Science, University of Bologna, Bologna, Italy, fabio@cs.unibo.it

Chapter 1
Introduction: Theory and Methodology in Legal Ontology Engineering: Experiences and Future Directions

Pompeu Casanovas, Giovanni Sartor, Maria Angela Biasiotti, and Meritxell Fernández-Barrera

1.1 Legal Ontologies *Come of Age*

Paraphrasing Deborah McGuiness' expression for referring to the maturity of the field of ontology engineering we can say that today legal ontologies have *come of age* (McGuiness 2003). A considerable number of research projects aimed at the application of semantic-web technologies to the legal domain have indeed enabled the accumulation of considerable experience in the field of ontology engineering, which is the activity (and the technology) meant to construct conceptual structures or ontologies (model of concepts and their relationships). Legal ontologies have been proposed as conceptual models for the most diverse legal applications, such as information retrieval, interoperability frameworks and inference drawing, among others. This explains the current wide typology of legal ontologies in terms of granularity (domain-specific vs. core), degree of formality (highly axiomatised vs. lexical or language-oriented), methodologies of development (top–down vs. bottom–up and middle-out), and knowledge sources for concept and term extraction (official legal sources vs. legal expert interview and ethnographic work).

However, as a field of study becomes mature, difficulties and shortcomings of current choices become visible and require collective reflection. The diversity of methodological approaches and theoretical underpinnings in legal ontology engineering indicate both that it is a fertile field in which diverse research programs, rooted in different disciplines, are flourishing (Natural Language Processing, Knowledge Management, Knowledge Engineering, . . .), and that there is a risk of losing coherence among these diverse disciplines if dialogue is not enhanced, with regard to a set of open issues. Firstly, we need to consider the interface between language and ontology, namely how close conceptual models of the law

P. Casanovas (✉)
Department of Political Science and Public Law, Institute of Law and Technology,
Autonomous University of Barcelona, Faculty of Law, Barcelona, Spain
e-mail: pompeu.casanovas@uab.cat

G. Sartor et al. (eds.), *Approaches to Legal Ontologies*, Law, Governance
and Technology Series 1, DOI 10.1007/978-94-007-0120-5_1,
© Springer Science+Business Media B.V. 2011

and their linguistic expression are and consequently what role automated terminology extraction can play in the construction of formal models for the law. Secondly, we need to manage the multilevel complexity of legal knowledge and in particular we need to address the connection between core legal ontologies, domain models and their textual representation. Thirdly, we need to justify epistemological choices regarding the definition of legal knowledge and the selection of its representative sources, and in particular we need to establish whether content patterns specific for the legal domain can be envisaged and are desirable. Fourthly, we need to examine to which extent the formal constraints imposed by ontological structures imply limitations on the complete and faithful representation of legal knowledge, and what is the place of legal ontologies in a comprehensive view of legal knowledge management systems. Furthermore, we need to investigate whether fruitful synergies between legal theory and formal ontological analysis can be obtained, provided that a common ground for reflection is clearly defined.

1.1.1 Legal Ontologies in Legal Thinking

Legal ontologies, while resulting from the new ICT developments above described (and first of all, from the need to bring legal knowledge into the Semantic Web, making it searchable and usable), are connected to some traditional concerns of lawyers and legal academics. On the one hand languages and methods for ontological engineering provide a new way of expressing ideas that have been traditionally part of legal thinking (the idea that legal concepts have a structure and are linked one to another) and on the other hand they enable a critical reassessment of legal thinking and its embodiment in different legal practices.

As it is well known there has been a vast debate in ontological research concerning the object of ontologies and their connection with scientific and common-sense knowledge.

Some of the most known ontologists, such as in particular Barry Smith, have adopted a realistic–scientistic approach. Ontologies must provide us with the structure of reality as it is discovered by science, and indeed ontology is understood as "the science of what is, of the kinds and structures of objects, properties, events, processes and relations in every area of reality" (Smith 2003). This rigorous approach is often contrasted with the view according to which ontologies are meant to provide the structures though which agents conceptualise (possibly wrongly) reality, rather than reality itself. These conceptualisations (regardless of how much there are scientific and objective characterisations of the reality to which they apply) have an interest on their own, especially when one wants to provide people with tools whose functioning reflects people's understanding and categorising of the world. Thus we have seen in recent years the emergence of folksonomies out of people's practice in using the Internet and tagging content. Ways of getting out of the extreme subjectivism to which the ontology-as-conceptualisation approach may lead can be identified in relying on people's consent (or negotiation aimed at consent) on the one hand, and on relying on the nature of our abstract cognitive competence (in the quasi-Kantian perspective developed by Nicola Guarino) or in the outcomes of experimental cognitive sciences (as suggested by Joost Breuker).

With regard to the law the contrast between realism and subjectivism takes a particular dimension. The law has indeed an ambiguous kind of existence: on the one hand it appears as an objective reality, which exists independently of individual desires and beliefs, and indeed constrains human actions; on the other hand it appears to emerge out of human commitments and beliefs, as a convention or an ideology (shared, in particular, among legal officers).

Often there is only a very partial convergence in assessing legal meanings: while on some points (e.g., on the idea that a contract is an agreement) there may indeed be convergence among most or all of the involved agents, with regard to other issues disagreement is ubiquitous (rather than a shared ideology the law appears as being constituted by a set of different views, sometimes overlapping, sometimes diverging, of different individuals and groups). The mixture of convergence and divergence is particularly clear in judicial law-making and in legal doctrine, where judges or authors mention precedents with which they agree but also those with which they disagree. And disagreement increases when one moves out of the legal professions, considering a broader pragmatic context (Casanovas 2009). A specific difficulty in dealing with the law consists indeed in the different perspectives through which the law is approached by people vesting different roles: a judge looks at concepts in order to understand what is the content of the law with regard to the case he is deciding (and to achieve the outcome he sees more legally just or equitable); an attorney tries to see whether such concepts can be given a meaning that supports her client's case; a citizen would like to anticipate the understanding of the judge or of his counterpart (to anticipate possible disputes), a company working in information retrieval focuses on the meaning that its intended users are likely to give to the terms they use in their searches, etc. It has been argued that the uncertainty about the content of legal concepts is only apparent, since it can be overcome by considering that the law itself constitutes its concepts, through its definitions and rules. However it is easy to see that this consideration does not solve the problems of constructing a legal ontology: first of all the law explicitly constitutes only some of its concepts and only in part (relying for the rest in common-sense and the knowledge of legal experts). Secondly, one needs to interpret the legal rules characterising legal concepts to establish how they determine the content of the regulated concepts: one needs concepts for understanding such concept-regulating norms.

It seems to us that the multi-level complexity and diversity involved in legal ontologies supports the main idea of this volume: there is no single approach to address the development of legal ontologies, but rather we have a cluster of problems, perspectives, instruments, and goals that require a plurality of approaches, motivated on theoretical but also on pragmatic grounds. Exploring the diversity of these approaches and how they complement one-another with regard to modelling and problematising legal concepts is indeed one of our fundamental objectives.

1.2 New Directions in Semantic Web Research: Rethinking Ontologies

The development of legal ontology engineering is not driven only by the curiosity of researchers, eager to use new tools to address the eternal problems of legal theory and legal practice. On the contrary, research on legal ontology engineering is mainly driven by the need to develop new computer applications, to better meet the demands of practitioners and citizens, in a framework characterised by an accelerated technological development. In the light of new trends in the broader landscape of semantic-web research the role and the utility of legal ontologies has indeed to be rethought. Research on the engineering of legal ontologies should in particular consider the recent developments questioning the need for a highly axiomatised and unified knowledge representation, and focusing instead on intelligence viewed as the ability to cope with heterogeneous and disperse data, based on different ontologies (Motta and Sabou 2006: 25; Fensel 2008: 3; d'Aquin et al. 2008: 22). This may lead to a new way of designing legal ontologies and of embedding them into architectures for legal information systems and other web services.

At present, more than sixty legal ontologies have been completed. The recent doctoral dissertations of Núria Casellas and Rinke Hoekstra focused on the field of legal knowledge representation and ontology building. More academic dissertations are under way, and several legal ontologies have been set within national and international EU Programs[1] (VI and VII Frameworks). Table 1.1 below reproduces the updating of thirty-three of them by Breuker et al. (2009: 12–14), based on the original André Valente's table (2005: 72).

This table certainly shows the strength and dynamicity of the domain. However, few of these ontologies have gone beyond the stage of advanced and refined prototypes, even scalable and ready for reusing. This is coherent with the industrial surveys on the Semantic Web (Cardoso et al. 2007) in which legal applications are almost invisible. Perhaps LKIF-core and the wide use of upper-top ontologies like DOLCE+ and SUMO in the legal domain are partial exceptions. We believe that this is going to change in the next future, but very likely, to be extensively applied, legal ontologies will have to be combined with other related techniques.

To develop ontologies into the next stage of the web, we have recently identified six challenges coming from the new generation of Semantic Web developers (Casanovas et al. 2010: 5–7): (i) the relationship between the Social Web (Web 2.0) and the Web of Data (Web 3.0); (ii) the construction of evolving and contextual legal ontologies (and their relationship with folksonomies); (iii) the construction of Semantic Legal Web Services (SLWS); (iv) bridging the gap between ITC law and ITC for lawyers; (v) grasping the changing and evolving nature of regulations through the convergence between Web 2.0 and Web 3.0; (vi) adding reasoning and applying dialectic systems to facilitate users' exchanges and legal operations through the web.

---

[1] See a summary of ALIS, ARGUGRID, ASPIC, BEST, DALOS, ESTRELLA, OPENKNOWLEDGE.META-SEARCH, SEAL and SEKT, in Sartor et al. (2008: 8–16).

Table 1.1 Extension of André Valente's table of legal ontologies (Breuket et al. 2009)

Ontology or project	Application	Type	Role	Character	Construction	Language
McCarty's language of legal discourse	General language for expressing legal knowledge	Knowledge representation, highly structured	Understand a domain	General	Manual	English
Valente and Breuker's functional ontology of law	General architecture for legal problem solving	Knowledge base in Ontolingua, highly structured	Understand a domain, reasoning and problem solving	General	Manual	English
Van Kralingen and Visser's frame ontology	General language for expressing legal knowledge, legal KBSs	Knowledge representation, moderately structured (also as a knowledge base in Ontolingua)	Understand a domain	General	Manual	English
Mommer's knowledge-based model of law	General language for expressing legal knowledge	Knowledge base in English very highly structured	Understand a domain	General	Manual	English
Breuker and Hoekstra's LRI-core ontology	Support knowledge acquisition for legal domain ontologies	Knowledge base in DAML+OIL/RDF using Protegé (converted into OWL)	Understand a domain	General	Manual	English
Hoekstra and Breuker's LKIF-core ontology	Support knowledge acquisition for legal domain ontologies	Knowledge base in OWL, highly structured	Understand a domain	General	Manual	English
Gangemi, Sagri and Tiscornia's JurWordNet	Extension to the legal domain of WordNet	Lexical knowledge base in DOLCE (DAML), lightly structured	Organize and structure information	General	Manual	Italian
Benjamins, Casanovas et al. Ontologiy of professional legal knowledge (OPLK)	Intelligent FAQ system (information retrieval) for judges (Iuriservice)	RDF. Knowledge base in Protégé, highly structured (converted in OWL)	Semantic indexing and search	Domain	Semi-automated	Spanish

Table 1.1 (continued)

Ontology or project	Application	Type	Role	Character	Construction	Language
Casellas et al. Ontology of professional judicial knowledge (OPJK)	i-FAQ for judges (Iuriservice, second version)	Last version in OWL. Knowledge base in Protégé, highly structured	Semantic indexing and search	Domain	Manual	Spanish
Lame's ontologies of French codes	Legal information retrieval	NLP oriented (lexical), knowledge base, lexical, lightly structured	Semantic indexing and search	Domain	Automated	French
Leary, Vanderverghe and Zeleznikow's financial fraud ontology	Ontology for representing financial fraud cases	Knowledge base (schema) in UML, lightly structured	Semantic indexing and search	Domain	Manual	English
Asaro et al. Italian crime ontology	Schema for representing crimes in Italian law	Knowledge base (schema) in UML, lightly structured	Organize and structure information	Domain	Manual	Italian
Boer, Hoekstra and Winkel's CLIME ontology	Legal advice system for maritime law	Knowledge base in Protégé and RDF, moderately structured	Reasoning and problem solving	Domain	Manual	English
Lehman, Breuker and Brouwer's legal causation ontology	Representation of causality in the legal domain	Knowledge base lightly structured	Understand a domain	Domain	Manual	English
Delgado et al. PROnto (Intellectual property rights ontology)	Integrating XML DTDs and schemas that define rights expression languages and rights data dictionaries	Knowledge base: first version in DAML+OIL (2001), current version OWL (2008)	Interoperability between digital rights management (DRM) systems	Domain	Manual	English

Table 1.1 (continued)

Ontology or project	Application	Type	Role	Character	Construction	Language
Teodoro, Binefa et al. e-Sentencias (Procedural ontology for multimedia in courts)	Ontology for representing procedural stages of Spanish civil hearings	RDF. Procedural knowledge within Spanish civil hearings (typology)	Diarization and content classification of the official video recordings (image and audio)	Domain	Manual	Spanish
J. Saias, P. Quaresma, Portuguese Attorney office ontology	Ontology to semantically enriching legal texts	OWL and logic programming (ISCO and EVOLP)	Organize and structure information	Domain	Automated	Portuguese
M. Klein, E. Uijtenbroek. A. Lodder, Laymen ontology	Ontology to represent laymen knowledge on liability cases	OWL and NLP. Knowledge base in laymen natural language	Understand a domain (tort law) and interoperability between NL and legal concepts	Domain	Semi-automated	Dutch
J. Breuker. A. Elhag's Crime.NL	Ontology of Dutch criminal law	OKBC	Main structure of (Dutch) criminal law; for comparing European CL	Domain/General	Manual	Dutch/English
S Despres. S. Szulzman Micro-ontology	Ontology to represent concepts in European directives	OWL and NLP (TERMINAE method)	Understand a domain	Domain	Semi-automated	French/English
UCC Ontology J. Shaheed. A. Yip. J. Cunningham	Ontology to represent top-level concepts (e.g. ownership)	NML top-level ontology based on NM	Organize and structure information	Domain (top-level)	Manual	English

Table 1.1 (continued)

Ontology or project	Application	Type	Role	Character	Construction	Language
E. Schweighofer, D. Liebwald's. CLO (Comprehensive legal ontology)	Ontology for information management	Some frame representation		General	Manual with support of legal core ontologies	English?
E. Melz and A. Valente's IRC ontology	Ontology of internal revenue code (USA)	OWL	Reasoning about tax cases	Domain	Manual	English

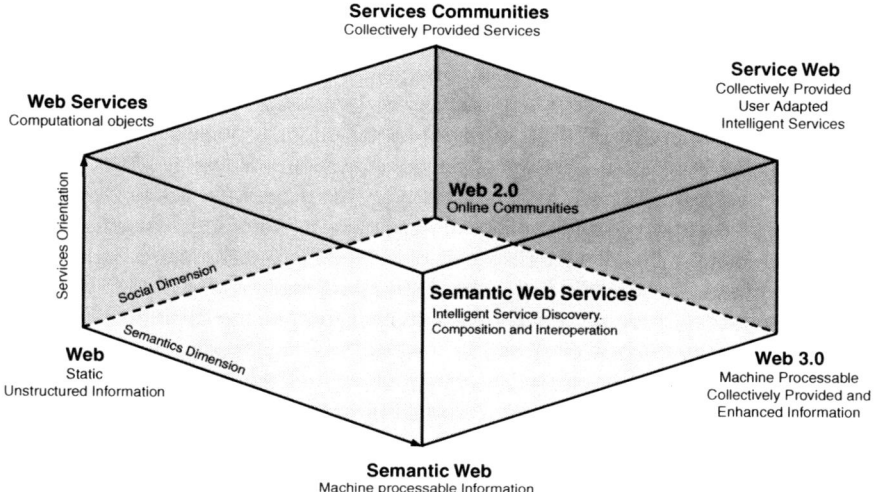

Fig. 1.1 Service web technological pillars. Source: Davies et al. (2009) (quoted with permission)

Especially point number three is interesting here. Web 3.0 is the product of the combination of semantic and social dimensions, and offering service communities is the product of the combination of semantic technology and web services. Figure 1.1 shows the vision of SWS, as recently plotted by SW developers (Davies et al. 2009). This would imply the transformation of Service-oriented Architectures (SOA) into an architecture comprised of billion of services, grounded into the worldwide sharing of content. Well, ontologies for IT law are playing a crucial role in this vision, because its technological features—reusability, autonomy, discoverability and composability—have to be mixed up with legal ontologies (on intellectual property principles, commerce, procedures, negotiation, mediation, security, contracting…) to be properly effective (ibid.). We think that the balance between services provided by humans and machines will be reached only if this new hybrid legal integration is provided.

1.3 Approaches to Legal Ontologies: Experience and Future Directions

Most of the chapters of this volume come from contributions to the workshop *Approaches to Legal Ontologies,* held in December 2008 at the European University Institute of Florence. The workshop gathered several research groups with experience in legal ontologies with the aim of setting up a space for presenting findings, sharing methodological concerns and exchanging ideas about the future of the field. The event was an occasion for bringing together different competences and backgrounds which play a role in legal ontology development. Thus the contributions collected in this book are a faithful representation of the diverse concerns that have driven research on legal-ontology building in recent years. They address the connection between legal-ontology engineering and a diverse set of other disciplines: legal theory, legal sociology, legal pragmatics, comparative law, complex systems theory, computational linguistics, cognitive science, multimedia and other technologies. In the following a brief sketch of the different contributions is presented.

In Chapter 2 Fernández-Barrera and Sartor analyse the value of legal doctrine and legal theory as an intellectual capital for ontology building. After acknowledging the fact that legal theory and legal doctrine represent just a part of legal knowledge, they proceed to analyse the characteristics of conceptual systems created and used by these disciplines. Some preliminary observations are made with regard to the utility of defining conceptual structures for legal contents despite the traditional criticisms based of contextual dependence and open-texture of legal concepts. Then, on the basis of an analysis of the historical works of several scholars different types of legal conceptual systems are identified, ranging from domain-specific to core conceptual structures, and from classical hierarchical organisations of concepts to more complex frame-based structures. The authors conclude that an important conceptual elaboration exists in doctrinal works which could be translated into formal ontological structures. However, due to the informal character of those conceptual systems, they should be carefully studied, problematised and specified before proceeding to their formalisation.

In Chapter 3 Casanovas, Casellas and Vallbé present a methodology for tackling the knowledge-acquisition bottleneck in legal ontology engineering. The *socio-legal* approach proposed by them is based on an empirical approach to data gathering which involves different actors such as legal professionals, legal theorists, socio-legal researchers and engineers. The focus on contextually situated legal knowledge reveals an underlying theory based on legal pluralism and pragmatism which questions the completeness of traditional doctrinal approaches to the law. The approach is illustrated through the description of the design of the Iuriservice system and the construction of the OPJK ontology. The system was aimed at providing Spanish judges in their first appointment with semantically-enhanced access to a repository of practical questions with their answers.

In Chapter 4 Joost Breuker and Rinke Hoekstra anchor the origins of ontology engineering in five disciplines which present different perspectives on the content and the use of ontologies: philosophical Ontology, information science, Artificial Intelligence, Knowledge Engineering, and Information Management. Different applications of ontologies and corresponding formalisms are envisaged by each one of those disciplines. However sometimes the chosen representation formalism is not suitable for the intended application and the authors adduce that this is due to an imprecise distinction between knowledge and semantics. Whereas the former refers to what people know about a term in general, the latter refers to the meaning a term acquires in a particular context. According to the authors, for understanding how terms acquire different meanings (which postulate different ontologies), we need to refer to cognitive science, i.e., to the basic architecture through which humans conceptualise the world according to their basic concerns. Cognitive science can provide the foundation for the most abstract ontological concepts. Thus a common-sense and cognitive-science based core ontology is needed for the legal domain such as the LKIF-Core.

In Chapter 5 Maurizio Ferraris presents a theoretical reflection on the nature of social objects which he conceives to be grounded on a theory of documents. The author starts by assuming that the existence of social objects is located in between physical objects and ideal objects. On the one hand, social objects do not fulfil the requirements for a mere physical existence, since they depend on men thinking about them. On the other hand, social objects, unlike ideal ones, occupy a portion of space and time. Thus Ferraris identifies two essential characteristics of social objects: firstly, their dependence on the existence on human minds; secondly, their dependence on their embedding in text. In this sense, the main conclusion is that social objects are *inscribed acts*

In Chapter 6 Ashley considers the components that an ontology for case-based reasoning systems should have and presents the state-of-the-art of ontologies in such domain. More concretely, the paper identifies three main tasks case-based reasoning ontologies should support: case-based comparisons; distinction between deep and shallow analogies; proposal and test of hypothesis. The extent to which current ontologies can fulfil those tasks is assessed on the basis of an example consisting on a legal classroom discussion that an imagined case-based reasoning system should be able to simulate with the aid of the adequate ontology. The paper concludes that the first task can be already addressed by current state-of-the-art technologies. However further research is needed for meeting the requirements of the other two tasks and in this line the paper contributes to the definition of future research efforts.

In Chapter 7 Mazzega, Bourcier, Bourgine, Nadah and Boulet introduce an innovative approach to legal ontologies inspired on complex systems theory. Their analysis starts from the observation that current legal ontologies are constrained by tree-like structures and thus offer a limited representation of the complexity present in any legal system. In this line, the paper presents a method for enriching a conventional ontological structure with further links between concepts independently of their a priori relations. This further links are based on the mutual information shared by the terms in the corpus, which is measured by information functions, having previously mapped the ontology to the corpus through a probabilistic measure of term occurrence. Furthermore, the analysis can be tailored to different scales, since these probabilistic measures can be applied to different levels of depth (from articles to the whole code or to the whole legal system).

In Chapter 8 Boella and Rossi analyse in detail the crucial role of legal ontologies for ensuring the interoperability of contents stored in different knowledge bases. The authors propose a procedural model based on the multi-level structure of legal information. A modular model of legal knowledge is thus proposed, which relies on the following layers: lightweight ontologies at the first layer, service ontologies at the second layer, an intermediate layer converting service concepts into domain concepts, and finally the fourth layer constituted by the core ontology. The model is illustrated through the research undertaken in the framework of the ICT4LAW project. Ontologies play a pivotal role in the project, since they enable the mapping between norms and the organisation's internal processes and regulations.

In Chapter 9 Biasiotti and Tiscornia approach the linguistic dimension of legal ontologies and its interaction with formal models of legal concepts. The authors put a strong emphasis on the importance of textual sources of the law, which determines the relevance of bottom–up approaches for legal ontology engineering. Ontology learning techniques are considered to be the most effective approach for bridging the gap between dogmatic conceptual constructions and lexical structures in legal sources. Besides the distinction between lexical meaning and conceptual meaning the authors address the challenge of embedding both meanings into modular architectures for legal knowledge representation.

In Chapter 10 Palmirani, Cervone and Vitali propose the enrichment of the CEN Metalex standard with LIDO (Legal Information Document Ontology), a legal-document ontology that enables the description of the legal meaning of textual components. This research is meant to bridge the gap between the mere representation of structural elements of legal text and the representation of their legal meaning. In particular, the LIDO ontology, based on the FRBR ontology, contains the following categories: legal actions affecting the document; legal temporal events; structure of the legal resource; semantic structure of the legal document.

In Chapter 11 Sancho Ferrer, Fernández Hernández and Mateo Rivero discuss the role of ontologies in search technologies for legal databases. The authors highlight the current limitations of ontologies for managing large legal databases since search engines are still unable to exploit them completely. One crucial issue for improving searches is understanding how expert knowledge affects the formulation of search queries. In this sense the paper explores the search behaviour of legal experts and explains why the system performance when using ontologies is still not adequate. The development of a legal dictionary for semantic processing is presented as a possible solution and future research directions are proposed.

In Chapter 12 Gangemi, Presutti and Blomqvist present two proposals for addressing design issues and supporting ontology engineering tasks: Ontology Design Patterns (ODPs) and the eXtreme ontology Design methods. Relying on the idea of design patterns originally developed in the domain of software engineering, ODPs provide solutions for types of problems that are frequently present in ontology design. The paper concentrates on CPs (content patterns), which are small ontologies to be used as basic building blocks in ontology engineering. The eXtreme ontology Design, a set of tools and methods that builds on ODPs for ontology development, is presented and applied in building an ontology for abusive discharges.

In Chapter 13 Francesconi presents a machine learning approach to extracting legal rules from legislative texts for the support of legal ontology building, on the basis of a semantic model of legislation. The semantic model distinguishes Domain Independent Legal Knowledge (which provides a classification of legal rules) and Domain Knowledge (which presents a description on the entities of a particular domain and the relations holding among them). A double methodology is implemented for knowledge extraction, both top–down, illustrated by the definition of a semantic model of legal rules, and bottom–up, consisting in the identification of rules instances in text. The goal of the paper is to strike a balance between consensus among legal knowledge engineers and authoritativeness in systems structured around legal rules by reducing human intervention in rule description.

In Chapter 14 Ferrario, Guarino and Fernández-Barrera reflect on the value of formal ontology for service science and more concretely, for the clear understanding of the legal implications in service-oriented systems. This goal derives from the observation that current service science is lacking suitable semantic representations of business processes in a machine-processable way. In this line, the paper analyses the concept of *service* by using the analytical tools of formal ontology with a particular emphasis on the legal aspects of the notion. A *service* is understood as a complex event where different agents play different roles and assume different responsibilities, and is distinguished from a *good* in the sense that the former is not transferable while the latter, being an object, is.

In Chapter 15 González-Conejero presents the potentialities of ontologies for managing, retrieving and searching multimedia legal files. Indeed, enhancing querying, management and storage capabilities of multimedia contents becomes a crucial issue in several institutional settings (for instance, in Spanish civil courts), when written files are substituted with electronic recordings. The MPEG-7 standard and multimedia ontologies are presented as possible solutions for managing multimedia contents even in the legal domain, provided that some particularities of the structure of judicial procedures are taken into account. The paper discusses the challenge of making explicit what is implicitly represented in images. It points to the role of pattern recognition and emotional speech analysis for tackling this challenge and bridging the semantic gap between concepts extracted from multimedia documents and their formalisation in an ontology.

References

Breuker, J., P. Casanovas, M.C.A. Klein, E. Francesconi (2009). The Flood, the Channels, and the Dykes: Managing Legal Information in a Globalized and Digital World. In J. Breuker et al. (Eds.) *Law, Ontologies and the Semantic Web. Channelling the Legal Information Flood*, Frontiers in Artificial Intelligence and Applications n. 188, IOS Press, Amsterdam, 2009, 3–20.

Cardoso, J. (2007). The Semantic Web Vision: Where We Are. *IEEE Intelligent Systems*, September/October, 2007, 22(5): 84–88.

Casanovas, P. (2009). The Future of Law: Relational Justice, Web Services and Second-generation Semantic Web. In M. Fernández-Barrera, N. Nuno Gomes de Andrade, P. De Filippi, M. Viola de Azevedo Cunha, G. Sartor, P. Casanovas (Eds.) *The Future of Law and Technology*. European Press Academic Publishing, Florence. 137–156.

Casanovas, P., U. Pagallo, G. Sartor, G. Ajani (2010). Introduction: Complex Systems and Six Challenges for the Development of Law and the Semantic Web. In P. Casanovas et al. (Eds.) *Artificial Intelligence and Complex Legal Systems*, LNAI 6237, Springer, Heidelberg, Berlin, 1–11.

Casellas, N. (2009). *Modelling Legal Knowledge Through Ontologies. OPJK: The Ontology of Professional Judicial Knowledge*, Doctoral Dissertation, UAB, 2009, available at http://idt.uab.es/%7Encasellas/nuria_casellas_thesis.pdf.

D'Aquin, M. et al. (2008). Toward a New Generation of Semantic Web Applications. IEEE Intelligent Systems, May/June, 2008, 23(3): 20–28.

Davies, J., M. Potter, M. Richardson, S. Stincić, J. Domingue, R. González-Cabero (2010). Towards the Open Service Web. *BT Technology Journal*, 26(2): 2009, Retrieved at http://www.btplc.com/Innovation/Journal/BTTJ/current/HTMLArticles/Volume26/25Towards/Default.aspx (2010).

Fensel, D. STI Technical Report 2008-01-10, STI Innsbruck, available at http://www.sti-innsbruck.at/fileadmin/documents/SemanticTechnology.pdf.

Hoekstra, R. (2009). *Ontology Representation: Design Patterns and Ontologies that Make Sense*. IOS Press, Amsterdam.

McGuinness, D.L. (2003). Ontologies Come of Age. In D. Fensel, J. Hendler, H. Lieberman, W. Wahlster (Eds.) *Spinning the Semantic Web: Bringing the World Wide Web to Its Full Potential*. MIT Press, Cambridge, MA.

Motta, E., M. Sabou (2006). Next Generation Semantic Web Applications. In R. Mizoguchi et al. (Eds.) [ASWC 2006], *The Semantic Web*, LNCS 4185, Springer, Heidelberg, Berlin, 24–29.

Sartor, G., P. Casanovas, N. Casellas, R. Rubino (2008). Computable Models of the Law and ICT: State of the Art and Trends in European Research. In P. Casanovas et al. (Eds.) *Computable Models of the Law: Languages, Dialogues, Games, Ontologies*, LNAI 4884. Springer, Heidelberg, Berlin, 2008, 1–20.

Smith, B. (2003). Ontology. In L. Floridi(Eds.)*Blackwell Guide to the Philosophy of Computing and Information*. Oxford, MA, Blackwell, 155–166.

Valente, A. (2005). Types and Roles of Legal Ontologies. In R. Benjamins et al. (Eds.) *Law and the Semantic Web: Legal Ontologies, Methodologies, Legal Information Retrieval, and Applications*, LNAI 3369. Springer, Heidelberg, Berlin, 2005, 65–76.

Chapter 2
The Legal Theory Perspective: Doctrinal Conceptual Systems vs. Computational Ontologies

Meritxell Fernández-Barrera and Giovanni Sartor

2.1 Introduction. Legal Doctrine and Legal Theory as a Source for Building Legal Ontologies

If ontologies are understood as the formal description of a domain of discourse (Antoniou and Van Harmelen 2008 [2004]: 11) then legal ontologies can be considered the formal description of the domain of legal discourse. A decision to make is, therefore, what counts as "legal discourse". However, it is difficult to identify one single legal discourse since it has been highlighted that different levels of legal language exist (Tiscornia 2005), among which we can identify the following: (i) the discourse of the legislator (laws and regulations); (ii) the discourse of the judges (judgements and other judicial decisions); (iii) the discourse of the doctrine (studies on several legal subdomains, systematising legislator and judges' discourses); (iv) the discourse of legal theory (legal works having a general content, not addressing a particular legal system).

Furthermore, limiting our view on legal discourse to the four previous kinds of discourse, amounts to having a restricted approach to the law, which only considers certain classes of legal documents as relevant sources of the discourse to be considered: the documents representing authoritative sources of the law (legislation and case law), plus the published academic comments on such sources and more abstract reflections (doctrine and theory). This corresponds to explicit legal knowledge, codified in specific and standardised ways by the legal community[1] (bills, laws, articles published in legal journals, judicial decisions, ...). Nevertheless, the law can be seen as well as a set of practices (actions, ways of reasoning, language uses ...) by legal professionals and of interactions between citizens (contracts, customs). In

---

M. Fernández-Barrera (✉)
Law Department, European University Institute, Florence, Italy; Institute of Law and Technology.
Autonomous University of Barcelona, Barcelona, Spain
e-mail: Meritxell.Fernandez@EUI.eu

[1] A rich literature exists on the definition of *explicit knowledge*, usually to contrast it with *implicit knowledge*. A landmark contribution to the distinction is (Polanyi 1966), where explicit knowledge is defined as codifiable knowledge due to its propositional form. On the contrary, implicit knowledge is usually non propositional and therefore difficult to codify.

G. Sartor et al. (eds.), *Approaches to Legal Ontologies*, Law, Governance and Technology Series 1, DOI 10.1007/978-94-007-0120-5_2,
© Springer Science+Business Media B.V. 2011

particular we can speak of an implicit or unspoken law that we can refer to as the discourse of legal practice. On the one hand, this includes practical legal professional knowledge[2] that goes beyond codified legal knowledge in the aforementioned forms (legislation, case-law, doctrine, legal theory) and consists in the know-how that tells how to apply codified knowledge in concrete situations.[3] Very much related to the paradigm of situated cognition,[4] this knowledge is acquired through experience rather than by formal training, it is unequally distributed among the members of the community and it is difficult to elicit. On the other hand, the discourse of legal practice includes the so-called "mute law", which has been frequently neglected by legal scholars and has rather been object of study by legal anthropology (Sacco 1995). This consists in common citizens' interactions beyond legally conceptualised situations and relations, thus including factual behaviours.

Written form accompanies sometimes as well these types of informal or implicit legal knowledge, but since it is not codified knowledge, its written forms are not archived orderly and in standardised formats (letters to clients and parties, summons, legal discussions over the Internet, etc.), so it is difficult to analyse them systematically. This is probably where the methods of legal doctrine require the contribution of the methodologies and approaches of legal sociology and legal anthropology,[5] for

---

[2]Not necessarily limited to traditional legal professions (lawyers, barristers, judges, . . .), but including other professionals having somehow to do with the law, such as mediators, economists, university professors, or the so-called *paralegal* professionals (Casanovas 1998).

[3]This corresponds to the notion of *personal knowledge and capability* as defined by Eraut (1997, 1998): "what individual persons bring to situations that enables them to think, interact and perform", and which includes: "Codified knowledge[0] in the form(s) in which the person uses it; know-how in the form of skills and practices; personal understandings of people and situations; accumulated memories of cases and episodic events (Eraut, 2000a, 2004e); other aspects of personal expertise, practical wisdom and tacit knowledge; self-knowledge, attitudes, values and emotions." (Eraut 2007). Similarly, in the legal field, "professional knowledge of a legal topic [. . .] involves a particular knowledge of: (i) statutes, codes, and legal rules; (ii) professional training; (iii) legal procedures; (iv) public policies; (v) everyday routinely cases; (vi) practical situations; (vii) people's most common reactions to previous decisions on similar subjects. (Casanovas et al. 2006: 266).

[4]*Situated cognition* is a transdisciplinary notion that applies to a wide range of scientific domains (social sciences, linguistics, animal cognition, evolutionary biology, . . .) and that more concretely was manifested in cognitive sciences and AI research as *systems thinking*, which implies studying things in a holistic way, as a dynamic and complex whole located in an environment (Clancey 2008). This approach has been very controversial in psychology and cognitive science as well as in AI (Ibidem), since it seems to question the orthodox physical symbol system hypothesis (for a theoretical analysis of the opposed views and an attempt to bring them together them see Slezak (1999); for a taste of the discussion see the response of Clancey (1992) to Sandberg and Wielinga's critical paper with regard to situated cognition (1992)). Situated cognition highlights precisely the non propositional and environmental aspects of knowledge and this is why it can be considered one of the foundations of a theory of practical legal knowledge.

[5]It is acknowledged that evidence of personal knowledge must come from observations of performance in order to have a holistic rather than a fragmented approach to knowledge, since the knowledge used in particular situations is available in a compiled form ready to be used (Eraut 2007).

instance ethnographic work on the ways of action and interaction of judges, lawyers in the institutional setting (at the court) and outside it (relationship with clients, . . .).

Bearing in mind that they cover just a part of the multilevel structure of legal knowledge, in this paper, we concentrate on the third and the fourth kind of legal discourse, namely, the discourse of doctrine and legal theory.[6] We think that in this kind of legal discourse (i) we find the intellectual roots of the conceptual structures used in legal reasoning; and (ii) we can find useful insights in order to build legal ontologies, either in the form of core legal conceptual constructions or domain-specific notions. Indeed, the particularity of legal doctrine and theory is that they try to identify, define and organise in broader conceptual structures the objects[7] of the domain. In this sense legal doctrine could be seen as an intellectual capital to be reused in ontology building in the same way that Ontology as a traditional branch of metaphysics contributes to the conceptual distinctions made in upper or foundational ontologies.

2.2 Legal Concepts: Striking a Balance Between Legal Interpretation and Ontological Categories

The possibility and the utility of constructing structures of concepts in the legal domain has always been controversial. One important reason for being sceptical about structuring legal concepts resides in the fact that this idea seems to presuppose that legal concepts have a certain degree of stability (context independence), i.e., that we can identify different occurrences of the same concept in legal texts and in legal practice (usually constituting the meaning of all occurrences of the same words in different legal texts). For instance, embedding the concept of "document" in a structure of legal concepts (while linking this concept to linguistic expressions to be found in legal discourse) seems to presuppose that it is possible to view this concept as the meaning of the different occurrences of the term "document".

If legal language was so context-dependent that the legislator would ascribe different meanings to each different occurrence of the term "document", and even different judges would express different meanings whenever using this term in motivating their decisions (concerning the validity of documents or other similar issues), then having the concept "document" in a conceptual structure would be of dubious utility: this concept would not provide the meaning of most occurrences of the word "document" in legal language, and similarly, the structural links pertaining to this concept might not apply to the (different) concepts expressed by the various occurrences of the word document.

As we shall see in the following, one may still want to provide a structure of concepts for legal thinking, but then one would abandon the goal of providing directly

---

[6]For a focus on the fifth type of legal discourse see Casanovas and Casellas socio-legal approach (Casanovas, Casellas and Vallbé 2010), in this volume.

[7]We will be using objects as a synonymous of concepts.

the meanings of the terms in legal language, and the semantic relationships between such meanings. One would rather provide a conceptual structure relatively independent from the practised legal language, which would have to be mapped to the different words used in legal discourse, and the different ways in which the occurrences of such words are used.

The idea that legal concepts have a stable meaning (which is maintained in the linguistic expressions of different norms, taking place in different contexts) is questioned by three characteristic aspects of the law:

– the dependency of legal concepts on legal norms
– the dependency of legal norms on (the interpretation of) terms in authoritative documents
– the dependency of interpretations of legal norms on the pragmatics of the different situations in which norms have to be applied.

In this section we shall consider how these dependencies impact on legal ontologies and how and within what limits we can save legal ontologies from this challenge.

2.2.1 The Mutual Dependence of Legal Concepts on Legal Norms

Legal concepts are dependant on legal norms since they may be expressly defined by legal norms, or since they may be implicitly defined by them. Let us firstly consider explicit definitions. For our purpose we may restrict our analysis of explicit definitions to the most evident forms of them, i.e., to those definitions having a metalinguistic form, i.e., ascribing a particular meaning to a term. Consider for example the following definition, contained in the EU data protection directive (Directive 95/46/EC of the European Parliament and of the Council):

(a) "personal data" shall mean any information relating to an identified or identifiable natural person ("data subject"); an identifiable person is one who can be identified, directly or indirectly, in particular by reference to an identification number or to one or more factors specific to his physical, physiological, mental, economic, cultural or social identity;

Here is the definition which can be found instead in the Italian legislation (art. 4a of the data protection code, Legislative Decree no. 196 of 30 June 2003)

(a) "personal data" shall mean any information relating to natural or legal persons, bodies or associations that are or can be identified, even indirectly, by reference to any other information including a personal identification number;

Let us observe the difference of the two definitions: they indeed do not identify the same concepts, the main difference being that "personal data" according to the EU definition only covers data concerning a physical person (a human) while the Italian definition also includes data concerning "legal persons, bodies or associations". One may also wonder whether the very different wordings of the two documents are meant to indicate conceptual difference or not. These two definitions exemplify two aspects of the typical legislative definition: the definition on the one hand characterises a concept, and on the other hand ties that concept to a term. In fact the usual normative effect of the definition is that all occurrences of the term within the text containing it have to be understood in the defined sense. This normative effect usually also applies to subsequent documents containing that term, unless there are reasons to the contrary, and it may cover as well preceding ones (if this fits with the purposes the new definition is aiming at, according to the assumed intention of the legislator) Thus a legislative definition is a norm that on the one hand establishes a concept (so that the concept is dependant on that norm) and on the other hand contributes to determine the meaning of other norms (so that these norms are dependant on the concept). This means that not only one needs to interpret the norms containing the defined concepts on the basis of the definition, but also that when interpreting the defining norm one must consider what impacts this will have on the norms where the term occurs. For instance, the Article 29 Data Protection Working Party (a body providing advice on data protection, established according to art. 29 of the Data protection directive, 95/46/EC) describes in this way the task of understanding the definition of the term "personal data": "Working on a common definition of the notion of personal data is tantamount to defining what falls inside or outside the scope of data protection rule". On the one hand the legislator, when defining a concept (the meaning of a legislative term) is performing a normative function, i.e., specifying the content of the norms in which the term to be defined appears, on the other hand the interpreter, when determining the meaning of the legislative definition, is participating in the same function.

Note also that the wording of a legislative definition is usually insufficient to enable a full characterisation of the defined concepts. With regard to the concept of "personal data", for instance the Article 29 Data Protection Working Party provides a 26 pages analysis, where it is discussed how this notion has to be understood, and applied to different cases. It must also be observed that it would be absurd, for the purpose of understanding the legal notion of "personal data", to rely only on the common-sense understanding of the terms from which the legislative definition results, i.e., "any information", "relating to", "an identified or identifiable". The abstract conceptual meaning of these terms (i.e. the meaning we may assign to them when they are not linked to a particular context) only is the starting point for understanding what they mean in the particular context we are considering (i.e., the context where they are providing the definition of "personal data" for the Data Protection directive). In other contexts—for instance, when the information to be regulated is technological know-how, when it is discussed whether an invention is "relating to" a particular industrial process, when it is required that the origin of a product is "identified or identifiable" for consumer protection—the same terms acquire distinct meanings (related to the different function they are performing), for which considerations developed in the Opinion of the Article 29 Working party have little or no relevance. For instance, in this opinion it is said that even dynamic IP addresses, assigned by Internet provides, are to be considered as pertaining to an identifiable person (even though they are assigned to a connection, rather than to a person, and only for the duration of that connection). Such considerations have little relevance for establishing when the producer of a good is identifiable from the label of that good. Since the purpose of the requirement of "identifiability" with regard to producers it to enable consumers to easily (without effort) identify the producer, a much clearer indication is needed for a producer to be "identifiable" from the good than for a person to be identifiable from his or her data: if a label included the indication "Manufactured by the producer owning the computer to which provider Wind assigned dynamic IP number 72.47.223.123 on 13 February 2009, from 12.00 to 13:00" we would not consider that it makes the producer identifiable for the purpose of consumer protection (though the producer will be identifiable, according to the Opinion of the Article 29 Working party, for the purpose of data protection).

Besides being defined explicitly, the meaning of a legal concept can also be defined implicitly, i.e., through its use within legal discourse (and in particular within legislative discourse). This happens in various ways. Sometimes the legal norm indicates that the concept applies to certain entities under certain conditions (that such entities, under such conditions count as instances of the concept); for instance, it may say that also a three wheeled vehicle is (counts as) a motorcycle, so that it may be driven with a motorcycle licence, or that a frog is a fish, so that the prohibition to take fish also applies to frogs. In other cases the law states what conditions originate the event or state of affairs described by a legal concept and what follows from such a normative state of affairs. Consider for instance the rules stating under what conditions a contract comes into existence, is terminated, and what the legal effects of a contract are, the rules establishing when citizenship is acquired and what is entailed by being a citizen, or the rules establishing when one acquires and loses ownership, and what are the rights and duties of an owner (for a discussion of some views on this issue, see Sartor 2009).

Consequently, legal semantics is determined (among other things) by legal doctrine, to the extent that doctrine determines, identifies or constructs legal norms on the basis of the sources of law. The discussion concerning the meaning of a legal concept in a legal system concerns establishing what norms -leading to, or departing from, the term expressing the concept- hold in that system. Since the inferential links holding in a legal system represent, or are derivable from, norms of such a system, this discussion is inseparable from the doctrinal issues concerning what legal norms belong to a legal system (given the available legal material, such as legislation, precedent, custom, and so on) and consequently constitute correct premises of legal reasoning with regard to that system. On the one hand, when we argue that in a given legal system certain preconditions determine the application of a concept and that certain consequences follow from it, we are arguing that certain norms exist in such a system, according to a certain interpretation. On the other hand, when we consider whether a certain norm exists in a legal system we must take into account the conceptual network in which the norm participates: if the norm links a conceptual qualification to certain preconditions, we must consider what consequences other norms connect to that qualification; if the norm provides consequences of a certain conceptual qualification, we must consider what preconditions entail this qualification.

In fact, by constructing in a certain way (through doctrinal interpretation/con\-struction) the meaning of a certain concept in a legal system we contribute to determining the substantive legal conclusions derivable according to that system. Consequently, we will argue for one or the other interpretative construction of the relevant norms, according to what conclusions, derivable according to such norms, we believe better fit (the values and principles we associate with) the considered legal system.

Consider, for instance, the recent debate about torture, where the absolute prohibition of torture[8] has been recently questioned with regard to the treatment of suspect terrorists. A lawyer believing that the law permits infliction of pain on detainees for the purpose of extracting useful information has two ways to go about showing that this is the case: the lawyer can take either a restricted view of the conditions for applying the concept of torture (requiring, for instance, that permanent physical damage is caused, so as to exclude that there is torture when pain is inflicted without such an effect) or a restricted view of the consequences of qualifying an act as torture (assuming that only certain kinds of tortures are always forbidden, while other kinds of torture are in certain circumstances permissible). Correspondingly, a lawyer believing, on the contrary, that the law never permits any infliction of pain for the purpose of extracting information will claim that every pain inflicted for this purpose qualifies as torture, and will claim as well that the law prohibits every act of torture regardless of the form it may take. The two lawyers, in offering what they view as justified conditions for qualifying an act as torture or as justified consequences following from this qualification, will characterise in different ways the concept of torture, and this will have relevant deontic implications (the first characterisation of torture permits certain actions on detainees, actions which the second characterisation prohibits). As this example shows, the characterization of legal concepts is no neutral activities: it concerns establishing what norms hold in a legal system and thus what norms have to be applied by judges and imposed upon the party. It is not an activity dealing with mere descriptive linguistics: it is rather a central aspect of legal interpretation.

---

[8] As stated in Art. 5 of the Universal Declaration of Human Rights: "No one shall be subjected to torture or to cruel, inhuman or degrading treatment or punishment."

2.2.2 Why Systems of Legal Concepts May Still Be Useful: The Interplay of Theoretical, Doctrinal and Sociological Analysis of Legal Contents

We cannot provide here a detailed analysis of the reasons why the endeavour of building structures of legal concepts can be challenged. Let us just mention some of these reasons (for a more detailed account see Sartor 2009):

- Legal change may question the validity of conceptual hierarchies. As the law evolves, new inferential links are introduced -by the legislator, by precedents, by custom- newly associating a legal concept to a certain condition or a certain effect, or dissociating the concept from one of its pre-existing conditions or effects. In introducing such new inferential links, conflicts with existing conceptual structures, as resulting from definition and from taxonomic inheritance, are inevitable, and inevitably legal evolution is to prevail over static conceptual hierarchies.
- Definition cannot fully capture the meaning of legal concepts. In fact to determine what preconditions and effects characterise a certain concept we must also consider what can be obtained through correct interpretation of laws and cases, what emerges from customs and other legally relevant social interactions, etc.
- a definitional approach to legal concepts appears even more unable to fully capture the legal meanings, if we include among the relevant inferential links those emerging from legal practice, such as non-verbalised attitudes of legal reasoners.
- the preconditions for applying a concept make the concept dependent upon the reasons justifying its application, while effects deriving from the application of the concept indicate what conclusions the concept is a reason for. Such reasons can be supported by rationales, and they can be attacked by contrary reasons (reasons why the concept should not be applied or why we should not, given certain situations, derive its conclusions). These underlying dialectics get lost when we take a definitional attitude.
- In order to enable the relevant values and interests to be realised through the application of the law in different contexts and across different subject matters, we need to shape legal inferential links (legal norms) in the ways that best promotes such values and interests. This may lead us to abandon terminological consistency: for instance, we may need to understand causality in different ways in private and criminal law, or to conceive good faith differently with regard to customers and to professionals, to differentiate notions of fault and negligence, and so on.

The considerations we have developed exclude that we can assume that any ontology fully captures the meaning of legal concepts, and the meanings of the words that in legal discourse are used for expressing such concepts. However, this does not make useless the attempt to organize legal meanings into conceptual structures. We need to be able to pack inferential information into legal terms, and to use this information according to terminological relationships. Without terminological information, we would not be able to make sense of the textual formulations of legal norms and of the connections between norms having different levels of abstraction. Without the inheritance across conceptual hierarchies, legal regulations would become a chaos of useless repetitions. And specifying the meaning of legal concepts and their relations helps us in better understanding legal norms and the commitments we undertake when representing legal information and addressing legal issues.

There is indeed a feedback circle involved in constructing legal norms, where the assignment of a meaning to a term and the teleological interpretation of the norms including that term go together: on the one hand we start with a preexisting understanding of the term at issue, then we refine our understanding of the term on the basis of teleological considerations concerning the norms where the term appears, which may lead us to revise the understanding of one or more instances of the occurrences of that term. There is also a complex relationship between common language and legal language, where the law inherits in principle the terminology of common language (words like "fish", "wine", "food", "harm", "pain", "parent", etc.), but then may redefine these words, either through the legislator's definitional or qualifying statements, or through legal interpretation.

Thus we need to consider the conflict between legal interpretation and ontology as a dialectical balance and co-evolution, rather than as a merely destructive confrontation. This requires that lawyers (and ontological engineers working with legal knowledge) have the ability to continuously adjust their onto-terminological constructions as the law evolves (taking into account the need to implement legal values), and at the same time to make conceptual analyses bear on the interpretation of legal norms and on the solution of legal cases.

In conclusion, the task of providing an analysis of the meaning of such legal concepts does not pertain uniquely or mainly to legal ontology as a separate discipline. It rather pertains to legal theory, legal doctrine and legal sociology, and such disciplines can use the tools provided by ontological research in order to better specify their proposals and findings. On the other hand work on computational ontology (for purposes such as information retrieval or knowledge representation) should use the inputs provided by legal theory, legal doctrine and legal sociology in order to develop legal conceptual structures appropriate to the purposes the ontologies being developed are meant to serve. Constructing systems of legal concepts involves thus different approaches to legal knowledge in a complementary way.

2.3 Systems of Legal Concepts in Legal Doctrine

The potential connection between computational legal ontologies and legal doctrine is the common concern for the conceptualisation of the law. Nevertheless, it cannot be trivially assumed that the formal structure of the conceptual networks found in doctrinal classifications is similar enough to the formal structure of computational ontologies and some kind of analysis is required to see how and to which extent the two structures can be mapped.

2.3.1 System of Concepts, Their Topological and Semantic Properties and Methodology for Exploring Them

In our analysis of legal concepts will rely on the following notion of *system of concepts* or *conceptual system*:

> A conceptual system can be conceived as a network in which each node corresponds to a concept and each line in the network corresponds to a link between concepts (Thagard 1992: 30).

Furthermore, since the links between concepts have a semantic nature, a conceptual system can be regarded as a semantic network. Two issues are thus relevant for the analysis of a conceptual system; on the one hand, the *topological structure* that it gives place to, i.e., the architecture of the links between the concepts (namely, a tree, a rooted tree –the one with a unique beginner or root element-, . . .); and on the other hand the *semantic relations* expressed by the lines that unite the nodes in the network[9] (this relation can be an inclusion relation –is-a-, a meronymic relation –part-of-, . . .). In this context, we should be able to answer these two questions:

- Are the conceptual structures of ontologies and doctrinal legal classifications equivalent with regard to their topological structure?
- Are the conceptual structures of ontologies and doctrinal legal classifications equivalent with regard to the semantic relations expressed by the links between their nodes?

With regard to the analysis of topological structure a methodological precision is required). Our analysis is limited to the explicit links made by the authors between concepts.[10] The definition of what counts as an explicit link is controversial, but here it will be assumed that two ways exist for expressing it: either textually or graphically. This has effects on the cognition of legal contents. In the first case it will be necessary to do a complete reading of the text in order to extract the elements of the system of concepts and infer their relations; in the second case the graphical representation makes easier the cognition of the classificatory structure. When an

---

[9] The relevance of the explicit understanding of the intended meanings for various types of arcs and links in semantic network structures has been highlighted by Woods (1975).

[10] Ontologies and databases are indeed constrained by an external set of rules whereas a graph is not necessarily constrained and can reflect an emergent system itself, with no external control (Bales and Johnson 2006: 453). If we limit ourselves to explicit conceptual systems as presented by legal doctrine, we are accepting the restrictions imposed by external rules of organisation of concepts, such as the correct construction of a taxonomy following the Aristotelian method of division by *genus* and *differentia*. The method of division is presented by Aristotle in *Posterior Analytics*: "It is such attributes which we have to select, up to the exact point at which they are severally of wider extent than the subject but collectively coextensive with it; for this synthesis must be the substance of the thing." Nevertheless, the method of division, consisting in the knowledge of how to divide forms into kinds, was already proposed by Plato in the *Phaedrus* and described in more detail in the *Sophist*.

explicit verbal description is made of a system of legal concepts, the author usually puts a special emphasis in marking linguistically the conceptual structure by using specific linguistic markers that describe the structure (such as *x **are divided in** y and z; there are **n types of** x*; . . .), for instance, in Gaius division of persons: *"The **principal division** of the ius of persons is the following, namely, that all men are **either** free **or** slaves"*. When the system of concepts is presented graphically through a schematic representation, the diagrammatic lay-out replaces linguistic markers and the information is transmitted directly through the interpretation of the image. Even if some instances can be found in legal history (see Fig. 2.1), the diagrammatic representation of systems of legal concepts is not very usual in the legal domain unlike in other domains.

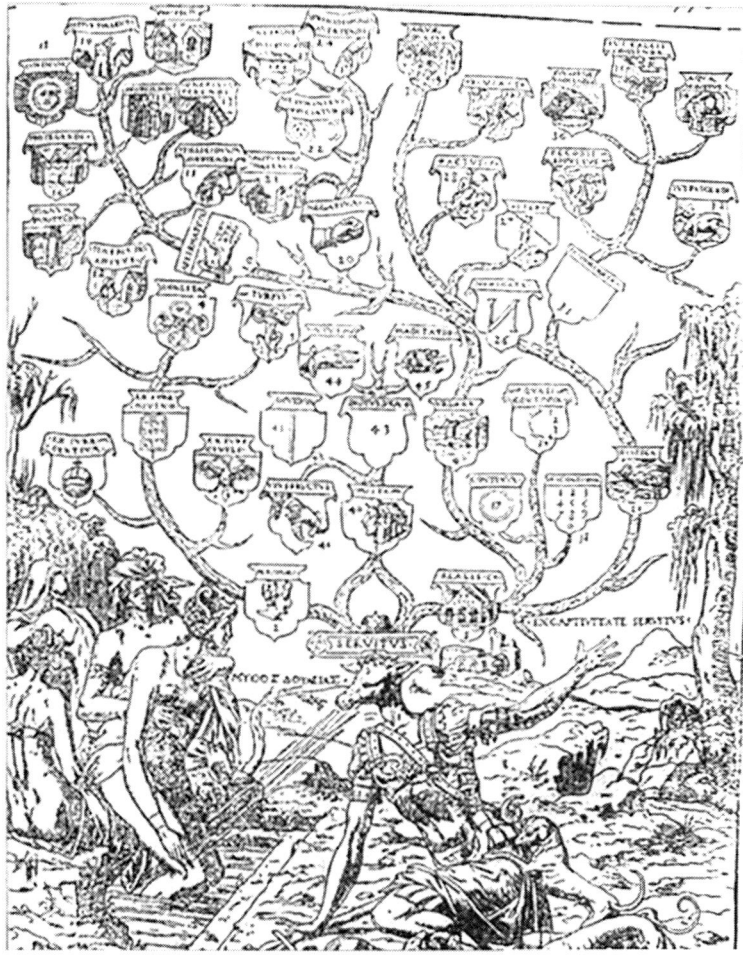

Fig. 2.1 Arbor servitutum. From the 1548–1550 edition of the Corpus Juris Civilis, Digestus Vetus, p. 770 (Source: Hayaert 2007: 319)

This is why the conceptual systems that will be presented in this paper have been manually constructed on the basis of explicit linguistic structures whereby the author of the text marks class subsumption, generic semantic relations or other semantic links.

However, it is conceivable that other more complex conceptual graphs can emerge from the statistical analysis of the corpuses composed by legal doctrinal texts. Further analysis in this direction using current statistical approaches combined with Natural Language Processing Techniques could reveal implicit conceptual systems emerging from doctrinal texts and propose new analytical approaches of traditional legal theory, as well as put them more accurately in connection with structural features of computational ontologies.

2.3.2 System of Concepts in Ontologies

A conceptual system, according to the definition provided above, consists of concepts and links between them. In ontologies the system of concepts follows a pre-established scheme, usually taking the form of a rooted tree, where concepts are organised vertically, from more general to more specific.

For instance, let us consider the fragment of the DALOS[11] domain ontology shown in Fig. 2.2: the topological structure is that of a rooted tree, with a single initial element (Thing) further divided into the branches of Activities, Agent, Object, Quality and Region. Other nodes span out from these branches, giving place to new branches. For instance, Object is divided into Physical-object and Social-object, from which further branches of the tree fan out.

The semantics of the arches linking the nodes of the tree in Fig. 2.3 is an inclusion or is-a relation, which is the creator of the ontological backbone: the taxonomy of entities. In the case of the DALOS ontology we can observe, for instance, that Social-Object is-a kind of Object, and Object is-a kind of Thing.

However, in DALOS ontology semantic cross-references -not directly represented in the tree-like structure of Fig. 2.2—are established through the definition of properties. For instance, the property *provides-information-on* has as its domain information-object and as its range has, among other concepts, agent. There exists, thus, in fact, a semantic relation linking agent and information-object, although these concepts are not directly linked through the *is-a* relation represented in the tree-like structure. Due to these further semantic links represented through properties the actual structure of the semantic network

---

[11]The EU DALOS project (Drafting Legislation with Ontology-Based Support) is aimed at providing legislators with control over legal concepts and the corresponding vocabulary across several European languages. The DALOS domain ontology represents the consumer law and was manually built with the aid of NLP support (Agnoloni et al. 2007, Francesconi et al. 2007).

```
Thing
      Activities
      Agent
              Legal-person
              Natural-person
   Object
          Physical-object
                  Immovable-property
                  Movable-property
                  Physical-agent
          Social-object
                  Economic-object
                  Information-object
                  Legal-object
```

Fig. 2.2 Fragment of DALOS ontology of consumer law

Fig. 2.3 Taxonomic
semantic relations (*is-a*) in
DALOS ontology

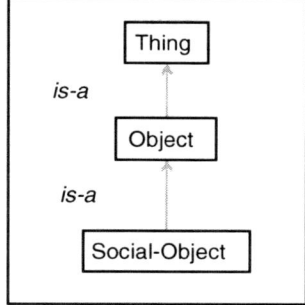

is much more complex than the initial taxonomy (although the network follows anyway the organizational schema established by the designer).

2.3.3 Systems of Concepts in Legal Doctrine

If we apply to the legal domain the definition of "systems of concepts" provided above we will obtain that:

A *system of legal concepts* or *legal conceptual system* is a network in which each node corresponds to a legal concept and each line in the network corresponds to a link between legal concepts.

In this sense, legal classification understood as the definition and organisation of legal objects or concepts is the task that gives place to systems of legal concepts. This is precisely one of the ways in which doctrine contributes to the systematisation of the legal system.[12] Doctrine builds theories in which each concept has its definition, for the classificatory order relies on the features specified in the definitions. For instance, contract theory will define: *contract* as a legal transaction with certain properties (and therefore as a subclass of *legal transaction*), *parties* as natural or legal persons that participate in a legal transaction (and therefore as a role of the classes *natural person* and *legal person*), and so on. The relevance of the definition and organisation of legal concepts is the design of a conceptual map of the domain, a structured universe of discourse shared by domain experts that enables their communication and mutual comprehension. In other words, it is the creation of a knowledge system.[13] In this sense, when a legal scholar speaks of *contract* any other domain expert should be able to recognise the concept and therefore know what kind of entity the term refers to. Nevertheless, the conceptual map of the domain does obviously not remain always the same, but a certain conceptual dynamics exists, a sort of evolution of legal conceptual systems due to changes in regulation or to judicial interpretation that either modifies the intensional[14] or extensional[15] definition of concepts, or creates new concepts. Sometimes even new subsystems will be created, like labour law, consumer law, ... (Collins 1997: 64). Doctrinal systems of legal concepts can be thus considered dynamic conceptual systems, just like scientific conceptual systems are (Thagard 1992).

The most significant efforts to provide the definition of a basic conceptual language of the law took place during the XIXth century. Indeed, partly influenced by the positivist paradigm, partly driven by the desire to give law a scientific methodology, decades of legal research were committed to this endeavour. Apart from the philosophical underpinnings of the effort, practicalities were as well at issue, for the development of a common terminology for legal reasoning was deemed essential for achieving clarity and correctness in legal thought. In the common law sphere several scholars refer indeed to the need of establishing a clear usage of legal terms that would free legal discourse from obscurity (for instance Bentham, Austin and Wigmore). This is the stream of thought corresponding mainly to analytical jurisprudence, with roots in Bentham's thought and that starting from Austin's *The*

---

[12]It has been highlighted that there exist different levels of legal systematization: (i) systematization of legal concepts; (ii) systematization of legal rules in institutions and branches of the law according to the piece of reality that they regulate; (iii) systematization of legal rules on the basis of the values they pursue and their justification; (iv) systematization of those values themselves, establishing an axiological hierarchy (Renauld 1958). Legal doctrine is not always clear as to the object of systematization or classification, as highlighted by Pound (1924: 941): "[...]it is not uncommon for analytical jurists, assuming to classify 'the law', to move, without apparent consciousness of the transition, from classification of legal precepts to classification of the subject matter of legal precepts, or to classification of the institutions by which that subject matter is made effective by means of legal precepts, and vice versa."

[13]On the idea of legal classification as a knowledge system see (Collins 1997: 57).

[14]For instance when a new act changes the definition of a concept like "environmental risk".

[15]Such as when case law establishes that a bicycle will be an instance of the concept of vehicle in the interpretation of a certain act.

Province of Jurisprudence determined (1832) leaded the quest for the main conceptual components of the law. In continental legal thought a similar line of thought was manifested in the works of the German pandectists. Represented by main legal scholars such as Savigny, Ihering, Puchta and Windscheid, and with origins in Hugo, it developed in the context of a strong debate on the suitability of codification which would eventually culminate in the German Civil Code, which has been considered more similar to a doctrinal treatise than to a legislative piece of work.[16] The weakening of this stream of thought can be traced back to the jurisprudence of interests, by Ihering, who had been one of the major figures of the conceptualist school.

The works produced by the main figures of both streams of thought provide useful data for an analysis of legal conceptual systems with a historical perspective. Together with some examples extracted from current legal doctrine they will be the material on which to run our analysis of the structural and semantic characteristics of doctrinal legal conceptual systems.

2.4 Types of Systems of Legal Concepts

In the present section we will compare legal conceptualisations on the basis of the degree of abstraction of their conceptual units and of the kind of semantic relationships connecting them.

2.4.1 Degree of Abstraction

From the point of view of content, systems of legal concepts can be more or less specific. That is, there exist, on the one hand, certain systems of legal concepts that deal with the concepts specific to a subdomain of the law, like works dealing with civil law or criminal law,[17] where the conceptual networks basically contain concepts particular of the domain.[18] On the other hand, there exist systems of legal concepts that aim at providing a general picture of the whole legal domain and therefore contain more abstract notions that require a more philosophical reflection and theoretical commitments.

---

[16]The BGB (German Civil Code) has actually been criticised as embodying an abstract system of private law, in accordance to the conceptual apparatus built by the pandectists rather than a system adapted to actual conditions of life in society (Wieacker 1995: 376).

[17]On the idea of doctrinal subsystems which aspire to consistence and coherence see (Collins 1997: 60–61).

[18]The same concept can even exist in different subdomains and have different meanings in each of them. Concepts like "wilful misconduct" and "negligence", for instance, are not the same in criminal theory and in civil responsibility theory) (Vernengo 1986: 235–236).

An early example of domain-specific conceptual systems is the tripartite division of the law established by Gaius, a Roman jurist of the second century AD.[19] Three are the main branches of the hierarchy as described in *The Institutes* of Gaius: persons, things and actions. Each of them is further divided into more specific classes. Persons are divided into free and slave, dependent and independent, in curatorship and in guardianship. Two subclasses span out from persons: freeborn and freedmen. And the latter are further classified into roman citizens, latins and dediticii. The scheme is methodologically followed, giving a systematic exposition of the law that faithfully respects the method of division by *genus* and *differentia* (Fig. 2.4).

Another early example of legal classification in private law is found in the Justinian Code, which inherited Gaius scheme. Figure 2.5 shows the classification of the sources of obligations according to the Justinian Code, which follows a quadripartition: Contract, Quasi-contract, Delictus and Quasi delictus.

During the XIXth century legal doctrine and legal theory developed both types of systems of legal concepts, namely, domain specific and more general. Figure 2.6 shows a fragment of Windscheid's classification of real rights according to private law.

More general systems of legal concepts were developed by several scholars during the XIXth century, which focused on the detailed and *logical*[20] analysis of rights and duties trying to provide a formal account of legal discourse and reasoning. The one to provide a complete and detailed framework for such notions and to go down in history for such achievement was Hohfeld (1917), although some other legal scholars had already dealt with those concepts for a while (among which Austin himself (1832), Holmes (1870, 1872 and 1873), Holland (1880), Langdell (1887 and 1900), Salmond (1902), Taylor (1908), Gray (1909)). This trend would die out at the turn of the century due to the shift from the so-called "expository paradigm" (Herget 1990) to the sociological paradigm represented in figures such as Holmes and R. Pound and very well illustrated by Holmes' momentous phrase: "the life of the law has not been logic: it has been experience" (Holmes 1881).

However, not only legal theory is concerned with the construction of abstract systems of legal concepts. Also scholars working in particular areas of the law often build networks of their concepts and ground them on general theories of the law. For instance frequently civil law works try to link the domain of private law to a

---

[19] The use of hierarchies for presenting legal concepts was actually already common before Gaius and there is evidence to believe that it was an influence of Greek philosophical thought on Roman Jurisprudence (Talamanca 1976, Grosso 1976, Gaudemet 1986).

[20] It has to be noted that that the sense in which the term logical was used in that period differs from its current formal understanding. In late XIXth century legal discourse the adjective "logic" was used to characterise something analytical, clear, ordered, not contradictory, but by no means included a precise reference to the properties of modern symbolic logic as derived from the works of George Boole (1854 *Laws of Thought*) and Gottlob Frege (1879 *Begriffsschrift*- usually translated as *concept writing* or *concept notation*), among others.

```
Law
    Persons
                Free
                            Freeborn
                            Freedmen
                                        Roman citizens
                                        Latins
                                        Dediticii
                Slave

                Independent
                Dependent

                In curatorship
                In guardianship
    Things

                Private
                Public

                Corporeal
                            Inheritance
                            Usufruct
                            Servitude
                            Obligations
                                        Legal
                                        Praetorian

                                        Contract
                                        Quasi-contract
                                        Wrong
                                        Quasi-wrong

                Mancipi
                Nec mancipi
```

Fig. 2.4 Gaius classification of the law

```
<Sources of obligations>
     <Contract>
            <by performance/ delivery of property –re->
            <verbally –verbis->
            <by writing –litteris->
            <by consent –consensu->
     <quasi contractus –similar to those founded on contract->
     <Delictus >
     <quasi delictus –similar to those founded on an offence->
```

Fig. 2.5 Classification of the sources of obligations according to the scheme of the Justinian Code

```
<real rights>
      <servitudes>
                  <positive: they oblige the land owner to accept something that the holder of the
                  easement is entitled to do>
                  <negative: they oblige the land owner to omit a certain behaviour >

                  <personal: for the benefit of a particular person>
                              <ususfructus>
                              <usus>
                              <habitation>
                  <praedial (real): for the benefit of a particular state>


                  <continuous>
                  <discontinuous>


      <pledge>
```

Fig. 2.6 Windscheid's classification of real rights (Windscheid 1930: 477 ff.)

general theory of the law and this way provide connections between domain specific concepts and more abstract concepts (for instance between contract and legal act; or between parties and legal person) (Fig. 2.7).

The particularity of this scheme is that it provides a comprehensive overview of the categories on which the law operates, reaching therefore a high level of abstraction (for instance the categories of facts or objects), but at the same time a connection remains to concrete categories of very specific domains of the law. The category of financial transactional act, for instance, is directly connected to the concept of contract, which is much more familiar to the practicing lawyer.[21]

2.4.2 Types of Semantic Relations

A further distinction of systems of legal concepts built by legal doctrine can be made on the basis of the semantic relations linking the concepts of the system. In this sense we can speak of:

(i) Systems of concepts that organise concepts in terms of generality giving place to a vertical ordering from more general to more specific concepts, known as well as classification by *genus* and *differentia*. In these systems the relation linking concepts is the inclusion or *is-a* relation, and

---

[21] The concept of legal transaction is actually more common in the analysis of legal doctrine than in the domain of practicing law, for it is not regarded as a legal category in various legal orders. On the historical origins and the presence of this category in the various legal systems see (Sacco 2005: 278 ff.).

```
<"FACT" natural reality
        <objects>
                <things>
                <human body>
                <intellectual work>
        <facts>
                <positive fact>
                <negative fact>
                <hypothesis>
                <(im)possibility>


                <non-legal facts>
                <legal facts>
                        <behaviour>
                                <act>
                                        <non transactional act>
                                                <tacit acceptation of in-
                                                heritance>
                                                <illicit act>
                                                <wrongful licit act >
                                                <abandonment of a thing >
                                                <delivery>
                                        <transactional>
                                                <financial>
                                                <non financial>

                                                <unilateral>
                                                <bilateral>
                                                <multilateral>

                                                <unipersonal>
                                                <pluripersonal>
                                                <complex party>
                        <other human facts>
                                <having certain qualities>
                                <facts of knowledge>
                        <event –natural->


<"DIRITTO" realtà giuridica>
```

Fig. 2.7 Classification of legal reality (Sacco 2005)

(ii) Systems of concepts that gather together the elements connected to a particular event regulated by the law, like contract. This last kind of organisation
can be called "operational family", in the sense that the nodes of the conceptual system have a functional role in the particular frame of an event regulated
by the law. For instance, in the case of contract, relevant members of the system would be: the requirements (form, agreement, capacity), the effects, the
parties, . . .

Fig. 2.8 Typology of
"disposant" (Source: Cornu
1990: 201)

Disposant
    À titre gratuit
        Testateur
        Donateur
    À titre onereux
        Vendeux

<Legal facts>
    <Private declarations of will: legal transactions>
        <Public declarations of will (by the judiciary or other
state bodies) >
    <By law: all other legal acts>
    <Illicit acts>
    <Passing of time>

Fig. 2.9 Windscheid's classification of legal facts (Windscheid 1930: 200–201)

Both kinds of conceptual systems are highlighted by Cornu (1990: 195 ff).
Firstly, an example of conceptual systems organising concepts on the basis of the
genus and differentia method of division is the following one (Fig. 2.8):

As to the semantic relations linking the concepts of the structure, they are *is-a*
relations. In this sense, thus, Donateur *is-a* Disposant-à-titre-gratuit,
and Disposant-à-titre-gratuit *is-a* Disposant.

This kind of semantic links is commonly found in the aforementioned works of
conceptual analysis developed during the XIXth century, as the following examples show. Figure 2.9 reports the concept of legal fact as conceptualised by
Windscheid and the set of its subtypes, which are linked to it through the inclusion relation so that: private declaration is-a legal fact; passing
of time is-a legal fact, and so on.

Similarly, Figure 2.10 shows the conceptualisation of person as presented by
Puchta. In this case concepts are structured in various degrees of depth forming hierarchical chains based on the inclusion relation: charitable foundations is-
a universitas bonorum; universitas bonorum is-a legal person;
legal person is-a person.

Secondly, operational families of legal concepts gather together concepts which
are semantically related and form a functional set.

The example presented in Fig. 2.11 includes the central concept of
obligation and related concepts like debt, object of the obligation or
payment.

In this case the semantic link is not anymore an inclusion relation, but a more
complex connection. Payment is not a kind of obligation, but a way of extinguishing the obligation. Neither is the object a kind-of obligation, which
can be rather considered the content of the obligation. In general terms, thus, we

\<Persons\>
    \<Natural\>
        \<Slaves\>
            \<statuliberi\>
            \<in libertate esse[1]\>
        \<Free\>
            \<Intermediate classes\>
                \<*de facto* servitude\>
                \<auctoratus\>
                \<adiudicatus\>
                \<*colono*\>
            \<ingenui\>
            \<freed (liberti)\>
        \<Roman citizens\>
        \<non Roman citizens\>
            \<latin\>
            \<peregrini\>
        \<sui iuris\>
        \<alieno iuri subiecti\>

    \<Legal\>
        \<universas personarum\>
            \<state\>
            \<corporations\>
            \<priest organisations\>/ \<curia\>/ \<legion\>
            \<church\>

Fig. 2.10 Puchta's classification of persons (Puchta 1841: 54 ff.; 6–9)

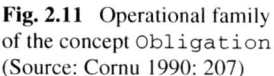

Fig. 2.11 Operational family of the concept Obligation (Source: Cornu 1990: 207)

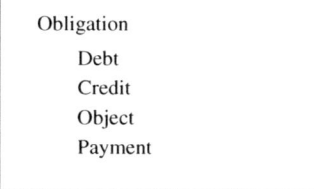

Obligation
Debt
Credit
Object
Payment

could say that the concepts belonging to the group are semantically related, and the specific relations holding between them will vary.

As to the topological structure of the different kinds of conceptual systems according to the semantic relations that unite their concepts, some differences can be highlighted. On the one hand, systems structured around the is-a relation will correspond to a rooted-tree, ideally with a single beginner and with new nodes fanning out from each node (Figs. 2.12 and 2.13).

On the other hand, operational families of concepts, will not necessarily follow the model of a rooted tree, and will acquire more diverse structures. This is due to

Fig. 2.12 Windscheid's
classification of real rights
(Windscheid 1930: 477 ff.)

```
<real rights>
    <servitudes>
        <positive >
        <negative >

        <personal >
                <ususfructus>
                <usus>
                <habitation>
            <praedial>

            <continuous>
            <discontinuous>

    <pledge>
```

Fig. 2.13 Structure of is-a
hierarchies

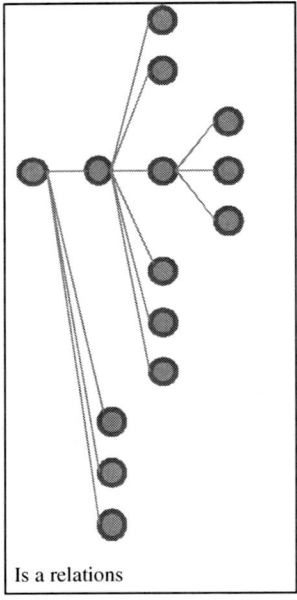

Is a relations

the fact that concepts in an operational family are not necessarily related to a single beginner, but can form looped structures. Indeed, we could say that in the operational family of `Obligation`, `obligation` is semantically related to `debt`; `debt` is semantically related to `credit`, and so on (Figs. 2.14 and 2.15).

Sometimes both types of systems of concepts, namely, is-a systems of concepts and operational systems of concepts will be mixed. In this case a variety of conceptual structures and semantic relations will be intermingled. In the following figure, for instance, we can see the operational family of `Contract` (contract

Fig. 2.14 Operational family
of the concept Obligation
(Source: Cornu 1990: 207)

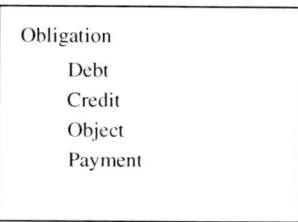

Fig. 2.15 Structure of an
operational family of
concepts

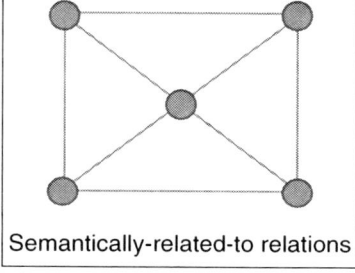

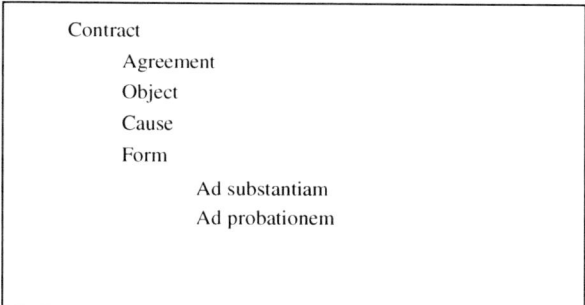

Fig. 2.16 Taxonomical and operational family of concepts

and its requirements, which are not linked by an inclusion or is-a relation) connected to an is-a hierarchy of the types of form (both form ad substantiam
–form required for the validity and the effectiveness of the contract- and form ad
probationem –form required to proof the existence of the contract- are types of
form) (Fig. 2.16):

2.4.3 Other Forms of Conceptual Organisation in Legal Doctrine

It is possible to think, however, of a global organisation of legal contents in which
a broader perspective is taken: this would be the case of the branches of law and

Fig. 2.17 Branches of private
law (Savigny 1886: 385 ff.)

<Private Law>
  <Real Rights>
  <Obligations>
  <Family law (pure and applied)>
  <Inheritance law>

legal institutions. At this layer, it is legal norms that are being assembled under a
common category because of the subject matter that they regulate, their goals and
their underlying values (Renauld 1958: 171–172).

Within the division of the law into different branches, it is necessary to distinguish two issues: on the one hand, the different areas in which the subject matter is
divided; on the other hand, the order in which those areas are presented in legal discourse (be it scholarly works or legislative texts). It is natural to think that these two
aspects will usually be connected, since from the moment that one starts to think
of the different main areas of which the law is composed, it becomes relevant to
imagine an ideal order in which those areas are to be presented.

As to the order in which legal materials are organised, there are two possible
options: either following the order established by the legislator or introducing a
new order that follows some kind of rational organisation. The former is typical of
doctrinal works extremely committed to the structure of the original text, whereas
the latter is characteristic of systematic expositions of the law, like those of XIXth
century German legal scholars.

Among the latter, both Savigny and Windscheid show special concern about the
division of the different branches of (private) law and their order of exposition. In the
case of Savigny private law is considered to be composed of "family law" (pure and
applied), "real rights", "obligations" and "inheritance law". Once he has identified
these different parts Savigny suggests the order that he considers more suitable for
their presentation and he states the need of developing a general part where the
common elements to other parts of the law (like legal capacity, modification and
extinction of legal relationships, ...) are assembled (Fig. 2.17):

Windscheid, at his turn, divides private law into: a general part, composed of
"of law in general", "of rights in general"; and a special part containing "law of
property" and "familiy law". The first part deals with legal principles applicable to
legal norms and to all types of rights, whereas the second part presents firstly, "law
of property", which is successively divided into "legal relationships over things";
"legal relationships between persons (obligations), and "inheritance"; and, secondly
"family law" (Fig. 2.18).

Aside from the noteworthy similarities between the two plans of organisation
of the law (they clearly share some categories: <Family law>, <inheritance law>,
<obligations> and the prevision of a general part) it is important to highlight the dif-
ferences between these structures and the models of legal concepts presented in the
previous sections. Whereas in the former categories refer to subject matters or broad
topics (for instance, <family law>), in the latter, categories refer to legal objects with

```
<Private Law>
     <General part>
            <of law in general>
            <of rights in general>
     <Special part>
            <the law of property>
                    <legal relationships over things>
                    <legal relationships between persons>
                           < obligations>
                    <inheritance law>
            <family law>
```

Fig. 2.18 Branches of private law (Windscheid)

regard to which normative assertions can be made (Ex: <natural person>, "a natural person shall be liable for negligence").

This leads us to an interesting observation with regard to the idea of "legal classification", namely, that it is an ambiguous notion for it us used to refer either to the classification of legal objects (concepts), or of thematic areas of the law. This ambivalence of the concept of classification was already noticed by Pound (1924: 940–941), who pointed to the existing confusion in some doctrinal works, where authors move in their classifications, from one level to another.

A mixture of classification of concepts and subject matter can be observed for instance in Holmes' classification of duties,[22] where some branches of the law are attached as subclasses to some of the types of duties, for instance, the "law of prize", or "criminal law" as subclasses of -duties of all the world- to the sovereign-, even if, clearly, "criminal law" is not a kind of duty, but a subject matter in which duties will be established by the legislator (Fig. 2.19).

As to the topological structure of this kind of conceptual system it corresponds to a rooted-tree, ideally with a single beginner and with new nodes fanning out from each node. In this sense, thus, it is quite similar to the informational structure of taxonomical is-a systems of concepts. Nevertheless, an important difference exists, since in this case the topological structure does not represent a completely consistent semantic architecture. In other words, the structural links do not stand in all cases for the same semantic relation (since, for instance, even if they are structurally placed in a similar way, "criminal law" and "contract" are not linked though the same semantic relation to the superclass Duties).

---

[22] One of the peculiarities of Holmes classification is the shift of perspective, for he tried to solve the problems in Austin's taxonomy by suggesting a classification of the law on the basis of duties instead of rights (Kellogg 1984: 6; Kellogg 2007: 67).

```
Duties
    <Of all the world>
            <To the sovereign>
                            <Law of prize>
                            <Military service>
                            <Criminal law>
            <To all the world>
                            <Law of libel and slander –civil actions->
                            <Injuries to the person –false imprisonment, ...>
                            <Some nuisances?>
                            <Fraud independent of contract or special relations>
            <To persons in particular situations or relations –some of them special applica-
            tions of <To all the world>>
                            <Law of offices- corporations>
                            <Monopolies –patent rights,....>
                            <Posession>
                            <Ownership. Easement. Rent?
                            <Contract>
                            <Domestic relations>

    <Of persons in particular situations or relations>
            <To the sovereign>
                            <of officers –impeachment,....>
                            <eminent domain>
                            <taxes on property>
            <To all the world –some are special applications of <To all the world>>

                            <Corporations>
                            <Duties of landowners to not make nuisances on their land,
            <To persons in particular situations or relations –including more special appli-
            cations of <to all the world>and <to persons in particular situations or relations>>
                            <Members of corporation to each other>
                            <Landlord and tenant,....>
                            <Trustee and cestue que trust>
                            <Contractor and contractee>
                            <Master and servant>
                            <Guardian and ward...>
```

Fig. 2.19 Holmes' classification 1872 (Source: Herget 1990)

2.5 A Mapping Between Doctrinal Conceptual Structures and Computational Ontologies

On the basis of the considerations made in previous sections, some conclusions may be drawn:

Firstly, there is a general topological correspondence between doctrinal conceptual structures and computational ontologies. Both are based on a taxonomic or is-a structure with further semantic cross-references that create more complex networks of concepts.

Secondly, in terms of reusability, special attention has to be paid to peculiar structures found in legal doctrine. On the one hand, sometimes legal classification refers to topics or thematic areas (the so-called "branches of the law") instead of referring to legal objects. On the other hand, sometimes legal classification mixes both "branches of the law" and legal objects. When translated into computational ontologies a clear distinction should be made between both, either creating different ontologies (one for topics and the other for entities) or creating a superclass `Topic` or `Legal_Topic` for the branches of the law, and another one for `Concept`/ `Legal_Concept`.

Thirdly, with regard to semantic types of relations, conceptual models of legal theory foresee not only is-a or inclusion semantic relations, but as well functional groups of concepts where semantic links can be of different types and can for looped structures. In this line, the relevance of frame-based structures of legal concepts has been acknowledged in the representation of legal knowledge. Framenet models for the law are thus already under development as a complement to legal ontologies (Venturi et al. 2009, Agnoloni et al. 2009).

Fourthly, if we now make a comparison of (i) the systems of legal concepts based on the semantic relation is-a and (ii) operational systems of legal concepts in terms of their suitability for being translated into a formal ontology, several observations can be made:

- the *is-a* are easy to transform, the operational systems of legal concepts are not;
- the reason is that the is-a can be directly represented in the languages for the formal representation of concepts (such as OWL), as an inclusion relation linking a class and its sub-class. Nevertheless it is important to note that not all the subclasses identified in a doctrinal classification will be formalised as subclasses in an ontology; some of them might, for instance, be roles instead of entities,[23] such as in the case of *citizen* or *free* with regard to the class *person*.
- in the case of operational systems of legal concepts it is not clear how to represent logically the relations linking concepts: what is the logical relation between `contract` and `parties`? Or between `contract` and `form`? It is clearly not an inclusion relation since, for instance, the parties are not a kind of contract, neither are the requirements for the contract to be valid. However, could the relation linking the requirements of a contract with the contract itself be considered a meronymic or part-of relation? Certainly not if we consider the meronymic relation as referring to a material or physical part, but in a wider sense of the notion of part such a conceptualisation might be possible. Indeed, if one understands the parthood relation as one in which a simpler event is part of a more complex event (see Varzi 2003), one could see the event of manifesting one's agreement through a specific form as an event that *is part of* the more general event of making a contract.

---

[23]The semantics of the is-a link has been an early topic of concern (Brachman 1983). See Guarino and Welty (2000, 2001) on the need of ontologically well-founded is-a links, based on philosophical criteria such as the notions of identity, unity, essence and dependence.

The ontological formalisation of an operational family of legal concepts requires indeed a much more elaborated analysis as it will be shown in the following example, where various classes of a foundational ontology (DOLCE[24]) are involved in the conceptualisation of a set of legal concepts. Let us imagine the operational family corresponding to the concept Contract. This set of concepts would include, besides Contract, other concepts that are traditionally regarded by doctrine as its requirements: agreement of the parties, object, cause and form.

There is a basic distinction in DOLCE that is useful for our purpose, namely, the distinction between *endurants* and *perdurants*. *Endurants* are entities that are wholly present at any time of their existence, that *are* in time, whereas *perdurants* are entities that *happen* in time, that is, that extend in time by accumulating different temporal parts (Masolo et al. 2003). On the one hand, the only possible relation between endurants and perdurants foreseen by DOLCE is the participation relation: endurants participate in perdurants. On the other hand, perdurants can be related to each other by the *parthood* relation, that is, a perdurant can be part of another perdurant.

From the perspective of legal doctrine, contract can be understood either as a legal act performed by the parties with the intention of producing certain effects, or as a set of normative specifications (*lex contractus*) that the parties accept.[25] For instance a sale contract may be viewed either as an event involving the parties (the event consisting in one party making an offer and the other accepting it) or as the normative regulation the parties state and intend to achieve (good *g* is transferred from party *a* to party *b*, party *b* has the obligation to pay the price *p*, etc.). There is also a third meaning in which the term "contract" is used to denote the document (the sheet of paper or the electronic file) which reports the statements of the parties.

If we follow the first option and we consider that contract is a legal act, we could define it ontologically as follows:

Contract: It is a perdurant. It can be seen as an event that has a certain extension in time.

Agreement: It is a perdurant as well. It consists of the action performed by the parties of declaring their will, so we have two declarations of will, understood as speech acts (Declaration 1 + Declaration 2), the contents of which are compatible.

Agreement is part of Contract.

Parties (Party 1 + Party 2): They are endurants.

Content of the declaration of will on which the agreement is based, that is, the norms accepted by the parties: It is an endurant. A non-agentive social object.

Form: The requirement of the form has to be understood as a requirement that the declaration of will takes a certain form. It might be a requirement of written

---

[24] Descriptive Ontology for Linguistic and Cognitive Engineering (Masolo et al. 2003).

[25] The distinction between contract as an act and contract as a norm was introduced by Kelsen (Díez- Picazo, Gullón 2001: 29).

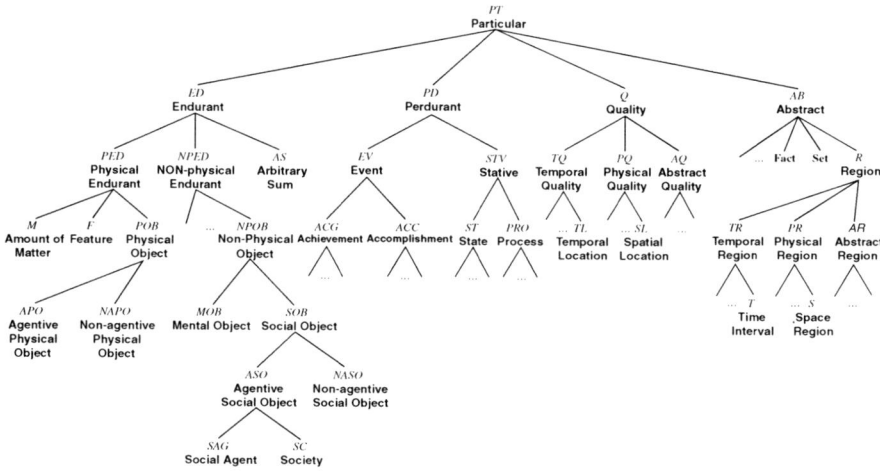

Fig. 2.20 Taxonomy of DOLCE top classes (Masolo et al. 2003: 14), showing the classes endurant and perdurant used to conceptualise the operational family of contract

form, or may consist, for instance, in the fact that the act is performed in front of a notary. Form could thus be understood as a property of the perdurant `agreement`.

`Object`: The object is an endurant to which the declaration of will refers. It can be a non-agentive physical object (such as a house in a contract of sale) or a non-agentive social object (like a right in a contract whereby the right of publication is sold) (Fig. 2.20).

Finally, in order to have effects it is required that the obligation arising from the contract has a `Cause`. This is a controversial concept, but let us consider the doctrinal approach according to which the cause of a contract consists in the shared goals that motivate the parties into performing the contract. This could be therefore characterised as a perdurant, more specifically a State of the party by which she has certain goals. These goals have to be licit and moral. Since it is difficult for the judge to know what are the internal goals of the parties, sometimes for each kind of contract a generic goal will be assumed. For instance, in the case of sale, the goal will be "acquiring/transfering the property over the thing", in the tenancy agreement the goal will be "having/giving the legal right to the use of the thing".

The `Cause` can then be formalised as a perdurant (of the type cognitive-State) previous or at least simultaneous to the agreement (Fig. 2.21).

2.6 Conclusions and Further Work

The main conclusion to draw on the basis of the previous observations is that legal theory and legal doctrine represent a precious intellectual capital with considerable potentialities in the development of computable legal ontologies.

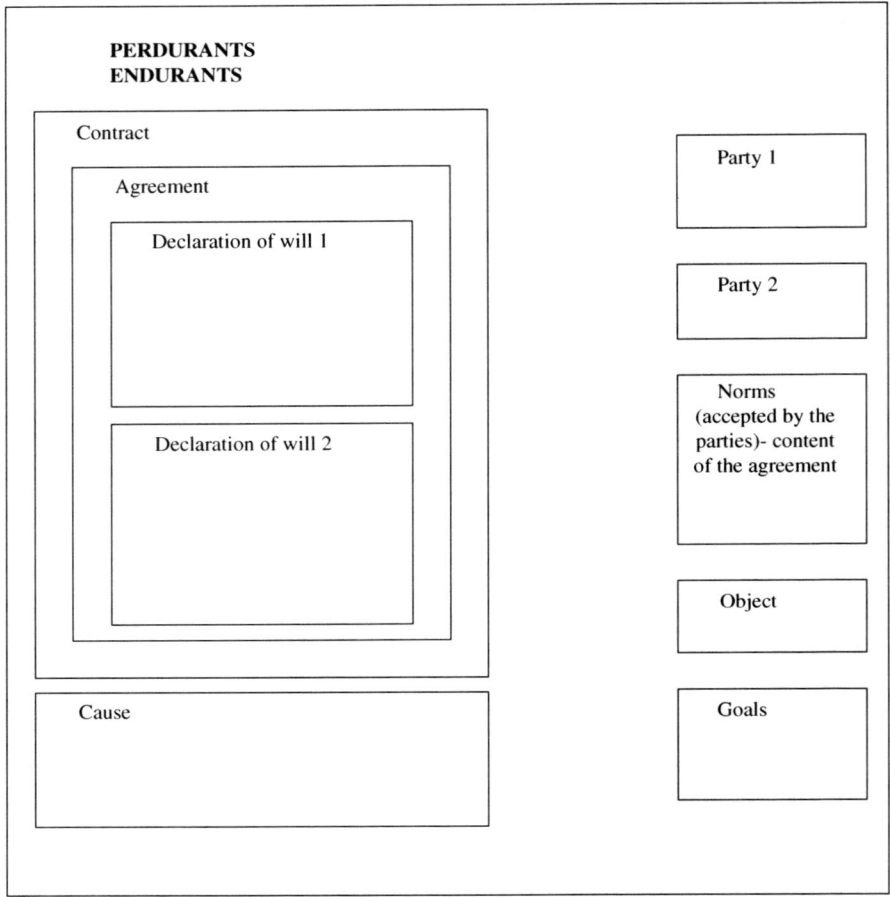

Fig. 2.21 The contract. Endurants and perdurants

The analysis of the topological and semantic characteristics of systems of legal concepts developed throughout the history of legal thought provides evidence for tracing some intellectual roots of legal ontology-building back to the history of legal thought. Indeed, similarities in the task of conceptual analysis performed by legal scholars and the type of conceptual modelling required by ontology engineering indicate that the former can provide fruitful insights to the latter. Nevertheless, as certain particularities of legal classifications previously shown indicate, reuse of doctrinal constructions is feasible only provided that their underlying formal structure is carefully analysed in order to translate it into appropriate logical-ontological forms, avoiding thus confusion between levels (concept vs. topic areas) and semantic relations (taxonomic vs. other types of semantic relations).

A hypothesis to be studied in further work is that systems of concepts provided by legal doctrine might be specially helpful for the construction of core legal ontologies, namely, ontologies providing general legal concepts, being used in different areas of the law. In fact, there are relatively few general legal concepts, which are often precisely characterised, so that their content can be expressed through the formal languages of computational ontologies. Furthermore, linking the concepts of a core legal ontology to doctrinal constructions would clarify the legal presuppositions determining certain choices in ontological modelling (ontological commitments). Finally, a core legal ontology would gain a high degree of justification, legitimacy and appeal, if it could be shown that it corresponds to systems of concepts used in legal doctrine, by leading authors.

In domain ontologies, concerned with the concepts peculiar to particular areas of the law, the reuse of doctrinal constructions might have disadvantages if compared to semi-automatic building approaches based on NLP techniques applied to big corpuses of legal texts. Firstly, because the number of concepts required by domain ontologies is usually higher than in core legal ontologies and, secondly, because usually systems of domain legal concepts built by doctrine are not very well specified and consequently their translation into formal languages becomes more difficult. Nevertheless, domain ontologies can draw inspiration from doctrinal constructions in order to structure and disambiguate lexical units extracted in a bottom-up fashion from big corpora.

Further inquiries will deal with the conceptual networks emerging from doctrinal works by applying the graph theoretic modelling paradigm, in order to see to which extent new conceptual graphs not subject to any hermeneutic external control arise. This could promote new analytical approaches to the traditional readings of legal doctrine and further enrich legal ontological models.

References

Agnoloni, T., L. Bacci, E. Francesconi, P. Spinosa, D. Tiscornia. S. Montemagni, G. Venturi (2007). Building an Ontological Support for Multilingual Legislative Drafting. In A.R. Lodder and L. Mommers (Eds.) *Legal Knowledge and Information Systems. Jurix 2007: The Twentieth Annual Conference*. IOS Press, Amsterdam, 9–18.

Agnoloni, T., M. Fernández-Barrera, M.T. Sagri, D. Tiscornia, G. Venturi (2009). When a FrameNet-Style Knowledge Description Meets an Ontological Characterization of Fundamental Legal Concepts. Jurix 2009, Rotterdam.

Antoniou, G., F. Van Harmelen (2008 [2004]). *A Semantic Web Primer*. Cambridge, MA; London, England: The MIT Press.

Austin, J. (1995 [1832]). *The Province of Jurisprudence Determined*. Cambridge, MA; New York, NY: Cambridge University Press.

Bales, M.E., S.B. Johnson (2006). Graph Theoretic Modeling of Large-Scale Semantic Networks. *Journal of Biomedical Informatics* 2006; 39(4): 451–464, available from: http://dx.doi.org/10.1016/j.jbi.2005.10.007.

Brachman, R. (1983). What IS-A Is and Isn't: An Analysis of Taxonomic Links in Semantic Networks. *IEEE Computer*, 16(10): 30–36.

Casanovas, P. (1998). Las formas sociales del derecho contemporáneo: el nuevo *ius commune Working Paper n. 146*, Universitat Autònoma de Barcelona.

Casanovas, P., N. Casellas, P. Vallbé (2010). Empirically Grounded Developments of Legal Ontologies: A Socio-Legal Perspective. In G. Sartor, P. Casanovas, M. Biasiotti, M. Fernández-Barrera (Eds.) *Approaches to Legal Ontologies*. Springer, Berlin. 49–68.

Casanovas, P., N. Casellas, J.-J. Vallbé, M. Poblet, V. Richard Benjamins, M. Blázquez, R. Peña, J. Contreras (2006). Semantic Web: A Legal Case Study. In J. Davies, R. Studer, P. Warren (Eds.) *Semantic Web Technologies. Trends and Research in Ontology-Based Systems*. Chichester: Wiley, 259–280.

Clancey, W.J. (1992). Representations of Knowing: In Defense of Cognitive Apprenticeship. A response to Sandberg & Wielinga. *Journal of AI in Education*, 3(2): 139–168.

Clancey, W.J. (2008). Scientific Antecedents of Situated Cognition. In P. Robbins, M. Aydede. *Cambridge Handbook of Situated Cognition*. New York, NY: Cambridge University Press.

Collins, H. (1997). Legal Classifications as the Production of Knowledge Systems. In P. Birks (Ed.) *The Classification of Obligations*. Oxford, MA: Clarendon Press, 57–70.

Cornu, G. (1990). *Linguistique juridique*. Montchrestien, Paris.

Díez- Picazo, L., G. Antonio (2001). *Sistema de Derecho Civil. Volumen II*. Madrid: Tecnos.

Eraut, M. (1997). Perspectives on Defining 'The Learning Society'. *Journal of Education Policy*, 12(6): 551–558.

Eraut, M. (1998). Concepts of Competence. *Journal of Interprofessional Care*, 12(2): 127–139.

Eraut, M. (2007). Theoretical and Practical Knowledge Revisited. *EARLI* 2007, Budapest.

Francesconi, E., P. Spinosa, D. Tiscornia (2007). A Linguistic-Ontological Support for Multilingual Legislative Drafting: The DALOS Project. In Casanovas P. et al. (Eds.) *Proceedings of LOAIT 07. II Workshop on Legal Ontologies and Artificial Intelligence Techniques*, CEUR Workshop Proceedings, Stanford University, Stanford 103 ff.

Gaudemet, J. (1986). Tentatives de systématisation du droit à Rome. *Archives de Philosophie du Droit: Le système juridique*. Sirey, Paris, 31.

George, B. (1854). *An Investigation of the Laws of Thought on Which are Founded the Mathematical Theories of Logic and Probabilities*. Walton and Maberly, London.

Gottlob, F. (1879). *Begriffsschrift. eine der arithmetischen nachgebildete Formelsprache des reinen Denkens*, Louis Nebert, Halle a. S.

Gray, J.C. (1909). *The Nature and Sources of the Law*. Columbia University Press, New York, NY.

Grosso, G. (1976). Influenze aristoteliche nella sistemazione delle fonti delle obbligazioni nella giurisprudenza romana. *Colloquio italo-francese: La filosofia greca e il diritto romano*, Roma, 14–17 aprile 1973, Accademia Nazionale dei Lincei.

Guarino, N., W. Christopher (2000). Ontological Analysis of Taxonomic Relationships. In A.H.F. Laender, S.W. Liddle and V.C. Storey (Eds.) *Conceptual Modeling- ER 2000*. Springer Berlin/ Heidelberg. 210–224.

Hayaert, V. (2007). Mens Emblematica et humanisme juridique: l'insertion d'emblemata dans l'édition Senneton du Corpus Juris Civilis (1548–1550). *Le Journal de la Renaissance*, 2007, 5: 301–321.

Herget, J.E. (1990). *American Jurisprudence 1870–1970*. Rice University Press, Houston, TX.

Hohfeld, W.N. (1917). Some Fundamental Legal Conceptions as Applied in Judicial Reasoning. *Yale Law Journal*, 26: 710.

Holland, T. (1880). *Elements of Jurisprudence*, Clarendon, Oxford 5.

Holmes, O.W. (1870). Codes and the Arrangement of the Laws. *American Law Review*, 5: 1.

Holmes, O.W. (1872). The Arrangement of the Law. Privity. *American Law Review*, 7: 46.

Holmes, O.W. (1873). The Theory of Torts. *American Law Review*, 7: 652.

Holmes, O.W. (1881). *The Common Law*. Little, Brown, and Co, Boston, MA

Kellogg, F.R. (1984). *The Formative Essays of Justice Holmes*. Westport, CT: Greenwood Press.

Kellogg, F.R, (2007). *Oliver Wendell Holmes, Jr., Legal Theory, and Judicial Restraint*. Cambridge University Press, Cambridge, NY.

Langdell, C. (1887). A Brief Survey of Equity Jurisdiction. *Harvard Law Review* I: 55.

Langdell, C. (1900). Classification of Rights and Wrongs. *Harvard Law Review* 13: 537–659.

Masolo, C., S. Borgo, A. Gangemi, N. Guarino, A. Oltramari (2003). *WonderWeb Deliverable D18. Ontology Library (Final)*. IST Project 2001-33052 WonderWeb: Ontology Infrastructure for the Semantic Web.

Polanyi, M. (1966). *The Tacit Dimension*. Garden City, New York, NY.

Pound, R. (1924). Classification of Law. *Harvard Law Review*, 37(8), 933–969.

Puchta, G.F. (1841–1847) *Cursus Der Institutionen, Breitkopf und Haertel*, Leipzig. Italian translation (1854) *Corso delle istituzioni* / di G.F. Puchta ; tradotto e preceduto da un discorso da A. Napoli, Turchiarulo.

Renauld, J.G. (1958). La Systematisation dans le raisonnement juridique. *Logique et Analyse* (NS) 168: 168–183.

Sacco, R. (1995). Mute Law. *The American Journal of Comparative Law*, 43(3): 455–467.

Salmond, J.W. (1902). *Jurisprudence, or the Theory of the Law, Stevens & Haynes*, London 4–5.

Sandberg, J., B. Wielinga (1992). Situated Cognition: A Paradigm Shift? *Journal of AI in Education* 3(2): 129–138.

Sartor G. (2009). Legal Concepts as Inferential Nodes and Ontological Categories. *Artificial intelligence and Law*, 17: 217–251.

von Savigny, F. (1840–1849). *System des heutigen roemischer Recht*. Italian translation (1886). *Sistema del diritto romano attuale*. Unione Tipografico-Editrice, Torino.

Slezak, P. (1999). Situated Cognition: Empirical Issue, "Paradigm Shift", or Conceptual Confusion? In J. Wiles, T. Dartnall (Eds.) *Perspectives on Cognitive Science: Theories, Experiments, and Foundations. Volume 2 of Perspectives on Cognitive Science. Volume 2 of Contemporary Studies in Cognitive Science and Technology*. Greenwood, Westport, CT, 806–811.

Talamanca, M. (1976). Lo schema 'genus-species' nelle sistematiche dei giuristi romani. Colloquio italo-francese: La filosofia greca e il diritto romano, Roma, 14–17 aprile 1973, Accademia Nazionale dei Lincei.

Taylor, H. (1908). *The Science of Jurisprudence*. Macmillan, New York, NY.

Thagard, P. (1992). *Conceptual Revolutions*. Princeton University Press, Oxford.

Tiscornia, D. (2005). Multilingual Semantic Metadata for Law. In Quaderni CNIPA, 2005, *3rd Workshop on Legislative XML* (Furore, 6–8 aprile, 2005).

Varzi, A. (2003). Mereology. *First published Tue May 13, 2003; substantive revision Thu May 14, 2009. Stanford encyclopaedia of philosophy.* [http://plato.stanford.edu/entries/mereology/]

Venturi, G., A. Lenci, S. Montemagni, E.M. Vecchi, M.T. Sagri, D. Tiscornia (2009). Towards a FrameNet Resource for the Legal Domain. In N. Casellas, E. Francesconi, R. Hoekstra, S. Montemagni (Eds.) *LOAIT 2009*, IDT Series, Barcelona, 67–76.

Vernengo, R.J. (1986). Systematization in Legal Dogmatics and Judicial Decisions. In *Rechtstheorie Beiheft 10. Vernung und Erfahrung im Rechtsdenken der Gegenwart*. Duncker & Humblot, Berlin, 231–239.

Welty, C., N. Guarino (2001). Supporting Ontological Analysis of Taxonomic Relationships. *Data & Knowledge Engineering*, 39(2001): 51–74

Wieacker, F. (1995). *A History of Private Law in Europe. With Particular Reference to Germany*. Clarendon Press, Oxford.

Windscheid, B. (1906). *Lehrbuch des Pandektenrechts in drei Bänden*. Auflage, Leipzig. Italian translation (1930). *Diritto delle Pandette*. Trad. Italiana di Fadda e Bensa. Torino, UTET.

Woods, W.A. (1975). What's in a Link: Foundations for Semantic Networks. In D.G. Bobrow, A.M. Collins (Eds.) *Representation and Understanding: Studies in Cognitive Science*. Academic Press, New York, NY, 35–82.

Chapter 3
Empirically Grounded Developments of Legal Ontologies: A Socio-Legal Perspective

Pompeu Casanovas, Núria Casellas, and Joan-Josep Vallbé

3.1 Introduction: Wrestling with the Angel

Dealing with data is far from easy. The definition of objects, measures and research processes have to be added to the problem of knowledge representation. There is at present a great deal of methodologies for ontology building. DOGMA, KACTUS, METHONTOLOGY, TOVE or DILIGENT, are well-known approaches to ontology engineering. All of them use to distinguish analytically types of activities, and phases or successive stages in the building process. METHONTOLOGY, e.g., includes the identification of the ontology development process, a lifecycle based on evolving prototypes, and techniques to carry out each of the management, development-oriented, and support activities (Gómez-Pérez et al. 2003: 125). DILIGENT separates as well these three types of distinct activities: ontology management, ontology development activities, an ontology support activities (Sure et al. 2006: 173).

Those are useful guidelines. However, as we have already stated (Casanovas et al. 2009), if ontology building is to be considered not only as an engineering process, but as a process of knowledge integrated in a wider field of research, sometimes these successive stages tend to be blurred into the dynamics of field research and the knowledge acquisition process.

We think that this is a difficult problem, because ontology-building is a complex process, which can require ongoing knowledge acquisition efforts. Therefore, lifecycles follow other patterns which may not be predicted in advance. At least, this has been our experience when conducting social science research on legal behavior and legal knowledge. Moreover, legal knowledge is dynamic. Therefore, grounding empirically the legal knowledge to be modeled through ontologies is also an evolving and ongoing process.

P. Casanovas (✉)
Department of Political Science and Public Law, Institute of Law and Technology,
Autonomous University of Barcelona, Faculty of Law, Barcelona, Spain
e-mail: pompeu.casanovas@uab.cat

G. Sartor et al. (eds.), *Approaches to Legal Ontologies*, Law, Governance
and Technology Series 1, DOI 10.1007/978-94-007-0120-5_3,
© Springer Science+Business Media B.V. 2011

This is not new. Experts systems faced a similar problem regarding the representation of common knowledge. Ed Feigenbaum called it the "knowledge acquisition bottleneck problem" (1977), and later on, "wrestling with the angel" (1992). Reflecting on their own experience, Forsyth and Buchanan (1989) suggested going beyond the traditional engineering methods and following the eliciting techniques of ethnomethodology and qualitative sociology.

More recently, ethnography has been seriously considered as a starting point. The assumption is that shared and implicit knowledge can be reassumed in *patterns of cooperative interaction* elicited by researchers to model and design computing e-government tools (Martin et al. 2002). These patterns consist of examples of similar social phenomena that serve as resources for defining, generalizing and reusing design concepts (e.g. "telling a story about the workplace", and they complement findings of field research). They may be defined as "regularities in the organisation of work, activity, and interaction among participants, and with, through, and around artefacts" (Martin and Sommerville 2004: 59).

In the Pragma-dialectics field, a similar ethnographic trend has been adopted by Jackson (1989) and Jacobs (2002) to produce detailed accounts on interactions in mediation processes. They reconstruct the *collaborative design of the disagreement space*. "We do not take the central problem of pragmatics to be how communicators assign functional meaning to specific messages or disambiguate speaker intention, but how is that people mutually negotiate social activity with language and thus participate in everyday life" (Aakhus and Aldrich 2002).

Common language, tacit and implicit knowledge, and the content of shared experiences and routines in everyday life seem to be the problems to be tackled before modeling. In this chapter, we will summarize the lessons learned in the construction of the ontology of IURISERVICE, an intelligent FAQ for judges in their first appointment. We could have taken other examples as well, stemming from other projects—the NEURONA (Casellas et al. 2009), E-SENTENCIAS (Casanovas et al. 2009) or ONTOMEDIA (Poblet et al. 2009) ontologies—. But, for the sake of synthesis, we will concentrate only on a single one, just to widen up the field in the last section.

In Section 3.2 we will define the socio-legal approach, including the conceptual problems of the sources and the boundaries of the legal domain. In Section 3.3, we will introduce the construction process of IURISERVICE. We will conclude by redefining the social-legal approach in Section 3.4.

3.2 The Socio-Legal Approach: Pluralism and Legal Culture

Legal scholars use to identify many sources of law. Discourses, rules, acts, events or documents are considered to be *legal*. Law and non-law are split up according to several criteria of identification or *validity*. Legal material, then, is classified according to the validity of the source, and according to three main positions— monism (normative positivism), dualism (facts/norms), and pluralism (plurality of legal sources).

3.2.1 Legal Pluralism

Typically, socio-legal scholars embrace a pluralist perspective and, following the first legal realism, they do not refer to a validity criterion or a validity rule to describe norms or rules as social artifacts.[1] They refer to law as a "political arena", "legal field", "political domain", "power construction" or "professional field".[2] This is a heritage from legal realism as well: what lawyers do (or what legal academics do)— as Trubek, Dézalay, Buchanan or Garth put it—reflects "what judges do" or "what officers do", the old mottos by Holmes and Llewellyn.

From this behavioral perspective, there are actually many *legal pluralisms* based on multiple regulatory forms referring to a plurality of aspects, according to different authors. Very broadly: (i) negotiations on rules, norms and rights; (ii) mechanisms stemming from different legal orders (especially in post-colonial states); (iii) selection of different jurisprudential places and procedural subjects (*forum shopping*); (iv) selection of different legal systems or norms (*répertoire normatif du juge*); (v) non-legal sources vs. legal sources (grounded on the state); (vi) increasing complexity of transnational orders and structures; (vii) semi-autonomous social fields (social ordered organisms or institutions) in industrial societies; (viii) differential regulations depending on class, race or gender; (ix) dialogue among cultures to grasp the different symbolic feature of regulations; (x) self-organizational or self-regulatory social or normative systems or sub-systems; (xi) implicit cultural models producing some social or institutional effects; (xii) folk models of law, institutions and rights.[3]

All these objects and aspects lead to different social approaches and methodologies too, opposed to the normative, deontic or "formalistic" methods of legal philosophy. During the twentieth century, this relationship has been sometimes difficult.[4] Law is not conceived as "a mirror of society that functions to maintain legal order" (Tamanaha 2001: ix).

However, from the technological point of view, monism and pluralism face similar problems. Legal knowledge representation, legal knowledge acquisition, and modelization have to be faced independently of which conception of law has been chosen.

Measures are another common problem. Ontology construction requires some kind of control of the different versions and steps of the process, and decisions have to be made at each step. There are no "task neutral ontologies" (Bench-Capon 2001). This means that, even for pluralists, some conception of law and regulation is *always* implemented. And, in the other way round, perhaps legal theory scholars

---

[1] See Friedman et al. (1995), and Abel (1995) for consistent readings on the field.

[2] The legal field is defined, e.g., as "the ensemble of institutions and practices through which law is produced, interpreted, and incorporated into social decision-making. Thus, the field includes legal professionals, judges, and the legal academy." (Trubek et al. 1994: 411)

[3] See for a summary of different kinds of pluralism, Casanovas (2002).

[4] See Abel (1995:1): "When asked what I study, I usually respond gnomically: everything about the law, except the rules."

have a natural trend to take ontology exclusively in a philosophical or pure conceptual sense,[5] without taking into account that the whole lifecycle comprehends usability and other tests of prototypes with potential and end users.[6] It is not clear yet how *regulatory ontologies* (ontologies on rules, norms and rights) rely on legal theory or socio-legal studies.

Besides, from an empirical point of view, there is a preliminary problem before any modelization takes place. What does "legal data" mean? How is the construction of legal data to be solved?

3.2.2 Legal Culture

Both legal scholars and computer scientists tend to use a conceptual intuitive starting point. Documents—as such *documents*—are selected according to their value as a legal source: laws and regulations, judgments and other judicial decisions, the discourse of the doctrine and jurisprudence and legal theory (Tiscornia 2005).[7] Peczenik's late theory, e.g., even points out to *coherentism*, adapting philosophy and reason to legal theory (rather than the reverse way). Therefore, *scientia juris* constitutes a privileged and entirely conceptual approach to legal documents (Peczenik 2000). Law *supervenes* as a "qualia", allowing their separation from other kind of non-legal ones (e.g. preparatory drafts, opinions etc. . .).[8] Still, this is the Puchta and Jhering way of dealing with legal concepts.

Socio-legal scholars take another perspective: some *legal data* (and metadata) are required to compare legal systems. This is called the *legal culture* perspective: legal knowledge is not to be inferred (or deduced) from the construction of a legal theory, but it is abductively or inductively operated through functional or professional practices that can be described and measured.

Legal culture means "the cluster of attitudes, ideas, expectations and values that people hold with regard to their legal system, legal institutions, and legal rules" (Pérez-Perdomo and Friedman 2003: 2). Since Friedman (1975), following Almond and Verba's related work on "political culture" (Almond and Verba 1963), "internal legal culture" (the culture of lawyers and jurists) may be distinguished from "external legal culture" (users, citizens, laymen. . .).

---

[5] "What does exist and what can exist? What is the essence of things, and what the conditions of their existence?" (McCormick 1991: vii).

[6] See the conception of "top ontology" developed by Hage and Verheij (1999).

[7] See Fernández-Barrera and Sartor (2010), Chapter 2, this volume, for a discussion of this perspective and the link between classical legal philosophy and the construction of legal-core ontologies.

[8] "What is law? That is, what are the criteria of law? [. . .] Law is a complex of interrelated components. Two kinds of component occupy a central position in this complex: norms and actions. There are also secondary components, that is, on the one hand, the legal values that justify and explain the norms and, on the other, the mental processes connected with our actions. Legal norms make up a system, and much theoretical literature deals with its structure [. . .]" (Peckzenik 2005: 92–93).

Blankenburg (1991, 1997) refined these concepts by introducing indicators on "law in the polls", "law in the minds", "law as body of laws", and "law as institutional fact". Thus, there are *patterns of legal cultures* (ibid. 1997), according to which cultures can be described as "litigation prone" (like USA, Germany and France) or "avoiding litigation cultures" (like Japan or the Netherlands): "legal behavior is determined by institutional supply rather than by popular demand" (ibid. 1997: 31). Professional behavior, litigation, the number of lawyers and judges, and legal beliefs are causally correlated and they can be statistically measured through social indicators.[9]

This kind of approach offers a quite detailed picture of the legal contexts and scenarios in which cognitive processes of memory, intention, planning and reasoning may take place. Before starting modeling processes and ontology building, it seems reasonable gathering as much data as possible about the actual functioning of institutional behavior.[10] However, this kind of data does not bridge by itself the gap between the normative approach and the social one.

As we will show in the next section, legal professional knowledge can be elicited and built up following complementary methodological trends aiming at obtaining accurate records of practices, routines, cases and (individual and collective) memories. The socio-legal approach turns out to be a *hybrid*, selective approach that uses different combinations of qualitative and quantitative methodologies according to the problems to be solved, the concrete objectives to be achieved, and the type of ontology that the technological system requires.

3.3 An Ontology-Enhanced Decision Support System for Judges: IURISERVICE

In this section we will briefly describe the methodological approach for the design of the IURISERVICE system, and the process of construction of the Ontology of Professional Judicial Knowledge (OPJK), a legal professional ontology grounded on empirical data and expert knowledge. The IURISERVICE application was designed to provide Spanish judges in their first appointment with on-line access to an FAQ (Frequently Asked Questions) system, which contains a repository of practical questions (problems) with their corresponding answers. The aim of the system was to discover the best semantic match between the user's question [input question] (formulated in natural language) and a stored question, so as to offer an answer that satisfied the user. Time and accuracy were critical issues and, to that end,

---

[9]"Law as a social system, that follows, is shaped by *institutional supply* rather than demand: by the infrastructure of legal services, by procedural conditions, by the costs and the ease with which the courts work and by how many alternatives to them are accessible" (Blankenburg 1991: 20).

[10]Regarding institutions, technology and the judiciary, judicial and administrative contexts are shaped through the interplay between human beings, formal regulations, behavioral patterns and the technology at hand (Fabri and Contini 2001, 2003; Contini and Lanzara 2009).

the main research had been based on the possibility of modelling the legal professional knowledge contained in the repository of questions through the use of ontologies. In order to find the question-answer pair that best matches the input question, the system was enhanced with the OPJK ontology and semantic distance calculation.

It is worthwhile to emphasize here that technical work was embedded since 2001 into a larger research on judges and the judiciary in Spain. This research started with the Observatory of Judicial Culture, and was followed up in the subsequent years by several national and international projects.[11] In all of them, the pragmatic focus was the structuring of practices and procedures of the judicial culture: how judicial professional knowledge is produced, shared and organized through formal and informal means (Poblet and Casanovas 2005). In this approach, the implication of judges and magistrates themselves turned out to be crucial.[12] But, as we will see, judges are not researchers. Thus, relying on a user-centered approach has undoubtedly positive effects on technology construction, but it has to be mentioned too that a higher level of uncertainty on the final result has to be assumed as well.

3.3.1 Empirical-Based Design and Knowledge Acquisition

The need for the IURISERVICE system and its initial design was established as a result of a thorough ethnographic survey carried out with the collaboration of the Spanish General Countrycil of the Judiciary [Consejo General del Poder Judicial, CGPJ]. The Spanish Young Judges [Jueces Jóvenes en España] survey[13] was conducted during 2002, it involved five Spanish Universities, [14] and its main objective was to gather information towards the implementation of a support network for judges.

In-depth interviews were made by judges still in training to a set of 129 judges with less than 4 years of experience, out of the total set of 352 young judges who had completed their studies at the Spanish School of the Judiciary from 1997 to 1999 and occupied at the time their first appointment. The questionnaire was designed by senior judges of the Spanish School of the Judiciary, experts of the Documentation Office and team members of the research group. To perform a comparative analysis a set of 139 senior judges was selected.

---

[11] See the Acknowledgments section.

[12] "The practical implication of cognitive apprenticeship is to refocus instructional research on the design process itself: We should design computer systems in partnership with students, teachers, and practitioners in the context of use, so we can produce programs that people can afford and want to use, that promote creativity, and that relate in an honest, pragmatic way to everyday life" (Clancey 1992: 139).

[13] Detailed information regarding this survey can be found at Ayuso et al. (2003) and Álvarez et al. (2005). Also Casanovas et al. (2004) includes some references to the data.

[14] Universitat Autònoma de Barcelona (UAB), Universitat de Barcelona (UB), Universitat Politècnica de Catalunya (UPC), Universidad de León, and Universidad de Burgos.

Table 3.1 Questionnaire for the 2002 survey

Domains	Number of questions	Examples
Training evaluation	18 closed questions and 3 open-ended questions	What is your opinion about the education received at the Law School? What is your opinion regarding the current system of access to the profession? What changes do you suggest in the training at the Spanish School of the Judiciary? Have you used the on-line continuous training system of the CGPJ?
Professional activity	13 closed questions and 16 open-ended questions	What was the most complex professional problem that you had during the first 3 months of appointment? Do you comment your cases if complex with other peers? Do you use Internet?
CENDOJ services	5 closed questions	Do you use the personal attention service of CENDOJ? Do you use legal databases?
Relationships	26 closed questions and 4 open-ended questions	Do you think that people are right when they say that "Justice is very slow"? Do you keep professional relationships with judges from your own class?
Comments on the profession	7 closed questions and 3 open-ended questions	What do you think it is a "good judge"? Why did you become a judge? Do you take your work home?

The questionnaire contained both open-ended and closed questions tackling several areas. Table 3.1 below includes some of the questions included in the questionnaire, adapted from Ayuso et al. (2003) and Álvarez et al. (2005).

Some of the results provided some insight towards which problems could a system for judges in their first appointment offer support. The analysis of the open-ended question "Explain the two most important doubts that you had during the first 3 months as a judge", reported that their questions referred to mostly to the on-call period [*guardia*] (Benjamins et al. 2005). During that period, usually a week per month, the judge must be available 24 h a day for any case that reaches the judicial office.

Thus, this on-call period doubts seem to refer mostly to practical situations regarding, for example, who is to keep the belongings of a detainee or a corpse? Or what is to be done when the prosecutor or the coroner does not attend an appointment? These on-call problems did not appear in the responses of the interviewed senior judges, suggesting that this type of knowledge was probably acquired with the day-to-day practice of the profession. Accordingly, the theoretical training that applicants endure to access judicial appointments does not contain this more 'practical' knowledge; neither does the training at the Spanish School of the Judiciary. This is also consistent with the findings of the survey regarding the changes proposed to the training received in the Spanish Judicial School at Barcelona: judges in their first appointment suggested educational changes towards offering a more practical teaching approach rather than the focus on theoretical study (Ayuso et al. 2003).

This, together with the fact that most judges in their first appointment declared to comment with peers (especially more experienced peers) their cases frequently (11.8%) or sometimes (72.7%), was thought to provide a ground for such a support system. Problems regarding on-call situations at late hours were difficult to consult or comment with others and access to a Frequently-Asked Questions (FAQ) repository containing this type of material could be of use, especially during the first months of appointment.

From the experience of this previous Spanish Young Judges survey, a further questionnaire and ethnographic campaign were designed, and performed during 2004. One Hundred and twenty four newly appointed judges around Spain conformed the sample (from a total of 248 judges of the 52th Class), and the semi-structured interviews were entirely carried out by the research team of the Institute of Law and Technology at the Universitat Autònoma de Barcelona (UAB). The new questionnaire was also organized in 5 sections, concerning professional training, professional activity, professional relationships, quality of life, and personal data. This time, the questionnaire contained some of the 2002 questions, together with questions directed towards gathering information on the requirements that a would-be system ought to have. Information regarding complex cases in civil or criminal law was included again, together with the inquiry regarding their comments with peers about the cases, and the use of Internet. However, new questions such as, "Could you explain specific doubts or problems that came up during the on-call period?", "What kind of professional information do you usually look for in the Web?", and "What would you expect from a web service/software that would provide professional assistance to judges?" were added.

According to the findings presented in Vallbé (2009) (initially analysed in Casanovas et al. (2004)), the use of the Internet was widespread among the interviewed judges, and the information search was mostly job-related, being the official websites (official legislative publications, the judicial power website, etc.) the sites most visited. Computer skills were generally at user level, and mainly regarding the use of text processors, databases and e-mail. The majority of interviewees also desired a system that could solve "doubts", although "corporate information", "judges' forum" and "doctrine" were also considered issues that a system could also offer.[15] Finally, in this survey, the interviewed judges were also asked to provide a list of problems (in the form of questions) that they had faced during their first appointment.

Moreover, different text-based analyses on junior judges' responses were carried out in order to verify the practical nature of these on-call problems and the domain for legal professional knowledge acquisition. In effect, through the combination of simple term-frequency lists, text-mining techniques, and text multivariate statistics—e.g., correspondence analysis—on judges' responses, it was concluded that the relevant terms used by judges pointed to actual references in the judicial

---

[15]The most up-to-date analysis of the data is contained in Vallbé (2009), although more nformation regarding the data and the results may be found in Casanovas et al. (2004, 2005).

Fig. 3.1 Representation of
the terms that describe a
typical problem during
on-call services (with a
$r = 0.4$ correlation threshold)

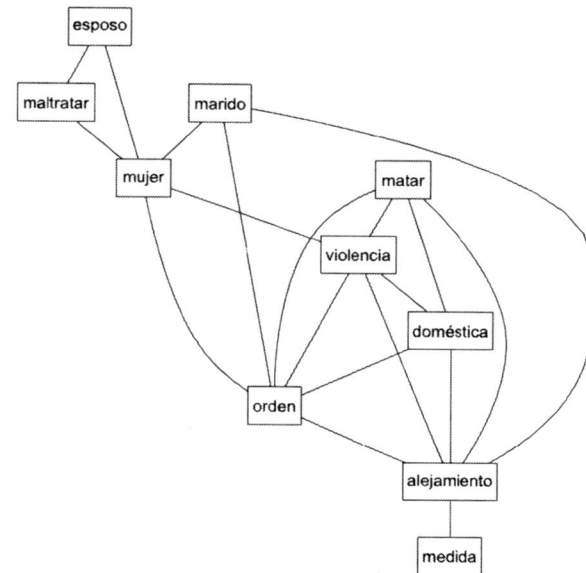

world, in the sense that these terms did not point to abstract instances such as *justice, good* or *evil*, but to instances that have a representation in the world, whether they be particular actors (e.g., forensic doctor) or actions (e.g., arresting a person).[16]

Figure 3.1 maps the correlation of a cluster of terms referring to a typical problem arisen during on-call services, namely conflicts regarding domestic violence. In it we can firstly observe the central role played by the terms *violencia* [violence], *orden* [order, injunction], and *mujer* which may be interpreted as representing three different dimensions of those situations. These analyses led us to the conclusion that problems junior judges do face when on call may be regarded as being of a behavioral, practical nature.

Therefore, the conceptualization process of the Ontology of Professional Judicial Knowledge was based on this conclusion and on this previous and careful knowledge acquisition stage, which comprehended the acquisition of the list of questions and the treatment of this corpus in order to obtain the relevant terminology related to practical problems faced by judges in their first appointment, through term extraction and ontology learning from the corpus of questions—problems— faced by judges. The treatment of the corpus and the extraction of relevant terms was preceded by the establishment of the ontological requirements—including competency questions, other knowledge sources such as materials used by judges

---

[16]Correlations among terms are based on similarity measures between objects within a dissimilarity matrix (Feinerer 2008). The search for correlations is carried out in the vector space computing the cosine between vectors interpreted as the *normalized correlation coefficient* (Manning and Schütze 1999)—with values between 0 and 1.

for their knowledge acquisition process: course syllabus, legislation, and doctrine, the study of existing legal ontologies towards reuse, etc. Detailed information regarding this process may be found at Casellas (2008).

The methodological steps recommended by most ontology development methodologies (Noy and McGuinness 2001; Sure 2003; Gómez-Pérez et al. 2003) and knowledge acquisition techniques (Schreiber et al. 1999; Sure 2003; Milton 2007) were followed and accounted for: (1) preparatory phase (specification of ontology requirements), (2) development phase (knowledge acquisition—experts, documents, reuse—, conceptualization—classes, relations, properties, instances—, validation and formalization), and (3) evaluation phase.

3.3.2 The Ontology of Professional Judicial Knowledge

The lists of questions gathered from these interviews provided the input list of questions for the system and, together with the answers that senior judges of the Spanish School of the Judiciary gave to these questions, they conform the repository of the system. As the aim of the system was to discover the best semantic match between the user's question or input question (formulated in natural language) and a stored question, so as to offer an answer that satisfies the user, the ontology to be developed was to provide better search capabilities than the mere keyword search and to be designed towards semantic indexing and search. This ontology, therefore, ought to represent the relevant concepts related to the problems that take place during the on-call period, the knowledge contained in the list of questions.

This main corpus for judicial professional knowledge modelling, which was acquired through semi-structured interviews, is constituted by nearly 800 practical questions formulated by the newly recruited judges. The interviews were recorded by the team of researchers, with the consent of the judges involved. Later, the recorded interviews were transcribed by the team. This corpus, the set of questions, contains the professional judicial knowledge gathered during daily practice at courts and constituted the repository of the application. The questions contain mainly problems or doubts arisen during the on-call period, although they also include other complex cases that junior judges had to face during their first year of practice. As an example,

- A doctor phoned to inform of someone who is not quite well and that would require internment (confinement). He asks for a court order on the phone. Can I grant it?
- Police is asking for a search warrant to enter a property to unblock a drainpipe, as the owner does not let them in. Should I grant that warrant?
- What is to be done if, while on-call, a corpse removal needs to be performed and there is not forensic doctor available?

Several tools were used in order to extract information regarding subdomains of knowledge and relevant terms of those domains, included in the questions.

Table 3.2   QTO topic and subtopic classification

Topic	Subtopics
Process	Competence conflicts, enforcement proceeding, quick trial, comision rogatoria
Judicial office	Public prosecution, hearing video recording
Gender violence	Restraining order
Immigration	Expulsion and extradition
Family	Internment and incapacitation, autopsy and corpse removal, minors

Correlations shown in Fig. 3.1, together with results from ALCESTE and OntoGen supplied subdomain information. Also TextToOnto, Text2Onto, AntConc, and Yoshikoder were used as tools to support term and ontology extraction.

For example, in order to gain some more insight towards the general contents of these questions, ONTOGEN was used on the corpus of questions to suggest concepts and relations, while the instances of those concepts were the questions themselves. This semi-automatic classification of the questions into different concepts (or topics) produced the following main topics: Oficina_Judicial [court office], Violencia_Domestica [gender violence], Extranjeria [immmigration], Proceso [process], and Familia [family]. A total of 17 classes (root, main topics and subtopics) were semi-automatically learnt by the OntoGen tool (see, for example, Table 3.2). This topic ontology (Question Topic Ontology) was used to support question classification within the IURISERVICE system. See, for more details, Blázquez et al. (2005) and Casellas et al. (2007).

Regarding relevant terminology, Yoshikoder and AntConc offered the initial list of 477 terms (later extended to include more than 900 terms), which supplied the initial terminological knowledge for term grouping, conceptual modelling and ontology formalization. This inital knowledge acquisition and grouping was informally validated by legal experts.[17]

Once the conceptual extractions were performed and as much information as possible was acquired on the corpus of questions, we proceeded at grouping and organizing the concepts in a taxonomy, taking into account the content of the corpus of questions (practical problems), the context of the questions (the judicial setting) together with background theoretical knowledge acquired during the training period of judges (from academic textbooks, legislation and examination and training course syllabuses), the established competency questions, and the insights provided by the analysis of several upper and core ontologies Casellas (2008).

---

[17]With Yoshikoder, the analysis of the document containing the full set of questions obtained an initial list 1,998 terms for the lemmatized text. To gather an initial more manageable set of terms, a threshold of 5 occurrences was established, 452 terms were obtained. AntConc obtained a similar list with 455 terms. The 455 list of terms from the AntConc analysis on the lemmatized corpus was manually revised to offer a first working set of terms, including a revision on multiple terms (N+Adj, N+prep+N, and N+prep+N+Adj forms).

Finally, the taxonomical structure was formalized in OWL using the Protégé ontology editor to allow future reuse or enrichment.[18] Two versions of OPJK, regarding their computational complexity, have been produced in order to facilitate computation capabilities and to obtain significant technical evaluation results in the future.

OPJK version 1.0 includes 74 classes, 73 `rdfs:subClassOf` relations and 912 instances, together with a total of 31 `owl:ObjectProperty` axioms (14 `owl:subPropertyOf` and 15 `owl:inverseOf`), 1 transitive and 1 functional `owl:ObjectProperty`. OPJK version 2.0 includes, as well, 1 `owl:equivalentClass` and 75 `owl:disjointWith` axioms, around 100 multiple class instantiation constructs, and, finally, 53 `owl:sameAs` axioms (Fig. 3.2).[19]

3.3.3 User-Centered Approach: Expert Involvement

Evaluation activities, both during conceptualization and after formalization were central to the development of the Ontology of Professional Judicial Knowledge. The participation and consultation of legal experts (academics, magistrates and lawyers), to validate the knowledge extracted, the modelling decisions taken, and the final OPJK ontology was key. There are different moments and levels of involvement of experts in the development process of the ontology. First, as explained above, the research team gathered the knowledge that constituted the corpus during the interviews with judges in their first appointment. Second, a first validation regarding the grouping of terms was performed with experts and, finally, the formalized ontology was evaluated by experts and refined accordingly. Moreover, usability and field tests were conducted.

Regarding validation, difficult and complex modelling decisions were discussed with the team of domain experts and ontology engineers, prior to formalization. We already explained that Yoshikoder and AntConc offered the initial list of 477 terms, which supplied the initial terminological knowledge for term grouping, conceptual modelling and ontology formalization. This initial knowledge acquisition and grouping was informally validated by legal experts. Taking into account most suggestions and revising the classifications offered by the legal experts, some changes were introduced to the groups towards conceptualization and further relevant extracted terms from the initial list were classified. It is worth to mention that expertise is a mixed up knowledge: common sense, procedural knowledge, legal interpretation and legal theory.

The evaluation included the evaluation of the OPJK classes, subclass relationships, properties and instances and a more general and experimental evaluation based on a usability questionnaire. The results of these evaluations, a 72.92

---

[18] Versions 3.3.1, 3.4 (beta) and 4.0 (beta) were used.

[19] OPJK versions 1.0 and 2.0 have a DL expressivity of *ALHIF+* and *SHOIF*, respectively.

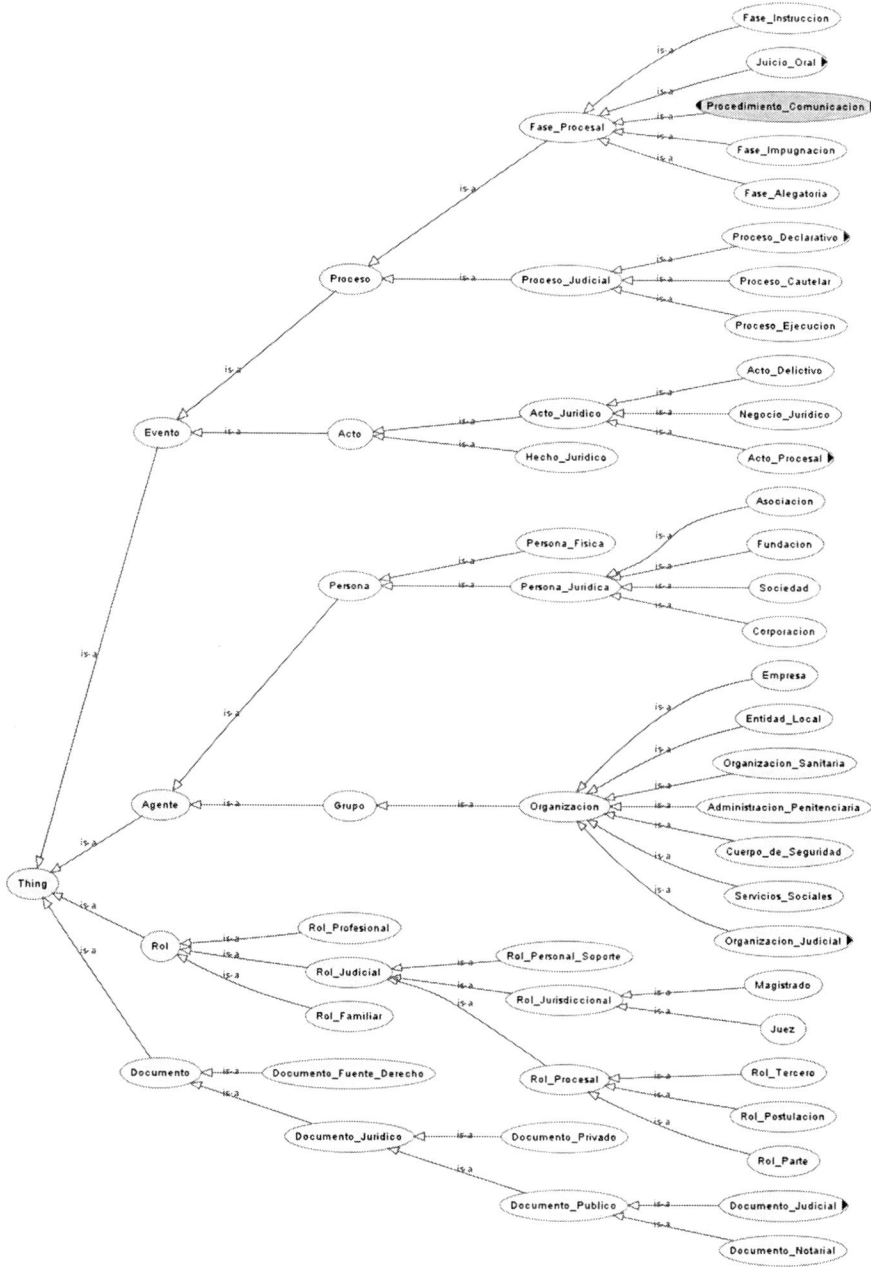

Fig. 3.2 OPJK class structure

Fig. 3.3 Usability tests in the
Spanish Judicial School, with
magistrates and researchers of
the IDT team. SEKT Project,
May, 2006

and 69.44% of agreement with the ontology, respectively, suggested that, although
there was general agreement, there was also some room for improvement regarding
class conceptualization which could offer more granularity and foster understanding and shareability amongst experts. With the evaluation results and the expert's

Fig. 3.4 Field tests with users in the Spanish Judicial School, with junior judges. SEKT Project,
February, 2007

suggestions the ontology was refined, several classes were added or modified (e.g., relabelled), some instances were redistributed; properties and disjoint axioms were modified or added.

Finally, several usability tests, such as Heuristic Evaluation and Cognitive Walkthrough (see Fig. 3.3) and users tests of the IURISERVICE application (see Fig. 3.4) were conducted with the involvement of magistrates from the Spanish Judicial School, trainee judges and legal experts (Casanovas et.al 2009b).

3.4 Final Remarks

We have come a long way since the first ontology and the first prototype of IURIS-ERVICE in 2002. The SEKT project (2003–2006) allowed us to build up a second reusable and more consistent ontology, and a second prototype. Two doctoral dissertations and more than 20 papers and international articles have been produced as a result of this extended research on the Spanish judiciary. But, so far, the system has not yet been implemented, because the initial design of the system, although semantically enhanced, was mainly envisaged as a Web 1.0 application. Moreover, new statutes regarding domestic violence, judicial organization, immigration, and health care have been promulgated, and the original questions and answers require a sound revision. Beyond professional changes in the Spanish political landscape, maintenance of the knowledge-base has been one of the main problems for the OPJK ontology and for the system as a whole.

Up-to-date maintenance of the FAQ requires that the magistrates of the School revise new questions and feed the system with new answers. Therefore, the system would benefit from some automated functionalities of the Web 2.0 and 3.0, and from collaborative development, and the dynamic flow of collective knowledge in a *community or network of users* (in this case, judges in their first appointment). Professional legal knowledge evolves sometimes faster than legal language.

All these practical problems do matter, because we think that the lifecycle of this type of ontologies that are grounded on ongoing institutional features has proven to be longer than we thought at first. The consequence is that we have extended the knowledge acquisition phase up to now, thus, we are in a third stage of IURISER-VICE. Relationships and ties with the Judiciary have been maintained; new studies are required to update the descriptions of judicial culture and behavior, and a new implemented prototype will come with a renewed set of tests.

We call this empirically grounded development of legal ontologies an *iterative and integrated pragmatic cycle*, with the following components:

- surveys and ethnographic fieldwork (carnets, reports, audio and video-tapes. photos, interviews, transcriptions...)
- statistical, textual and visual analysis
- intervention (professional, technological–ontology building, prototypes...)

- ontology validation and evaluation
- usability tests (cognitive walkthrough, *focus groups*, protoype testing...)
- users tests (field tests...)
- refinement (ontology, hypothesis and prototype)

Feedback from users is crucial, but it cannot be completely planned and controlled, because organizations, corporations and institutions have their own dynamics. Sometimes the cycle can be followed almost sequentially, but very often cannot. It depends on the dynamics, complexity and development of the research in which ontologies are built up for precise purposes.

Acknowledgements The research presented in this paper has been developed within the framework of the following projects: SEC2001-2581-C02-01; FIT-150500-2002-562; FIT-150500-2003-198; EU-IST 2003-506826 SEKT; SEJ2006-10695; FIT-350101-2006-26.; FIT-350100-2007-161; TSI-020501-2008, 2008–2010; CSO-2008-05536-SOCI.

References

Aakhus, M., A. Aldrich (2002). Crafting Communication Activity: Understanding FeliCity in 'I wish I...' Compliments. *Research on Language and Social Interaction*, 35(4): 395–425.

Abel, R.L. (Ed.) (1995). *The Law & Society Reader*. New York University Press, New York, NY.

Abel, R.L. (1995). What We Talk About When We Talk About Law. In R. Abel (Ed.) *The Law & Society Reader*. New York University Press, New York, NY, 1–10.

Almond, G., S. Verba (1963). *The Civic Culture. Political Attitudes and Democracy in Five Nations*. Princeton University Press, Princeton, NJ.

Álvarez, R., M. Ayuso, M. Bécue (2005). Statistical Study of Judicial Practices. In V.R. Benjamins, P. Casanovas, J. Breuker, A. Gangemi (Eds.) *Law and the Semantic Web. Legal Ontologies, Methodologies, Legal Information Retrieval, and Applications*, LNCS, vol. 3369. Springer, Berlin, Heidelberg, 25–35.

Amselek, P., N. MacCormick (Eds.) (1991). *Controversies About Law's Ontology*. Edinburgh University Press, Edinburgh.

Ayuso, M., M. Bécue, R. Álvarez, O. Valencia, R. Álvarez, M.L. Hernández, M. Santolino (2003, Septiembre). Jueces jóvenes en españa (2002). Análisis estadístico de las encuestas a los jueces en su primer destino (promociones 48/49 y 50). Análisis comparativo con jueces de mayor experiencia. SEC-2001-2581-C02-01/02 informe interno Report n.2, Consejo General del Poder Judicial [General Countrycil of the Judiciary].

Bench-Capon, T.J.M. (2001). Task Neutral Ontologies, Common Sense Ontologies and Legal Information Systems, 2nd International Workshop on Legal Ontologies. In Verheij, B. (Ed.) *Legal Knowledge and Information Systems: Jurix 2001: The Fourteenth Annual Conference*, Frontiers in Artificial Intelligence and Applications, IOS Press, Amsterdam.

Benjamins, V.R., P. Casanovas, J. Contreras, J.M. López-Cobo, L. Lemus (2005). Iuriservice: An Intelligent Frequently Asked Questions System to Assist Newly Appointed Judges. In V.R. Benjamins, P. Casanovas, J. Breuker, A. Gangemi (Eds.) *Law and the Semantic Web. Legal Ontologies, Methodologies, Legal Information Retrieval, and Applications*. Number 3369 in Lecture Notes in Computer Science, Springer, Berlin, Heidelberg, 205–222.

Blankenburg, E. (1991). Legal Cultures Compared. In E. Blankenburg, J. Commaille, M. Galanter (Eds.) *Disputes and Litigation*, Oñati Proceedings n.12, IISJL, Oññanti, 11–21.

Blankenburg, E. (1997). *Patterns of Legal Culture: The Netherlands Compared to Neighboring Germany*, Duitsland Institute, Universiteit van Amsterdam.

Blázquez, M., R. Peña-Ortiz, J. Contreras, R. Benjamins, P. Casanovas, J.-J. Vallbé, and N. Casellas (2005, December). D10.3.1 Legal Case Study: Prototype. Sekt ist-2003-506826 Deliverable,

SEKT, EU-IST Project IST-2003-506826, Intelligent Software Components S.A. (iSOCO) and Universitat Autonoma de Barcelona (UAB).

Casanovas, P. (2002). Dimensiones del pluralismo jurídico, IX Congrés d'Sntropologia FAAEE, Barcelona, available at http://www.ub.edu/reciprocitat/GER_WEB_CAS/Actividades/Actividades%20Simposio%202002/Ponencia-Casanovas.pdf (accessed 10/5/2010)

Casanovas, P., X. Binefa, C. Gracia, E. Teodoro, N. Galera, M. Blázquez, M. Poblet, J. Carrabina, M. Monton, C. Montero, J. Serrano, J.M. López-Cobo (2009a). The E-Sentencias Prototype: A Procedural Ontology for Legal Multimedia Applications in the Spanish Civil Courts. In P. Casanovas, J. Breuker, M. Klein, E. Francesconi (Eds.) *Channelling the Legal Information Flood. Legal Ontologies and the Semantic Web*, vol. 188. Frontiers in Artificial Intelligence and Applications, IOS Press, Amsterdam, 199–219.

Casanovas, P., N. Casellas, J.J. Vallbé (2009b). An Ontology-Based Decision Support System for Judges. In P. Casanovas, J. Breuker, M. Klein, E. Francesconi (Eds.) *Channelling the Legal Information Flood. Legal Ontologies and the Semantic Web*, vol. 188. Frontiers in Artificial Intelligence and Applications, IOS Press, Amsterdam, 165–175.

Casanovas, P., M. Poblet, N. Casellas, J. Contreras, R. Benjamins, M. Blázquez (2005). Supporting Newly-Appointed Judges: A Legal Knowledge Management Case Study. *Journal of Knowledge Management*, 9(5): 7–27.

Casanovas, P., M. Poblet, N. Casellas, J. Vallbé, F. Ramos, R. Benjamins, M. Blázquez, L. Rodrigo, J. Contreras, J. Gorroñogoitia-Cruz (2004, December (January 2005)). D10.2.1 Legal Case Study: Legal Scenario. Sekt ist-2003-506826 Deliverable, SEKT, EU-IST Project IST-2003-506826, Intelligent Software Components S.A. and Universitat Autonoma de Barcelona.

Casellas, N., J.-E. Nieto, A. Meroño, A. Roig, S. Torralba, M. Reyes de los Mozos, P. Casanovas (2010). Ontological Semantics for Data Privacy Compliance: The NEURONA Ontology, *Intelligent Information Privacy Management. Papers from the AAAI Spring Symposium, Stanford 23rd–25th of March 2010, Technical Report SS-10-05*, AAAI Press, Menlo Park, California, 34–38.

Casellas, N. (2008, December). *Modelling Legal Knowledge Through Ontologies. OPJK: The Ontology of Professional Judicial Knowledge*. Ph.D. thesis, Departament de Ciència Política i Dret Públic, Facultat de Dret, Bellaterra, Barcelona.

Casellas, N., P. Casanovas, J.-J. Vallbé, M. Poblet, M. Blázquez, J. Contreras, J. M. López-Cobo, V. R. Benjamins (2007). Semantic Enhancement for Legal Information Retrieval: Iuriservice Performance. In *Proceedings of the Eleventh International Conference on Artificial Intelligence and Law. ICAIL 2007, June 4–8, Stanford Law School, California*, 49–57. Association for Computing Machinery.

Clancey, W.J. (1992). Representations of Knowing: In Defense of Cognitive Apprenticeship. *Journal of Artificial Intelligence in Education*, 3(2): 139–168.

Contini, F., G.F. Lanzara (Eds.) (2009). *ICT and Innovation in the Public Sector. European Studies in the Making of E-Government*. Palgrave, Macmillan, Houndmills.

Fabri, M., F. Contini (Eds.) (2001). *Justice and Technology in Europe: How ICT is Changing the Judicial Business*. Kluwer Law International, The Hague.

Fabri, M., F. Contini (Eds.) (2003). *Judicial Electronic Data Interchange in Europe: Applications, Policies, and Trends*. IRSIG-CNR, Lo Scarabeo, Bologna.

Feigenbaum, E.A. (1977). The Art of Artificial Intellegigence: I. Themes and Case Studies of Knowledge Engineering. STAN-CS-77-621 Heuristic Programming Project Memo, 77–25.

Feigenbaum, E.A. (1992). A Personal View of Experts Systems: Looking Back and Looking Ahead, Knowledge System Laboratory, Report n. 92-41 KSL, Stanford.

Feinerer, I. (2008). *tm: Text Mining Package* (R package version 0.3-3 ed.).

Fernández-Barrera, M., G. Sartor (2010). The Legal Theory Perspective: Doctrinal Conceptual Systems vs. Computational Ontologies, Chap. 2, this volume.

Forsyth, D.E., B. Buchanan (1989). Knowledge Acquisition for Expert Systems: Some Pitfalls and Suggestions. *IEEE Transactions on Systems, Man, and Cybernetics*, 19(3): 435–442.

Friedman, L.M. (1975). *The Legal System: A Social Science Perspective.* Russell Sage Foundation, New York, NY.

Friedman, L.M., S. MacAulay, J.A. Stookey (Eds.) (1995). *Law and Society Reader: Readings on the Social Studies of Law.* Norton and Co, New York, NY.

Friedman, L.M., R. Pérez-Perdomo (Eds.) (2003). *Legal Culture in the Age of Globalization. Latin America and Latin Europe.* Stanford University Press, Stanford, CA.

Gómez-Pérez, A., M. Fernández-López, O. Corcho (2003). *Ontological Engineering. With Examples from the Areas of Knowledge Management, e-Commerce and the Semantic Web.* Advanced Information and Knowlege Processing. Springer, London.

Hage, J., B. Verheij (1999). The Law as a Dynamic Interconnected System of States of Affairs: A Legal Top Ontology. *International Journal of Human-Computer Studies,* 51 (6): 1043–1077.

Jacobs, S. (2002). Maintaining Neutrality in Dispute Mediation: Managing Disagreement While Managing Not To Disagree. *Journal of Pragmatics,* 34: 1403–1426.

Jackson, S. (1998). Disputation by Design. *Argumentation,* 12: 183–198.

Manning, C.D., H. Schütze (1999). *Foundations of Statistical Natural Language Processing.* The MIT Press, Cambridge, MA/London, UK.

Martin, D., M. Rouncefield, I. Sommerville (2002). Applying Patterns of Cooperative Interaction to Work (Re)Design: E-Government and Planning. In *Proceedings of CHI 2002.* Publications of the ACM, Minneapolis, MN.

Martin, D., I. Sommerville (2004). Patterns of Cooperative Interaction: Linking Ethnomethodology and Design. *ACM Transactions on Computer-Human Interaction,* March 2004; 11(1): 59–89.

Milton, N. (2007). *Knowledge Acquisition in Practice. A Step-by-Step Guide.* Decision Engineering. Springer, London.

Noy, N.F., D.L. McGuinness (2001). Ontology Development 101: A Guide to Creating Your First Ontology. Technical Report SMI-2001-0880, Stanford University School of Medicine.

Peczenik, A. (2000). Scientia Juris. An Unsolved Philosophical Problem. *Ethical Theory and Moral Practice,* 3(3): 273–302.

Peczenick, A. (2005). *Scientia Juris. Legal Doctrine as Knowledge of Law and as a Source of Law.* In *A Treatise of Legal Philosophy and Legal Jurisprudence,* vol. 4. Springer, Heidelberg, Berlin.

Poblet, M., N. Casellas, S. Torralba, P. Casanovas (2009). Modeling Expert Knowledge in the Mediation Domain: A Mediation Core Ontology. In N. Casellas, E. Francesconi, R. Hoekstra, S. Montemagni (Eds.) *Proceedings of 3rd Workshop on Legal Ontologies and Artificial Intelligence Techniques (LOAIT2009), Barcelona June 8, 2009, IDT Series,* vol. 2, 19–28. (Available at: http://www.huygens.es/site/service4.html).

Poblet, M., P. Casanovas (2005). Recruitment, Professional Evaluation and Career of Judges and Prosecutors in Spain. In G. di Federico (Ed.) *Recruitment, Professional Evaluation and Career of Judges and Prosecutors in Europe: Austria, France, Germany, Italy, The Netherlands and Spain.* IRSIG-CNR, Lo Scarabeo, Bologna, 185–214.

Schreiber, G., H. Akkermans, A. Anjewierden, R. de Hoog, N. Shadbolt, W.V. de Velde, B. Wielinga (1999). *Knowledge Engineering and Management. The CommonKADS Methodology.* A Bradford Book. The MIT Press, Cambridge, MA/London, England.

Sure, Y. (2003). *Methodology, Tools and Case Studies for Ontology Based Knowledge Management.* Ph.D. thesis, Fakultät für Wirschaftwissenschaften der Universität Fridericiana zu Karlsruhe.

Sure, Y., C. Tempich, D. Vrandecić (2006). Ontology Engineering Methodologies. In J. Davies et al. (Eds.) *Semanic Web Technologies. Trends and Research in Ontology-based Systems,* Chichester, Wiley, 171–190.

Tamanaha, B.Z. (2001). *A General Jurisprudence of Law and Society.* Oxford University Press, Oxford, MA.

Tiscornia, D. (2005). Multilingual Semantic Metadata for Law. In Quaderni CNIPA, 2005, *3rd Workshop on Legislative XML* (Furore, 6–8 aprile, 2005).

Trubek, D.M. (1990). Back to the Future: The Short, Happy Life of the Law and Society Movement. *Florida State University Law Review*, 18(1): 1–55.

Trubek, D.M., Y. Dézalay, R. Buchanan, J.R. Davis (1994). Global Restructuring and the Law: Studies of the Internationalization of Legal Fields and the Creation of Transnational Arenas. *Case Western Reserve Law Review*, 44(2): 407–498.

Vallbé, J.-J. (2009, July). *Models of Decision-Making: Facing Uncertainty in Spanish Judicial Settings*. Ph.D. thesis, Departament de Dret Constitucional i Ciència Política. Universitat de Barcelona, Barcelona.

Chapter 4
A Cognitive Science Perspective on Legal Ontologies

Joost Breuker and Rinke Hoekstra

4.1 Introduction

Ontological engineering has several origins. In this article we identify five, and all five still play a major role in ontology engineering. Each of these roots gives a different perspective on content and use of ontologies, but as these roots are hardly ever explicit, they are a source of much confusion. In the past, one has tried to solve this confusion by defining what an ontology is: much in the spirit of ontology engineering iself. There is little consensus and the best definitions leave much underspecified. As we will show in Section 4.2, these five roots take different perspectives on what ontologies aim to capture. Philosophical ontology is concerned with "reality"; Information science with systematic terminology; Artificial Intelligence (AI) with terminological knowledge and Information Management with semantics. These differences may look subtle but have different consequences for the use of these ontologies, which ranges from analytic clarification to automated reasoning. This is also manifest from the different representation formalisms used. If these uses were consistent, we would not have to bother, but as will be shown in Section 4.4, mismatches occur between the representation formalism used and the aim of the application. These mismatches can often be traced to an unclear distinction between knowledge and semantics. In developing standards for the Semantic Web (SW) this confusion is reinforced by taking a knowledge representation formalism as a standard for ontologies, while current practice—mainly information management—could have done with a more expressive formalism. We explain the difference between knowledge and semantics, i.e. the use of knowledge in context, in Section 4.3 using a simple cognitive architecture for natural language production.

In Section 4.5 we will focus on an area of ontology engineering where a cognitive science perspective is well suited and should be taken more serious: the area of top/upper/foundational/core ontologies. These ontologies cover the abstract, general

J. Breuker (✉)
Leibniz Center for Law, University of Amsterdam, Amsterdam, The Netherlands
e-mail: breuker@science.uva.nl

G. Sartor et al. (eds.), *Approaches to Legal Ontologies*, Law, Governance and Technology Series 1, DOI 10.1007/978-94-007-0120-5_4,
© Springer Science+Business Media B.V. 2011

concepts that are applicable to (almost) any domain, like time, space, causation, agent, matter, process, etc. Here also the distinction between knowledge and semantics fades. Thus far, this area of research has shown a large divergence of approaches and results. In many respects it is reminiscent of age long discussions in philosophical ontology; on the other hand the concerns are about representations, powerful to feed content-specific reasoning e.g. about spatial and temporal configurations. These kinds of concepts are also the drivers or cores of common sense, and sometimes an explicit common sense view is proclaimed (e.g. in DOLCE (Gangemi et al. 2002) and in CYC (Lenat 1995)). For both a philosophical perspective (e.g. Sowa's ontology (Sowa 2000), and to some extent SUMO (Pease and Niles 2002) and also DOLCE (!)), and a common sense perspective no external, empirical evidence is cited to support claims on the selection of concepts and their structuring. At the same time Cognitive Science has moved from an almost exclusive concern about cognitive processes to (the development of) the basic content of our shared cognitions and emotions, and a wealth of empirical data and theoretical insights have been reported. In the last Section of this article we will give some examples and refer to our still ongoing work on a common-sense based core ontology for legal domains: LKIF-Core (Hoekstra et al. 2007; Hoekstra 2009).

In summary, we will present two perspectives from cognitive science to ontology engineering. The first one comes from the architecture of human cognition in which one can argue that knowledge and semantics are not the same thing and should be treated differently: both with respect to formal-machine representation as to the kind of applications that should be fueled by ontologies. The second one concerns a valid identification of the basic concepts that constitute our deep common sense.

4.2 Origins of Ontological Engineering

In temporal order we can trace the following origins of ontology engineering:

4.2.1 Philosophy (1) Ontology

Ontology as a branch of metaphysics is concerned with (categories) of being, i.e. about existence and reality. Although the term "ontology" only appears in the seventeenth century, its endeavor is more than two millennia old (Parmenides; Aristotle). It has been emphasized already in the beginning of the 90-ies that ontologies (i.e. ontology engineering) and Ontology should not be confounded. The former is about (machine-readable) structures of concepts, while the latter is about "existing entities". Despite this difference, philosophical ontology has found a place in ontology engineering, often referred to as "formal ontology". This is also due to the fact that (philosophical) logic and theories of knowledge representation have come close enough to compare work. Ontology brings a wealth of analyses of concepts to ontologies. An excellent review of concepts relevant for ontology engineering can be found in Sowas book (2000). However, it also brings on board the speculative and argumentative nature, due to the lack of an applied or empirical perspective.[1]

4.2.2 *Philosophy (2)* Lingua Universalis Philosophica

The existence of different languages—the curse of Babel—was not only a serious obstacle for universal understanding, but also the fact that words have ambiguous and variable meanings was already a preoccupation of many philosophers in the Middle Ages (e.g. Ockham). In the Seventeenth century several proposals were made to construct a language whose terms would be well defined, and moreover, whose form would transpire its semantics. The best example of this approach is the unique work by John Wilkins (1668) who published a thesaurus, structured as a taxonomy of about 2,000 well-defined and cross referenced concepts, starting from 40 main categories. In fact we can see this work as far more in line with current ontology engineering than philosophical ontology, and the book (hard to get) could still serve as a useful source of inspiration for constructing top-ontologies. Its influence in philosophy was very small, but it inspired the construction of thesauri, in particular Roget's thesaurus (1852) and it is one of the origins of information science. According to Wilkins an important cause for the confusions inherent to natural language was the fact that words were arbitrary labels for concepts: their morphology did not indicate the underlying semantics. Given his taxonomy new words could be composed by descending a path in the taxonomy. For instance, "zita" would stand for "dog", composed from z for "animal", i for "beast", t for "canine" and a for "dog".[2] Leibniz immediately ordered this book, but instead of creating semantically transparent words, he proposed to use numbers which could be automatically processed by mechanical calculators, using combinatorics. This *calculus ratiocinator* is based upon prime numbers and is binary, previewing computer cryptography. Leibniz himself improved Pascal's calculator to include division, and concluded farsighted, but overly optimistic:

> "Once the characteristic numbers of most notions are determined, the human race will have a new kind of tool, a tool that will increase the power of the mind much more than optical lenses helped our eyes, a tool that will be as far superior to microscopes or telescopes as reason is to vision" (G. Leibniz, Philosophical Essays)

In summary: current views and practice in ontology engineering have more affinity with these *Lingua Universalis Philosophica* views on taxonomies of concepts and mechanical reasoning, than with Ontology.

---

[1] Paradoxically formal ontology is sometimes called 'applied ontology'! see Wikipedia under wikipedia.org/wiki/Applied_ontology

[2] The reader is referred to (Ecco 1997) for a detailed review.

4.2.3 Artificial Intelligence

In a classic paper McCarthy and Hayes (1969) discuss the definitions of a small set of central concepts of common sense: causation, fluents, action and its epistemological consequences. This work was further taken up in an influential paper—"naive physics manifesto"—by Pat Hayes (1985) in which he argued that in common sense views of the physical world small sets ("clusters") of concepts formed the basic ontology for interpreting physical events. Although this proposal was never taken up in its full consequence, in the beginning of the 80-ies reasoning about physical systems became a major research issue. In Qualitative Reasoning (QR) (Weld and de Kleer 1990) and in Model Based Reasoning (MBR) (Hamscher et al. 1992) it is necessary that the system is able to interpret situations and to reason from the structure of these situations and its current states what will or can happen, i.e. to make predictions about its behavior. To be able to do so, it should be equipped with basic notions of its physical domain (e.g. gases, containers, and temperatures, or electricity, connections and components). These basic concepts should be defined in such a way that the relevant properties of the entities involved could be inferred. Therefore, the knowledge base of a QR/MBR systems contains an ontology (which is not necessarily well separated from the rest of the knowledge) (Forbus 2008). Ontological knowledge is used to identify what instances (individuals) are, and to infer properties and other relationships with other individuals to be able to interpret a situation. Ontologies in AI are therefore constructed to perform reasoning. Note that in natural language processing, the meaning of words has a similar status. However, in Section 4.3 we will point out that there is a subtle but important difference between word senses in natural language and concepts used in predicting situations.

4.2.4 Knowledge Engineering

The most direct ancestor of ontology engineering is the knowledge engineering community. In methodologies for building knowledge systems, in particular CommonKADS (Schreiber et al. 1993), ontologies were used as specifications of domain terminology, i.e. a conceptual documentation for constructing a domain knowledge base (Van Heijst et al. 1997). Languages were constructed to handle these ontologies in machine manageable form: CML[3] and Ontolingua (Gruber 1993). The latter language was based upon KIF (Knowledge Interchange Format; now: CommonLogic), a machine readable version of predicate logic, intended to be used as a translation interlingua for various Description Logic (DL) based knowledge representation (KR) systems. Casting ontologies in Ontolingua also enabled reuse of domain ontologies via the publicly available Ontolingua repository. A side effect of these developments was that these ontologies could very well be used in supporting knowledge and information management (Schreiber et al. 2000).

---

[3]Conceptual Modeling Language for CommonKADS (Breuker and Van De Velde 1994)

4.2.5 Semantic Web

A real boost to the development of ontologies occurred when Tim Berners-Lee (1999) was "dreaming" aloud and proposed to extend the current Web with semantic support:

> "The first step is putting data on the web in a form that machines can naturally understand, or converting it to that form. This creates what I call a Semantic Web – a web of data that can be processed directly or indirectly by machines" (Berners-Lee 1999: 191)

Ontologies were supposed to provide these semantics that should enable this machine-understanding, and a new, state of the art Web Ontology Language (OWL) was designed (Bechhofer 2004). OWL is a DL based knowledge representation language, carefully conceived to enable decidable reasoning (Horrocks et al. 2003).

From this overview of the roots of ontologies, it becomes understandable why we have such a large variety of kinds of ontologies, and that there is so little agreement about what ontologies are or should be. First, the aims differ considerably. Some are aimed at reasoning (see e.g. (van de Ven et al. 2008) for legal reasoning); most others are for information management and retrieval, in particular for (Semantic) Web applications. Second, is the re-usability perspective. The most abstract and general (upper-, top- or foundational) ontologies are supposed to be applicable to almost any domain. Philosophical ontology is here often the main source of inspiration (e.g. DOLCE (Gangemi et al. 2002), SUMO (Pease and Niles 2002)). Core ontologies capture some clusters of concepts that are typical for some field of activities, such as medicine or law (Hoekstra 2007), which makes them re-useful for domain ontologies of the field. Third, there is a large range of formalisms into which ontologies are cast, varying from typical KR formalisms (e.g. OWL-DL, Topic Maps, RDFS); to interchange formalism (KIF, CommonLogic), and to conceptual specification languages (UML, CML). However, as we will see in Section 4.4, the choice of the language is in many cases not motivated by the job the ontology is supposed to perform. Fourth, the ontologies differ much in detail of representation. Some are no more than class-subclass structures of terms, while others have dense specifications of (structured) properties and relations.

4.3 Knowledge and Semantics

In the overview of the roots of ontology engineering, ontology appears to capture successively: reality, knowledge and/or semantics. All three are closely interrelated. To identify or to belief that certain categories refer to reality we must know about these. Semantics reflect our understanding of expressions, and this understanding is based upon our knowledge and beliefs in general. However, we must make an important distinction between knowledge and semantics, i.e. between what we know and belief about some term (concept) and what a term means in some expression. We can illustrate this by the different senses that a simple, rather concrete term like "car" can take. We know lots of things about cars (and maybe even more about individual cars). However, in the following statements, the meanings of the term car are totally different:

1. Driver: "I will take my car". (car is a vehicle)
2. Mechanic: "This car has a defective carburetor". (car is a device)
3. Salesman: "This car is a bargain". (car is a commodity)
4. Insurance inspector: "This car is a wreck". (i.e. no longer to be viewed as a car)

It is not difficult to add new perspectives, dependent on the focus of a property (e.g. energy consumer; polluter, status symbol, killer, etc). The properties that are *relevant* with each view (superclass) of "car" have little in common. Vehicles are for transport; devices have a structure and causal behaviors; commodities imply trade; wrecks are to be recycled, etc. Therefore the semantics of terms in expressions are the result of *using* knowledge in a specific context. These contexts may even bring "logical" conflict with what we know the term can mean, as in metaphorical expressions: e.g. "This car never abandoned me". Leaving metaphor for practical reasons aside (however important it is in our reasoning and communication, e.g. (Lakoff 1987; Pinker 2007)), we can see the semantics of a term as a subset of what we know a concept to be. This means that for instance a reusable ontology that should capture the semantics of a term in various contexts should contain multiple classifications. That is exactly *not* what current practice shows in ontologies aimed at information management of documentation, in particular when these applications have to operate on the Web, where contexts can be highly diverse. They do not recognize contexts, nor do they select specific meanings of terms. The problem is not that we do not have the technology available to do so: it is the fact that it is extremely costly and complex to construct ontologies that have multiple views on board. Multiple classification is necessary, but not sufficient to obtain this automatic machine understanding that Tim Berners-Lee was dreaming about. We will return to this issue in the next section, but first we will give a short account of the kind of knowledge stores that have evolved to enable us to come to context sensitive communication, i.e. the use of natural language.

Figure 4.1, adapted from (Levelt 1993), presents a very simplified cognitive architecture for generating natural language. The spatial and the kinesthetic representational systems are perceptual systems that interpret information from the eyes, respectively sensors that identify the positions of our body parts, including the body with respect to gravity. These two systems can integrate the information abstracted from these senses so that body movements in space can be coordinated. They include very short term, sensory memories. Many animals who have these kinds of receptors have these systems. In humans a new kind of representational system evolved that works like an interlingua between these perceptual systems: a propositional representation system. It allows us to state that we see a chair, hear footsteps, etc. With "propositional" is meant that its representations no longer contain perceptual elements. This propositional system is the human knowledge base.[4] This knowledge

---

[4]Another term has been: long term memory. At least three subsystems can be distinguished: episodic memory, containing past memories (instances); semantic memory (which contains generic

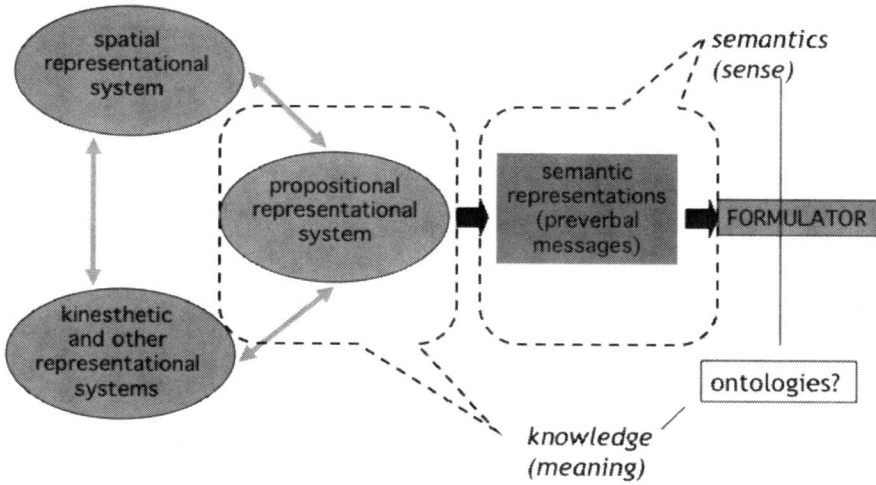

Fig. 4.1 Knowledge stores in natural language generation. After Levelt (1993)

store is used to create a "preverbal message". It is constructed from a (sequence of) speech act(s), reflecting intention; the communication content of these speech acts is derived or selected from the propositional system. This content is what semantics are about. In its simplest version they are selections from this propositional system, but often new constructs emerge, as e.g. in the use of metaphors, analogies, etc. We discuss here this architecture not only to explain how in psycholinguistics semantics are distinguished from knowledge. As it becomes more and more evident that we share this propositional store with some of our close ancestors, we may become interested in the genetic knowledge seeds which guide humans in developing their interpretations of the physical and social world. To be continued in Section 4.5.

4.4 Formalisms, Reasoning and Information Management

With a few exceptions, applications fueled by ontologies are used for information management. They are used for finding or indexing (tagging) what documents are about, or to filter data, but they are not used for reasoning. Reasoning with ontologies can take two forms. The first one is for modeling situations and for problem solving: as in QR and in MBR. The second one is to use ontology as the vocabulary in natural language processing: as in Tim Berners-Lee's proposal for the Semantic Web. This dream has created a paradox and an impasse. The ontology language, OWL(-DL), is extremely well suited for this first kind of reasoning, and moreover, one can trust blindly its reasoning capabilities. This is for

---

knowledge, facts and beliefs), and an associative memory that accounts for skills and other empirical contingencies. These sub-sytems work relatively independently. For instance amnesia, due to damage of specific areas of the brain, is a disturbance of episodic memory; not of semantic memory.

Ontolingua	XML	RDF/S	DAML+OIL	OWL
FBO & FO-Law	TOF, TOV & Ontology French Law	e-Court O. (RDF(S)/OIL), Multi Tier Contract O. (RDFS/DAML) & Consumer Protection Ontology (RDF/OWL)	OCL-NL, LRI-Core, IPROnto & AGO IR O.	LRI-Core (OWL-DL), LOIS, IPROnto (OWL-DL), Copyright O. (OWL-DL), BEST-User O., LKIF-Core (OWL-DL), SIAP Legislative O., OnProc (OWL-DL), Ontolegis & Ontojuris, Patent O., Ontology Fundamental Legal Concepts (OWL-DL), US UCC, Ontology Legal CBR (OWL-Lite), Oral Hearing O., Greek Public Adm. O. (OWL/OWL-S) & ALIS IP O.

Fig. 4.2 Legal ontologies and the representation formalisms used, copied from (Casellas 2010)

nstance of importance for systems that have to operate autonomously, as e.g. in Deep Space. However, enabling machines to "understand" documents, which will nvolve usually some natural language processing, will always have a heuristic and 'incomplete" flavor for which we do not require this trust on complete, consistent reasoning. This is important, because OWL has a limited expressivity that brings all kinds of problems. For instance identifying individual entities as being identical can only be approximated using tricks (Hoekstra and Breuker 2008; Hoekstra 2009). Maintaining identity in natural language processing (NLP) is a major issue (e.g. context bound unique naming; pronoun reference assignment). Full NLP is still too hard a nut to crack, especially in the highly heterogeneous environment of the Web. Attempts to have some superficial approximation to this problem (e.g using case structures) have shown minimal improvements in the efficiency of retrieval. OWL may not be the representation format for entering this information management arena, it is highly popular for representing ontologies for information management, as Fig. 4.2 shows for an almost complete list of published legal ontologies.[5] A reason to cast these information management ontologies in OWL can be that it allows one to do consistency checking, e.g. to find that properties of a subclass conflict with those of a superclass. However, real logical consistency checking requires a strong commitment with (many) properties which provide sufficient definitions. That is what information management ontologies lack in general. Consistency checking should be a necessary verification step for top ontologies, as it is very important

---

[5]As DAML+OIL, and RDFS/OWL are in fact (precursors to) OWL, we can state that except for Ontolingua (history) and XML all these ontologies are OWL based.

that no inconsistencies can propagate to lower levels when they are used to structure domain ontologies. By their philosophical ancestry many top ontologies are written in KIF/CommonLogic or Ontolingua. However, for these systems no complete consistency checking is available, and in translating these into OWL-DL most properties get lost in translation.

4.5 A CS Perspective for Top Ontologies

Top ontologies have two roles. The first one is to provide a structure of classes where a domain ontology can hang its main concepts as subclasses. It gives a starting position for more detailed modeling. The second role is even more interesting: by inheritance one gets already defined properties for free, which helps in consistency checking. Moreover, top structures may imply "special inference", i.e. inference rules that are bound to some set of terms. For instance, by defining a set of terms for spatial positions, such as "left-of (A,B)" is equal to "right-of (B,A)" etc. one can easily generate all tautologies. However, current practice does not show such "reuse" benefits. There are many reasons such as the chosen formalism (see above); little commitment in specifying properties; too few resources, and finally little agreement and much argument about the often slowly emerging points of departure. The history of the SUMO top ontology is probably the best worked out case, because its development started about a decade ago under the blessings and ambitions of IEEE. SUMO originally was SUO, and stood for Standard Upper Ontology. Meetings and mailing showed profound disaccord under the participants, and it went as far that some voting was proposed. This was a reason for many to leave this arena. A core of researchers still involved grabbed most of the available (pieces of) top ontology and integrated these in SUMO, where the S no longer stands for Standard, but for the less authorative Suggested. The M stands for Merged. Problem in most of these debates was that they had the same flavor (and also lots of the content) of the age old philosophical debates. It was not only philosophical. It also included practical arguments for powerful representations. In our opinion, these debates could continue for ever as there were no or hardly any empirical criteria available to decide on issues; the more because the idea was that these abstract terms were neutral with respect to any application. We will argue here for taking a cognitive science perspective. This provides not only rich resources for empirical grounding but is highly appropriate when it concerns human knowledge, and in particular: common sense.[6] For instance, by far the majority of what is available on the Web. We all have common sense, so it seems that anyone can participate in this enterprise. That

---

[6]It is hard to state what is not constrained by the primitive dispositions to interpret the world on which human builds in order to act effectively. However, we have obtained a more "conscious", "rational" way to interpret the world by delayed reflection. This has for instance ended in models of reality which have become even inconceivable, as in quantum theory. See for instance on 'physical ontology: http://en.wikipedia.org/wiki/Physical_ontology. Also core ontologies with a highly specialized technical domain may make shortcuts, see e.g. (West 2004).

is a major thesis in the development of folksonomies. It is a naive view because we have no direct access to the structure of concepts that make up this top. We even do not know whether this top is coherent. We can only reconstruct this by trying to trace its development: not only in humans, but over evolution as it has become apparent that we share many basic concepts with (higher) animals, and that these are not explicitly laid down in some ready made form, but rather have the character of instincts: i.e. they need experiences and cultural parametrization to get a specific shape. This is typically the area of evolutionary psychology which draws heavily on experimental work in developmental psychology, etiology and anthropology. A good example of this work can be found in Pinker's book on the "stuff of thought" where he argues that (and how) concepts of space, time and causation make up these conceptual, heritable predisposition (Pinker 2007). We share notions about agent causality (i.e. actions vs. processes), intention, power and fairness. Most of his arguments come from use of language. An even larger range of concepts and even stronger anchored in empirical research over the aforementioned disciplines can be read in Marc Hauser's book on the emergence of moral beliefs, which also throws a perspective on notions of justice in the legal domain (Hauser 2006). What these studies reveal is how a number of concepts evolve, both in an evolutionary as in a cultural way. They show that unexpectedly early distinctions are made for instance between a physical world and a social-psychological world on the basis of observing moving objects. Objects that move "by themselves" are agents. Directions of movement are indications of intention, etc. Note that the number of concepts that must be assumed to be driving these identifications already represent a substantial top-structure.

However, the interpretation of these findings for constructing a top ontology must be taken with care, as they do not show how later, cultural influences may extend or modify the nature of these concepts.[7] A good example is the introduction of the notion of "energy" in our common sense vocabulary due to our insights in and experiences with electricity as a source for heat, light and movement. Energy unifies the original notions of power/impuls for movement, fire for heat and light, etc. In the notion of "energy" we have apparently found a new "superclass".

On the other hand, the distinction between physical and agent causation (processes vs. actions) is extremely well maintained, even if the distinction is sometimes hard to assess in concrete cases (e.g. guilt in criminal cases; football offenses that merit a card or not). Mental concepts, like belief, knowledge, intention and emotion are also part of the early repertory of babies: they constitute a "Theory of Mind" which attributes intentions and knowledge to others, but ultimately is also the source of attributing these also to one-self to explain ones own behavior. This wealth of insights has been a leading guide in the construction of the LKIF-Core ontology for legal domains, where a physical and a mental world form starting points (Breuker and Hoekstra 2004; Hoekstra et al. 2007; Breuker et al. 2007).

---

[7]Thus far we have not read about cases where such a concept gets "overwritten" by new information in the common sense domain.

A good example of how a CS perspective leads to different representations than in other ontologies (in particular: SUMO) is the conceptualization of space. During the construction of SUMO, arguments were raised whether space should be represented "3D", i.e. having three dimensions, or 4D which would include time, to provide for histories in the spatial world. There is a special 4D version of SUMO. In fact, we cannot conceptualize a 4D world straightforward: we have to leave out one dimension and imagine a kind of flatland moving forward in time. This means that a 4D representation is not a direct representation of common sense: it is an abstract, geometrical rendering of the fact that both time and space can be viewed as having dimensions. However, from a human cognitive point of view space is not a uniform concept. There are two kinds of spaces. (1) The space that physical objects take. The basic concept here is "size", which can be big, small, etc. This concept may be equated with "volume" (e.g. relevant for fluids) so that a 3D picture may finally emerge. (2) This is different from, but compatible with viewing space as marking positions of objects. Space is here not outer space, but on earth, which is a floor or landscape on which objects are stacked. This is the consequence of the fact that we live in a largely flat world permanently under the influence of gravity. Left-of/right-of plays here a minor role and explains why we get easily confused in discriminating between these. It also explains why we have the illusion that a mirror image switches left–right, where it in reality switches the front-back "dimension" of the observer. These simple facts (gravity, eyes "in front" of our head) have given rise to concepts of positions in space (for an extensive CS literature on this subject, see McManus (*nomen est omen?*) book on "left hand, right hand". (McManus 2002). In other words, 3D is applicable to the extension of objects; for marking positions we have a 2D "map" view on which objects rest. As a consequence we should have two kinds of ontologies for space. One about size, and one about position. By performing measurement we can relate these.

4.6 Some Paradoxes for Conclusions

Ontology engineering is not a uniform field of research and development. and it is full of paradoxes. The first one is of course that where ontology is aimed at providing clear definitions, it has not succeeded in defining itself. Philosophical ontology still plays an important role, while a much closer ancestor in ("natural") philosophy—the *Lingua Universalis* movement—aimed at taxonomic and mechanized reasoning is forgotten and has only an indirect impact via Information Science. Philosophers who could benefit from automated consistency checking use formalisms that do not really allow for this. On the other hand, applications aimed at information management, e.g. searching the web, use very often formalisms which have traded correct reasoning for expressivity, while these applications do not require reasoning. A major paradox is the fact that in developing top ontologies that claim to cover common sense, the main sources of inspiration are introspection and philosophical analyses. No reference is made to the empirical data available from Cognitive Science, which are far more valid than those speculations. Finally, the reader may also find it paradoxical that we use in the title "legal" but hardly any reference is made to the domain of law. That is true. First, it should be noted that the domain of law is rather advanced in the world of ontologies. The fact that OWL-DL is used may seem an unnecessary complication, but it also enables this community to move effortlessly to applications that need trustworthy automated reasoning. An example is HARNESS, a legal assessment system that runs completely in OWL-DL (van de Ven 2008). Second, in the core concepts of law, many common sense concepts are hidden, as cognitive studies on moral and legal concepts show (Hauser 2006).

References

Bechhofer, S., F. van Harmelen, J. Hendler, I. Horrocks, D.L. McGuinness, P.F. Patel-Schneider, L.A. Stein. OWL Web Ontology Language Reference. W3C Recommendation, World Wide Web Consortium, February 2004. URL http://www.w3.org/TR/owl-ref/. In M. Dean, G. Schreiber (Eds.).

Berners-Lee, T. (1999). *Weaving the Web: The Past, Present and Future of the World Wide Web.* Orion Business Books, London.

Breuker, J., R. Hoekstra. (2004). Core Concepts of Law: Taking Common-Sense Seriously. In A.C. Varzi, L. Vieu (Eds.) *Proceedings of Formal Ontologies in Information Systems (FOIS-2004.* IOS-Press, Torino, Italy, 210–221.

Breuker, J., W. Van De Velde (1994). *CommonKADS Library for Expertise Modeling: Reusable Problem Solving Components.* IOS-Press/Ohmsha, Amsterdam/Tokyo.

Breuker, J., R. Hoekstra, A. Boer, K. van den Berg, R. Rubino, G. Sartor, M. Palmirani, A. Wyner, T. Bench-Capon (2007). OWL Ontology of Basic Legal Concepts (LKIF-Core). Deliverable 1.4, Estrella, www.estrellaproject.org.

Casellas, N. (2010). *Legal Ontology Engineering.* Springer, New York, NY.

Ecco, U. (1997). *The Search for the Perfect Language.* Blackwell Publishers, Oxford.

Forbus, K. (2008). Qualitative Modeling. In F. van Harmelen, V. Lifs-chitz, B. Porter (Eds.) *Handbook of Knowledge Representation.* Elsevier, San Diego, CA, 361–394.

Gangemi, A., N. Guarino, C. Masolo, A. Oltramari, L. Schneider. (2002). Sweetening Ontologies With DOLCE. In A. Gomez-Perez, V.R. Benjamins (Eds.) *Proceedings of the EKAW-2002.* Springer, Heidelberg, 166–181.

Gruber, T.R. (1993). A Translation Approach to Portable Ontology Specifications. *Knowledge Acquisition,* 5: 199–220.

Hamscher, W.C., L. Console, J. de Kleer (Eds.) (1992). *Readings in Model-Based Diagnosis.* Morgan Kaufmann, San Mateo, CA.

Hauser, M. (2006). *Moral Minds: The Nature of Right and Wrong.* Harper Collins, New York, NY.

Hayes, P.J. (1985). Naive Physics I: Ontology for Liquids. In J.R. Hobbs, R.C. Moore (Eds.) *Formal Theories of the Common Sense World.* Ablex Publishing Corporation, Norwood, 71–108.

Hoekstra, R. (2009). *Ontology Representation: Design Patterns and Ontologies That Make Sense.* IOS Press, Amsterdam.

Hoekstra, R., J. Breuker (2008). Polishing Diamonds in OWL 2. In A. Gangemi, J. Euzenat (Eds.) *Proceedings of the 16th International Conference on Knowledge Engineering and Knowledge Management (EKAW 2008),* LNAI/LNCS. Springer, Berlin, 64–73.

Hoekstra, R., J. Breuker, M. Di Bello, A. Boer (2007). The LKIF Core Ontology of Basic Legal Concepts. In P. Casanovas, M.A. Biasiotti, E. Francesconi, M.T. Sagri (Eds.) *Proceedings of the Workshop on Legal Ontologies and Artificial Intelligence Techniques (LOAIT 2007),* June 2007. Stanford University, Stanford. CEUR Workshop Proceedings.

Horrocks, I., P.F. Patel-Schneider, F. Van Harmelen (2003). From *shiq* and **RDF** to OWL: The Making of a Web Ontology Language. *Journal of Web Semantics: Science, Services and Agents on the World Wide Web Semantics,* 1: 7–26.

Lakoff, G. (1987). *Women, Fire and Dangerous Things.* University of Chicago Press, Chicago, IL.

Lenat, D.B. (1995). CYC: A Large-Scale Investment in Knowledge Infrastructure. *Communications of the ACM,* 38(11): 33–38.

Levelt, W.J.M. (1993). *Speaking.* Cambridge University Press, Cambridge, MA.

McCarthy, J., P. Hayes. (1969). Some Philosophical Problems from the Standpoint of Artificial Intelligence. In B. Meltzer, D. Michie, M. Swann (Eds.) *Machine Intelligence* vol. 4. Edinburgh University press, Edinburgh, 463–502.

McManus, C. (2002). *Right Hand, Left Hand.* Weidenfeld and Nicolson, London.

Pease, A., I. Niles. (2002). IEEE Standard Upper Ontology: A Progress Report. *Knowledge Engineering Review,* 17: 65–70. Special Issue on Ontologies and Agents.

Pinker, S. (2007). *The Stuffofthought.* Allen Lane, London.

Schreiber, A.Th., B.J. Wielinga, J.A. Breuker (Eds.) (1993). *KADS: A Principled Approach to Knowledge-Based System Development,* vol. 11 of *Knowledge-Based Systems Book Series.* Academic Press, London. ISBN 0-12-6290407.

Schreiber, G., H. Akkermans, A. Anjewierden, R. de Hoog, N. Shadbolt, W. Van den Velde, B. Wielinga (2000). *Knowledge Engineering and Managament: The CommonKADS Methodology.* MIT Press, Cambridge, MA.

Sowa, J.F. (2000). *Knowledge Representation: Logical Philosophical, and Computational Foundations.* Brooks Cole Publishing Co, Pacific Grove, CA.

van de Ven, S., J. Breuker, R. Hoekstra, L. Wortel (2008). Automated Legal Assessment in Owl 2. In *Legal Knowledge and Information Systems. Jurix 2008: The 21st Annual Conference,* Frontiers in Artificial Intelligence and Applications. IOS Press, Amsterdam, December 2008.

Van Heijst, G., A.Th. Schreiber, B.J. Wielinga (1997). Using Explicit Ontologies for kbs Development. *International Journal of Human-Computer Studies,* 46(2/3): 183–292.

Weld, D., J. de Kleer (Eds.) (1990). *Readings in Qualitative Reasoning About Physical Systems.* Morgan Kaufman, San Mateo CA.

West, M. (2004). Some Industrial Experiences in the Development and Use of Ontologies. In *Proceedings of EKAW-2004 workshop on Core Ontologies,* Whittlebury Hall, Northamptonshire, UK.

Wilkins, J. (1668). *An Essay Towards the Real Character and a Philosophical Language.* Gellibrand, London.

Chapter 5
Social Ontology and Documentality

Maurizio Ferraris

5.1 Introduction

Encyclopedia entries, bets, gains and losses, research projects, books, lessons, relationships, votes, credits, exams certificates, exams, records, academic degrees, students, professors, art works and consumerist literature, cathedrae, aulas, application forms, hiring, revolutions, workshops, conferences, dismissals, unions, parliaments, stock societies, laws, restaurants, money, property, governments, marriages, elections, games, cocktail parties, tribunals, lawyers, wars, humanitarian missions, voting, promises, buying and selling, prosecutors, physicians, perpetrators, taxes, vacation, medieval soldiers, presidents. What are all those objects made of? And, first of all, are they objects? Some philosophers would say they are not, since—according to them—only physical objects exist. Other philosophers would dare say that even physical objects are socially constructed, since they are the result of our theories. For real, thus, the world would be Prospero's world: *We are such stuff/ As dreams are made on and our little life/Is rounded with a sleep.* That is not the case, though: social objects exist indeed, the proof being the difference between thinking to promise something, and actually promising something: once you give your word, the promise keeps on existing, even in case you forget about it, or—as more frequently happens—you change your mind.

The first aim of this article is to expand on the nature of social objects, as contrasted with physical and ideal objects, and to spell out the steps that lead to their discovery. Secondly, I will illustrate and criticize the major contemporary theory on social objects, John Searle's theory, and compare it with another theory, according to which social objects are a kind of inscription. Lastly, I want show how, from this standpoint, a social ontology evolves naturally into a theory of documents, which I propose to name "documentality".

M. Ferraris (✉)
Department of Philosophy, University of Torino, Turin, Italy
e-mail: maurizio.ferraris@labont.it

I would like to thank Giuliano Torrengo for important comments on the theses contained in this article.

5.2 Physical, Ideal and Social Objects

For a long time philosophers have underestimated the dimension of social objects, focusing exclusively on physical and ideal objects. This fact, probably is a consequence of an ambiguity concerning the nature of social objects, which is apparent as soon as we confront them with two other classes of objects into which reality can be divided. Physical objects, such as tables, lakes, occupy a place in space and in time, and exist even if we do not think about them; ideal objects, such as numbers, relations or theorems, differently from physical objects, do not occupy any place in space and in time, but, as much as physical objects, exist even if we do not think about them. Social objects, on the other hand, such as marriages and graduations, occupy a modest amount of space (more on this later: it is, roughly, the amount of space a document occupies) and a more or less extended portion of time—they cannot be eternal though (differently from ideal objects, social objects seem to tend towards their own end: the theorem of Pythagoras is meaningful exactly because it is eternal, a promissory note for the opposite reason, i.e. because it will expire sooner or later; although there may be social objects, such as the Roman Empire or the Egyptian Dynasties, that last longer than the life of an individual). Thus, social objects looks like being somewhere in between the materiality of physical objects and the immateriality of ideal objects. I explain in details this point later. What I would like to underline in the first place, both in order to explicate why philosophers, and common people with them, have discovered social objects so late, and to draw attention to the most peculiar aspect of social objects, is the following: *differently from physical and ideal objects, social objects exist only in so far as there are men thinking that they exist*. Without men, mountains would remain what they are, and numbers would have the same properties they actually have—but it would be complete nonsense to talk about offences and loans, Nobel prizes and years in jail, art works or pornography. This feature has been misconstrued, and this fact has lead to the spreading out, in various ways, of a conceptual ambiguity. That is, the idea to the effect that social objects are utterly relative, or that they are nothing over and above a manifestation of the will. What is denied to social objects here is their object-like nature: they are reduced either to something indefinitely interpretable or to a bare psychological act.

We can find out how little true this reduction is thanks to a simple experience. I can decide to go to the cinema; if, eventually, I change my mind, this decision does not constrain me in any way. It is really just an expression of the will, which, since it has no outward manifestation, has a purely psychological dimension. Things are different if I propose to someone to come along with me to the cinema; if I change my mind, I have to tell her or him and provide a justification. What I have constructed, then, is an object that is not nullified by a bare change of my will. Let us further assume that my invitation had the form of a promise; for instance, I have told my son: "I promise you that, if you keep on being a good boy, I take you to the movie tonight". Now, if I had told him only "I promise that", I would have not promised; a promise has a beginning only when there is an object of reference, and a time limit, if only a vague one ("I promise you that sooner or later I quit smoking").

If, on the other hand, social objects were utterly relative constructions, they would not carry within them any necessity, and it should be possible for "I promise" to be a promise, but "I promise" is just the first singular person of the indicative present tense form of the verb "to promise".

5.3 The Discovery of Social Objects

This phenomenology of social objects should enable us to detect the features of social objects (Di Lucia 2003; Ferraris 2003b; Gilbert 1989 and 1993; Johansson 1989; Kim-Sosa 1999; Moore 2002; Smith 1998, 1999, 2002; Tuomela 2002) that motivated their discovery. We are not dealing here, strictly speaking, with a historical progression (none of the following authors is likely to have ever read any of the others), but rather with a theoretical progression.

The first stage of the history consists in recognizing the specificity of social objects, and the first one who did this is the Italian Giambattista Vico (1668–1744) (Vico 1744), who—quarreling with Cartesian rationalism and naturalism—defended the original character of the sphere of human interaction. In order to individuate this sphere, which identifies the passage from animal to man, and from nature to culture (the latter, thus, is essentially meant to be social progress), Vico points towards marriages, tribunals and burials. Those are social acts, that do not describe anything nor add anything new to the physical or ideal world, nonetheless they trace the change from the animal to the man, and from nature to culture.

The second stage of the history concerns the Scottish philosopher Thomas Reid (1710–1796) (Reid 1785), who underlines the autonomy of social objects, distinguishing them from mere psychological constructions or manifestations of the will. Reid claims that the premise for the constitution of a social object is an act concerning at least two people. As in the previous example, thinking about going to the cinema is not, whereas proposing someone to go to the cinema is, a social act.

The third stage, in the middle of the Nineteen hundred, amounts to the theory of linguistic acts, by the English philosopher John L. Austin (1911–1960) (Austin 1962). Linguistic acts are somehow an explication of the specific character of social acts. Social acts, insofar as they require to be expressed, are linguistic acts (we will see how this conclusion is partly misleading); and since they are not just a description of something (think in the "yes" said at a wedding ceremony, a paradigmatic example), but they produce something, they possess an original feature with respect to other parts of language. While saying "this is a chair" does not amount to acting upon the chair in any way, saying "the meeting is open" or "I hereby declare you doctor in philosophy" produces an object that was not there before.

The fourth stage of our history, relatively eccentric if compared with the previous ones, is provided by the German philosopher and law theorist Adolf Reinach (1883–1917) (Reinach 1913; see Mulligan 1987), who proposes a typology of social objects, described as a priori derivable (namely as endowed with a logical form, roughly what I was underlining when I made you notice that "I promise" is not a promise), and insists upon the fact that what is produced by social acts is not a self-contained *praxis*, but it is a *poiesis*, the construction of an enduring object (a graduation or a marriage, with respect to other social events, such as a party or a ruffle in which nobody gets seriously injured, have consequences that reach farther than the event).

5.4 X Counts as Y in C

In the contemporary debate, the standard theory of social objects has been proposed in the nineties by the American philosopher John R. Searle (n. 1932) (Koepsell–Moss 2003; Smith 2003a.). The building up of this ontology can be described as a strategy in four steps.

The first step is set at Oxford, during the fifties, at the school of—among the others—John Austin, and continues at Berkeley during the sixties and seventies. Here Searle's activity focused on linguistic acts, an especially subtle part of language. When I say "yes" at a wedding ceremony, I am not describing anything that is already there, I am constructing something that is born in that very instant.

The rhapsodic analyses of Austin get a systematic dimension in Searle's work. Searle offers a complete classification of them (Searle 1969, 1975), but this is not the only thing he is doing. On the one hand (and the upshots in social ontology derive from here), Searle does not limit himself to a classification of linguistic acts, but he acknowledges also the existence of objects that may be borne to life by performative acts—a particular kind of linguistic acts. A marriage and a conviction, for instance, understood as rites, may last just a few minutes in their culminating moment. The corresponding social objects may last years though, and it is the philosopher's task to account for those objects' existence. By doing this, however, a philosopher should deliver a theory of mind too (Searle 1980, 1983, 1992), since the peculiar feature of objects such as marriages or penal convictions, differently from cows or mountains, is that they exist only if there are minds believing that they exist.

And here it is Searle's second step, set in Berkeley, during the Eighties. Austin was exclusively concerned with language (and perception), Searle, I have just suggested, was seeking a theory of mind. Could a computer passing the Turing test get married? Is a computer used in a betting shop really betting? Can it christen a boat? Can it bequest something to another computer? The obvious answer to all these questions is "no". And this depends on the fact that human mind has something that computers do not have: intentionality. Intentionality is the capacity to refer to things in the world, by using the representations we have at our disposal here, roughly, under the hair, beyond the eyes, and between the ears—namely in our minds. Intentionality, however, is not a ghost, a feeble mist descending on the world as postmodernists uphold, when they claim that Being is reducible to Language. Not at all, it is something as real as photosynthesis or digestion is. We should not misunderstand this point, because one thing is maintaining that human mind is not a computer, and quite another maintaining that Darwin was wrong. This is a very delicate knot, because claiming that the *individual I* is in many cases the result of a collective intentionality does not mean that reality is constituted in an inter-subjective way. Not at all, there are pieces of reality perfectly capable of staying by themselves, and they do not depend on language or conscience. Other pieces, surely, do depend on them. Still, we should not mix up those two cases, if we do not want every honest philosophy to come to an end.

The third step is set here and there around the world between the seventies and the eighties (Searle 1993a, b, 1998). Searle assists—not inert, but astonished—to postmodernists spreading through the departments of comparative literature, under the risk that sooner or later they would get to philosophy departments too. Here is the crowd: who says that the Being that can be understood is language, and who says that nothing exists outside texts, and you would eventually meet a fun-loving person maintaining that there are no facts, but only interpretations. In conclusion, the moral seems to be that—quite paradoxically—words, but not things, exist; concepts exist, but not the objects they refer to.

We would be mistaken in seeing in this reaction to the postmodern idealism simply a polemical phase, since it is in this framework that Searle elaborates the theory of reality as "background" (Searle 1999). Reality is something that does not require to be demonstrated, because it is at the ground of our demonstrations. Reality constitutes the basic element of Searle's general ontology, it delivers us the deep sense of his realism—and, at the same time, the deep sense of the non-realism of the postmodern speaker who, with their laptop, on the plane, polishes the talk s/he will give at a conference in an American University, on the topic of the non-existence of the external world.

And here the last step comes (Searle 1995), which is set in Paris. During the nineties Searle enters in a Café, and pronounces a French sentence "*Un demi, Munich, à pression, s'il vous plaît*". Searle makes us notice that this very simple sentence triggers a huge invisible ontology: the social exchange between he and the waiter, a lattice of norms, prices, fares, rules, passports and nationalities, an universe of such a complexity that would have had Kant shivering, if only Kant had thought about it. We are at the postmodernists' antipodes. If postmodernists dissolve tables and seats by reducing them to interpretations, Searle's ontology asserts that also things such as promises and bets, shares and debts, medieval knights and Californian Professors, tenures and symphonies possess their own specific reality. They are neither ghosts, nor movements of the consciousness or of the will (given that promises exist when we sleep, and in case we change our mind too, and contracts can bind institutions independently from the people who run them), they are higher order objects with respect to physical objects, in accordance with the rule "X counts as Y in C"—meaning that the physical object X, for instance a colored piece of paper, count as Y, a 10 euro banknote, in C, the Europe of the year 2006.

It is not hard to see how here we are approaching the closure of a system. The philosopher of language who has studied linguistic acts comes across performative acts, and notices that with them we can construct social objects; the philosopher of mind, who has studied intentionality, understands intentionality's role in the construction of social reality; the anti-postmodern polemist, in turn, elaborates a realist ontology that enables us to understand that—for some reasons and our intentions and hopes notwithstanding—it is useless to try to avoid paying the beer by saying that reality (social and maybe physical reality as well) is socially constructed. The last move was left for the social ontologist: discovering this new reign of objects that—please notice—cannot be defined as "mental" just because they need human minds.

5.5 No (Social) Thing Exists Outside Texts

Very well. Now, we know that this theory (and Searle knows it very well too) has counterexamples, together with the general difficulty of clarifying the key notion of "collective intentionality".[1] Even if we limit ourselves to considerations concerning the object, the problem is twofold: it is not obvious at all how, from the physical object, we manage to get to the social object; and it is not clear at all how, given the social object, we should individuate a corresponding physical object.

In order to explain the shift from the physical to the social, Searle makes the example of the transformation of a wall into a boundary. The idea is the following: firstly, there is a physical object, a wall that divides the inside from the outside, and defends a community. Then, step by step, the wall deteriorates, and only a line of stones is left—unhelpful as a physical shelter—to identify a social object, namely a boundary: the very same that, later on, will be the yellow line that in the post-offices and airports allocates an insuperable threshold. Now, we can understand how a wall, by falling apart slowly, can, in certain circumstances, turn into a boundary. But it is not at all evident how, on the ground of this simple analogy—a lucky chance that who knows how few times occurred—the yellow line or the center line of the road are born. The question is further complicated by the following consideration: if really a physical object can constitute the origin of a social object, then *every* physical object would turn into a social object, every wall would signify a prohibit on. But clearly this is not the case, as everyone who decides to tear down a wall in their house can verify, provided that the demolition would not contradict certain norms—which not necessarily concern the physical solidity of the wall. And, lastly, we should not forget that one of the most famous walls in contemporary history, the Berlin Wall, was begot by a boundary—the opposite of what should have happened according to Searle's explanation.

As for the second aspect of the problem—the aspect concerning the reversibility from the social to the physical sphere—it is rather intuitive to assert that a banknote is also a piece of paper, or that a president is also a person. As much as it is true that when Searle is alone in a hotel room there is only a physical object, but many social objects (a husband, an employee of the state of California, an American citizen, a driving license holder...). In this case, the passage back from Y the social) to X (the physical) goes smoothly. However, things change in different, although not very peculiar, situations. How should we deal with vague (Williamson 1994, 1998) or

---

[1] I have criticized at length this aspect of Searle's theory in Ferraris (2005). Collective intentionality has been originally elaborated by the Finnish philosopher Raimo Tomela (1995), whereas the psychologist M.E. Bratman (1992) was concerned with "shared intentionality".

vast entities, such as a State, a battle, a university? And how about negative entities, such as debts?

The English philosopher Barry Smith (born 1952) (Smith 2003b) has rightly pointed out that in many cases we have to acknowledge the existence of Y independent entities, namely entities that do not ontologically coincide with any part of physical reality. Here, according to Smith, we are dealing with "representations". In order to better define the notion of "representation", Smith qualifies it as a "quasi-abstract entity", providing as an example, a chess match played at random. The idea is that chess may be played independently from any physical support. You can play in Internet, where the chessboard is not "present" as a physical chessboard is (for instance, it has two localizations, corresponding to the two computers). Moreover, two experts can play by heart, without there being even a chessboard represented on a screen, but rather through two barely thought chessboards. Smith expands the model to the paradigm of money. Also in this case, from a certain moment on (and more and more as technology develops), we loose the physical counterparts, substituted by traces on the computer. Also in this case there is a social object to which it does not correspond any physical object, but rather a representation.

This is all fine, but really the computer *blips* are not physical at all? Are they really a *res cogitans* utterly detached from a *res extensa*? It takes only visiting a technological cemetery (a huge Chinese landfill, or the corridor of a Department where out of order computers have been stored) to realize how much plastic and silicon is necessary for magnetic traces to exist. And, unless we want to say that computers have souls, separated from their bodies, the *blips* will be material things as well. Indeed, it is difficult—nay, impossible—to uphold that, in the case of money that is transformed into traces on a computer, there are only representations, and not a physical thing sustaining them, although something endowed with a rather light physicality. But let as suppose that this is indeed the case, that representations do not need anything physical. Then, there would be no way to answer the question: *how should we distinguish in principle 100 real thalers from 100 ideal thalers?* How are we to distinguish the representation of 100 thalers from 100 merely imagined, or dreamed of, thalers?[2]

The difficulties emerging both out of Searle's theory and Smith's correction help us to spot the way to the solution of the problem of social objects, which I propose to develop after the theory of the French philosopher Jacques Derrida

---

[2]If one maintains that it is false that a social object depends on a particular physical substrate, but it is true that every social object generically depends on some physical substrate (namely an inscription of some sort), one can keep on criticizing Searle's position (that concerns rather the fact that Searle points to the "wrong" physical substrate, somehow), and at the same time avoid Smith's "representational" conclusions. The chess match does not depend on a particular chessboard, neither does it depend it on two particular computers, or some particulars neurons. Still, if a match is there, then some physical substrate is also there, and therefore the match generically depends on some physical substrate. On the distinction between particular and generic dependence see (Simon 1987: 296–307).

(1930–2004) (Derrida 1967; see Ferraris 2003a, 2006. On the social role of writing see Ong 1982). Derrida has elaborated a philosophy of writing that finds its most correct application in the social sphere. What is more interesting is that Searle knew this theory, but the alliance was rendered impossible by a reciprocal misunderstanding. Actually, Derrida dedicated an essay to Austin's linguistic acts (Derrida 1971). Those acts, Derrida observed, are mostly inscribed acts, since without records of some sort the performatives would not produce social objects such as conferences, marriages, graduation ceremonies, or constitutions. The point is simple, if we imagine a graduation or a wedding ceremony in which there are no registers and testimonies, it is difficult to maintain that a husband, a wife, a graduated person has been produced. This amounts to saying that social objects turn out to be (as much as the ideal ones) closely linked to the forms of their inscription and recording. That article irritated Searle, who few years after replied (Searle 1977) (the reply was followed by an exceedingly long response by Derrida (1988)) against what to him was nothing but a misunderstanding of Austin. Thus, the meeting seemed not to bring anything to the point. Still, we can see in it the solution of Searle's puzzle.

Indeed, the problem in Searle's social ontology depends on not having investigated the hypothesis that the physical counterpart of a social object is a trace, namely exactly what Derrida has brought attention to during all his career—be it a trace on the paper, or a trace in the brain, an inscription in the memory that remind us a promise, a debt, a duty or a fault. Derrida, having at hand the evidence to the effect that money has turned into inscribed paper, although not yet the (more striking) evidence to the effect that it would have turned into computer bytes, provided as soon as 1967, through his hypothesis on the nature of writing, the ground of an extremely powerful ontology. However, Derrida was wrong in claiming that "nothing exists outside texts" (and Searle was entitled to reproach him on this). Actually, as we have seen, physical and ideal objects exist independently from every recording, as much as independently from there being a humanity. This is not the case for social objects, which depend tightly on records and the existence of humanity. It is in this sense that, by weakening Derrida's thesis, I propose to develop a social ontology starting from the intuition that no *social* thing exists outside texts.

5.6 Object = Inscribed Act

Keeping this in mind, my thesis (Ferraris 2005) is that, contrary to Searle's idea, the constituting rule of a social object is not *X counts as Y in C* (social objects are higher order objects with respect to the underlying physical objects), but *Object = Inscribed Act*: social objects are social acts (concerning at least two people) characterized by the fact of being inscribed, in a document, in a computer file, or simply in people's heads. With respect to Searle, we solve all the problems of the shift from the physical to the social; with respect to Smith, we have a way to distinguish an actual social object from a purely thought one; with respect to Derrida, we acknowledge a specific sphere of social objects, separated by physical and ideal objects. The essential lines of this theory are the following: in the world there are subjects and there are objects. The subjects refer to objects (the former represent, think about, somehow deal, with the latter), namely they possess intentionality; objects do not refer to subjects.

Objects come in three kinds: (1) physical objects (mountains, rivers, human bodies, and animals) that exist in space and in time, and are independent from subjects knowing them, even though they may have built them, as for artifacts (chairs, screwdrivers); (2) ideal objects (numbers, theorems, relations) that exist outside of space and time, and are independent from the subjects knowing them, but which, after having been discovered, can be socialized (for instance, a theorem can be published: still, it is the publication, not the theorem, that has a beginning in time); (3) social objects, that do not exist *as such* in space, since their physical presence is limited to the inscription (money is such because of what is written on the coin, on the banknote, on the memory of the credit card), but last in time, and whose existence depends on the subjects who know, or at least can use, them and who, in certain cases, have constituted them. This latter circumstance displays to us the fact that social objects, for which construction is necessary, depend on social *acts*, whose *inscription* constitutes the *object*.

As I have indicated through the law Object = Inscribed Act, social objects consist in the recording of acts that encompass at least two people, and are characterized by being inscribed, on a physical substrate whatsoever, from marble to neurons, passing through paper and computers. I do not consider obnoxious the idea that also brain processes are to be described in terms of a sort of writing, since they manifest to us exactly in those terms, as it is revealed also by the fact that the mind has always been described as a *tabula rasa*, i.e. a writing table.

From this standpoint, and weakening Derrida's axiom, one can state that "no social thing exits outside texts". Physical as much as ideal objects exist independently from inscription and records, but this is not the case for social objects. Without some sort of recording it is impossible to conceive any kind of society, and—even more so—any social object. However, the recording is a necessary but not sufficient condition for the existence of social objects: without recordings there are no social objects, but not necessarily a recording (for instance a recollection of mine) constitutes a social object

Social objects are constituted by inscribed acts, but not every inscription is a social object. Fingerprints become social object when they are registered by the police and used as evidence in a trial, and in this case they are actually part and parcel of an inquiring procedure. And when fingerprints are taken on a passport, they become part of a document, which is endowed with an even more evident social character, since it incorporates this social character—so to speak. From this standpoint, the document has to be conceived, rather than as something which is done once for all, and constituting a class of stable objects, as a teleological end of a theory of social objects. Not all inscriptions are documents, but there is no inscription that, in certain conditions and once it has acquired a certain social power, cannot become such.

5.7 Documentality

If all this is true, then a theory of social objects develops naturally into a theory of the document, understood as an inquiry centered on the definition of what I call "documentality", namely the properties that constitute, in each case, the necessary and sufficient conditions (starting from two very general conditions: being an inscription and being a document or a "documental" thing) to be a social object. At last, there is no society if there are no documents, and documents are records with a particular social value. On this ground, a theory of documentality can develop along three directions. The ontological dimension, answering the question: what is a document? The technological dimension, concerning the means through which documentality can be spread in a complex society. The pragmatic (and forensic) dimension, which concerns the care of documents in a society characterized by the explosion of writing, and in world dominated by information technology (Koepsell 2000, 2003).

1. As for the first question—what is a document?—we need to articulate the law Object = Inscribed Act. Documentality comprises a sphere encompassing so different things as memories, notes (a memo can, although not necessarily must, acquire social value), and international treaties; all such things can be realized through the most different media (paper writing, electronic writing, pictures . . .); they can refer to the most different activities (borrowing a book, getting married, being named, declaring war. . .). In the vast majority of those realizations it is possible to spot the structure of documentality: first of all, a physical substrate; then, an inscription, which obviously is smaller than the substrate and which defines its social value; finally, an idiomatic thing, typically a sign (and its variation, such as the electronic signature, the debit card's or mobile's PIN, . . .), which guarantees its authenticity.

It is important here to single out a point. Sounds, signs, and thoughts are not physical objects as hefty as States or persons. They possess far less molecules. Still, they are not completely void of physical bulk: a sound needs vibrations, a thought requires electric activity in the brain, and this, obviously holds for signs over a piece of paper too (even more manifestly so). This last circumstance, if one thinks over it a while, is more relevant than it is generally believed, since paradigmatic social objects such as banknotes are "signs over a piece of paper": banknotes qualify as social, and not only physical, objects because of few molecules, those in the inscription and possibly in the thread-mark too. Actually, the really important aspect of a banknote, what turns it from a physical object—a drawing, let us say—into a social object, are the few molecules of the inscription that declare its value, along with the ones of the signature of the governor who states its validity—and not the bunch of molecules constituting its form and matter—proof being that a very big banknote may have lesser value than a much smaller one. Those few molecules, moreover, are not very different from the *blips* in the computer of a bank: they are objects of the same sort, showing similar characteristics; and this holds also for what Searle calls "status indicators", such as, for instance, passports and driving licenses. At the same time, those molecules are *something*, although there is only a little amount of them, and not just a representation. Those few molecules account for Smith's expression "quasi-abstract entity": the entity must be recorded somewhere in space. At the ontological level, my proposal is to spot in documentality five ascending degrees (from physical to social): traces, recordings, inscriptions, documents, idioms.

I call a "trace" what, endowed with a rather small number of molecules, serves as the physical substrate of a record. Only for social objects the trace has a constitutive value. In the world of physical objects, there are traces only for minds that are able to recognize them. In the world of ideal objects, traces operate only in the socialization of an entity that does not depend on an inscription. Things are different for the constitution of a social object, since the trace openly indicates a beginning in time, and moreover it motivates the chronology of the object also beyond the intentions of the people involved in its constitution, and the length of their life.

A trace, in a mind or for a mind, becomes a record; this record can, in certain circumstances, acquire social value, for instance when the agents of the scientific police transform a piece of DNA attached to a cigarette butt into a proof. But, indeed, the mere recording is not, as such, a social thing.

An "inscription" is a record with a social value. Within a society, spoken or written words, as much as hand-shakings, can be relevant things. The inscription possesses the following laws of essence: it is the necessary but not sufficient condition of the social object; it is smaller than its substrate; its size has no bearing on the size of the corresponding social object; the inscription is true if it is idiomatic.

Inscriptions that can acquire a legal value are documents, which are, along with Smith's perspective (Smith 2006), acts fixing. [3] And here it is the last ingredient of our ascending hierarchy: the idiom. With "idiom" I mean a specific way of presentation of an inscription that links a particular inscription to an individual. Its more evident model is the signature (on a document, a check, a banknote: an element that is almost everywhere in social reality, although it is often unobserved), but it can also be a specific way in which someone expresses themselves, for instance their normal tone of voice. Its aim is the object's individuation, and exactly in so far as it individuates an object it can play the role in the validation of social objects, which, thanks to the signature, emerge as the expression of the intentionality of someone.

---

[3] According to Smith (2006), thus, it is possible to develop a theory of what he calls "document acts", i.e. a theory "1. of the different types of document, ranging from free-text memos to standardized forms and templates, and from single documents as self-contained collections of information to bodies of documents incorporating various sorts of riders, codicils, protocols, addenda, amendments, endorsements and other attachments, including maps, photographs, diagrams, signatures and other marks, 2. of the different types of physical medium or bearer for a document's content (most important here is the distinction between paper and electronic documents), 3. of the different sorts of things we can do to documents (fill in, sign, countersign, stamp, copy, notarize, transfer, invalidate, destroy), 4. of the different sorts of things we can do (achieve, effect) with documents (establish collateral, create organizations, record the deliberations of a committee, initiate legal or military actions), and of the different ways in which, in performing such acts, we may succeed or fail to achieve the corresponding ends, 5. of the institutional systems to which documents belong (marriage, property, law, commerce, trade, credentialing, identification, movement of goods and people), and of the different positional roles within such systems which are occupied by those involved in the performance of the corresponding acts, 6. of the provenance of documents (of what distinguishes an original, authentic document from a mere copy or forgery)."

2. As to the second question—how documentality can be spread in a complex society?—if it is true that in our developed society the demand for documentality is growing at a fast pace, it is also true that our society is provided growing resources from the electronic supports, which enhance and multiply the law Object = Inscribed Act.

This element is apparent in financial transactions, and in all that can be done through them. On a financial level, and already in an economy based on paper supports, documents are what fix the values, compose different values within a single system, stir resources and energies, relate people, protect transactions (De Soto 2000). On this ground, a shift from the paper support to the electronic support de-locates the operations by extending the capacity of writing. It becomes, thus, possible to accomplish differently natured operations: paying taxes, fines, bills (also those that, differently from power and gas bills, cannot be domiciled in a bank, such as the garbage tax) and union fees (for every kind of employee); booking medical visit, lawyers, public office; obtaining certificates (family state, identity documents, house certificates); doing bank transactions; obtaining postal services (at a virtual counter you can send a registered letter, a telegram, and, in general, a letter that will be delivered in a paper form); and purchasing on line (in this case, physical commodities—we are delivered our shopping on line—, as much as events or social objects: plane tickets, museum tickets, concert tickets).

The problems concerning identification are tougher. Electronic documents are not localized, or, at least, they are far less localized than paper documents. If I fill on line an application form in a public administration site, the form will be the same whether I fill it at a computer in Italy or in Mexico, but, then, where exactly is the form? Moreover, who answers me is not a person (someone will read the form only later, if anyone), but a program. And a program cannot talk, unless it has been enabled to do so through another program, that is a written thing. The document is not any longer the transcription of a voice localized in a physical person, it is a written thing de-localized in each computer through which we can access it. In this framework, we find the issue of the digital signature, which constitutes a remedy to the impersonality and de-location of the digital, and which sums up within itself exactly two fundamental features of the document: individual reference (idiomaticity) and deontic power.[4]

---

[4] See the characterization of the digital signature to be found in the Italian Legislation (Art. 24, March 5th 2005, n. 82, Digital Administration Code). The digital signature ought to univocally refer to one and only subject and to the document or set thereof to which it is affixed or associated. The affixing of a digital signature integrates and substitutes the affixing of seals, stamps, and marks of whatever kind, and used to every aim to which the current normative applies. For the generation of the digital signature, a qualified certificate has to be used, whose validity, at the time of the subscription, is not expired, revoked, or suspended. The validity of the certificate, along with the identifying elements of the titular, of the certificating officeholder, and possibly the constraints on its use has to be established through the qualified certificate itself, according to the technical rules established by article 71.

3. Finally, let us face the third question. How are we to take care of documents in a world characterized by the explosion of writing? The growing problems of privacy in the advanced societies are usually read from the stand point of a Big Brother, namely a big watching eye, in accordance with the model of Bentham's Panopticon, but this image is partly misleading. Actually, it is true that there are more and more cameras observing (also with an infra-red eye) our everyday life, in banks, stations, supermarkets, private buildings, and satellites. But the strength of this eye would be nothing, were it not accompanied with the capacity of recording,—which is exactly what turns an act of vision into a document. In this case too, the debates on the interceptations are just the tip of the iceberg: democracy requires to be investigated through the central questions rising within the category of "documentality".

All this suggests two complementary, although contrasting, considerations. On the one hand, the growing role of documentality shows undoubtedly why it is so bad being "sans papier"; it is exactly the lack of those paper—which are more and more turning into computer blips—the starting point of the process leading to the bare life, namely the offended life, a life liable to anyone's offence. In this sense, then, documentality looks like a safeguard. On the other hand, obviously enough, documentality deprives us of the right to a secret and private sphere, it creates a sort of universal control. Therefore, what has been called the *habeas data*, namely the acknowledgement of the privacy of the records concerning us (Rodotà 2006), turns out to be not less important than the acknowledgement of the *habeas corpus* that was ratified 800 years ago.

5.8 Conclusions

I maintain to have demonstrated that the critical category for social ontology is the category of "documentality", in accordance with the constitution law Object = Inscribed Act. Through this category it is possible to develop a unified theory of social objects, going over the difficulties found in the previous theories.

References

Austin, J.L. (1962). *How to do Things with Words*. Oxford University Press, Oxford.
Bratman, M.E. (1992). Shared Cooperative Activity. *The Philosophical Review*, 101: 327–341.
Derrida, J. (1967). *De la grammatologie*, Ed. de Minuti, Paris.
Derrida, J. (1971). Signature, événement, contexte. Communication au Congrès international des Sociétés de philosophie de langue française (Montréal, août 1971). Then, in (1972) Marges de la philosophie, Paris, Ed. de Minuit.
Derrida, J. (1977). *Limited Inc.: Abc*. Johns Hopkins University Press, Baltimore, MD.
De Soto, H. (2000). *The Mistery of Capital. Why Capitalism Triumphs in the West and Fails Every Where Else*. Basic Books, New York, NY.
Di Lucia, P. (Ed.) (2003). *Ontologia Sociale. Potere deontico e regole costitutive*. Quodlibet. Macerata.

Ferraris, M. (2003a). *Introduzione a Derrida.* Roma-Bari, Laterza.
Ferraris, M. (2003b). Oggetti Sociali. *Sistemi Intelligenti*, XV(3): 441–466.
Ferraris, M. (2005) *Dove sei? Ontologia del telefonino.* Bompiani, Milano.
Ferraris, M. (2006). *Jackie Derrida.* Bollati Boringhieri, Torino.
Gilbert, M. (1989). *On Social Facts.* Routledge, New York, NY.
Gilbert, M. (1993). Group Membership and Political Obligation. *The Monist*, 76: 119–131.
Johansson, I. (1989). *Ontological Investigations. An Inquiry into the Categories of Nature, Man and Society.* Routledge, London; 2a ed. Frankfurt: M. Ontos-Verlag 2004.
Kim, J., E. Sosa (1999). (Eds.) *Metaphysics: An Anthology.* Blackwell, Oxford.
Koepsell, D.R. (2000). *The Ontology of Cyberspace.* La Salle, Open Court.
Koepsell, D.R. (2003). Libri e altre macchine: artificio ed espressione. In R. Casati (Ed.) Sistemi Intelligenti, 3: 429–440.
Koepsell, D.R., L.S. Moss (Eds.) (2003). John Searle's Ideas About Social Reality, monography. *American Journal of Economics and Sociology*, 62: 285–309.
Moore, M.S. (2002). Legal Reality: A Naturalist Approach To Legal Ontology. *Law and Philosophy*, 21: 619–705.
Mulligan, K. (1987). (Ed.) *Speech Act and Sachverhalt. Reinach and the Foundations of Realist Phenomenology*, Nijhoff, The Hague.
Ong, W.J. (1982). *Orality and Literacy. The Technologizing of the Word.* Methuen, London/New York, NY.
Reid, Th. (1785), *Essays on the Active Powers of the Human Mind*, in Id., *Philosophical Works*, 1967. Olms, Hildesheim.
Reinach, A. (1913). Die apriorischen Grundlagen des bürgerlichen Recht. *Jahrbuch für Philosophie und philosophische Forschung*, 1: 685–847.
Rodotà, S. (2006). *La vita e le regole.* Hildesheim, Milano.
Searle, J.R. (1969). *Speech Acts.* Cambridge University Press, Cambridge, MA.
Searle, J.R. (1975). *A Taxonomy of Illocutionary Acts.* Cambridge University Press, Cambridge, MA.
Searle, J.R. (1977). Reiterating the Differences: A Reply to Derrida, *Glyph*, I: 172–208.
Searle, J.R. (1980). Minds, Brains and Programs. *Behavioral and Brain Sciences*, 3: 417–58.
Searle, J.R. (1983). *Intentionality. An Essay in the Philosophy of Mind.* Cambridge University Press, New York, NY/Cambridge, MA.
Searle, J.R. (1992). *The Rediscovery of the Mind.* Bradford Books, Montgomery, VT.
Searle, J.R. (1993a). Rationality and Realism, What is at Stake ? *Daedalus*, 122(4): 55–83.
Searle, J.R. (1993b). The World Turned Upside Down, and Reply to Mackey. In G.B. Madison (Ed.) *Working Through Derrida.* Northwestern University Press, Evanston, IL, 170–188 and 184–188.
Searle, J.R. (1995). The Construction of Social Reality. *New York, Free Press.* The Free Press, New York, NY.
Searle, J.R. (1998).*Postmodernism and Truth.* TWP BE *(a journal of ideas)*, 13: 85–87.
Searle, J.R. (1999). *Mind, Language and Society. Philosophy in the Real World.* Basic Books, New York, NY.
Smith, B. (1998). Ontologie des Mesokosmos: Soziale Objekte und Umwelten. *Zeitschrift für philosophische Forschung*, 52: 521–540.
Smith, B. (1999). Les objets sociaux. *Philosophiques*, 26: 315–347. http://www.erudit.org/erudit/philoso/v26n02/smith2/smith2.htm English version: Social Objects http://wings.buffalo.edu/philosophy/ontology/socobj.htm.
Smith, B. (2002). The Ontology of Social Reality. http://ontology.buffalo.edu/smith//articles/searle.PDF, 2002
Smith, B. (2003a). John Searle: From Speech Acts to Social Reality. In J. Searle (Ed.) Id., Cambridge University Press, Cambridge, MA.
Smith, B. (2003b). Un'aporia nella costruzione della realtà sociale. Naturalismo e realismo in John R. Searle. In P. Di Lucia (Ed.) Ontologia Sociale, Potere deontico e regole costitutive. Macerata: Quodlibet (2003): 137–152.

Smith, B. (2006). "Document Acts". http://ontology.buffalo.edu/document_ontology/.

Simons, P. (1987). *Parts. A Study in Ontology.* Clarendon Press, Oxford, MA.

Tomela, R. (1995). *The Importance of Us,* Stanford University Press, Stanford, CA.

Tomela, R. (2002). *The Philosophy of Social Practices.* Cambridge University Press, Cambridge, MA.

Vico, G.B. (1744). *La scienza nuova,* in Id., ed., N. Abbagnano, *La scienza nuova e altri scritti,* Torino, Utet 1952, 247–748.

Williamson, T. (1994). *Vagueness.* Routledge, London.

Williamson, T. (1998). a c. di, *Vagueness,* fascicolo monografico. *The Monist,* 81: 193–348.

Chapter 6
The Case-Based Reasoning Approach: Ontologies for Analogical Legal Argument

Kevin D. Ashley

6.1 Introduction

This paper addresses the state of the art in ontologies for case-based models of legal reasoning. It attempts to answer the question, "If one were to build a case-based legal reasoning system today, what kind of ontology should one use and what kinds of ontologies or guidance for building them are available?"

Today, one would not develop a system for case-based legal reasoning without considering the need for an ontology. A lesson learned over decades of research designing rule-based legal reasoning systems is the need for an ontology to organize the concepts and manage their interactions. Most likely, the same lesson is true for building a system to reason with legal cases, although the field seems to have learned more about rule-based, rather than case-based, ontologies. It seems hard even to specify what an ontology for case-based legal reasoning should provide.

This paper is an attempt to *demonstrate* what an ontology should provide with an extended example. Section 6.2 defines "ontology," outlines the general roles ontologies serve, and proposes three specific roles for ontologies supporting case-based legal reasoning. Section 6.3 presents the extended example, and Sections 6.4 and 6.5 distill the requirements an ontology needs to model the example's case-based argument. As summarized in Section 6.6, some requirements appear to have been met or nearly so in recent work. Others require considerable further innovation, but the concrete example may help to focus and define appropriate goals.

6.2 Definitions and Roles

By "ontology", we mean "an explicit, formal, and general specification of a conceptualization of the properties of and relations between objects in a given domain (citations omitted)" (Wyner 2008). In order to focus on the level of ontology under

K.D. Ashley (✉)
Learning Research and Development Center, Intelligent Systems Program, and School of Law, University of Pittsburgh, Pittsburgh, PA, USA
e-mail: Ashley@pitt.edu

G. Sartor et al. (eds.), *Approaches to Legal Ontologies*, Law, Governance and Technology Series 1, DOI 10.1007/978-94-007-0120-5_6,
© Springer Science+Business Media B.V. 2011

discussion, either abstract and fundamental or specific and applied, it is convenient to distinguish between: (1) an ontological framework that specifies the fundamental types of things that exist for purposes of the system, sets out the relations among these types or concepts, and defines a conceptual syntax for representing more complex concepts; and (2) a domain ontology that specifies objects, predicates, relations, and semantic constraints for a given domain.

Depending on the purpose of the case-based legal reasoning system under development, the ontology might serve a number of general roles, to:

- facilitate exchange and re-use of knowledge and information among knowledge bases and other resources which may be distributed over the Internet and the Web (Breuker et al. 2004).
- make assumptions about concepts explicit so that the program can reason with them and manage relations and distinctions among concept types (Breuker et al. 2004).
- help generate natural language explanations (Wyner 2008).

More specifically, however, since case-based legal reasoning involves drawing inferences by comparing a problem with cases, a CBR ontology should help to:

1. *Support case-based comparisons*: Find relevant cases, compare them with the problem, draw inferences based on the comparisons, and make arguments how to decide the problem.
2. *Distinguish deep and shallow analogies*: Identify cases that are relevant despite superficial dissimilarities or irrelevant despite superficial similarities.
3. *Induce/test hypotheses*: Induce defensible hypotheses about how to decide a problem from a database of suitably represented cases, and evaluate and modify the hypotheses (e.g., using hypothetical reasoning).

The next sections present an extended example to illustrate each role, and discuss recent work on how ontologies can satisfy the role.

5.3 Extended Example

The goal of the new case-based legal reasoning system is to simulate arguments that a law professor and students might reasonably make in discussing a legal case in class. It should generate the kinds of arguments students make in explaining how the case should be decided and that a professor makes in probing those arguments. More specifically, given the facts of a legal dispute, the system outputs an extended argument about how the case should be decided. The arguments include proposing tests or rules for deciding the case, drawing analogies to past cases (i.e., precedents), justifying the analogies in terms of principles and policies underlying the legal domain, challenging the proposed tests by posing hypotheticals and responding, for instance, by modifying the proposed test (Ashley et al. 2008).

Here, a "proposed test" is a rule that advocates or judges might reasonably propose for deciding the case and defend as consistent with past cases and underlying principles and policies. It is a hypothesis about how to decide the case. A "hypothetical" is an imagined situation that involves such a hypothesis (i.e., a proposed test), either exploring its meaning or challenging it as too broad or too narrow.

The example illustrates the intended output for a case drawn from a "family" of cases centered on *Pierson v. Post*. That case deals with an issue of common (i.e., judge-made as opposed to statutory) law: under what circumstances may hunters have property rights in the animals they pursue. Often treated in first year property law courses, *Pierson* and related cases have been a focus of discussion in AI and Law research (Berman and Hafner 1993; Gordon and Walton 2006; Atkinson and Bench-Capon 2007). The problem scenario focused on here is *Popov v. Hayashi*, as introduced in Atkinson and Bench-Capon (2007).

The example is intended to convey an intuitive sense of the kinds of case-based inferences and arguments the system would model. The intended output of the system is an argument presented here as a natural language text in ten parts. Four tables show excerpts of the types of "ammunition" the class participants could employ in making arguments for and against the plaintiff (P), the party that asserts a legal claim in court against the defendant (D), who defends against it. Table 6.1 shows the

Table 6.1 Cases/hypotheticals

Case name	Facts (and factors-side favored)	Decision
Pierson v. Post, 3 Caines R. (N.Y.1805) (C)	D, knowing that the plaintiff was pursuing a fox with horse and hound on open land, intercepted the fox and killed it. (NC-D, OL-D, MCI-P, KCI-P, II-P, N-P)	D
Keeble v. Hickeringill, 103 Eng.Rep. 1127 (K.B. 1706) (C)	P property owner used decoys on his part of the pond to lure ducks. D used guns to scare ducks away. (NC-D, OWL-P, L-P, MCI-P, KCI-P, II-P)	P
Young v. Hitchens, 6 Q.B. 606 (1844) (C)	P commercial fisherman closed net on fish. When the opening was still a few fathoms wide, D went through the opening and caught fish. (NC-D, OL-D, L-P, C-D, MCI-P, KCI-P, II-P)	D
Flushing quail (H)	D, knowing that P was pursuing quail by flushing them out on open land and shooting them, intercepted the quail and killed them. (NC-D, OL-D, L-P, C-D, MCI-P, KCI-P, II-P)	?
Competing school-masters (H)	D school master of competing new school frightens boys on way to old school of P master. (*NC-D*, OL-D,L-P,C-D, *MCI-P*, *KCI-P*, II-P)	?
Escaping boar (H)	D possessed wild boar that escaped and damaged P's crops (NC-D, OWL-P, L-P, *N-D*)	P
Popov v. Hayashi, 2002 WL 31833731 (Cal. Superior, 2002) (H)	When Barry Bonds' record-breaking 73d home run ball was struck into the crowd, P caught it in the upper part of the webbing of his mitt, but was tackled by other fans. D (not one of the tacklers) picked up the ball and put it in his pocket. (*NC-D*, *OL-D*, *MCI-P*, *KCI-P*, *II-*P)	Split proceeds

name, facts, and decision of the *Popov* and *Pierson* cases and other real and hypothetical cases. Table 6.2 lists a variety of principles or policies in this area of property
law that courts take into account in deciding such cases. Table 6.3 lists some factors, stereotypical fact patterns that strengthen or weaken a side's claim for property
rights. Table 6.4 lists some proposed tests that the arguers (and a court) might plau-
sibly maintain for deciding such a case. We assume that the students would have
encountered *Popov* and *Pierson* and some of the other cases in Table 6.1 in reading
the part of their casebook dealing with First Possession (See, e.g., Singer 2005).

Example, Part 1. The discussion begins with the facts and plaintiff's claim in
the *Popov* case. The plaintiff showed that, when Barry Bonds' record-breaking 73d
home run ball was struck into the crowd, plaintiff caught it in the upper part of the
webbing of his baseball mitt, but then he was tackled by other fans. In the scuffle,
the defendant, who was not one of the tacklers, picked up the ball and put it in his
pocket. Plaintiff claimed a property right to the baseball with which the defendant
interfered (Table 6.1, Cases/Hypos). A question for the court—and for the class—is

Table 6.2 Principles/policies

Principles or policies	Meaning
Protect fair play	Discourage unsportsmanlike conduct and unfair competition
Reduce nuisance pests	Encourage eradication of deleterious pests
Promote certainty	Maximize rule's ease and clarity of application
Protect livelihood	Protect livelihood of working parties
Avoid property rights on public property	Avoid assigning property rights to things on public property
Promote economic competition	Promote economic competition among businessmen
Protect free enterprise	Protect free enterprise of businessmen
Legally protectable interests	Only protect interests the law recognizes
Protect landowner's rights	Protect the rights of the landowner on his own land

Table 6.3 Factors

Factors	Short name (abbreviation)	Side favored
Animal not caught or mortally wounded	NotCaught (NC)	D
Open land	OpenLand (OL)	D
Own land	OwnLand (OWL)	P
P pursuing livelihood	Livelihood (L)	P
D in economic competition with P	Competes (C)	D
P manifestly closes in on goal	ManifestClosingIn (MCI)	P
D knows P closes in on goal	KnowsClosingIn (KCI)	P
D intentionally interferes physically with P's closing in on goal	Intentional interference (II)	P
Animal is a nuisance pest	Nuisance (N)	D

Table 6.4 Proposed tests (i.e., hypotheses)

Proposed tests	Short name
If plaintiff manifestly intended to gain possession of something of value, and the defendant intentionally interfered causing plaintiff to fail, then he can recover	Manifest Intent
If plaintiff manifestly intended to gain possession of the baseball, and the defendant intentionally interfered causing plaintiff to fail, then he can recover	Manifest-Intent-1
If plaintiff did not gain possession of the baseball (e.g., by catching and securing it), then he cannot recover	Possession
If plaintiff did not gain possession of the quarry (e.g., by catching and securing it), then he cannot recover	Possession-1

the appropriate legal test (if any) for deciding if the plaintiff has such a property right and whether it is satisfied on these facts.

Example, Part 2. A student advocating for the plaintiff proposes a test: "If plaintiff manifestly intended to gain possession of something of value, and the defendant intentionally interfered causing plaintiff to fail, then plaintiff can recover," (Table 6.4, Proposed Tests, Manifest Intent). In order to justify the test, the advocate might argue that it is consistent with underlying principles and past cases: it Protects Fair Play (Table 6.2, Principles/Policies) and is analogous to the *Keeble* case (Table 6.1, Cases/Hypos) in which plaintiff won where the defendant scared away ducks plaintiff had lured to its part of a pond. The student might draw a factual analogy in terms of relevant factors the cases share: Manifest Closing In, Knows Closing In, and Intentional Interference (Table 6.3, Factors).

Example, Part 3. The professor might probe the proposed test as too broad by posing a hypothetical: Suppose a defendant school master of a competing new school frightens boys on their way to the old school of the plaintiff schoolmaster. Should the plaintiff schoolmaster recover? (Table 6.1, Cases/Hypos). If so, would that not contradict the law's goal to promote economic competition? (Table 6.2, Principles/Policies).

Example, Part 4. The pro-plaintiff student might respond by distinguishing the *Popov* case from the Competing Schoolmasters hypothetical (Table 6.1, Cases/Hypos), arguing that the plaintiff and defendant are not in economic competition (Table 6.3, Factors) and thus a pro-defendant factor applied in the hypothetical that does not apply in *Popov*. He might go on to modify his proposed test by making it apply more narrowly to errant "baseballs" rather than to "something of value." (Table 6.4, Proposed Tests, Manifest Intent-1).

Example, Part 5. Another student might respond to the pro-plaintiff student's argument (Part 2) in another way by distinguishing the *Keeble* case, emphasizing any pro-plaintiff factors present in that case not shared in *Popov*. For example the plaintiff in *Keeble* was pursuing his Livelihood on his OwnLand (Table 6.3, Factors). This matters, the student argues, because the court may have aimed to Protect Livelihood and Landowner's Rights (Table 6.2, Principles/Policies). He might also suggest that Protects Fair Play, although morally relevant, is not a Legally Protectable Interest (Table 6.2, Principles/Policies). Continuing to advocate for the defendant, the student might cite the *Pierson* case where the defendant won (Table 6.1, Cases/Hypotheticals) *despite* the shared facts associated with Manifest Closing In, Knows Closing In, and Intentional Interference (Table 6.3, Factors).

Example, Part 6. If the professor asks for the defendant's advocate's test, the student might propose one like the court in *Pierson* actually employed: "If plaintiff did not gain possession of the baseball (e.g., by catching and securing it), then he cannot recover" (Table 6.4, Proposed Tests, Possession). The student might concede that his test is inconsistent with *Keeble*, but emphasize that applying it in the *Popov* facts would Promote Certainty by discouraging litigants who "almost caught" the ball or "should have had it", and Avoid Property Rights in Public Property (Table 6.2, Principles/Policies), a consideration not present in *Keeble*.

Example, Part 7. Posing a hypothetical based on a real case, the professor might challenge the student's proposed pro-defendant test as too narrow. Suppose the plaintiff were a commercial fisherman, closing his nets on a school of fish, when another fisherman swooped in with a fast boat and scooped up the fish with a smaller net. Wouldn't such a plaintiff fisherman also fail to recover?" (*Young* case, Table 6.1, Cases/Hypos.)

Example, Part 8. In response, the student might broaden his test to cover failing to catch and secure not just baseballs but any quarry including fish (Table 6.4, Proposed Tests, Possession-1). He would justify his proposed result in *Popov* by analogizing *Young* where the defendant won because of a failure to catch or secure the quarry and despite the shared facts associated with Manifest Closing In, Knows Closing In, and Intentional Interference (Table 6.3, Factors).

Example, Part 9. The pro-plaintiff student of Part 2 might object by distinguishing the *Young* case, where the defendant was in economic competition with the plaintiff, a factor that favored defendant in *Young* where there was a policy to promote economic competition that did not apply in *Popov* (Table 6.2: Principles/Policies).

Example, Part 10. The pro-defendant student might respond that while the plaintiff and defendant are not in the business of selling baseballs, they were in economic competition, since Barry Bonds' last home run ball is worth a fortune.

6.4 Requirements for a Case-Based Legal Ontology

The example illustrates ways in which an ontology could address the first specific role for a CBR ontology (Section 6.2): *Support case-based comparisons*, and foreshadows issues raised by the other roles: *Distinguish deep and shallow analogies* and *Induce/test hypotheses*. The requirements for an ontology differ depending on the goals; the behavior in the example could be modeled at various levels of sophistication. As a basic assumption, the system should at least be able to generate a discussion of how to decide any of the cases or hypotheticals in Table 6.1 taken as the problem case, and to incorporate into the discussion as precedents or hypotheticals any of the other real and hypothetical cases in Table 6.1. Additional assumptions about the system's level of sophistication are discussed below.

6.4.1 For Representing Cases

A basic task for the case-based ontological framework is to specify and organize classes of concepts for representing the Table 6.1 cases and hypos. This includes concepts for representing case Names, Parties, Legal Claims (e.g., to enforce a property right) Decision, etc. but also concepts for representing case facts. Here, much will depend on the nature and grain size of the desired fact representation.

As illustrated in the example, factors have proven to be useful abstractions for representing case facts. A number of CBR programs employ lists of expert-supplied factors to represent legally relevant patterns (e.g., Ashley 1990; Rissland and Skalak 1991; Aleven 2003; Chorley and Bench-Capon 2005; Ashley and Brüninghaus 2006; Wyner 2008). As noted, each factor captures a stereotypical pattern of facts that has legal significance in cases involving a particular claim; each represents a relevant similarity or difference and makes it possible to model comparing cases in terms of set theoretic operations over the sets of factors in each case. This is preferable to using quantitative feature weights, since selecting relevant cases and comparing them in terms of sets of factors facilitates explaining the comparisons in arguments. For instance, using factors, the *Keeble* case is analogized to the problem in Part 2 and distinguished from it in Part 5; also in Part 5, the *Pierson* case is cited as a "trumping" counterexample; it shares all the factors with the problem that *Keeble* does but reaches an opposite result (Ashley 1990; Aleven 2003). For the class of factors, the domain ontology will represent at least the name and side favored by the factor.

Factors will not be sufficient, however. Since the example involves hypothetical cases designed to challenge proposed tests, the domain ontology needs to support a more complex fact representation, especially if the system will pose its own hypothetical scenarios. Cases could be represented in structured formats, composed of facts at least some of which are represented at a finer grain size. As suggested in the Table 6.1 Cases/hypos, the domain ontology will have to represent some fundamental categories of human agency (See Breuker and Hoekstra 2004b) such as:

> INTERFERENCE: not interfering, interfering physically with, preventing someone's reaching a goal
> INTENTIONALITY: acting unintentionally, negligently, knowingly or intentionally
> OBJECTIVENESS OF INTENTION: hiding ones intentions, being ambiguous about them or manifesting them clearly

This domain ontology needs to support analogous activities across the domains covered by the Table 6.1 Cases/hypos. It covers factual classes and values specific to hunting (or "catching") (The asterisks (*) indicate concepts introduced in order to relate the hunting and fishing domains of the cases fan's to catching a homerun ball in the stands—or a schoolmaster's luring away a tuition-paying student):

> HUNTING/CATCHING VENUES: land; pond; ocean; ballpark stands*
> RESTRICTIONS ON VENUES: open; privately owned; subject to regulatory restriction; by invitation only*
> QUARRY: animals (wild, domestic, edible, nuisance pests, fox, quail); quarry; baseballs*; students*; something of value*; economic goals*
> HUNTING/CATCHING STEPS RE POSSESSION: seeking quarry; closing in on quarry; catching and securing quarry (in a mitt*, by killing, in a net hauled in); missing quarry
> HUNTING/CATCHING OCCUPATIONS: pursuing livelihood; competing economically; by avocation

With a domain ontology like this, a hypothetical could be created by a coordinated substituting of slot values in the structured case facts or be compared in terms of the corresponding slot values across two cases. The ontology's factor representation could include focal slots whose values are key to the factor's application (Ashley 1990). For instance, the professor's hypothetical in Part 3 substitutes "students" for "baseball" in the quarry slot of the problem and schoolmasters for fans who caught the baseball in an avocational activity. The changes seem small, but they may have significant implications. The Livelihood and Competition factors kick in, a change whose significance is discussed below.

5.4.2 For Explaining Case Decisions

Case decisions need to be explained, and a CBR ontology needs to support those explanations. In the example, the decisions are explained in terms of the proposed test (i.e., legal rule) a decision instantiates, the principles and policies which inform the decision and of which it represents a tradeoff, and the inferences drawn from case comparisons and the reasons why the comparisons matter.

Since tests need to be composed, compared, and modified, it is natural to represent them as logical formulae with concepts drawn from the ontology. This includes factual concepts for case representation such as "quarry" or "baseball" and legal terms or *intermediate legal concepts*. If a rule specifies factual requirements for the application of a particular legal term, and that legal term, in turn, is a requirement in another rule that implies the legal or normative consequences, the legal term is an intermediate legal concept. A concept like "ownership, citizenship, guardianship, trusteeship, possession, etc." "stands as a mediating link between the requirements and the consequences" (Lindahl 2004; See Wyner 2008).

The ontology contains and organizes all of the general factual and intermediate legal concepts for formulating the tests (e.g., possession, manifestly intended, intentionally interfered, causing, and quarry.) A primary task of the ontology is to coordinate the ordinary and legal institutional descriptions of events and, from the context, to keep track of the factual and legal senses of apparently identical terms. Some intermediate legal concepts may appear the same as general factual concepts. For instance, "causing" may have both an ordinary commonsense and a technical legal meaning as an intermediate legal concept. Such technical legal concepts are open-textured; their meanings are subject to argument.

Typically, ontologies organize concepts according to generality (e.g., fox and fish are animals and also each is a kind of quarry as is a baseball or a tuition-paying student.) Generality, however, is not the only useful ordering criteria. Some orderings characteristic of the "hunting or catching" domain are important, such as certainty of possession (e.g., catching and securing vs. seeking or closing in). Orderings characteristic of the legal domain would also be valuable. Intermediate legal concept classes could be ordered by legal effect or "inclusiveness".

For instance, requiring that an intention's OBJECTIVENESS OF INTENTION be manifest is more stringent than allowing it to be ambiguous or hidden. Similarly, the ordering of the INTENTIONALITY class (i.e., (1) unintentionally, (2) negligently, (3) knowingly or intentionally) corresponds to a legal effect: A rule that penalizes certain actions only if performed knowingly or intentionally is less inclusive than one that penalizes even unintentional actions that have negative consequences.

Since explaining a case decision also involves explaining the extent to which it is consistent with underlying principles, the ontology needs to support reasoning with and about principles. This means categorizing the principles (e.g., arguably, Protects Fair Play is a moral principle, not a Legally Protectable Interest in Part 5).

The ontology should also organize and track hierarchical relationships among the explanatory concepts, including factual concepts, factors, intermediate legal concepts, and principles/policies. Thus, the values of factual concepts in a case or case comparison may trigger the application of factors and intermediate legal concepts which, in turn, trigger the application of principles. For instance, as the value of HUNTING/CATCHING VENUES switches from pond or ocean to ballpark stands and the corresponding values of RESTRICTIONS ON VENUES from privately owned to open or subject to invitation , different factors will apply such as Open Land or Own Land. These, in turn, trigger different principles/policies. Open Land (Table 6.3, Factors) is connected with Avoid Property Rights in Public Property (Table 6.2, Principles/Policies); Own Land relates to Protect Landowner's Rights as employed in explaining the *Keeble* decision and distinguishing it from *Popov*, Parts 5 and 6. Similarly, as the value of QUARRY varies from fish to fox to homerun baseball to tuition-paying students to economic goals, particular factors and their related principles and policies switch on or off: Fox triggers the Nuisance factor and the policy of Reducing Nuisance Pests. Quail triggers Livelihood and the policy of Protect Livelihood. Values for INTENTIONALITY, INTERFERENCE, and OBJECTIVENESS OF INTENTION such as "knowingly interfering physically with a person's manifest attempt to catch a fish" trigger the policy of Protect Fair Play. This makes sense: factors represent similarities and differences and are legally relevant in part because they indicate that different principles and policies are at stake.

Intermediate legal concepts employed in the proposed tests are also implicated by values of factual concepts and relate to factors and principles/policies. For instance, "Intentionally interfered" relates to Intentional Interference (Table 6.3, Factors) and to Protect Fair Play (Table 6.2, Principles/Policies.) "Nuisance pests" connects with Nuisance and Reduce Nuisance Pests. "Possession" is associated with Not Caught and with Promote Certainty.

The ontology has to record and organize these hierarchical relationships in the manner of the Factor Hierarchy in CATO (Aleven 2003) and hierarchical domain model in IBP (Ashley and Brüninghaus 2006). In addition, the ontology must enforce constraints on values and combinations of values. For instance, some venues are subject to private property ownership and some are not. A pond can be privately owned; the ocean cannot be. Sometimes these distinctions will be quite subtle. A ballpark may be privately owned but still open to the public; fans may come in, watch the game, purchase a beer, and even catch a fly ball that strays their way and take it home. They may not take home the seat they are sitting in, however. How to represent such considerations raises design issues; these considerations combine commonsense and legal reasoning and probably should not be dealt with at the ontological level, but that is a design decision based in part on whether the system is aimed at modeling reasoning about them. Finally, the ontology must support translating the values associated with a case or comparison of cases into explanations, probably using explanation-oriented semantic networks that represent the relations among facts and reasons in a more structured way (see, e.g., Falkenhainer et al. 1989; Branting 2003; McLaren 2003; Ashley and McLaren 1995).

6.4.3 For Representing Case-Based Arguments

These explanations will be woven into case-based legal arguments using a set of argument schemes capturing typical, schematic domain-specific inferences (Prakken 2006). The legal inferences based on case comparisons in Parts 2 and 5 are examples of case-based argument schema. The ontology should represent classes of concepts for use in the argument schema to denote features of the case comparisons for purposes of drawing and explaining inferences. For instance, the ontology in Wyner (2008) includes *partitions*, explicit features of the comparison of a pair of cases that capture set-theoretic relationships of the factors in each case and that condition or bias the legal conclusion drawn from the comparison.

6.5 Using the Ontology to Model Arguments with Hypothetical Cases

A recent survey reports a distinction between ontologies designed for models of case-based legal reasoning that focus on rule-extraction versus those that focus on case comparison:

When cases are considered as authoritative sources of rules (as in the rule extraction method), . . ., the extracted rules are applied, just like other rules. From an ontological point of view, the rule extraction method treats cases basically as sets of rules. In the method of case comparison, cases are considered differently, namely as authoritative sources of arguments and decisions. . . . Ontologically, the case comparison method views cases basically as sets of arguments and decisions. (Roth and Verheij 2004: 635)

The method illustrated in the extended example represents an amalgam of these two conceptions of case-based legal reasoning. Rules may be derived from cases and applied deductively, but the important point is that there are arguments about what the rules mean; the rules can be challenged, changed, and reinterpreted through a process of case comparison. Rather than an authoritative source of a rule, the case is seen as an authoritative result given a set of facts from which a range of rules can be extracted in light of prior decisions and underlying principles/policies. A test is proposed that deductively leads to a desired decision. The test is subjected to a process of interpretive investigation with, among other things, hypothetical examples that tease out the meaning of its terms and assess its fit with the past decisions and principles. The test is applied deductively to the hypothetical and prior case facts, but that is only part of the process.

The result must be assessed in light of underlying domain principles and policies. As the example suggests, the decision of a case is frequently more consistent with some principles and policies than with others. A hypothetical can be used to change the balance in order to demonstrate that a proposed test is too broad or too narrow (Ashley et al. 2008). In turn a proposed test can be modified to ameliorate the over or under breadth.

The case comparison guides that process of modifying the test. As per the model in Ashley et al. (2008) and as illustrated in Part 4, if the test has been challenged as too broad, an advocate can distinguish the hypothetical example from the case at hand, argue that they should have different results, and, guided by the distinction, add a condition or limit a concept definition so that the narrowed test still applies to the current fact situation but does not apply to, or leads to a different result for, the hypothetical example. If the test has been challenged as too narrow, as illustrated in Part 8, an advocate can analogize the hypothetical to the case at hand, concede that the result should be the same in each and, guided by the analogy, eliminate a condition or expand a concept definition so that the test applies to both with the same result.

An ontology that represents the connections among factors, concepts and principles/policies, as described above, could support computationally modeling these phenomena of argument. Hypothetically changing an appropriate fact takes the case out of one policy and into another. For instance, in Part 3, switching the QUARRY from baseball to tuition-paying student and applying the Manifest Intent test suddenly leads to a result that protects fair play but at the expense of discouraging economic competition! This involves commonsense reasoning when judges do it; the switch could be modeled in terms of simple ontological moves. The ontological ordering of terms by abstractness and legal effect or "inclusiveness" also guides comparing or modifying test versions. For instance, "baseball" is substituted for "something of value" in modifying the Manifest Intent test in Part 4 into Manifest Intent-1 (Table 6.4), thus removing the over breadth. In Part 9, the modification of Possession to Possession-1 with the liberalization of the quarry from baseballs to "baseballs" and "fish" or "quarry" accommodates the hypothetical and is, again, inspired and supported by connections in the ontology.

As presented in Ashley et al. (2008) the model of hypothetical reasoning illustrated in the extended example explains some features of U.S. Supreme Court oral arguments, common law decision making (Eisenberg 1988; Gewirts 1982), and American legal education, but it may apply as well to aspects of civil law legal reasoning especially in the highest courts dealing with constitutional issues (MacCormick and Summers 1997: 528–529).

6.6 Challenges for a CBR Ontology

As a goal, an ontology and computational model that could generate the example represents an advance over existing case-based legal reasoning programs in AI and Law research whose outputted arguments do not include such features as reasoning with proposed tests and hypotheticals and which have tended not to have elaborate ontologies (see, e.g., McCarty and Sridharan 1981; Ashley 1990; Rissland and Skalak 1991; Aleven 2003; Branting 2003; Bench-Capon and Sartor 2003; Chorley and Bench-Capon 2005, Ashley and Brüninghaus 2006). An exception is the recent OWL-based ontology in Wyner (2008). It comes nearest to satisfying the ontological requirements in a program, AS-CATO, that is a reworking of two programs, CATO (Aleven 2003) and IBP (Ashley and Brüninghaus 2006), all of which implement some of the behaviors illustrated in the example. Neither the ontology nor the AS-CATO program address reasoning with proposed tests, hypotheticals or underlying principles and policies.

The two remaining roles of a case-based ontology, distinguishing deep and shallow analogies and inducing/testing hypotheses present challenges that the example helps to frame.

Distinguish deep and shallow analogies. In order to distinguish deep and shallow analogies, the ontology will need to represent classes of claims and issues as well as an explanation of what the court decided. For example, from a superficial viewpoint, given the relevance of the *Pierson* case, the Escaping Boar case (Table 6.1) may also appear relevant. It involves *possession* of a *wild animal* and, like *Pierson*, arguably, even a *nuisance pest*. At a deeper level, however, the scenario, claim, and issue of the Escaping Boar case are quite different; the claim is negligence (or strict liability without fault) and the issue involves whether the defendant possessor of the escaping animal who escaped through (or even absent) the defendant's negligence is liable for injury sustained by his plaintiff neighbors. As suggested in Table 6.5, in order to discriminate among superficially similar cases, the ontology should support representing in a more structured way the relations among the parties, defendant's injuries and the way plaintiff's actions caused them, and the relevant claims and

Table 6.5 Explanation of some cases, issues, claims, factors

Case name	Explanation	Factors
Popov v. Hayashi	Where defendant pocketed a very valuable baseball that plaintiff had caught, plaintiff won a *claim* of interference with property despite the *issue* of possession where plaintiff had not completely secured the ball before being knocked down, but was awarded only half the proceeds of sale of baseball.	*Not caught, open land, manifest closing in, knows closing in, intentional interference*
Young v. Hitchens	Where defendant commercial fisherman caught fish from within the still open nets plaintiff commercial fisherman was closing around the fish, defendant won *claim* of interference with property due to *issue* of plaintiff's possession where plaintiff had not captured the fish.	Not caught, *open land*, livelihood, competes, manifest closing in, knows closing in, intentional interference
Keeble v. Hickeringill	Where defendant used guns to scare away ducks that land owner lured to his part of the pond, plaintiff won claim of interference with property despite issue of possession where plaintiff had not killed or mortally wounded ducks.	Not caught, own land, livelihood, manifest closing in, knows closing in, intentional interference
Pierson v. Post	Where defendant killed a fox, a nuisance pest, that plaintiff hunted for sport, plaintiff lost *claim* of interference with property on *issue* of possession where plaintiff had not killed or mortally wounded the fox.	Not caught, open land, manifest closing in, knows closing in, intentional interference, nuisance
Escaping boar case	Where defendant possessed a wild animal nuisance pest that damaged plaintiff's property, plaintiff won *claim* for negligence/strict liability on *issue* that animal escaped through/without defendant's fault.	Not caught, own land, livelihood, *nuisance*
Competing School masters hypothetical	Where defendant schoolmaster scared away pupils from attending plaintiff's school, plaintiff won?/lost? a *claim* for interference with a property interest where an *issue* involved whether the plaintiff had a property interest in students attending his school.	*Not caught, open land, livelihood, competes, manifest closing in, knows closing in,* intentional interference

issues. Explanation-oriented semantic networks would be a suitable representation for this type of information (see, e.g., Branting 2003; McLaren 2003; Breuker and Hoekstra 2004a). In order to assess whether cases that share some terms and factors are similar at a deeper level, the program could then map the explanations from one case to another.

By contrast, in the *Popov v. Hayashi* case, as we have seen, the issue re possession in a claim for enforcing a property interest are similar, even though the tackling fans are the only "wild animals" involved: defendant intercepts the "quarry" (in this case a baseball) as plaintiff closes in. The court cited the *Pierson* and *Young* cases because they involved a similar issue of possession.

If the decisions in *Pierson* and *Young* are represented as structured explanations as suggested in Table 6.5, and if the ontology supported matching explanations expressed in increasingly abstract versions, the deeper analogies would be revealed. For one thing, "baseball" would be seen as a kind of quarry like a "fox" or "fish" and "putting in one's pocket" a kind of interference with plaintiff's property interest. Factors would also need to be matched more abstractly. The italicizing of the factor names for the *Popov* case in Tables 6.1 and 6.5 indicates that the *Not Caught*, *Open Land*, *Manifest Closing In*, *Knows Closing In*, and *Intentional Interference* factors all have somewhat different senses in the context of a fan's catching a homerun ball in a baseball stadium's stands versus hunting a fox in a meadow or catching fish in the open sea. A baseball may be caught but will not be mortally wounded. Hunter's close in on their living prey or interfere with one another's attempts in a different way. And, as noted above, a baseball stadium is not Open Land, although fans are invited in and may catch homeruns that come their way. Similarly, the factors in the Competing School Master hypothetical of Part 3, with its human or economic "quarry," are italicized in Tables 6.1 and 6.5 because the case does not involve animal quarry, the venues are not hunting venues in the usual sense, "closing in" has a different connotation, "catching" is metaphorical, and even the manner of ones livelihood and competition is somewhat different from the hunting scenarios.

How can this kind of abstract matching be managed? The factors should be expressed in terms of more abstract schema that deal with closing in on ones goals and being frustrated by external intentional interference (See, e.g., Breuker and Hoekstra 2004b). These could be mapped flexibly to different kinds of scenarios achieving analogical mapping and reuse across multiple legal domains.

The underlying principles/policies associated with factors could also inform the analogies, but they, too, would need to be matched abstractly. For instance, the *Young* case pits the policy of Protecting Livelihood against Promoting Economic Competition, arguably presenting a deeper analogy to the Competing Schoolmasters hypothetical than to the *Pierson* case. "Once the purpose of the rule is understood, analogous cases setting forth the rights of school masters become more relevant than cases dealing with foxes." (Berman and Hafner 1993). If the abstract schema associated with these competing principles or their associated factors (i.e., Livelihood and Competes) are seen abstractly as applying to the *Popov* case with its struggle over a potentially extremely valuable baseball, then a fruitful line of argument is revealed. Of course, the ontologically-supported mapping across cases that are similar at a deeper level despite superficial differences would seem to be a subject for argument itself raising issues similar to ontology alignment (Laera et al. 2006).

Induce/test hypotheses. The remaining role for the ontology is to support the generation and assessment of hypotheses, namely, the proposed tests. Designing systems to induce (or abduce) reasonable legal tests or rules (and other abstractions such as issues and factors) from the decided cases and their facts, suitably represented, has been the focus of research in AI and Law. For instance, the IBP program generated and tested hypotheses predicting a winner based on a logical model of a legal claim, legal issues, and cases represented with factors (Brüninghaus and Ashley 2003). The rules derived in Chorley and Bench-Capon (2005) reflected value preferences in past cases. Generating legal hypotheses is more challenging than ordinary machine induction, because the tests must be susceptible to being explained in terms of expert legal knowledge: principles/policies, precedents, their facts and decisions, issues and other legal rules.

As illustrated in the extended example, one way to model the kind of incremental, explainable induction that characterizes legal reasoning is to focus on the process of proposing tests and evaluating them with hypotheticals. The hypothetical reasoning process is driven by argument schema applied to problem cases and is supported by the ontology. The primary adaptive mechanism involves substituting facts and concepts from the ontology to make the hypotheticals and modify the tests. This is like case-based adaptation (Kolodner 1993: 7), except the solution is not a case decision alone but includes the test as proposed or modified; the hypothetical case is a case adaptation that helps evaluate if the test is consistent with past cases, underlying principles and policies, and anticipated future cases. A robust computational model of the process would integrate and extend techniques for constructing hypotheticals (Ashley 1990), broadening or narrowing a legal rule (Rissland and Skalak 1991) and for reasoning with values (Atkinson and Bench-Capon 2007; Bench-Capon and Sartor 2003).

A comprehensive ontological organization of the legal and factual concepts to guide substitutions would be essential, but it may not be enough. In fashioning proposed tests and tailoring them to past cases, principles, and policies, human participants in the process, such as advocates, judges, professors, and students, commonly invent new intermediate legal concepts. The extended example does not illustrate the advocates' inventing new legal concepts, but it is interesting to think how an ontological framework and domain ontology might support that commonplace of legal argument. In drawing analogies across cases from different legal domains, concepts employed in rules of abstractly analogous cases could be adapted to the new domain with the assistance of the ontological organization. Alternatively, the ontology might support a process of composing existing terms in its ontological organization. Ontology-based automated combinations of elements have been discussed in the literature, such as causal case explanations in terms of actions and intentions (Breuker and Hoekstra 2004a) and transformation rules (i.e., weak rules of inference abstracting and formalizing procedures empirically discovered in solving cases) (Zarri 2007). It is a matter of determining appropriate guidelines and constraints for the process so that the results can be evaluated.

6.7 Conclusions

In order to help specify what an ontology for case-based models of legal reasoning and argument should provide, this paper has presented an extended example based on a legal classroom discussion the yet-to-be invented CBR system should simulate, supported by an appropriate case-based ontology. The example illustrates three roles for the ontology in supporting case-based comparisons, distinguishing deep and shallow analogies, and inducing and testing hypotheses. The paper has distilled the ontological requirements for modeling the example's case-based arguments and reviewed current research relevant to meeting those requirements. The first role is nearly within reach of current AI and Law technology; work still needs to be done in modeling the proposing of tests for deciding a case and the role of hypotheticals in evaluating and modifying the test in light of prior cases, principles and policies. The last two roles present challenges that will necessitate advancements in the design of ontologies and the kinds of reasoning they support.

The concrete example helps to define and focus on goals for future developments in designing CBR ontologies. It comprises a family of related, and some unrelated, or apparently unrelated, cases. The cases are almost all based on real legal cases, almost any of which could be used as a problem scenario with the other cases cited as precedents or the seeds of hypotheticals. In this sense, the extended example captures a limited but realistic argument "world" and, thus, might be an appropriate tool for designing and building a working case-based ontology. Such examples can illustrate a wide range of legal reasoning behaviors and domains providing a concrete context for modeling ontological operations. The extended example can be made more complex in an incremental way so that, as new features are built into the ontology, more advanced behavior can be simulated, tested, and accommodated.

References

Aleven, V. (1997). *Teaching Case-Based Argumentation Through a Model and Examples*, Ph.D., University of Pittsburgh.

Aleven, V. (2003). Using Background Knowledge in Case-Based Legal Reasoning. *Artificial Intelligence*, 150(1–2): 183–238.

Ashley, K. (1990). *Modeling Legal Argument: Reasoning with Cases and Hypotheticals* (The MIT Press). Based on (1988) Ph.D. Tech. Rep. No. 88-01 COINS, U. Mass.

Ashley, K., S. Brüninghaus (2006). Computer Models for Legal Prediction. *Jurimetrics Journal*, 46: 309–352.

Ashley, K., C. Lynch, N. Pinkwart, V. Aleven (2008). A Process Model of Legal Argument with Hypotheticals. JURIX 2008. Firenze.

Ashley, K., M. McLaren (1995). Reasoning with Reasons in Case-Based Comparisons. In M. Veloso, A. Aamodt (Eds.) ICCBR-95 LNCS (LNAI) 1010. Springer, Heidelberg, 133–144.

Atkinson, K., T. Bench-Capon (2007). In Proceedings of the Eleventh International Conference on Artificial Intelligence and Law (ICAIL), June 4–8, 2007, Stanford Law School, Stanford, California.

Bench-Capon, T., G. Sartor (2003). A Model of Legal Reasoning with Cases Incorporating Theories and Values. *Artificial Intelligence*, 150: 97–143.

Berman, D., C. Hafner (1993). Representing Teleological Structure in Case-Based Legal Reasoning: The Missing Link. In *ICAIL 1993*. ACM Press, New York, NY, 50–59.

Branting, L.K. (2003). A Reduction-Graph Model of Precedent in Legal Analysis. *Artificial Intelligence*, 150: 59–95.

Breuker, J., R. Hoekstra (2004a). DIRECT: Ontology-Based Discovery of Responsibility and Causality in Legal Cases: In T. Gordon (Ed.) *Proceedings JURIX-2004*. IOS-Press, Amsterdam, 115–126.

Breuker, J., R. Hoekstra (2004b). Epistemology and Ontology in Core Ontologies: FOLaw and LRI-Core, Two Core Ontologies for Law. In *Proceedings of the EKAW04 Workshop on Core Ontologies in Ontology Engineering*, 15–27.

Breuker, J., A. Valente, R. Winkels (2004). Legal Ontologies in Knowledge Engineering and Information Management. *Artificial Intelligence and Law*, 12(4): 241–277 Springer.

Brüninghaus, S., K. Ashley (2003). Predicting the Outcome of Case-Based Legal Arguments. In G. Sartor (Ed.) *Proceedings of the 9th International Conference on Artificial Intelligence and Law* (ICAIL-03) ACM Press, New York, NY, 234–242.

Chorley, A., T. Bench-Capon (2005). AGATHA: Automated Construction of Case Law Theories Through Heuristic Search. In *ICAIL 2005*. ACM Press, New York, NY, 45–54.

Falkenhainer, B., K. Forbus, D. Gentner (1989). The Structure-Mapping Engine: Algorithm and Examples, *Artificial Intelligence*, 41(1): 1–63.

Eisenberg, M. (1988). *The Nature of the Common Law*, vol. 99. Harvard University Press, Cambridge, MA.

Gewirtz, P. (1982). The Jurisprudence of Hypotheticals. *Journal of Legal Education*, 32: 120 f.

Gordon, T.F., D. Walton (2006). Pierson vs. Post Revisited—A Reconstruction Using the Carneades Argumentation Framework. In P.E. Dunne, T. Bench-Capon (Eds.) *COMMA 2006*. IOS Press, Amsterdam.

Kolodner, J. (1993). *Case-Based Reasoning*. Morgan Kaufmann, San Mateo, CA.

Laera L., V. Tamma, J. Euzenat, T. Bench-Capon (2006). Arguing Over Ontology Alignments. In *Proceedings of the First Workshop on Ontology Matching*, Athens, GA, 49–60, URL http://ceur-ws.org/Vol-225/paper5.pdf.

Lindahl, L. (2004). Deduction and Justification in the Law. The Role of Legal Terms and Concepts. *Ratio Juris*, 17: 182–202.

MacCormick, D., R. Summers (Ed.) (1997). *Interpreting Precedents*. Ashgate/Dartmouth, Brookfield, VT.

McCarty, L.T., N.S. Sridharan (1981). *The Representation of an Evolving System of Legal Concepts: II. Prototypes and Deformations*. LRP-TR-11. Lab. for CS Res. Rutgers U.

McGinty, L., B. Smyth (2002). Comparison-Based Recommendation. In S. Craw, A.D. Preece (Eds.) *ECCBR 2002*. LNCS (LNAI), vol. 2416. Springer, Heidelberg, 575–589.

McLaren, B. (2003). Extensionally Defining Principles and Cases in Ethics: An AI Model. *Artificial Intelligence*, 150: 145–182.

Prakken, H. (2006). Artificial Intelligence and Law, Logic and Argument Schemes. In D. Hitchcock, B. Verheij (Eds.) *Arguing on the Toulmin Model*. Springer, Dordrecht.

Rissland, E.L., D.B. Skalak (1991). CABARET: Rule Interpretation in a Hybrid Architecture. *International Journal of Man-Machine Studies*, 34(6): 839–887.

Roth, B., B. Verheij (2004). Cases and Dialectical Arguments. An Approach to Case-Based Reasoning. On the Move to Meaningful Internet Systems 2004: OTM 2004 Workshops. In R. Meersman, Z. Tari, A. Corsaro (Eds.) *WORM'04: The Second International Workshop on Regulatory Ontologies*. LNCS, vol. 3292. Springer, Heidelberg, 634–651.

Singer, J. (2005). *Property Law: Rules, Policies & Practices*, 4th ed. Aspen Press, New York, NY.

Wyner, A. (2008). An Ontology in OWL for Legal Case-Based Reasoning. *Artificial Intelligence and Law*, 16: 361–387.

Zarri, G. (2007). Ontologies and Reasoning Techniques For (Legal) Intelligent Information Retrieval Systems. *Artificial Intelligence and Law*, 15(3): 251–279.

Chapter 7
A Complex-System Approach: Legal Knowledge, Ontology, Information and Networks

Pierre Mazzega, Danièle Bourcier, Paul Bourgine, Nadia Nadah, and Romain Boulet

7.1 Introduction

The need for the development of legal ontology is increasing together with the diversity of applications of legal knowledge management (Casanovas et al. 2007), ranging from document retrieving, data and text mining, computer-assisted legal drafting, rationalization of legal fields (e. g. codification), modeling legal reasoning, multi-agent simulations, development of decision support systems for environmental or resource management, etc. The design of a particular ontology depending on the targeted application, we postulate—in quite elusive terms—that the complexity attached to any ontology is mirroring the complexity of the application field. At the same time the training in and practice of the modeling of complex systems develop a particular sensibility in the approach of scientific issues. For example the possibility to build universal tools for the analysis and management of such systems is often considered with suspicion. Indeed on the one hand the a priori setting of a time-independent frame representing a system is discarded for the accounting of its truly dynamical—and eventually idiosyncratic—nature; on the other hand the isolation of a sub-system from its wider context—even when justified on methodological arguments—is revisited with care and possibly criticized, relying on the idea that the whole is only seldom just the sum of the parts.

We will introduce two main ideas. First, concerning the legal field, jurists deplore the complexity of Law and claim for a better quality of knowledge management (see e.g. Surden et al. 2007) able to deal with legal systems as complex systems (Doat et al. 2007). In particular it is believed that the complexity is threatening the legal security (see e.g. in the French context, Conseil d'Etat 2006; de Claussade 2007). A legal corpus is also difficult to manage because it is a dynamical network (Zhang and Koppaka 2007). Consequently, any ontology-building process should include the complexity of the relationship between ontology and corpus.

Second, the web-based technologies and their applications are ever more requiring a complete access to the available information which is heterogeneous and

P. Mazzega (✉)
Université de Toulouse, UPS (OMP) CNRS IRD, Toulouse, France; LMTG, Toulouse, France
e-mail: mazzega@lmtg.obs-mip.fr

G. Sartor et al. (eds.), *Approaches to Legal Ontologies*, Law, Governance
and Technology Series 1, DOI 10.1007/978-94-007-0120-5_7,
© Springer Science+Business Media B.V. 2011

distributed. Legal ontology has been based on closed retrieval-based systems. But applications are now evolving toward the exploitation of operational multi-agent systems. Moreover, the need for linking source texts and legal contents becomes more pressing. For example, the French legal data bank LEGIFRANCE (2008), able to facilitate free access to Codes and Laws does not provide links to jurisprudence (judge's cases) or author's literature on the web.

From these introductory remarks we consider in Section 7.2 the production of legal ontology and comment on cases of ontology building (with the automatic treatment of natural languages or *via* differential principles) and uses. In Section 7.3 we precise the new needs emerging from the process of building ontology in connection with their use in the automated exploitation of large textual data bases structured in complex networks. A complementary approach is proposed in Section 7.4 that actually maps an ontology in a corpus of legal texts *via* a probability measure. More precisely we first associate to every concept in the ontology-tree or network a posterior probability of occurrence in the various parts of the legal corpus of interest. Then it is possible to estimate the mutual information given by one concept about another concept in this particular corpus, independently from the cognitive or logical links represented between them in the *prior* ontology. An information function has already been used in relation to ontology building but with no connection to the complex cognitive and structural properties inherent to a legal corpus (Lame and Desprès 2005).

In Section 7.5 we show how such endowing of an ontology with information functions provides any ontology with some plasticity and adaption capacity that responds to their use in complex cognitive environments. Indeed endowing ontology with information functions allows to estimate the pertinence of some general ontology with regard to any particular legal corpus, to evaluate the strength of the links between concepts of the ontology on the basis of their use in the corpus or by comparison in different corpuses, and possibly to update and/or recover new concepts as well as concept links unsuspected in the a priori ontology, and correlatively to tie an ontology for specific applications to a particular corpus of texts. In Section 7.6 we couple the view on a large legal corpus as a complex network with explicit or latent structures, with the mapping of ontological terms and the association of probability and information functions at different organizational levels. Finally in Section 7.7 this complex-system approach to legal ontology, information and networks is recast in the present-day evolution of the information technologies and impacts on the practice of Law, in particular the *enactive web* in the field of legal ontology.

7.2 Ontology Development: Dealing with Natural Language

Before building an ontology for knowledge management, it is necessary to specify the specific field that we want to represent and the goal of the representation, this choice commanding the selection of the pertinent concepts and of their mutual links.

Ontology building is performed in a collaborative workspace involving at least a computer scientist and an expert of the (legal) domain. The expert has the theoretical and practical knowledge of the field and the computer scientist brings methods and tools to represent it. They share data (ontology resources like textual corpora, transcription of interviews, formalized knowledge, other prior ontologies, etc.) but also their respective knowledge and skill by the mediation of a natural language. The natural language is a fundamental component in this process and a vector for knowledge sharing in ontology development. Indeed, the many subtleties of the Natural Language allow to define and to emphasize the complexity of a field.

Technically speaking, building ontology means indexing a corpus and/or defining some relationships between a set of terms of the corpus. In some cases the ontology building process relies on larger knowledge fields or disciplines like philosophy or legal theory. Anyway at this technical level too, the good practice for ontology building consists in delimiting a *field* and an applicative *aim*. In our research team, (Nadah et al. 2007), current ontology designs are based on a particular structure and a finite number of logical relation types, say:

- Generic structure: tree-like graphs + references;
- Small set of relations: list + references (Fig. 7.1).

Many legal ontologies use the resources of automatic treatment of natural languages or alternatively the guidelines of differential principles. The methods for

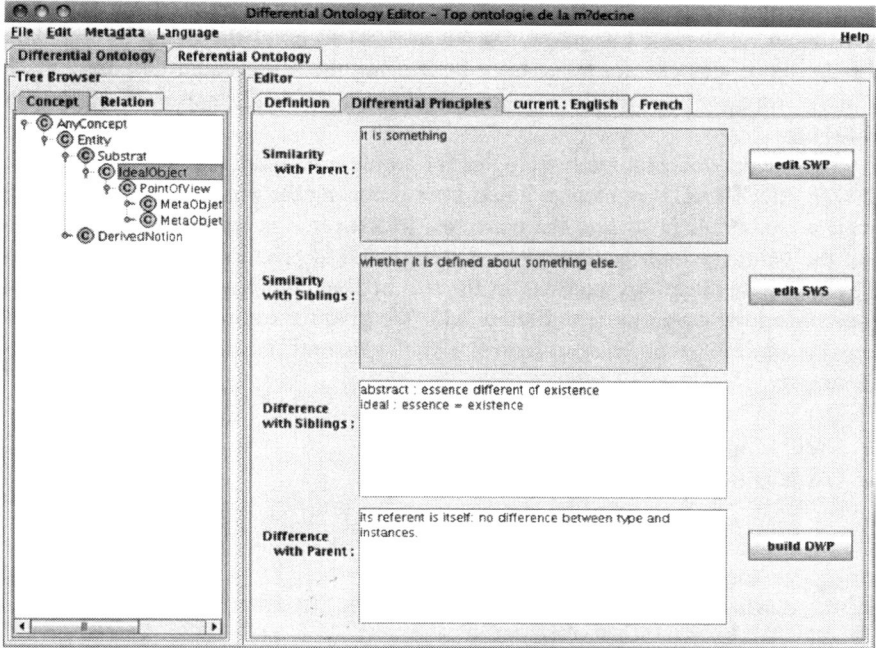

Fig. 7.1 Differential principles at work in the differential ontology editor

training ontologies from texts or Web pages may be classified according to the following criteria: (i) the type of sources (textual corpus, documentation from the Web, etc.); (ii) using or not using existing sources (taxonomy, thesaurus, other ontologies); (iii) technical ways used to extract the concepts, relations, axioms and instances. The linguistic methods are based on tools for corpus analysis (see e.g. SYNTEX, Bourigault et al. 2005). They take as input a corpus and provide a list of terms which are suitable for being concepts of the ontology. After this grammatical and terminological analysis, other tools (e.g. *Terminae*; Després and Szulman 2006) allow to start building ontologies from the results of the terms extractors. Some of these tools (like *Terminae*) provide a link between the termino-ontological resources and the corpus. Unfortunately, most common ontology editors do not provide a way to keep this link during the ontology development.

In Nadah et al. (2007), we describe an example of an ontology designed for licensing digital contents,[1] based on the concept of differential ontology. We intended to seek the relevant level for a generic ontology between existing formats and legal systems. It is obvious that, according to this goal, we had to start working from the existing standards, from use-cases and from law rules. Existing standards (RELs) are based on Right Data Dictionaries (RDD). Those are not based on ontologies, neither on legal rules. So, we had first to define the relevant notions to be kept in the ontology of licenses by giving a definition to each notion in natural language. Because of the resources we had to work with, it was not possible to start building the ontology with an automatic or semi-automatic system. We did not have at our disposal a corpus that would be used for Automatic Treatment of Natural Language. So we decided to build the ontology manually. Furthermore, this ontology has been built using the Differential Ontology Editor (DOE, Troncy et Isaac 2002)[2] according to the ARCHONTE[3] approach (Bachimont 2004).

There exist different methodologies for building ontologies (Guarino and Welty 2002). ARCHONTE is more a guide for structuring the concepts of the ontology than a methodology to find the concepts. Moreover it is based on semantics and so, the ontology built according to ARCHONTE is primarily a "linguistic ontology". The methodology consists in the use of four differential principles to help structuring the ontology (see Figure 7.1). We give for each concept of the ontology his similarities and dissimilarities with the "parent" concept and the "brothers" concepts:

- SWP: Similarity with parent;
- DWP: Difference with parent;

---

[1] The aim was to create a Right Expression Language (REL) based on an ontology, taking both the existing standards (ODRL Ianella 2002; XrML CONTENT GUARD 2002; Creative Commons) and applicable legislations into consideration.

[2] http://homepages.cwi.nl/~troncy/DOE/

[3] ARCHtecture for ONTOlogical Elaborating

- SWS: Similarity with siblings;
- DWS: Difference with siblings.

   This information is given in Natural Language, so the resulting ontology called "differential ontology" is at a linguistic level. Then, the ontology was formalized using Protégé.[4] Protégé does not provide specific fields for linguistic information. So we changed the DOE OWL-export to allow the user to keep the linguistic fields while using Protégé (see Figure 7.2). By this way, it is possible to continue building and formalizing the ontology with the Protégé Editor though referring to the linguistic notions. These notions are relevant for the development of the ontology because they give information about the semantics associated to the ontological concepts. The DAFOE[5] project aims at developing an open-source platform that will take into account the results of term extractors and provide to the user a link between the corpus and the ontology. It will be a further step to capture the information extracted from the natural language during the ontology building process.

   However most of the time, the rich expertise gained during the ontology-building process is partly lost when the ontology is represented in a machine. Ontology builders ever more need to keep a full track of the *cognitive* process that led to the selection of particular links in the ontological structure. In brief, natural language is

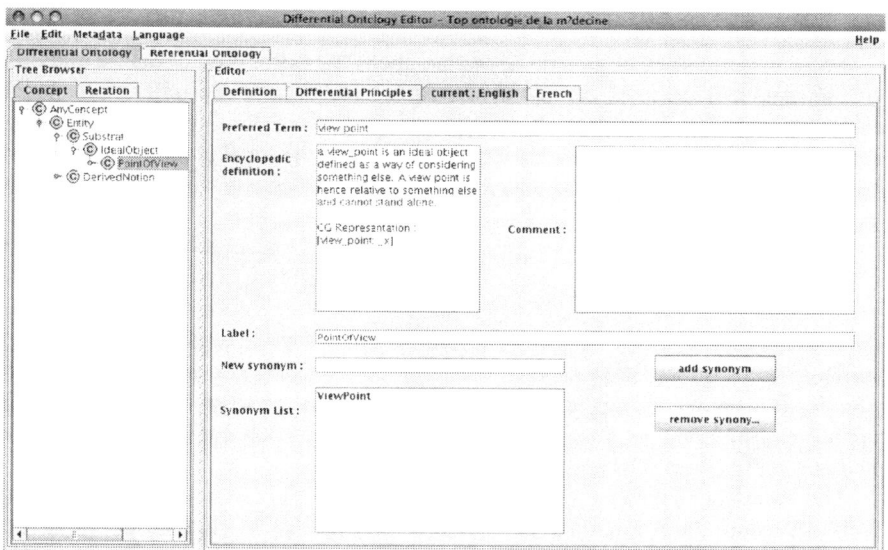

Fig. 7.2 Linguistic information at work in differential ontology editor

---

[4]http://protege.stanford.edu/
[5]http://www.dafoe4app.fr/

relevant to emphasize relationships between concepts of the ontology. However even in this new generation of linguistic ontology, some relevant relations or notions of the field may remain implicit within the text and not take into account the likely evolution of the corpus and then, the dynamics of the ontology. We will show how these characteristics—dynamics is at the core of the legal knowledge—can be integrated in an extended approach of ontology-building.

7.3 A Complex-Systems Approach Applied to Legal Corpus and Legal Ontology

Legal knowledge has a main feature: though well-structured (easily available for designing "logical" ontology) it is generally considered as being scattered in a complex way in large textual corpuses. We have already proposed to objectively define the complexity in legal domains by: (a) a large number of interacting components; (b) a partial knowledge of the (dynamical) links between components; (c) a limited predictability of the system evolution and/or outputs; (d) a dependency of the system properties when observed at different levels (scales) of its organization (Bourcier and Mazzega 2007a). Note that so doing we do not separate the two main sources limiting our representation of a complex system, say its organization or structure intricacy and its intrinsic instability and our limited knowledge of the components ties and evolution rules.

More importantly this general approach opens the possibility to define quantitative measures of the legal complexity inspired from numerous studies dedicated to the analysis and characterization of complex systems (continuous or discrete, natural or artificial; see e.g. Badii and Politi 1997). Can the legal complexity deplored by jurists be measured and visualized? What are the effects of this configuration on the ontology of a field?

Usually a rich diversity of cognitive patterns and conceptual neighborhoods or clusters is emerging during the process of ontology-building. Such forms exceed the possibilities offered by the traditional representation of operational ontology in basically tree-like structures. In spite of recent improvements in legal knowledge, such limits in the representation of legal ontology correlatively constrain the way complex legal corpuses are exploited or mined. Indeed we observe that legal corpuses are structuring complex networks of inter-relationships that are legally meaningful and rationally based (Ost and van de Kerchove 2002).

The mapping of the concepts of an ontology on a corpus and its endowing with (sets of) information functions present several advantages: (1) they conserve and exploit the existing ontology, whatever the limits set on its representation (like tree-like structures); (2) they allow to automatically retrieve links between any pair (or m-element groups) of concepts even not a priori expected form the ontology; (3) they can be represented as a weighted complex graph with the corpus as support (see below) in an informative layer. These functionalities preserve the full complexity of the legal field as illustrated in the following sections.

7.4 Mapping an Ontology on a Corpus
via a Probability Measure

We assume that various properties of an ontology can be measured by information functions in a corpus of texts. Statistical tools, namely those presented in the following section, can map dynamics and interaction between *terms*, *set of terms* and *contexts* either in the same corpus, or between corpuses. In the following example, we show how the tangled meanings of the "*reproduction*", "*representation*" and "*placing at the disposal*" (*mise à disposition*) that are difficult to represent in a legal ontology of the field of the Intellectual Property Rights, can be tracked in a legal corpus (here the French Code of the Intellectual Property, CIP for short) and their mutual information sharing measured.

The French legal codes, like the CIP which is the corpus C in our example, are usually divided in a legislative and a regulatory part. The legislative part of main interest for us is subdivided in books, titles, chapters, sections and articles. This hierarchical organization of a code corresponds to a tree-like structure. Now let x be a notion or a concept in an ontology (in our example x="*reproduction*" or "*representation*", etc.), and a_k the *kth* leaf (e. g. the *kth* article) in the corpus C. We associate with x the number n of its occurrences in the text a_k, say:

$$n[x(a_k)] = \text{number of occurrences of } x \text{ in } a_k \qquad (7.1)$$

$n[x(C)]$ being the total number of occurrences of the concept x in the corpus C (the union of all the a_k), we can associate to x the probability P of occurrence over any text a_k (or union of texts) of the corpus by estimating the ratio:

$$P[x(a_k)] = n[x(a_k)]/n[x(C)] \qquad (7.2)$$

Obviously if x is not appearing in a_k the associated probability is 0. If x is not appearing in some subset $c \subset C$ we similarly have $P[x(c)] = 0$.[6] Conversely if x is appearing in a_k only we have $P[x(a_k)] = 1$. Several comments are worth developing from here. In the way we build it, the probability P is neither a theoretical nor an a priori probability function but an *empirical* or *posterior* probability, estimated from the observed frequency of occurrence of x on a definite corpus C.[7] Nevertheless some theoretical properties of P are valid, and more elaborate statistics can be used as shown below (information functions). Indeed, by construction, we necessarily have $0 \leq P \leq 1$, and the probability of the union of two independent events is the sum of the probabilities associated to each event. But the most decisive step we have accomplished is elsewhere. By using a legal corpus C as a *support* for the definition

---

[6]Note that if C is a large legal corpus, the zero occurrence of a concept x somewhat disqualifies x as a component of the legal ontology (though x is likely to belong to a core ontology).

[7]We find the intuitive notion of a *measure* that was elaborated by E. Borel in the development of a mathematical theory of measure funding the probability theory (see Halmos 1974).

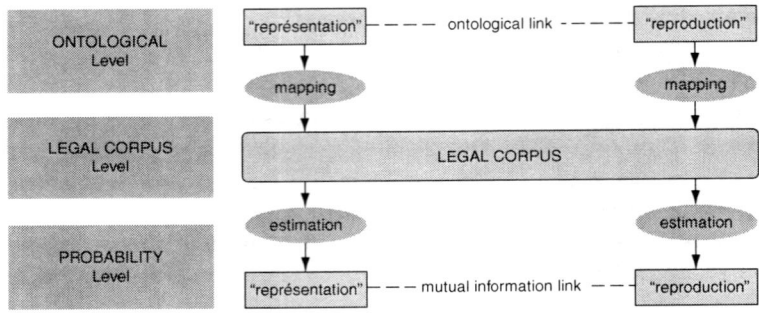

Fig. 7.3 Schema of the association of probability measures to concepts in an ontology. In this particular example *representation* and *reproduction* are concepts of an ontology developed from the intellectual property rights, related by some ontological link (for ex. they are instances of the same class "exploitation rights"). These concepts are looked for in the corpus (mapping) and the posterior probabilities of occurrence are estimated. Finally the average mutual information between these two terms in the whole corpus or local mutual information in part of it is estimated and used to weight the a priori ontological link

of a probability function associated to events of concept-occurrence, we directly link an ontology with a corpus through a measure (as schematized in Fig. 7.3).

The probability P can be associated to any other concept y. When y is an instance of x considered as a class of object, we intuitively understand that looking at the way the mapping over C of the probability $P[x(a_k)]$ changes into the mapping of $P[y(a_k)]$ provides a kind of visualization of the downscaling process in the ontology levels over C (respectively up scaling process when substituting the map associated to y for the map associated to x). Of course such transformation must be operationally defined. For example, we can translate the definition of the generic event "class x is appearing in a_k" by a univocal definition "class x appears in a_k if any of the instances of x appears in a_k", and we count as an individual event every such occurrence. More specific counting rules—and so forth probability definitions—can be proposed depending on the purpose of the combined corpus and ontology analysis.

Within the ontology the link between x and y (if any) can also be of a general type of relation (e.g. *subsumption* that induces tree-like graphs, or *meronymy* that induces directed acyclic graphs in the ontology) or of a specific type related to the analyzed context.[8] As explained now, the statistical significance of such link over C can also be measured with the appropriated tools.

From the joint event of x and y occurring in the text a_k, we define the joint probability $P[x(a_k), y(a_k)]$. Considering the sum of the contributions of the constitutive texts a_k we also have the joint probability over the corpus C, say

---

[8]For example we might be interested in analyzing the legal relationships between the various administrative courts or between different legal bodies in charge of the management of the Intellectual Property Rights in the French or European legal systems. These relationships are themselves relevant legal concepts.

$$P[x(C), y(C)] = \sum_k P[x(a_k), y(a_k)]$$

In the case x and y only seldom appear together in the texts, the joint probability will be near zero (exactly 0 if they never occur together in any text a_k). Now we can define the averaged mutual information (hereafter *AMI* for short) function between x and y over the corpus C by:

$$I_{AMI}[x, y]_C = \sum_k P[x(a_k), y(a_k)] \ln \left\{ \frac{P[x(a_k), y(a_k)]}{P[x(a_k)]P[y(a_k)]} \right\} \qquad (7.3)$$

Note that removing the sum provides the estimate of the information content over the single text a_k (with a lower level of statistical significance). If the occurrence of x and y are independent from each other, then the average mutual information drops to zero (the argument of the logarithm *ln* function is 1). An interesting property of I_{AMI} is that it can reach quite high values even when the probabilities of occurrence of x and of y are low: if the joint probability is much larger than $P[x]$ and $P[y]$, then the mutual information is high. Indeed in such case the rare events of occurrence of x or of y tend to happen simultaneously, a clue for a high local level of mutual information. I_{AMI} is an *average* information measure because it sums the information content over a set of texts (sum over the articles a_k).

It is a *mutual* information because it is symmetric in x and y (formally, $I_{AMI}[x, y]_C = I_{AMI}[y, x]_C$). In other words, x says on average as much about y as y says, on average about x.[9] The *AMI* function is a measure of the information that x (*resp.* y) contains about the concept y (*resp.* x) over the corpus C. It is also an abstract measure of the reduction of uncertainty that the knowledge of concept x brings to the knowledge of concept y (or the reverse). The I_{AMI} function can be mapped or visualized over the corpus C by representing its value on each constitutive text a_k. Moreover the definition of I_{AMI} is compatible with any geometry of the probability support: C can be a tree-like graph like in Fig. 7.4 a network of texts, a non organized set of texts, etc.

Before shifting to the interpretation and meaning of this figure, it should be noted that the information function (eq. 7.3) can be easily generalized at least in two main directions. First, in the same way we have estimated the joint probability of 2-component events "x and y", it is possible to evaluate the joint probability of a m-component event. For $m=3$, we count the number of occurrence of the three terms x, y and z in each article a_k and then normalize this number by its total number of occurrence in the corpus C. This gives us the joint probability $P[x(a_k), y(a_k), z(a_k)]$. The definition of the 3-component average mutual information function is then easily derived from such m-variables joint probability (see eq. 7.3). Second, conditional information functions can be also estimated, starting from conditional probability functions and proceeding similarly. The conditional event $x(a_k)/y(a_k)$ is counted

---

[9] $I_{AMI}[x, x]_C$ the self-information function is not trivially 1 and can be mapped as well on a corpus.

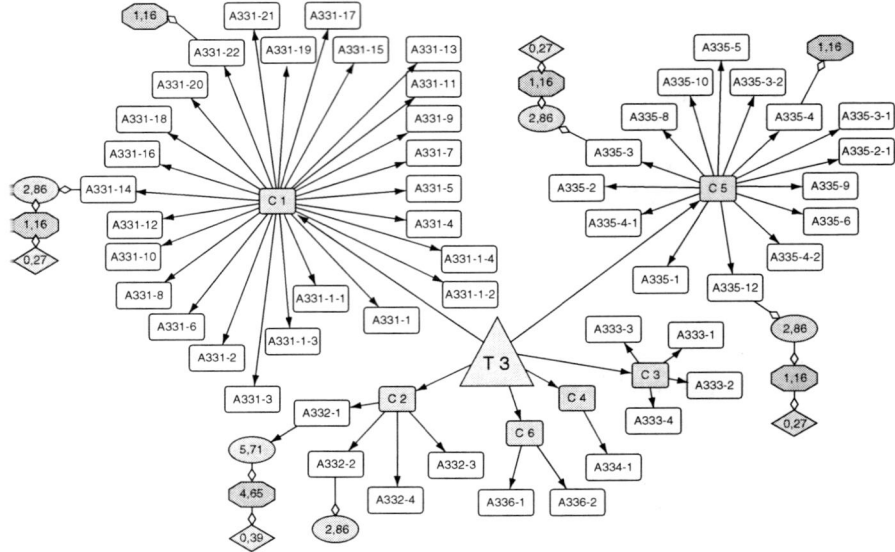

Fig. 7.4 Part of the structure of the code of the intellectual property is represented: the 3rd title of the 3rd book of the legislative part of the CIP is the root of the tree structure. This title (triangle T3) is subdivided in 6 chapters (*round rectangles* C1–C6). Each chapter is composed of several articles (*round rectangles* A "*number*"). The posterior probability of occurrence of the term "representation" (respectively "reproduction") is given in the ellipse (respectively *octagon*). The local mutual information between these two terms in this corpus is given in the *diamond-shaped* vertices. (Note that no symbol is drawn for zero probabilities or information)

when $y(a_k)$ occurs if $x(a_k)$ has occurred. Conditional probabilities can be estimated from the counting and normalization of the occurrence of conditional events.

Then in a way similar to eq. (7.3), conditional average mutual information functions can be estimated. Here also, m-component conditional probabilities and information function can be formed and used too for a finer mapping of the groups of ontological concepts in the corpus.

7.5 Ontology, Information and Legal Corpus

Some very interesting applications of the AMI function can be foreseen. Indeed the functional link so created can be used in two ways: (1) from the ontology to its mapping support (the corpus); (2) from the corpus to the ontology.

First it is observed that the meaning of some concept tends to evolve under the pressure of historical or social transformations. For example among many others, the concept of "family" is subject to an internal transformation due to the nowadays possibility to have surrogate mothers; our concept of the environment is surely much changed with regard to the dominant acceptation in the 60's or even 80's; intellectual property rights are facing the completely new opportunities of reproduction, representations and placing at the disposal of many individuals thanks to the development of new information technologies, etc. The probability mapping over a large legal corpus efficiently identifies those parts of the Law system the most prone to direct impacts, consecutive to the semantic changes. Further considering the graph structures associated to text hierarchy (tree-like) and cross-quotations (network), the areas where these impacts are likely to propagate into the corpuses are also identified. The mutual information function provides clues about the mutually informative concepts related—in our simple example—to the *reproduction* or to the *representation* that will be necessarily revisited. This effect of information propagation is most unpredicted when looking at the sole ontology, but efficiently *anticipated* when considering the mutual information of pairs (or *m-plets*) of concepts on a given large legal corpus.[10]

Second, let us consider the link from the corpus to the ontology. It is likely that a legal ontology—even a complex one—lacks some important relations between concepts (implicit relations). From a legal cognitive point of view two concepts can be issued from very different parts of Law, or have emerged from more or less independent historical process but still be mutually informative, or "close", over a given corpus. Such mutual information content can be automatically detected over a corpus, matching in turn all pairs of terms in the ontology, irrespective of the eventual links (whatever they represent) or absence of links being a priori set between them (see Fig. 7.3 where the ontological link and the informative link are intentionally distinguished).

Let us work a short illustration. In the French Code of the intellectual Property the concepts of *reproduction* and *representation* are distinguished. Obviously there is no direct or trivial link between the two notions (neither can we identify a short path of relations leading from one concept to the other), except at the level of root classes. In Fig. 7.4, we limit the representation of the analyzed corpus to the 3d Title (see the central node named T3) of the 3d Book of the CIP[11] (version of April 2009). We count 35 (resp. 86) valid occurrences of the term "*representation*" (resp. "*reproduction*") in the whole CIP. Consequently the probability associated to a single occurrence in an article is 1/35=0.0286 or in percentage 2.86% (resp. 1/86 or 1.16%). The average mutual information over the CIP is

$$I_{AMI} \left[\text{representation, reproduction}\right]_{CIP} = 3,51 \qquad (7.4)$$

This is the measure of a significant mutual information content (remember that the mutual information between independent terms drops to zero) between these two terms. But proceeding to the estimate of the AMI between the terms "*reproduction*" and "*placing at the disposal of*" we find an even higher level of mutual

---

[10]Considering these examples, the jurisprudence would be a very interesting corpus to explore with such information mapping tools, with also the possibility to consider particular periods of special social interest or technological developments.

[11]In this work we only consider the Legislative Part of the CIP.

information[12] (say 5.80). This higher AMI level or loosely speaking, higher proximity of these two last terms is likely to result from the corpus, say a code regulating the Intellectual Property Rights. In this context the reproduction of a work of art for example is, from a legal point of view, directly related to its placing at the disposal of the public for example. Conversely at the ontological level, the concepts of *representation* and *reproductions* will be much probably felt as in a narrower neighbourhood.

The posterior probability of occurrence of the "*representation*" and "*reproduction*" terms in the articles of the 3d Title 3d Book of the CIP are mapped in Fig. 7.4 together with the AMI level found at the scales of the articles. The article L332-1 of the CIP (noted *A332-1* in Fig. 7.4) is simultaneously exhibiting the higher probabilities for the separate terms and the higher local AMI level. This article is mainly presenting legal dispositions to be taken in the case of infringement. It is obvious that it is this context of occurrence that enhances the mutual information between these two terms, a configuration that could be hardly anticipated from any ontology-building process.

Many other tools can be designed and implemented in order to link an ontology and its mapping. Among others: (a) looking for the concept that maximizes the mutual information with a chosen concept x; (b) building higher level information functions like conditional mutual information (mutual information between x and y conditioned by the occurrence of z), chain rules for information (the mutual information between the chain of concepts $x_1 x_2 \ldots x_q$ and the concept y), etc., these functions basically evaluating the information brought by one concept about groups of concepts (in a conditional or non conditional manner).

Note that the probability and *AMI* functions can be defined on any support geometry, on trees as in Fig. 7.4, but also on networks or mixed graphs. The difficulty—and interest—is well illustrated on the estimation of joint probabilities. There are at least two ways for their estimation. We can consider as an event the presence of both the x and y concepts in the same article, a computational strategy corresponding to a statistically-based estimate of the I_{AMI} function. Or we only consider as a countable event their simultaneous occurrence within a semantic link (as in the present example). The second option is computationally much more difficult to implement but allows to proceed to semantically-based estimates of the mutual information between ontological concepts in a corpus.

7.6 Scaling Issues in the Ontology Mapping

The smaller scale objects that are represented in Fig. 7.4 are law articles. Because the French legal codes are internally organized as a hierarchy of levels (from the bottom

---

[12]It is interesting to note that this higher mutual information level is still resulting from a smaller number of occurrences of the joint event [*reproduction, placing at the disposal of*] with regard to the joint event [*representation , reproduction*]. The reason is that the systematic joint occurrence of rare terms is highly mutually informative.

Fig. 7.5 Same as Fig. 7.4 but
the smaller scale objects in
the corpus representation
being chapters (articles in
Fig. 7.4). The probability
estimates and average mutual
information are aggregated at
the level of chapters

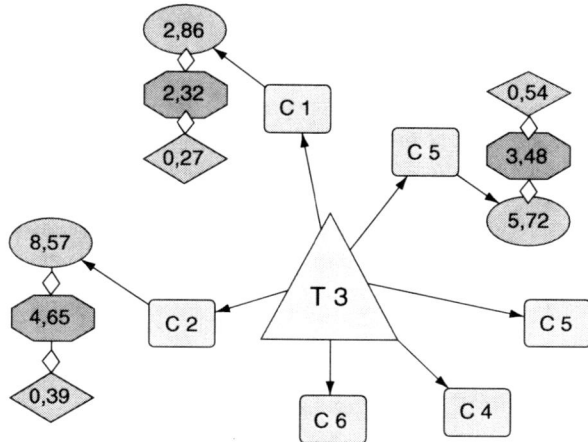

up: articles, chapters, titles, books and parts), the corpus is a tree-like structure,
the articles being the leaves. Basically we also associate the *posterior* probability
of occurrence of a term to the supporting articles, as well as we do for the AMI
between any pair of terms. The too large number of articles in the CIP[13] dissuaded
us from representing this corpus up to the resolution of the articles. An alternative
representation would be to aggregate the probability (or information) at the scale of
chapters and draw the resulting map, as illustrated in Fig. 7.5.

Now imagine that we take a look at a larger scale. The first larger scale entity
that we shall see will be the whole CIP itself: in this picture (not drawn), all the
chapters of the CIP will appear with the associated probabilities of the ontological
terms of interest. Looking further at a larger scale we shall see the *"nearest"* codes
as can be seen from a map of the code locations in some abstract space. Indeed in a
recent study we have shown that considering the quotations between codes, the set of
the French codes presents an underlying structure (Mazzega et al. 2009): ten codes
are constituting the kernel of the legal system (a code community that, following
the expression in use in the analysis of social networks, we call the rich club) as
being strongly tied together and the most quoted and quoting codes. Then two stable
communities of respectively 12 and 11 codes also appear, the first one most relevant
for the social and economical issues, the second one rather centred on the territories
and resources (Boulet et al. 2009). However the CIP is preferentially linked to the
first community but without being in the stable pool of codes: depending on the
formal criterion used to partition the graph into community, the CIP does or does
not belong to this community of "socio-economical" codes.

---

[13]This is a general property of most codes. For example there are 1,266 articles in the 2007 version
of the legislative part of the Environmental Code (Bourcier and Mazzega 2007b).

Still moving to a larger scale view, we shall find the legal system of all the French codes that form a dense network of corpuses. Once again, considering terms of interest for a given enquiry, the probability of occurrence and the mutual information can be estimated and mapped on the network of corpuses.

At this level the number of chapters present in all the codes will be high and it might be decided to sacrifice some resolution in order to improve the readability of the ontological mapping, considering only Books as the identity of smaller resolution. Even larger view would take into the picture the legal systems of the European Union Member Sates, and then the full international legal system that without doubt constitutes a large complex network.

7.7 Discussion and Perspectives

We will first discuss the novelty of these tools compared to the traditional approach of legal ontology built from natural language corpus. Then we shall pursue our discussion on the relevance of complex systems approach to build legal ontology.

7.7.1 Discussion about Information Functions in Ontology Building

Using measure to embed an ontology to a corpus is not opposed but complementary to the "traditional" use of ontology. The choice of the concepts for which we might wish to associate a probability of occurrence or estimate the mutual information may be driven by the ontology. In the previous sample, the concepts "*representation*" and "*reproduction*" were selected because any expert of the domain knows that those concepts are "linked". Conversely, measuring the occurrence probability and Average Mutual Information of concepts allows finding new relations between the concepts of the ontology, or making implicit relations explicit. As explained in Section 7.2, traditionally ontology building is based on human analysis at some stage of its development. We do not aim at automating the building of legal ontology. However given the fact that some domains are cognitively and/or structurally complex, we need other tools to capture and preserve this complexity as a characteristic of the field. A probabilistic reading of such field can enrich the linguistic one.

In the field of legal ontology building, the logical level can be enriched by the statistical level to compare and improve ontology or to do ontology fusion. In our example in the domain of Intellectual Property Rights the terms reproduction and representation are stable: however if we consider beyond the context the dynamics, in the corpus in IPR the content and the associated links of *reproduction* are continuously changing (between statute law, case law, legal literature, any legal authoritative interpretation). Moreover the term *reproduction* can also link new various legal sets of terms or *contexts* (following the evolution of multimedia supports).

7.7.2 The Complex Systems Approach and the Human Expertise

The objective of the complex system approach is however radically different from the traditional approach due to several aspects: we can integrate the dynamics of legal concepts, we use the huge capacities of corpus on the web and we avoid the human expertise as an a priori construction.

A legal ontology can be thus represented as *continuous* in dynamic networks such as the semantic web. Then we should attempt to answer the two following questions: In what way and to what extent the meanings of the same expression are similar and different, according to the *context* given by the whole sentence? How can this meaning move through *time*? Human experts have the remarkable skill to interpret the meaning of an expression depending on its context through long range interactions and on the date of the text. The increasing quantity of texts makes this encyclopaedic knowledge less and less tractable for human experts with bounded capacities of reading or memorizing

In the next steps, a generic automatic method for transforming any corpus into an *enactive web*, continuously *emerging* with the activity of the experts or users communities can be applied. Enactive web means to represent or perform in or as if in a play; to act out. For example, any new configuration in a sub-field of law will be able to produce a new map. It makes possible to extract "bottom-up" dictionaries and *continuous contextual ontology* produced by the platform enable to measure the rates of evolution and co-evolution of law, jurisprudence, legal doctrine and legal dictionaries into and between different European countries. It could help the European legislator to compare (almost *on line*) the evolution of legal European ontologies.

Acknowledgments R. Boulet benefits from a post doctoral grant of the Institut National des Sciences de l'Univers (CNRS, Paris). This study is partly funded by the Réseau de Thématique de Recherche Avancées « Sciences et Techniques de l'Aéronautique et de l'Espace » (RTRA STAE) in Toulouse, France, under the MAELIA project (http://www.iaai-maelia.eu/). The yEd Graph editor has been used for producing the Figs. 7.3 and 7.4.

References

Bachimont, B. (2004). *Art et sciences du numérique: ingénierie des connaissances et critique de la raison computationnelle.* Mémoire d'habilitation à diriger des recherches, Université de Technologie de Compiègne.

Badii, R., A. Politi (1997). *Complexity—Hierarchical Structures and Scaling In Physics.* Cambridge Nonlinear Sciences Series 6. Cambridge: Cambridge University Press.

Boulet, R., P. Mazzega, D. Bourcier (2009). Analyse d'un graphe juridique dense—Le monde concentré des codes législatifs. In M. Latapy (ed.) *Technique et Science Informatiques*, n spécial Graphes de Terrain. *sous presse.*

Bourcier, D., P. Mazzega (2007a). Toward Measures of Legal Complexity. In *Proceedings of 11th International Conference on Artificial Intelligence and Law.* Stanford Law School, ACM Press, New York, NY, 211–215.

Bourcier, D., P. Mazzega (2007b). Codification Law Article and Graphs. In A.R. Lodder, L. Mommers (Eds.) *Legal Knowledge and Information Systems, JURIX 200.* IOS Press, Amsterdam, 29–38.

Bourigault, D., C. Fabre, C. Frérot, M.-P. Jacques, S. Ozdowska (2005). Syntex, analyseur syntaxique de corpus, *Actes des 12èmes journées sur le Traitement Automatique des Langues Naturelles*, juin 2005, Dourdan (France), tome 2, 17–20.

Casanovas, P., P. Noriega, D. Bourcier, F. Galindo (Eds.) (2007). *Trends in Legal Knowledge—The Semantic Web and the Regulation Of Electronic Social Systems*. European Press Academic Publication, Florence, Italy.

de Clausade, J. (2007). Sécurité et complexité du droit: le développement des lois techniciennes », *Les Petites Affiches*, 5 juillet 2007, n° 134, 4.

Conseil d'Etat (2006). Rapport Public 2006—Sécurité juridique et complexité du droit, La Documentation française, Etudes et Documents 57: 233.

CONTENT GUARD (2002). Xrml 2.0. Technical Overview.

Després, D., S. Szulman (2006). Terminae Method and Integration Process for Legal Ontology Building. In *Proceedings of the 19th International Conference IAE/AIE*, Special Session on *Ontology and Text*, Nantes, France.

Doat, M., J. Le Goff, Ph. Pédrot, *dirs.* (2007). *Droit et Complexité—Pour une nouvelle intelligence du droit vivant*, Presse Univ. Rennes, France.

Guarino, N., C. Welty (2002). Evaluating Ontological Decisions with OntoClean Commun, ACM 45, 2 (Feb. 2002), 61–65. DOI= http://doi.acm.org/10.1145/503124.503150

Halmos, P.R. (1974). *Measure Theory*. Springer Verlag, New York, NY.

Ianella, R. (2002). Open Digital Rights Language (Odrl) Version 1.1.

Lame, G., S. Desprès, (2005). Updating Ontologies in the Legal Domain. ICAIL'05, June 6–11, 2005. ACM Press, Bologna, Italy, 155–162.

LEGIFRANCE (2008). Service Public de la Diffusion du Droit, http://www.legifrance.gouv.fr/.

Mazzega, P., D. Bourcier, R. Boulet (2009). The Network of French Legal Codes, *Proceedings of the International Conference Artificial Intelligence and Law ICAIL 2009*, Barcelona, Spain, ACM Press, 236–237.

Nadah N., M.D. de Rosnay, B. Bachimont (2007). Licensing Digital Content with a Generic Ontology: Escaping From the Jungle of Rights Expression Languages. *Procedings of the 11th International Conference on Artificial Intelligence and Law*, Stanford Law School, ACM Press, New York, NY, 65–69. DOI= http://doi.acm.org/10.1145/1276318.1276330

Ost, F., M. van de Kerchove (2002) *De la pyramide au réseau ? Pour une théorie dialectique du droit*. Publ. Faculté Univ. Saint-Louis, Bruxelles.

Surden, H., M. Genesereth, B. Logue (2007). Representational Complexity in Law. ICAIL'07, June 4–8, ACM Press, Stanford, CA, 193–194.

Troncy R. et A. Isaac (2002). DOE: une mise en oeuvre d'une méthode de structuration différentielle pour les ontologies, *Procedings of the 13th Journées Francophones d'Ingénierie des Connaissances (IC'02)*, 28–30 Mai 2002, Rouen, France, 63–74.

Zhang, P., L. Koppaka (2007). Semantics-Based Legal Citation Network. ICAIL'07, June 4–8, ACM Press, Stanford, CA, 123–130.

Chapter 8
The Multi-Layered Legal Information Perspective

Guido Boella and PierCarlo Rossi

8.1 Introduction

This paper tries to lay the basis for a procedural model that could contribute to improve the interoperability of legal ontologies. At the same time it focuses on critical points of current use of legal ontologies due to the fact that often the practice of law is disregarded.

Generally speaking, ontologies respond to diverse functions. One is related to the structuring of information; another is for reasoning and problem solving. There are ontologies aiming at information retrieval; while others are aimed at semantic integration. Finally, ontologies are useful for knowledge discovery or for the domain understanding (Valente 2005). As to the legal domain, all of these ontologies may play a role, according to the tasks for which they are applied. Legal ontologies are very varied, according to their building methods (such as bottom up v. top down approach), to their levels of formalisation (lightweight v. heavyweight ontologies), to their granularity (by the means of data amount and representation subjects).

This state of affairs is normally justified by the recourse to the diverse functions of ontologies. However, the ascertainment on what the law is inevitably impinges on several ways to build legal ontologies. We do not refer here to the philosophical debate on the nature of law. Normativity is a relevant phenomenon of law and normativity is communicated by linguistic means. Norms, too, exist in a non-linguistic sense: rights are intersubjective facts which emerge from behaviors and they can be rendered explicit by linguistic means. The real question is the operational understanding about the content of normativity. Such content is a social product because our experiences of intersubjectivity are not simply a set of sense-data, but rather the result of our application of socially-influenced conceptual frameworks to the interpretation of that sense-data. Different conceptual frameworks may change our notion of which legal rules should be applied in a single instance and how they could

G. Boella (✉)
Dipartimento di Informatica, Università di Torino, Torino, Italy
e-mail: guido@di.unito.it

G. Sartor et al. (eds.), *Approaches to Legal Ontologies*, Law, Governance and Technology Series 1, DOI 10.1007/978-94-007-0120-5_8,
© Springer Science+Business Media B.V. 2011

be detected. These frameworks are normally underestimated in ontology engineering, subsuming them into the general cognitive or philosophical tenets at the basis of top level ontologies, or reducing them to the specific content at the basis of task level ontologies.

It is precisely because law is inherently multilevel, that we need to maintain several levels in the ontological structure in order to explain the different aspects of law. Although, of course, we can only produce incomplete subsets of the multilevel account of law.

8.2 The Interoperability Issue

Semantic interoperability is one of the main issues about knowledge engineering in order to avoid the construction of numerous contents not properly communicating with each other. Knowledge represented in a specific format should be interoperable with other knowledge bases.

The context of web applications such as e-commerce transactions requires an effective communication among different knowledge bases.

Beyond the syntactic dimension constituted by the varied representation languages, such as RDF, OIL, OWL, XML, XOL, a shared vocabulary and a similar knowledge model are needed.

To achieve the "legal interoperability" one could argue that ontologies should represent all the concepts and instances of any legal domain and, then, create a knowledge model to ensure the correspondences. Large knowledge bases are difficult and expensive to build. Consequently, ontology developers are normally devoted to find a knowledge model that could be applied independently by single domain requirements. This choice implies that effective applications needed by final users are often based on content dependent vocabularies and taxonomies without sufficient matching with knowledge models.

Numerous knowledge models have been proposed according to two approaches. The first is devoted to the identification of a core ontology of law that can clarify the fundamentals of law. Among the most well-known core ontologies, FOLaw (Functionnal Ontology of Law) (Valente 1995), LRI-Core (Breuker and Winckels 2003), CLO (Core Legal Ontology) (Gangemi et al. 2003) may be mentioned.

The second one is devoted to the adaptation of foundational ontologies to the particularities of the legal domain. Top-level ontologies have recently been the subject of much research, as they facilitate the representation of commonsense necessary for human-like understanding and reasoning. This work has been concentrated to the enrichment of commonsense notions with legal biases, extensions and occurrences, such as LLD (McCarty 1989), or NM-L (Shaheed et al. 2005).

All these solutions aim at improving an unitary conceptualization of law, according to the main tenets of ontology developers. A well known definition of "ontology" is "formal and explicit specifications of a shared conceptualization" (Gruber 1995).

However, shared conceptualizations of law are difficult to be detected. One reason is that conceptualizations cannot be inferred only from legal texts. Several legal contents are present in the diverse jurisdictions and different legal systems support the production, interpretation and implementation of such contents. The corpus of laws in effect in each jurisdiction does not give us any clear indication of the legal rules operating in that legal order. Despite the fact that legal norms are ultimately based on formal sources, a meaningful understanding of a legal order requires also the comprehension of other rules influencing the legal process. They are related to the institutional context (such as the functioning of the judiciary, the influence on the legislative process of bureaucratic elites and so forth) and to the socio-cultural context (such as the legal education system, the role of the ideology on legal practice, and so forth).

A discussed topic in the knowledge engineering literature is that ontology axioms only indirectly account for a conceptualization. A large part of the intended meaning of the ontological concepts will remain implicit between ontology developers (Guarino 1998). In the same way, to encode the rules pertaining of the legal domain, the conceptualization of all legal rules should be explicit. Unfortunately, part of these rules are not rendered explicit, because institutional and socio-cultural contexts are always the preconditions of the legal process and jurists are not completely aware of them, even if these work as conceptual frameworks. Comparative law as well as, more recently, ethnographic research (Benjamins et al. 2004) are enriching legal knowledge engineering with instruments for legal rules explicitation. However, the results from comparative law and legal anthropology demonstrate that within and without any legal system there are self-differentiating legal patterns and historical traditions. The unitary compulsion of national authoritative law drove to cover over difference, but today many scholars insist upon the pluralism of any legal experience.

Another reason is constituted by the nature of legal language that can be misleading whether ontology developers stress its representational feature. Legal language has many usages indeed. It can be used to represent something (such as legal doctrine), to manipulate someone (such as the rhetorical communication in judicial claims), to do things in the social world (such as "commands" in legislative or judicial texts). There are not tight boundaries between these usages: persuasive opinions of legal scholars may influence the legal provisions in the enactment of a statute, as well as the performative nature of judicial opinions in common law systems may be shifted by the recourse of distinguishing in further decisions. Legal scholars and practitioners surf the translation from a language of factuality to that of normativity, from cases to doctrine and to policy. In contemporary legal debate, the question of how law should be conceptualized for theoretical versus pragmatic purposes remains, by and large, unresolved. This consideration implies that law is always fragmented in several conceptual frameworks with different features and objectives. And these conceptual frameworks may change according to time and events in the practice of law.

Therefore, any effort to improve the legal interoperability may begin by integrating the current solutions by a different perspective.

8.3 The Multilayered Legal Information Perspective: A Tentative Procedural Model

Legal knowledge can only be established through a knowledge-producing process. This process is determined by the intertwined effects of diverse pre-existing conceptual frameworks, institutional practices, prior normative commands, decisions of the legal actors, influences from other social and economic forces that are interested and determined by the legal process itself. Moreover, all elements may change in relation to different legal systems or different domains (like labour protection or financial services regulation) where the legal process is involved.

In consideration of this complex picture, ontology developers may prefer to analyse those elements that are quantitatively or qualitatively prevalent in the legal process. However, any explanatory priority for some elements may hinder the interoperability if other elements, underestimated in the knowledge model, are prevalent in different legal systems or domains.

Nevertheless, legal knowledge cannot be considered as a monolithic entity. A modularization of legal knowledge is more useful to manage large concepts with efficient reasoning. The introduction of modules with local semantics may help to analyze diverse legal systems or domains, providing a basis for the development of methods for localizing inference.

In the model we propose, lightweight ontologies are normally built, reviewed, and maintained by several types of knowledge experts, according to the expertise of different legal systems or domain experts. This constitutes the first layer (L1) that represents information about legal content as interpreted at a certain time by a certain community of experts. In our current project Legal Taxonomy Syllabus (Rossi and Vogel 2004; Ajani et al. 2007, 2010) we have lightweight ontologies of European different legal vocabulary and concepts (EU and five national jurisdictions) related to specific domains, such as consumer law. L1 allows multiple representations of the same domains, according to several extensional ontologies obtained by the legal literature.

The second layer (L2) is constituted by service ontologies, enabling the definition of roles and behaviours for agents in charge of executing tasks related to the specific domains considered by L1.

The third layer (L3) is devoted to link L1–L2, allowing to convert service concepts into/from domain concept ones, through a refinement in terms of ontological relations. The four layer (L4) is constituted by the state of art in core concepts ontology, but it is constantly enriched by the results of intensional semantics derived from the outcomes of the procedural model (L1–L3) applied to numerous legal systems and domains. The L4 is based on a set of orthogonal concepts that provide a basis for defining the legal process in a more complex way, independently from single applications.

8.4 A Scenario

In this section, we illustrate the model by analysing a scenario from regulatory compliance. We are inspired for this example by the ongoing work in the project

ICT4LAW.[1] The domain of the example is the Markets in Financial Instruments Directive (MiFID) 2004/39/EC, a European Union law that provides harmonised regulation for investment services across the Member States of the European Economic Area.

Large enterprises like banks and financial intermediaries are being subject to principles and regulations issued by national and supranational institutions (e.g. European Union). These oblige them to manage the risks of not being compliant to regulations, whose number increase continuously and which are of an ever-growing complexity. Enterprises are requested to set up specific functions to monitoring compliance, like, for example, the compliance management office. The non-compliance risk is the operative risk of being subject to penal or administrative sanctions, to relevant monetary losses, or to reputation damages for violating laws or self regulations. Risk is the possibility of being damaged due to circumstances which can be foreseen or not and are related to the probability of a damage event and risks are proportional to the seriousness of the damage.

Once a year the appointed offices have the task of identifying and evaluating the major risks of conformity and to plan the proper management actions.

Regulatory compliance requires the following steps. The compliance manager has:

1. To identify the legal provisions in order to evaluate the relevant regulation, in particular each time there is a new regulation, and to evaluate its impact. To evaluate the relevance for the business domains. To establish their normative interpretation and identify the prescriptions.
2. To identify the different domains of business: in particular, to identify roles which are responsible for risks and processes and activities of different domains.
3. To map prescriptions onto processes in order to detect the risks in the business processes; to define and apply methodologies to evaluate the risks.
4. To monitor the performance of rules and procedures to deal with risks.
5. To report to top offices according to the compliance program and to all offices involved in the compliance management.

The first three steps obviously seem to require the use of ontologies for facilitating the mapping between regulations and processes: building an ontology for the regulations, an ontology for the internal organization processes and business rules of the enterprise that have to show to be compliant, and to make the two ontologies interoperable.

However, this intuitive strategy is not viable in this naive formulation.

First of all, as many other regulations, MIFID is a multilevel regulation: the norms in the European Directives are then implemented by the national legislator (e.g., in Italy, TUF 98/58, Reg. Consob 16190 Intermediari, Reg. Consob 16191 Mercati).

---

[1] The ICT4LAW project, "ICT Converging on Law: Next Generation Services for Citizens, Enterprises, Public Administration and Policymakers", is a Converging Technologies 2007 project funded by Regione Piemonte.

From the ontological point of view this leads to the necessity of a double level ontology to represent both the concepts from the European point of view and the concepts from the national point of view. The European and national concepts may or may not be associated with the same terms. For example, a term in the Italian version of the directive may be translated in the implementation with a different Italian term, still maintaining the same meaning at the two levels, maybe because the same concept was already present in the system named with a different term. Vice-versa, a term from the directive which is directly imported in the national implementation without any change can assume a different meaning. Finally, the term can be translated in the national implementation with a different term with a different meaning. As a small example consider Art. 28 of Italian language version of Directive 2006/73/EC implementing Directive 2004/39/EC in comparison with Art. 35 of Reg. Consob 16190 where "supporto durevole" is implemented as "supporto duraturo".

These shifts in terminology could be motivated by different situations: an Italian term in the directive could have already a different meaning in the national system, so another one has been used in the implementation to identify the concept introduced at the European level. Otherwise, the term is introduced in the national system with the same meaning as in the European directive, then due to a different legal interpretation, the concept in practice may assume a diverse meaning.

This implementation process gives place to further problems in case of enterprises working at the transnational level, since not only the MIFID can be implemented in different ways in different countries, but also the socio-cultural contexts in which legal rules of MIFID are transferred will have an influence on the ontology of the law implementing the directive. Thus, such enterprises will get a plurality of ontologies which possibly diverge.

From the point of view of the representation by means of ontologies of such legal knowledge, the above discussion raises several issues. First of all, legal ontologies must be multilevel, to take into account the differences between the European level and the national implementations.[2] Second, the ontologies must be multisystem, to take into account the ontological differences between the different national systems. Third, approaches that aim at annotating legal texts with formalizations of rules in languages like LKIF-rule, RuleML, RIF, SWRL, etc. concerning definitions or prescriptions must beware to consider such rules as the ones which compose the legal system, since the legal culture interpreting them must be considered too. Otherwise they will fall in the still recurring positivistic illusion.

Some approaches to legal ontologies are compliant to these requirements, like the Legal Taxonomy Syllabus, where the European vs national levels and the multisystemic issues are considered. This is realized by means of separated ontologies, a common one for the European level, whose concepts have linguistic realizations

---

[2] We disregard the possibility of conceptual ambiguity among the different translations of a Directive in the different languages. Alas, such assumption is not always true, and there can be conceptual differences already in the different linguistic versions of the same directive.

in the different languages of the EU, and distinct ones for the national systems, whose concepts have linguistic realizations in the respective national languages. The European and national levels are related via an implementation link between concepts to indicate how the national system has implemented a concept present in a directive and with which terminology. The translation between the terms of the different languages in the meaning they have at the European level is realized via the common ontology, while the translation at the national level is possible only if explicit links are added between the corresponding concepts in the separated ontologies at the national level.

Moreover, in the Syllabus rather than attaching the definition of concepts as rules inside single legal texts, concepts are defined independently on the basis of the knowledge extraction from different sources like statutory laws, case law and legal literature. These sources are related to the concept to support the interpretation leading to its meaning, which can differ from the literal one proposed by single legal texts. At the same time, the norms supporting a concept constitute the context in which the term denoting the concept assumes such a meaning. It is well known, in fact, that terms, like, e.g., "withdrawal" in Directive 97/7/EC and Directive 90/314/EEC change their meaning depending on the norm defining them. This approach does not prevent, however, to represent the meaning of a term as given by the literal interpretation of a norm, since this situation can be represented by specifying the norm as the only context of the concept. The feasibility of such a flexible approach rests in the fact that the Syllabus provides a temporal stratification of concepts (Ajani et al. 2010), where the same concept can evolve over time depending on the modifications of the norm defining it, or on the interpretation provided by case law or doctrinal reconstructions, which can be added as subsequent sources of the meaning after the initial norm defining the concept.

Coming back to the regulatory compliance scenario, there is a further problem concerning ontologies. The conventional wisdom suggests that it is possible to have a legal ontology with a full description of the regulated process in the bank or insurance companies. It cannot be found in the MIFID provisions. The legislator is not able to foresee all processes to be regulated, so it cannot commit to a specific ontology when designing a law. By recourse to legal interpretation we can partially overcome the incompleteness of statutory law. The abovementioned double level ontology of Syllabus corresponds to L1 of the procedural model. It permits to elaborate extensional ontologies related to the described domain.

Alternatively, someone may consider the feasibility of building an ontology of the processes implied by MIFID regulation within the interested companies. Therefore, this ontology could be enriched by the concepts from MIFID, mainly sanctions for non compliance. This vision however is not correct. It is already difficult to assume that it is possible to construct a coherent ontology of the organizational structure and processes of companies, given the temporal stratification of legacy information. Much more critical is the assumption that processes may couple the schemes provided by the MIFID regulation.

Conversely, the definition of the roles and behaviours for agents in charge of executing tasks related to the scope of MIFID (L2), without considering the need of matching this ontology with the ontology of L1, gives the possibility to work in L3 with a contrastive comparison. This comparison may allow to discover the misalignments between internal company organisation as shown in L2 and the legal statements about company organisation provided by L1. In this way, the ontology of legal potentialities may emerge in the particular company choices, the black letter rule of the law and the legal interpretation about it.

The verification of these potentialities can be done by the orthogonal concepts of L4 that may offer solutions adopted in similar cases by the means of broader conceptual frameworks.

Thus, the ontology that can be constructed adopting the proposed model can be a partial one and a specialised one. Our experience with the ICT4LAW project is that rather than employing a unified knowledge model starting from one single perspective, it is better to work on the several single layers without assuming their reducibility to another layer or not.

This method follows a bottom–up approach, but it allows to make new knowledge emerge from the interplay between several dimensions, such as regulation vs business processes, and it facilitates the mapping between the specialised knowledge bases and the various conceptual frameworks.

The prospective objective of the proposed model could be to reconstruct conflict situations in accordance with basic principles of understanding that are the product of a sufficient consensus among explicit conceptualizations instead of a search for objectivity from a single theory of legal normativity.

References

Ajani, G., L. Lesmo, G. Boella, A. Mazzei, P. Rossi (2007). Terminological and Ontological Analysis of European Directives: Multilinguism in Law. In *The 11th International Conference on Artificial Intelligence and Law, Proceedings of the Conference ICAIL'07*, 43–48. ACM 2007, Stanford, California.

Ajani, G., G. Boella, L. Lesmo, M. Martin, A. Mazzei, D. Radicioni, P. Rossi (2010). Multilevel Legal Ontologies. In E. Francesconi, S. Montemagni, W. Peters, D. Tiscornia (Eds.) *Semantic Processing of Legal Texts: Where the Language of Law Meets the Law of Language*. LNCS 6036, Springer, Berlin, 136–156.

Benjamins, V.R., J. Contreras, M. Blázquez, L. Rodrigo, P. Casanovas, M. Poblet (2004). The SEKT Legal Use Case Components: Ontology and Architecture. In T. Gordon (Ed.) *Legal Knowledge and Information Systems. Jurix 2004: The Seventeenth Annual Conference*. IOS Press, Amsterdam, 69–77.

Breuker, J., R. Winkels (2003). Use and Reuse of Legal Ontologies in Knowledge Engineering and Information Management. In *ICAIL 2003 Workshop on Legal Ontologies & Web based Legal Information Management*, 2003.

Gangemi, A., A. Prisco, M.T. Sagri, G. Steve, D. Tiscornia (2003). Some Ontological Tools to Support Legal Regulatory Compliance, With A Case Study. In *Workshop WORM Core*. LNCS, Springer, Berlin.

Gruber, T. (1995). Toward Principles for the Design of Ontologies Used for Knowledge Sharing. *International Journal Human-Computer Studies*, 1995; 43(5–6): 907–928.

Guarino, N. (1998). Formal Ontology in Information Systems. In *Proceedings of FOIS'98*. IOS Press, Amsterdam, 1998, 3–15.

McCarty, L.T. (1989). A Language for Legal Discourse, I. Basic Features. In *Proceedings of the Second International Conference on Artificial Intelligence and Law*. Vancouver, Canada, 180–189.

Rossi, P., C. Vogel (2004). Terms and Concepts (2004). Towards a Syllabus for European Private Law. ERPL, 293–300.

Shaheed, J., A. Yip, J. Cunningham (2005). A Top-Level Language-Biased Legal Ontology. In J. Lehmann, et al. (Eds.) *LOAIT—Legal Ontologies and Artificial Intelligence Techniques*, Bologna 2005, IAAIL Workshop Series No 4, Bologna 2005, 13–24.

Valente, A. (1995). *Legal Knowledge Engineering: A Modelling Approach*. IOS Press, Amsterdam, The Netherlands, 1995.

Valente, A. (2005). Types and Roles of Legal Ontologies. In Benjamins et al. (Eds.) Law and the Semantic Web. Berlin, Heidelberg, New York: Springer, 65–76.

Chapter 9
Legal Ontologies: The Linguistic Perspective

Maria Angela Biasiotti and Daniela Tiscornia

9.1 Introduction

The representation of legal concepts in ontological frameworks helps the under-standing, sharing, and re-use of knowledge bases, as it makes explicit assumptions about legal knowledge, mediates storage of legal rules and supports reasoning on them. Since legal domain is strictly dependent on its own textual nature, a method-ology for ontology construction must privilege a bottom–up approach, based on a solid theoretical model. Such a model expresses in a coherent way the links among the conceptual characterisation, the lexical manifestations of its components and the universes of discourse that are their proper referents. Considering the complex-ity of the law, methodologies based on ontology learning techniques seems to be the most promising way to fill the gap between dogmatic conceptual models and lexical patterns extracted from texts.

Ontology learning techniques are tools for automatically extracting information from texts and for giving a structured organisation to such knowledge; this means combining lexical information and formal semantics, by codifying relations between concepts, their linguistic realisations and the contexts that contain them. To grasp the characteristics of the legal world, the requisites of such a methodology require specific approaches able to capture the multi-layered structure of the discourse, the extensional semantics of open textured concepts and the ontological characterization of the interpretative process in concepts construction.

The aim of this article is, therefore, to set out, through a description of some of the projects that have been implemented by the authors, the methodological routes for constructing legal ontologies in applications that, due to the tasks they intend to achieve, should maintain a clear reference to texts. The article is divided in six sections[1]: from Sections 9.2, 9.3, 9.4, and 9.5 we address methodological issues, by

M.A. Biasiotti (✉)
Ittig, CNR, Florence, Italy
e-mail: mariangela.biasiotti@ittig.cnr.it

[1] Daniela Tiscornia is author Sections 9.1, 9.2, 9.3, 9.4, and 9.5 and Maria Angela Biasiotti is author of Section 9.6.

G. Sartor et al. (eds.), *Approaches to Legal Ontologies*, Law, Governance and Technology Series 1, DOI 10.1007/978-94-007-0120-5_9,
© Springer Science+Business Media B.V. 2011

analysing the relations between language and law and the semantic relations among the levels of legal discourse (Section 9.2); we set out models of analysis of legal documents and coherent methods for processing them (Section 9.3); in Section 9.4, we describe the outcomes of recent projects, focussing on the role of a middle-out conceptual level for connecting lexical and ontological layers; in Section 9.5, we discuss issues with our results and introduce frame semantic as a conceptual interface between contexts and legal concepts. Section 9.6 goes into details on the complexities of legal knowledge and shows, through several examples, how to map, in a consistent way, the linguistic structures extracted from texts with external ontology design patterns. Finally, in the conclusion, we comment on the lessons we have learnt and indicate the future directions of our research.

9.2 Language and Law

There is a strict connection between law and language, characterised by the coexistence of two autonomous but structurally similar systems: both are endowed with rules that underlie the construction of the system itself, that guide its evolution and guarantee its consistency. Both are conditioned by the social dimension in which it is placed, whereby they dynamically define and fix their object in relation to a continually evolving social context.

The interrelation between language and law is not symmetrical because there is a strict dependence of the law on its linguistic expression: the law has to be communicated and social and legal rules are mainly transmitted through their oral and written expression. Even in customary law, there is almost always a phase of verbalisation that enables it to be identified or recognised; even if the law cannot be reduced to a language that expresses it, nonetheless, it cannot escape its textual nature.

Another characteristic of the law is that it is expressed through many levels of discourse:

- legislative language is the "object" language because it is the principal source of positive law that, in the broad sense, also includes contracts and so-called soft law; the constitutive force of written sources derives from the stipulative nature of legislative definitions and of authentic interpretations that assign a conventional meaning of legal concepts in relation to the domain covered by the law that contains them;
- Judges interpret in an "operative" sense legal language in order to apply norms to concrete cases: the main function of judicial discourse lays, therefore, in populating the extensional dimension of the object language, instantiating cases throughout judicial subsumption., that is, linking general and abstract legislative statements to their linguistic manifestation, or, in other words, mapping legal case elements to the kinds of descriptions that may classify them;
- the language of dogmatics is a reformulation of legislative and jurisprudential language aimed at the conceptualisation of the normative contents: whilst being a metalanguage with respect to legislative and judicial language, it is a linguistic

object as well, based on the analysis of the universe of the discourse; in turn, the conceptual models of dogmatics constitute the main semantic interpretation (the universe of the discourse) of legal theory;

- legal theory expresses the basic concepts, the systemic categories of the legal system (for example, subjective right, liability, sanction, legal act, cause, entitlement...). The building blocks and construction rules of legal theory are independent of an observable reality, but also of positive legal systems, which constitute possible models of them. Their role is mainly syntactic, since they provide a systematic structure to the regulative organisation of social communities (Ross 1951). Legal theory may, therefore, be constructed as a formal and axiomatic system, made up of concepts and assertions in the theory, whose scope is explanatory of positive legal systems. This function occurs thanks to links either to dogmatic or to extra linguistic entities as they emerge trough the sociological analysis of law (Ferraioli 2007: 47);
- and finally, there is the discourse of philosophy of law, expressing both general principles and value judgements as well as their ordering criteria.

On the (meta)theoretical level, the border between legal theory and dogmatic may be seen as a genus/species relationship, or in a model-theoretic interpretation as a relation between a logical theory and its models; legal theory has an explanatory and prescriptive function (in the broad sense) because it constructs concepts independently of the normative statements and interpretative operations, whilst the conceptual models of dogmatic arise out of the analysis of legal texts, that produces interpreted knowledge and are therefore not susceptible to being generalised in an axiomatic theory.

One of the most obvious demonstrations of this distinction is the creative role of legal translation, halfway between term equivalence setting and concepts comparison. Legal terminology used in the various legal systems, both European and non-European, expresses not only the legal concepts which operate there, but further reflects the deep differences existing between the various systems and the differing legal outlook of lawyers in each system. Given the structural domain specificity of legal language, we cannot speak about "translating the law" to ascertain correspondences between legal terminology in various languages, since the translational correspondence of two terms satisfies neither the semantic correspondence of the concepts they denote nor the requirements of the different legal systems.

Transferred into the computational context, the boundary between the conceptualisations of legal theory and dogmatic becomes purely methodological. The former entities, the kernel legal concepts, are modelled in the so called core ontologies, while the latter are the object of domain ontologies. Both are expressed by the same languages and by the same cognitive perspectives: computational ontologies are means of communication, aiming at making explicit a set of meaning assumptions shared by a social community; therefore we do not claim that a domain ontology is the "true" conceptualisation, but that it is nothing more than a partial and not-exclusive interpretation of a piece of social reality.

Since the focus of this article is to analyse legal ontologies from the perspective of language, we will not go into details about consolidated core legal ontologies; instead, we will concentrate on the design of a methodology that best reformulates, in a computational context, the process of conceptualisation proper of legal dogmatics, a process strongly based on legal language analysis.

9.3 Legal Text Analysis

In analysing legal documents, the basic aspect that must be elicited is the relation between meaning (norm) and form (text); norms are conceived as the interpreted meaning of written regulations that correspond to a partition in legal text, like articles, subsections, etc.; or a norm can be built by interpretative activities on a set of logically entailed linguistic expressions, for instance, the decision in a judgement, or set of legislative statements).

A general methodology for meaning extraction must be framed through a modular architecture, where different aspects refer to specific analytic models and to appropriate NLP tools.

9.3.1 The Semantics of Textual Structures

Despite the lack of specific rules governing the use of language, several legal documents have indeed fixed narrative structures, so that it is possible to detect semantic templates from typical linguistic structures, on the basis of a finite set of linguistic expressions and syntactic structures that can be considered in some way domain independent. More specifically:

As for legislation, we can define:

- a model of the logical structure of legislative texts, understood as a set of statements, that enable the following elements to be identified:

  - information about the document structure: enacting authority, class of source, time, publishing date, versioning, subject, partitions, etc. (Agnoloni et al. 2007),
  - classification of legislative statements according to their illocutive function (to define, to prohibit, to oblige, to sanction . . ..) (Biagioli et al. 2008).
  - distinction of language levels, for example, norms that talk about other norms (to repeal them, to amend them, etc.); (Spinosa et al. 2009).

dependency relations between classes of statements (for example, between a definition and a norm that uses the defined concept, between a norm that obliges and one that provides sanctions in the case of the breach of the obligation, etc.) (Biagioli et al. 2008).

- a model of inner structure of legislative statements, based on:

  - the interpretation of syntactic elements (even if, unless, notwithstanding, and/or, but otherwise, after, . . .) in terms of logical connectives among propositions (Allen 1986), expressing disjunctions or conjunctions of factual conditions, linked by logical implication to a legal effect or a legal qualification of a status;
  - the distinction between the deontic classification of behaviour and the set of regulated behaviours: the former is knowledge domain independent, the latter expresses common sense knowledge (Francesconi 2009).

Case law requires a different profile:

- analysis of rhetorical structures in legal judgements, to identify the basic components: facts of the case, decisions, arguments and grounds (Wyner 2008);
- distinction among arguments and non arguments (facts, complaints, reason for and against the decision) (Wyner 2008);
- extraction of the logical argumentative structure of the case, argument and rule, on which build a grammar of argument for automatic argument extraction (Wyner 2009);
- identification of factors in semantic terms, i.e., relevant elements on which the decision for or against a side in a case is based (see Chapter 6 by Ashley, this volume).

9.3.2 The Construction of Legal Concepts

Legal concepts are the product of the creative activity of dogmatics. Only in few cases legal concepts are elicited from the core meaning of a single norm, but, more frequently, they are built on set of norms, through a process of abstraction and generalisation, by collecting sets of normative conditions, to be linked to sets of legal effects.[2] Normative contexts are, therefore, descriptions, that, in the process of concept construction:

- constrain the common sense meaning of a term: Directive 97/7/EC, Article 2. "Definitions. For the purposes of this Directive: 'consumer' means any natural person who, in contracts covered by this Directive, is acting for purposes which are outside his trade, business or profession".
- state the condition of applications of a concept, typically, a state of affair (action/event, agent(s), temporal/spatial circumstances): "Directive 97/7/EC, Article 6. 1. For any distance contract the consumer shall have a period of at

---

[2]A reformulation of Ross theory on legal concepts in terms of ontological analysis is in Sartor (2007).

least seven working days in which to withdraw from the contract without penalty and without giving any reason."
- specify the extension or consequences of a legal status/effect in term of right, duties, sanctions. "Directive 97/7/EC, Article 6. 2. Where the right of withdrawal has been exercised by the consumer pursuant to this Article, the supplier shall be obliged to reimburse the sums paid by the consumer free of charge."
- contain assertions about the instance of concepts. Judgment of the Court (First Chamber) of 10 March 2005. "The answer to the question referred must therefore be that Article 3(2) of the directive is to be interpreted as meaning that 'contracts for the provision of transport services' includes contracts for the provision of car hire services."

One can expect that both the semiotic characterisation of normative statements trough syntactic parsing and the classification of their narrative roles would support content patterns detection. Unfortunately, there is no correspondence between the semiotic distinction of norms and their linguistic expression, the main distinction being that between regulative rules vs. constitutive rules. Regulative rules provide normative setting to existing forms of human behaviours, while constitutive rules creates new form of behaviours, or new legal entities (Searle 1969). In their linguistic realisation, the expression X is Y may introduce a new concept (as in definitions: (X is Y in context C) or in a mandatory way for a status of affair to be legally relevant (X must be Y).

As a consequence, we can assume neither that norms have always events (including both legal facts and acts in a wide notion of event) as their object, nor that the distinction between constitutive and regulative norms implies the identification of legal facts and individuals (qualified by constitutive rules) and legal acts (regulated by prescriptive rules). And this makes the computational process of meaning extraction even more difficult.

9.3.3 The Computational Models

Computational frameworks, covering the whole scenario outlined above are quite difficult to find in the literature on AI and law. Traditional rule-based and case-based approaches developed in the '80s were interested in capturing the inferential aspects of legal knowledge more than in expressing the conceptual components and dependencies among kinds of knowledge.

Proposals at theoretical level adopted frame-based descriptives formalisms, which at the present, turn out to be more easily reformulated in ontological languages. Normframe (van Kralingen 1993) is a general structure, where frame elements (slots) expressing properties of legal documents are distinguished from the attributes (frame elements) of norm components. The Functional Ontology of Law, (Valente 1995; Breuker et al. 2004), even if presented as a core ontology, is more addressed to describing the epistemological aspects of law as a control system of social behaviours.

These models are embedded in core legal ontologies, usually built top-down with the goal of representing intensional descriptions of legal concepts as classes for guiding the interpretation of the world and explaining common sense reasoning. Formal ontologies are composed of a relatively small set of concepts, defined by a high number of constraints which encode the relations between individuals of classes through cardinality restrictions, property range and domain, disjointness, transitive and symmetric properties. The LKIF Core LKIF-Core ontology,[3] developed within the ESTRELLA project is a modular collection of basic legal concepts aimed at supporting the implementation of rule-based knowledge bases for regulatory decision support systems. (Hoekstra et al. 2007). The Core Legal Ontology (CLO) (Gangemi et al. 2003) organises legal concepts and relations on the basis of formal properties defined in the DOLCE+ foundational ontology library (Masolo et al. 2002)[4]

Core ontologies are normally built on the knowledge elicited from legal experts and include the formalisation of basic concepts with which legal theory commonly agrees. In their specialisations in domain ontologies, the choice about the levels of generalisation is left to the developers; it mainly depends on the kind of applications and the results one expects to achieve, as they are expected to support classification, reasoning and the decision making process.

Both core and domain ontologies include clear assumptions about the normative knowledge, the ideal view of law about reality, and the world knowledge composed by entities, belonging either to physical or social reality, over which norms act by imposing constraints. One of the main concept necessary to understand this distinction is that of role. Norms can be viewed as roles itself or composed by roles, as social behaviours and social organizations are explained as (consisting of) roles (Breuker 1994, Masolo et al. 2004). Even if roles have a relational nature, a distinction should be made between role as a relationship and role as a concept, i.e. what roles mean. Roles are behavioural requirements on role execution and on qualification of role taking (Breuker 1994). While role execution (agents participating in events) pertains to world knowledge, role assignments pertain to normative knowledge: they classify agents and events according to such requirements. A legal Agent(a role itself) can play several roles at the same time (owner, employee, seller, heir, etc. . .) and correlatives roles are played by Agents involved in the same situation (buyer/seller). In the same way as in dogmatics legal concepts are built on norms, in core legal ontologies legal concepts, (and legal roles), are the reification of role-relations; for instance, deontic classification of behaviours (obliged, forbidden, etc..) are in CLO relations expressing the attitudes that (players of) roles can have towards a legal status/tasks, while right, duty, obligations are legal concepts which encompass a set of normative attitudes towards a legal effect.

---

[3] http://www.estrellaproject.org/lkif-core (Breuker et al.2007)
[4] http://dolce.semanticweb.org.

9.4 A Bottom–Up Methodology for Ontology Building

While several knowledge elements listed in Section 9.6.1 can be (semi) automatically recognized and extracted by means of machine learning and text mining tools, we cannot expect that automatic acquisition of knowledge elements would be able to capture the complete meaning of normative statements; therefore, ontology construction still require large amounts of knowledge to be manually drafted. The best solution in practical applications seems to be a middle out methodology, where text processing techniques and knowledge formalisation methods interact, throughout an iterative process of ontology learning and enrichment.

Many currently available Natural Language Processing (NLP) applications are rapidly evolving from the traditional processing of the formal aspects of language (part of speech tagging, syntactic parsing) towards automated analysis of meaning, by implementing tools for "ontology learning"; the term denotes a suite of methodologies and procedures for extracting the semantic structure from linguistic objects. The parsing process works in layers of increasing complexity, exemplified in the so-called "ontology learning cake" (Gomez-Perez and Manzano-Macho 2003) and explained in Buitelaar et al. (2006: 10) as: "ontology development is primarily concerned with the definition of concepts and relations between them, but connected to this also knowledge about the symbols that are used to refer to them. In our case this implies the acquisition of linguistic knowledge about the terms that are used to refer to a specific concept in the text and possible synonyms of these terms. An ontology further consists of a taxonomy backbone and other, non-hierarchical relations. Finally, in order to derive also facts that are not explicitly encoded by the ontology but could be derived from it, also rules should be defined (ad if possible acquired) that allow for such derivations."

9.4.1 Lexical Ontologies

At the lower layer, terms are extracted and organised in semantic lexicons. A de facto standard for building lexical ontologies is WordNet (Fellbaum 1998), a lexical database which has been under constant development at Princeton University. ' In fact WordNet merely attempts to map the lexicon into a network organized by means of relations ... A lexicon can be defined as the mappings of words onto concepts...". (Felbaum and Vossen 2008). "EuroWordNet (EWN) (Vossen et al. 1997) is a multilingual lexical database with wordnets for eight European languages, which are structured along the same lines as the Princeton WordNet[5]".

Our experience in building a multilingual wordnet in the legal domain deals with the realisation of the LOIS data base,[6] composed by about 35,000 concepts in five European languages (English, German, Portuguese, Czech, and Italian, linked

---

[5] wordnet.princeton.edu and www.globalwordnet.org
[6] Lois, *Lexical ontologies for legal information sharing* (EDC 2026–2001–02)

by English) (Peters et al. 2007). In LOIS, a concept is expressed by a synset, the atomic unit of the semantic net. A synset is a set of one or more uninflected word forms belonging to the same part-of-speech (noun, verb, adjective) that can be interchanged in a certain context. For example, {action, trial, proceedings, law suit} form a noun-synset because they can be used to refer to the same concept. More precisely, each synset is a set of word-senses, since polysemous terms are distinct in different word-senses, e.g., {diritto_1(right)} and {diritto_2(law)}; {property_1, attribute, dimension} and {property_2, belongings, holding}. Each word sense belongs to exactly one synset and each word sense has exactly one word that represents it lexically, and one word can be related to one or more word senses A synset is often further described by a gloss, explaining the meaning of the concept.

In monolingual lexicons, terms are linked by lexical relations: synonymy (included in the notion of synset), near-synonym, antonym, derivation. Synsets are structured by means of hierarchical relations (hypernymy/hyponymy) and non hierarchical relations of which the most important are meronymy (between parts or wholes), thematic roles, instance-of.

There are two basic approaches for automatic multilingual alignment of wordnets (Vossen 1999), the extend approach, from the source lexicon to target wordnets by means of term-to-term translation, and the merge approach, that we have adopted in building the LOIS db, according to which an independent wordnet for a certain language is first created and then mapped to the others. This approach, adopted in the EuroWordnet project, determines the interconnectivity of the indigenous wordnets by means of the Inter-Lingual-Index (ILI), a set of equivalence relations of each synset with an English synset. Cross-lingual linking indicates complete equivalence, near-equivalence, or equivalence-as-a-hyponym or hyperonym. Unlike the wordnets, the ILI is a flat list and, unlike an ontology, is not structured by means of relations. ILI entries merely function to connect equivalent words and synsets in different languages.

This solution seems coherent with the assumption that, in legal language, every term collection belonging to a language system, and any vocabulary originated by a law system is an autonomous lexicon and should be mapped through equivalence relationships to a pivot language, which acts as the interlingua. Language-specific synsets from different languages linked to the same ILI-record by means of a synonym relation are considered conceptually equivalent. The LOIS database has been built in a semi-automatic way, by means of NLP techniques for morfo-syntactic parsing and conceptual clustering, to extract syntagmatic and paradigmatic relations between terms; from the output, sets of candidates for synonyms, taxonomies and non-hierarchical relations was further manually refined.

Computational lexicon, even if sometime called lightweight ontologies, are in fact able to capture only the lexical semantic of terms, whose meaning merely depends on their position in the network and on semantic relations[7]; cross-lingual

---

[7]"A lexicon is not a very good ontology. An ontology, after all, is a set of categories of objects or ideas in the world, along with certain relationships among them; it is not a linguistic object.

equivalence is still language dependent, since driven by the English gloss and not explained, because of the lack of an explicit meaning representation. Nevertheless, they provide a powerful support for semantic classification, cross-lingual retrieval, terms extraction, etc. . . Given the wide diffusion of the wordnet model and the growing relevance of semantic resources in knowledge acquisition processes, several initiatives for the formal specification of the wordnet structure have been proposed, to allow a consistent integration between individual wordnets.[8]

In legal domain, the shallow semantic characterization of synsets generate ambiguities or loss of information in cases where domain and linguistic information overlap. To give some examples, in LOIS sub-class relations (between rental contract and contract), and semantic specialisation (between unfair competition and competition) are not distinct, as well as the semantic notion of functional equivalence and the legal notion of similarity in functions, as among Camera dei Deputati, Assemblée nationale, Congreso de los Diputados. Most of the semantic combinatorial properties of lexical items are not explicitly represented and multi-words, like: place of contract conclusion, offer acceptance, contract infringement, etc. . .) cannot be expressed. A further overlapping is that every definition, as a conventional assignment of a new meaning is considered in the same way as the introduction of a new sense (Tiscornia 2006). The lesson learned from the Lois experience brought us to the conclusion that semantic soundness and consistent integration of semantic lexicons must be supported by a domain-specific ontology, in order to make it explicit in the way in which legal concepts belonging to different systems share analogies and set differences.

9.4.2 Anchoring Terminologies to a Reference Ontology

Our experience of interfacing lexicons and ontologies on the Dalos project (Agnoloni et al. 2007) arose from the task the project intended to perform: a terminology control tool in the multilingual drafting of Community legislation, where the institutional texts expressed in the 25 languages of the European Union are deemed semantically (and, therefore, normatively) equivalent.

The aim of DALOS (Drafting Legislation with Ontology base Support[9]) is to provide a knowledge and linguistic resource for legislative drafting. The main outcome is the definition of a semantic framework, where the use of words and the

---

A lexicon, on the other hand, depends, by definition, on a natural language and the word senses in it..[. . .] Despite all the discussion in the previous section, it is possible that a lexicon with a semantic hierarchy might serve as the basis for a useful ontology, and an ontology may serve as a grounding for a lexicon. This may be so in particular in technical domains, in which vocabulary and ontology are more closely tied than in more-general domains" (Hirst 2004).

[8] The Owl meta.ontology for conneting Wordnets is composed by three classes: Synset, WordSense and Word. Each Synset object is a set of WordSense objects since polysemous terms are distinct in wordsenses http://www.w3.org/TR/wordnet-rdf/

[9] www.dalosproject.eu

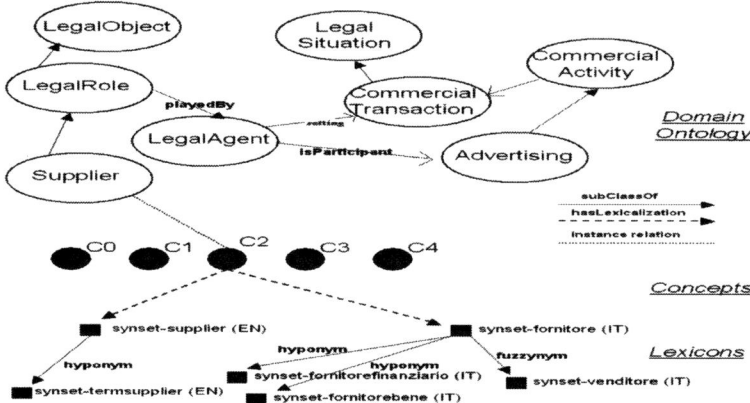

Fig. 9.1 Knowledge base architecture

underlining meaning assumptions are made explicit Such knowledge, embedded in a specialised drafting tool, will provide law-makers with a clear overview of the consolidated lexicon in a regulative domain and of the semantic properties of concepts, thus facilitating the harmonisation of legal knowledge and lexicons between the EU and Member States. It also support the dynamic integration of the lexicon by the legislator and the monitoring of the diachronic meaning evolution of legal terminology. The Knowledge base, as shown in Fig. 9.1, is composed of:

- the Lexical Layer which contains lexicons extracted by means of NLP tools[10] from a set of parallel corpora of EU legislation and case law in the sub-domain of consumer protection, chosen as a case study (16 EU Directives, 33 Court of Justice Judgments and 9 Court of First Instance Judgments[11]). Extracted terminologies[12] have been manually refined, producing four monolingual

---

[10]The tools, specifically addressed to process English and other EU language texts, are GATE and T2K. GATE supports advanced language analysis owned/provided and maintained by the Department of Computer Science of the University of Sheffield. T2K is a terminology extractor and ontology learning tool for the Italian language jointly developed by CNR-ILC and the University of Pisa.

[11]In order to guarantee the linking of acquired domain terms to the individual textual partitions rather than to the individual act, the corpus to be processed was segmented into 8,192 files corresponding to 2,583 directive partitions (sub-paragraphs) and 5,609 case law partitions.

[12]The selected minimum frequency threshold for both single and multiword terms was 5, the percentage of selected terms from the ranked lists was 20% in the case of single terms (both single and multiword terms), terms and 70% for multiword terms. The Italian TermBank is composed of 1,443 of which 1,168 are multiword terms of different complexity. The number of extracted hyponymic relations is 623 referring to 229 hypernym terms, whereas the number of identified related terms is 1,258 referring to 279 terminological headwords. The processing of the English corpus resulted in a set of 3,012 terms, which consists of 1,157 multi word units and 1,855 single word terms. This set has an overlap of 572 terms with the LOIS vocabulary. Crosslingual alignment computes

terminologies (in Italian, English, Dutch and Spanish), structured along the lines of WordNet, and formally codified as sets of instances of the Noun-Synset class, identified by a URI and described by OWL object properties that translate WordNet relations. Each Wordsense is also linked to its textual referent, a texts fragment codified as instance of class Partition (see Bacci et al. 2008).

- the Ontological Layer built on top of the lexicon is composed of:

    - the Concept Layer: it is a flat list of synset, linked by has-lexicalization relation to monolingual synsets in lexical layer; it acts as pivot, like in Wordnet ILI, in order to align synsets of different languages. They provide the extensional characterization of concepts but thy do not carry any kind of semantic information, which is provided by the ontology;
    - the ontological layer formally describes the intensional meaning of core elements in the consumer law domain. In selecting candidates for the ontology, we have assumed that all concepts defined in the legislative corpus are relevant, as well as several concepts used in the definitional contexts, expressing the basic properties of the domain, which has been modelled around the notion of "commercial transaction", relying on the basic state of affairs (legal situations) regulated. The role of the ontological layer is to assign a domain specific characterization to entities at conceptual levels, and consequently, to 'explain' and validate terminological choices at lexical layer.

Through the double-layered representation, concepts expressions (provider, producer, importer; produttore, fornitore, distributore, etc.) extracted from documents are "assigned" to the same conceptual entity "supplier", whose basic properties are formally codified in the ontology. In this way, meaning constraints imposed by legislative definitions (see Section 9.6 for examples) can be anchored to their normative scope and misleading alignments or diverging lexicalizations can be detected and explained (Francesconi and Tiscornia 2008).

9.5 The Next Step: Frames Detection

The connection between the two layers in Dalos has been manually performed.

In the current evolution of the project, we are looking at further solutions towards gradually reducing manual intervention by: (a) progressively strengthening knowledge extraction techniques from terms extraction to situations detection and (b) by using external semantic resources, in order to provide a structure that supports systematic, incremental, modular knowledge development (Peters 2009).

---

the overlap between the different languages according to two criteria: (a) the positional similarity in the texts; (b) (near)equivalents on the basis of translations (through WordNet) or, if they share some elements, that are translations. More details are in Agnoloni et al. (2009).

An approach that intends to provide solutions to both these goals is based on frame semantics. Frame semantics offers a formal framework for the interface between linguistic and content patterns, widely adopted in ontology learning, because it provides a formal semiotic representation of linguistic patterns. Our on going project, still at the beginning (Venturi et al. 2009), aims at re-using and specialising Framenet, (Baker et al. 1998; Fillmore and Baker 2001) a well-known lexicographic resource[13]: "The Berkeley FrameNet Project is creating an online lexical resource for English, based on the principles of Frame Semantics and supported by corpus evidence. A semantic frame is a script-like structure of inferences, which are linked to the meanings of linguistic units (lexical items). Each frame identifies a set of frame elements (FEs), which are frame- specific semantic roles (participants, props, phases of a state of affairs). Our description of each lexical item identifies the frames which underlie a given meaning and the ways in which the FEs are realized in structures headed by the word. The FrameNet database documents the range of semantic and syntactic combinatory possibilities (valences) of each word in each of its senses, through manual annotation of example sentences and automatic summarization of the resulting annotations.[. . .] The FrameNet database now contains information about more than 4,000 lexical units (senses of words) based on the annotation of more than 100,000 sentences". (Narayanan et al. 2003).

FrameNet aims at supporting NLP extraction, allowing the semantic annotation of large corpora and thus creating a reference corpus able to support the detection of linguistic patterns at text level. Through automatic procedures of Role Labelling, the mapping of all the semantic information associated to words in a given context (in terms of semantic roles and event participants) to the evoked frames or to more general concepts, the suggestion of content patterns would rise. To gie an example,the frame Commerce_Scenario, its definition and its Core Frame Elements (in bold) are reported below:

Commerce_Scenario: Commerce is a situation in which a Buyer and a Seller have agreed upon an exchange of Money and Goods (possibly after a negotiation), and then perform the exchange, optionally carrying it out with various kinds of direct payment or financing or the giving of change.

The following is an example of an annotated fragment of legislation, Directive 2008/48/EC, instantiating the Commerce-scenario Frame (FEs tags in square brackets): "provisions of this Directive should apply to natural and legal persons (credit intermediaries [Buyer]) who, in the course of their trade, business or profession, for a fee[Money], present or offer credit agreements [Goods]to consumers [Seller]".

Even if Framenet codifies common sense knowledge, our approach aims at specialising and instantiating a set of frames from Framenet without creating a large number of domain specific frames. Basically, we expect to specialize common sense frames by means of insertion of FEs and by labelling FEs with domain-specific Semantic Types. Our idea is to map Semantic Types into external legal ontologies,

---

[13]http://framenet.icsi.berkeley.edu/~framenet/

l ke CLO, LKIF or into domain ontologies, as in the case of the Dalos ontology (see (Dolbey et al. 2006) for a similar approach in biomedical domain).

Examples below introduce some preliminary hints:

- mapping frames to classes in legal ontologies: PROIBITING and BEING_ OBLIGED match Permission and Obligative_right in LKIF Core and normative positions in CLO.
- BEING_OBLIGED: Directive 2008/48/EC, Art. 9: Each Member State [Responsible_party] shall in the case of cross-border credit [Condition]ensure access [Duty]for creditors from other Member States to databases used in that Member State for assessing the creditworthiness of consumers.
- introducing FEs: in BEING_OBLIGATED a further FE: Beneficiary has been added to express the recipient of the obligation performed by the responsible_party:
- BEING_OBLIGED Directive 1999/44/EC, "Art. 2: The seller [responsible_party], must deliver goods[Duty] to the consumer [Beneficiary] which are in conformity with the contract of sale".
- linking a Frame to different classes to disambiguate ontological distinction: the 3 instances below, instantiate different FEs of DOCUMENTS: if mapped onto legal document in CLO it inherits the distinction between the normative content (legal document is a subclass of informative object, instantiated by contexts 2 and 3) and its physical realisation (as sub-class of text, instantiated by context 1):

1. Directive 2008/122/EC, Art.5: Member States shall ensure that the contract [document]is in writing, on paper or on another durable medium[medium], and drawn up in the language or one of the languages of the Member State in which the consumer is resident or a national, at the choice of the consumer, provided it is an official language of the Community.
2. Directive 2008/122/EC, Art. 8: "the exercise of the right of withdrawal by the consumer terminates the obligation [obligation] of the parties [bearer]to perform the contract".
3. Directive 2008/122/EC, Art. 10: "2. From the second instalment payment onwards, the consumer [bearer]may[right] terminate the contract [obligation]without incurring any penalty by giving notice to the trader [issuer]within fourteen calendar days of receiving the request for payment of each instalment".

- defining domain specific Semantic Types. Our intuition is that the lexical notion of roles expressed in FEs can be ontologically characterized trough Semanti Types. For instance, qualifying FEs as Legal role will pose constrains over the type of fillers, while allowing the distinction between the Agent (legal or natural person) performing the action and the role(s) assigned to them by law. For instance:

– FEs of COMMERCIAL_goods_transfer: Directive 97/7/EC 'consumer'[FE: buyer; SemType: Legal role] means any natural person [FE: Agent;SemType: Legal Subject]who, in contracts covered by this Directive, is acting for purposes which are outside his trade, business or profession;
– extensions of Lexical Units. Links to lexical ontologies will allow us to extend LUs by mapping terms into legal wordnets and conversely, to constrain FEs fillers by links to synsets hierarchies, for instance, FE: Agent can be linked to top synsets in Lois, like: natural person or legal person, which includes public body, organization, authority and their hyponyms.

We expect to obtain two results from the instantiation and specialization of Framenet: (1) an annotated corpus of legal documents, able to guide Role Labelling procedures for the detection of typical patterns from the occurrences in a corpus and (2) a corpus-based lexicon (a set of the Lexical Units), in which the meaning of the terms is manifested through the association of the linguistic structures (semantic roles) with the corresponding domain structures (roles assigned by norms). The process of corpora annotation, frame detection and specialisation must be understood as a recursive process, where the structured lexicon will be constantly enriched by the expansion to new Lexical Units and spans, and the systems of frames further detailed.

9.6 The Gap Between Text and Knowledge

Part II goes into details on the complexities of legal knowledge and shows, through several examples, which is the effective gap existing between the linguistic meaning of a term and its semantic/domain meaning and how to bridge this gap. Methodologies to be applied for consistently mapping the linguistic structures extracted from texts with external ontology design patterns are also proposed.

9.6.1 Bridging the Gap Between Text and Knowledge

Lexical Meaning

Term --------------- Concept

Legal Domain Meaning

Ontology development is primarily concerned with the definition of concepts and relations between them, but connected to this also knowledge about symbols that are used to refer to them. This implies the acquisition of linguistic knowledge about terms that are used to refer to a specific concept in a given domain and text as well as possible synonyms of these terms. In this scenario, of course, terms are the linguistic realisation of a domain-specific concept. Dealing with lexical or linguistic ontologies (that is, lightweight ontologies) also means facing a specific gap that exists between terms/concepts and their meaning in the referred domain. There is a difference between the linguistic meaning and the semantic meaning of the concept as well as the one existing between terminology and ontology. Often a concept in a given domain seems to have a more extended meaning than the one expressed by its linguistic meaning; on the contrary, some times the concept does have a more restricted meaning in the referred domain with respect to the linguistic one. The two meanings appear to be the same at times. For instance, goods are items held for sale in the regular course of business, as in a retail store whilst the ordinary and accepted meaning of the word goods is that of "items circulated on the commercial market intended for sale." In the consumer law domain goods that can become the object of a consumer contract or transaction can only be "consumer goods" which are defined as "any tangible movable item with the exception of goods sold by way of execution or otherwise by the authority of law—water and gas where they are not put out for sale in a limited volume or set quantity, electricity". Therefore the ordinary and common understanding of the term goods becomes in the given consumer law domain something different less wide and more narrow.

As can be noted, there is a substantial gap between the linguistic definition of goods given by the common definition and the one given by the EU set of legal definitions within the specific consumer law domain. The relationship between the linguistic meaning of the term and the semantic meaning may be that one narrows or extends the other.

This gap becomes very significant within the legal domain where norms are applied when/if facts or behaviours are relevant for the law. Then knowing the exact meaning of the term/concept, its extensions or restrictions appear to be essential in order to realise if the situation analysed is the one foreseen by the legislator or by a judge in his/her decisions.

Solutions for bridging this gap between the textual meaning and the conceptual or semantic meaning appear to be methodologies able to somehow capture the intended, not explicit or hidden meaning of the concept. The following may all be possible solutions to be adopted with a different degree of consistency with respect to a given domain:

- termontography strategies: the termontography is a middle-out approach combining domain expertise (top–down) with information provided in natural language (bottom–up). This approach allows us to ideally capture and represent knowledge acquired from texts. First of all, in close collaboration with field specialists of the domain which is subjected to ontological analysis, an initial framework of categories and inter-categorial relationships is actually developed top-down. Initially, this categorisation framework serves as a template for the manual and semi-automatic extraction of knowledge from a corpus. However, it will gradually evolve in an enriched and more fine-grained network of semantic relations, reflecting culture-specific categorisations, as the knowledge elicited via textual material is then confronted with the categorical frame (a bottom–up analysis). The results of this analysis are reflected in a termontological database, which can, for instance, be used as a supportive resource for formal knowledge engineering

(Temmerman et al. 2009). For instance, when building an ontology or compiling a terminological database, both ontologists and terminographers will start from the identification of their purposes, the restriction in the scope of the domain, the specification of the user requirements as well as the acquisition of domain knowledge needed for the extraction and understanding of categories and terms;

- covert categories approach: this strategy implies adding categories that are unlexicalised in the language upon which the lexicon is based: covert categories (unlexicalised concepts) relying on the definition find frequently recurrent patterns that could signal the reification of a covert category (Barrière and Popowich). Type hierarchies are important structures used in knowledge stores to enumerate and classify the entities from a domain of interest. The hierarchical structure establishes de facto a "similarity space" in which the elements of a same class are considered close semantically, as they share the properties of their superclass. An important task in Natural Language Processing (NLP) is sentence understanding. This task relies partly on comparing the words in the sentence among each other as well as the words in previous sentences and words in a knowledge store. A type hierarchy consisting of words and/or word senses can be useful to facilitate these comparisons and establish which words are semantically related. The problems of using a type hierarchy for evaluating semantic distance come from its dependency on the available words of a specific language, and on the arbitrariness of its classes and of its depth, which leads to the development of semantic distance measures giving arbitrary results. We propose a way to extend the type hierarchy, to give more flexibility to the "similarity space", by including non-lexical concepts defined around relations other than taxonomic relations. We also suggest a method for discovering these non-lexical concepts in texts, and present some results;

- exctracting the key-phrase from documents: this associates key relevant terms to documents (Gangemi and Presutti 2008). Extracting key phrases from documents is a very well established technique in Natural Language Processing (NLP). In the literature, several methodologies have been proposed, ranging from applying supervised learning techniques, to pattern based approaches. Key-phrases are in general noun compounds, usually composed of 2 or 3 words, and they can be identified by specifying syntactic patterns. Statistical measures are, in general, adopted to measure the internal coherence among words of the same terms and the distributional properties of the term as a whole inside documents in a corpus;

- meaning/description of the concept: (legal) definitions (Van Kranlinger). The description of acts and act frames has already brought us into the realm of concept descriptions: act descriptions are a specific form of concept descriptions. A concept description determines the meaning of a concept. In the legal domain, the concepts that need description are usually specific legal terms. This type is referred to as the (legal) definition. A concept description comprises seven elements. The first element is the concept to be defined: every concept description describes a concept or term. It does so by either stating the conditions under which a concept is applicable or by naming some instances of a concept (combinations are also possible). An important element of the concept description is the concept type. Four concept types can be distinguished: legal definitions, deeming provisions, factors, and meta concepts. Deeming provisions are used to introduce legal fictions. Deeming provisions allow things which are not true to be true and vice versa. According to this approach from the point of view of a generic ontology, it is interesting that the vocabulary can be divided into two parts: a generic and a statute specific part, whereas some of the categories in the vocabulary only have generic meaning, others have both generic and statute-specific meaning;

- mapping linguistic and content pattern approaches: this strategy implies the extraction of linguistic patterns from texts, to identify definitional contexts by mapping definitional techniques and related linguistic structures (assign a sign to a symbol) to derive a context of use from linguistic frames. This allows us to detect actions/agents/roles in the factual component of regulative propositions as well as to extract semantic information from syntagmatic and paradigmatic relations and to map frames into ontology content patterns (CPs) (Gangemi and Presutti 2008), specialising content patterns for legal sub-domains (e.g., incriminating rules, sanctioning, process compliance assessment).

9.6.2 Some Practical Applications

All the analyzed solutions or methodologies seem to have as a crucial and starting point the legal definition giving the concept a specific meaning within a given domain or identifying the context of use of that concept. Therefore, the definition itself seems to be the point from which to start for rendering the legal meaning of a term/concept explicit and for matching the linguistic meaning with the domain in a consistent way.

9.6.2.1 Definitional Techniques

Definitions can be either lexical (descriptive) or stipulative. In principle, the difference is simple. A lexical definition reports actual linguistic usage. Therefore, it can be correct or incorrect (i.e., true or false, although that terminology is seldom used). A stipulative definition reports how the definer is going to use a term, or how he/she recommends others to use it. A stipulative definition cannot be correct or incorrect, but it can be enlightening or confusing, fruitful or barren, adequate or inadequate. It is often difficult to draw a sharp line between lexical and stipulative definitions. How, for instance, should we classify the extensive philosophical literature on the meaning of "knowledge"? Do the authors aim at a lexical definition describing what we mean by "knowledge" in ordinary language, a lexical definition of what "knowledge" means in philosophy, a stipulative definition for a fruitful concept in philosophy, or perhaps even a real definition (i.e., a definition of the essence of what it is to know something, rather than a definition of the word "knowledge" or the concept knowledge)? In practice, this is often far from clear. A major reason for this is that stipulative definitions are circumscribed by linguistic practice. Lexical and stipulative definitions tend to differ in how they treat the ambiguities and unclarities of ordinary language. A lexical definition should, at least in principle, exhibit actual uses even when they are unclear or even confused. If a term has several different meanings or uses, they should be listed and distinguished between. In contrast, stipulative definitions are usually developed in order to eliminate ambiguity and vagueness. A definition has three constitutive parts. It consists of the definiendum (that which is to be defined), the definiens (that which defines) and a defining connective. Hence, in the definition "A bachelor is an unmarried man", "a bachelor" is the definiendum, "an unmarried man" the definiens and "is" the defining connective. There are at least three different attitudes that a stipulative definer can take to the lack of clarity in ordinary language. First, one can choose to do essentially the same as in lexical definitions, namely, to accept but clarify what is confused or obscure in ordinary usage. This approach is justified when it can be shown that the lack of clarity is not a disadvantage given the purpose of the definition. Secondly, one can restrict the meaning of the word, thirdly, one can split the concept by introducing new terms that distinguish between different meanings of the word under scrutiny. Applied to the analysed gap, the result will be that it will:

- clarify, when the linguistic meaning and the domain/semantic meaning are quite the same or at least equivalent;
- restrict the meaning, when the linguistic meaning is wider than the semantic one or vice versa (narrowing actions);
- split the concept introducing new terms that distinguish between different meanings in all other cases (extending actions).

Considering the different relationships that could arise between the lexical meaning and the semantic one here below an overview of situations existing as to the legal domain is provided.

9.6.3 Narrowing Lexical Meaning

The narrowing action serves to restrict a lexical meaning which is wider than the semantic one.

The worker who according to a linguistic definition is a person who works at a specific occupation (Lexical Def. ILI GLOSS) according to the definition given by several European Union Directives workers also becomes the following:

- worker_2: any person who, in the Member State concerned, is protected as an employee under national employment law and in accordance with national practice;
- worker_ 3: any person employed by an employer, including trainees and apprentices but excluding domestic servants;

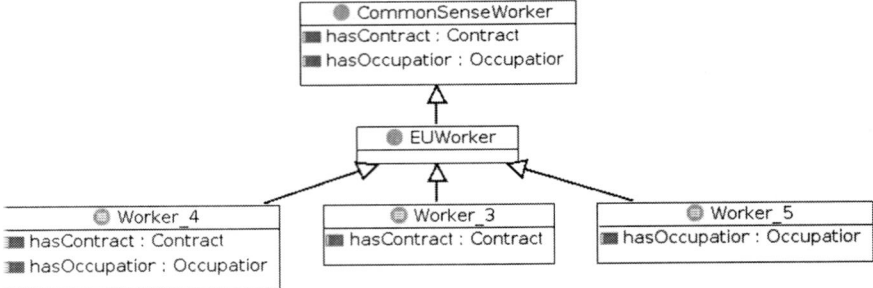

Fig. 9.2 Worker UML representation

- worker_4: any person carrying out an occupation on board a vessel, including trainees and apprentices, but excluding port pilots and shore personnel carrying out work on board a vessel at the quayside
- worker_5: any worker as defined in Article 3 (a) of Directive 89/391/EEC who habitually uses display screen equipment as a significant part of his normal work (Fig. 9.2).

Therefore Worker is to be considered from the legal point of view, and therefore protected by the employment law, not just any person who simply works at some occupation but only those persons who are employed in a certain way, with a certain contract identifying certain tasks. The specifities characterizing each type of worker contribute to narrow the lexical meaning of the concept worker within the legal domain. Therefore the gap between the linguistic meaning and the semantic meaning do correspond to a different substantial legal coverage of real situations.

9.6.4 Extending Lexical Meaning

The extending action in the opposite sense serves to extend a lexical meaning which semantically appears wider and comprising further entries:
Directive 1985/374/EEC, Art. 2: Definition of Producer

1. The manufacturer of a finished product, the producer of any raw material or the manufacturer of a component part and any person who, by putting his name, trade mark or other distinguishing feature on the product presents himself as its producer.
2. Without prejudice to the liability of the producer, any person who imports into the Community a product for sale, hire, leasing or any form of distribution in the course of his business shall be deemed to be a producer within the meaning of this Directive and shall be responsible as a producer (Fig. 9.3).

The lexical meaning of the term producer could never have allowed us to consider as such the importer of a specific product nor the leaser of the product. The semantic

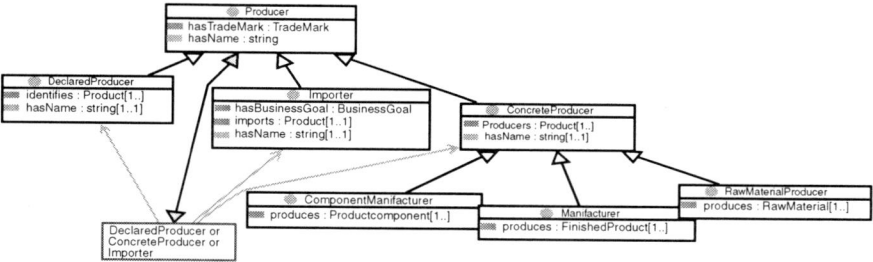

Fig. 9.3 Producer UML Representation

meaning arising directly from the definition given by the norm of the concept "producer", on the contrary, says that the norm is also to be applied to those persons who lexically are not included within the meaning of "producer" but who nevertheless are to be intended as such. Therefore, all subjects considered as producers by the norm and according to the semantic meaning of the concept are required to observe all legislative dispositions and obligations.

9.6.5 Outcomes

The analysis of the gap existing between the lexical and the semantic meaning of a term/concept within the legal domain allows us to track the possible relationships between linguistic resources and ontologies.

The importance of incorporating linguistic resources in ontology engineering has been stressed by Jarrar (2006): "Linguistic resources (such as lexicons, dictionaries and glossaries) can be used as consensus references to root ontology concepts. The importance of using linguistic resources in this way lies in the fact that a linguistic resources renders the intended meaning of a linguistic term as it is commonly agreed among the community of its language".

The set of concepts that a language lexicalizes through its set of word-forms is generally an agreed conceptualization. Usually, lexicographers and lexicon developers investigate the repeated use of a word-form (e.g. based on a comprehensive corpus) to determine its underlying concept(s).

Therefore from one side linguistic resources (such as lexicons, dictionaries, and Thesaurus, and dictionaries) are indeed important resources for identifying concepts and can be used as consensus references to root ontology.

From the opposite point it can be affirmed that lexical resources and semantic resources such as ontologies need each other and are complementary one to each other as ontologies allow to represent the complex relationship between the lexical and the semantic meaning of a term. More specifically the representation made by ontologies enables first of all to migrate from the term to the concept, which is something more consistent from the semantic point of view; secondly they enable to disambiguate the meaning of the concept setting it in a specific domain. This procedure seems to be very useful in the legal domain where the lexical meaning of a term hardly ever corresponds to the semantic one. Therefore the need to narrow or to extend the lexical meaning can be realized also from the formal point of view by representing the domain by using ontologies.

9.6.6 Discussion

The article describes the problems related to the construction of legal ontologies beginning from the illustration of analytical profiles of legal texts to arrive at the description of approaches, models and computational tools that seem more reliable because they are close to the processes for the formulation of the concepts elaborated by legal authority, in particular, in recognising that contexts of use play a fundamental role.

What above outlined is expected to be a further step towards the shift from lexical to formal knowledge, by means of tools and procedures that enable the two levels to be brought close together, so diminishing both the burden of the manual work and the arbitrary nature of links.

Nevertheless, our intuition is that, besides solutions at operational level, a deeper analysis of mapping relations between lexical and conceptual knowledge is necessary from the methodological level. In ontology engineering meta-ontologies for integrating heterogeneous lexical resources with formal ontologies have been already proposed and discussed (Picca et al. 2008). In the field of law a meta-model would clarify relations between different kinds of conceptual entities: as outlined above, in computational applications "legal concepts" are either intellectual artefacts or roles, sets of word-sense, sets of frame structures; either extensional or intensional characterization has been adopted for making distinctions in their semantics; the assumption is that changes in intension/extension in legislative definitions create new conceptual entities and that the role of judicial interpretation is to assign instances to classes. Finally, all activities directed to the representation of meanings belong to legal interpretation, but an ontological reformulation of a theory of interpretation and of legal concept construction seems not yet been completed.

References

Agnoloni, T., E. Francesconi, P. Spinosa (2007). xmLegesEditor: An OpenSource Visual XML Editor for supporting Legal National Standards. In *Proceedings of the V Legislative XML Workshop*, 239–251. Florence: European Press Academic Publishing.

Agnoloni, T., L. Bacci, E. Francesconi, W. Peters, S. Montemagni, G. Venturi (2009). *A Two-Level Knowledge Approach to Support Multilingual Legislative Drafting.*In J. Breuker, P. Casanovas, E. Francesconi, M. Klein (Eds.) *Law, Ontologies and the Semantic Web.* IOS Press, Amsterdam.

Allen, L.E., C.S. Saxon (1986). Analysis of the Logical Structure of Legal Rules by a Modernized and Formalized Version of Hohfeld's Fundamental Legal conceptions. In A.A. Martino, F. Socci (Eds.) *Automated Analysis of Legal Texts: Logic, Informatics and Law*, North-Holland, Amsterdam, 385–450.

Baker, C., F. Collin, C.J. Fillmore, J.B. Lowe (1998). The Berkeley FrameNet Project. In *Proceedings of the 17th International Conference on Computational linguistics*, Montreal, Quebec, Canada 86–90.

Buitelaar, P., P. Ciiano, B. Magnini (Eds.) (2006). Ontology Learning from Text: An Overview. In *Ontology learning*. IOS Press, Amsterdam.

Bacci, L., E. Francesconi, T. Agnoloni (2008). Ontology Based Legislative Drafting: Design and Implementation of a Multilingual Knowledge Resource. In A. Gangemi, J. Euzenat (Eds.) *Knowledge Engineering: Practice and Patterns, Proceedings of the 16th International Conference EKAW 2008*, Springer, Berlin, 364–373.

Biagioli, C., D. Grossi (2008). Formal Aspects of Legislative Meta-Drafting. In E. Francesconi, G. Sartor, D. Tiscornia (Eds.) *Legal Knowledge and Information Systems—JURIX 2008: The Twenty-First Annual Conference*. IOS Press, Amsterdam, 192–201.

Breuker, J., A. Valente, R. Winkels (2004). Legal Ontologies in Knowledge Engineering and Information Management. *Artificial Intelligence and Law*, 12(4): 241–277.

Breuker, J., R. Hoekstra, A. Boer, K. van den Berg, R. Rubino, G. Sartor, M. Palmirani, A. Wyner, T. Bench-Capon (2007). *OWL ontology of basic legal concepts (LKIF-Core)*. Deliverable 1.4, Estrella.

Dolbey, A., M. Ellsworth, J. Scheffczyk (2006). BioFrameNet: A Domain-specific FrameNet Extension with Links to Biomedical Ontologies.In *Proceedings of KRMed*. Baltimore, Maryland, USA.

Fellbaum, C. (Ed.) (1998). *WordNet: An Electronic Lexical Database*. MIT Press, Cambridge, MA.

Fellbaum, C., P. Vossen (2008). Challenges for a Global WordNet. In*Online Proceedings of the First International Workshop on Global Interoperability for Language Resources* (ICGL 2008), City University of Hongkong, January 8–12, 2008, 75–82.

Ferraioli, L. (2007). *Teoria del diritto e della Democrazia*. Volume primo, Laterza.

Francesconi, E., D. Tiscornia (2008). Building Semantic Resources for Legislative Drafting: The DALOS Project. In P. Casanovas, G. Sartor, R. Rubino, N. Casellas (Eds.)*Computable Models of the Law*. LNCS, vol. 4884. Springer, Berlin.

Fillmore, C.J., C.F. Baker (2001). Frame Semantics for Text Understanding. In *Proceedings of WordNet and Other Lexical Resources Workshop*, NAACL. Pittsburgh, PA, USA.

Gangemi, A., M.-T. Sagri, D. Tiscornia (2003). A Constructive Framework for Legal Ontologies. In V.R. Benjamins, P. Casanovas, J. Breuker, A. Gangemi (Eds.)*Law and the Semantic Web: Legal Ontologies, Methodologies, Legal Information Retrieval, and Applications*. IOS Press, Amsterdam, 97–124.

Gangemi, A. (2009). Introducing Pattern-Based Design for Legal Ontologies. In J. Breuker, P. Casanovas, M.C.A. Klein, E. Francesconi (Eds.) *Law, Ontologies and the Semantic Web—Channelling the Legal Information Flood*. Frontiers in Artificial Intelligence and Applications 188 IOS Press, Amsterdam, 53–71.

Gomez–Perez, A., D. Manzano-Macho (2003). *A Survey of Ontology Learning Methods and Techniques*,Ontoweb Deliverable 1.5.2003.

Hirst, G. (2004). Ontology and the Lexicon. In S. Staab, R. Stude (Eds.) *Handbook on Ontologies in Information Systems*. Springer, Berlin, 209–230.

Hoekstra, R., J. Breuker, M. Di Bello, A. Boer (2007). The LKIF Core Ontology of Basic Legal Concepts. In *Proceedings of LOAIT 2007*. Stanford University Palo Alto, CA, USA.

Jarrar, M. (2006). Towards the Notion of Gloss, and the Adoption of Linguistic Resources in Formal Ontology Engineering. In *Proceedings of the 15th International World Wide Web Conference*. WWW2006, ACM press, Barcelona.

Mustafaraj, E., M. Hoof, B. Freisleben (2006). LARC: Learning to Assign Knowledge Roles to Textual Cases. In *Proceedings of 19th FLAIRS Conference*. 11–13 May 2006, Melbourne Beach, FL.

Masolo, C., S. Borgo, A. Gangemi, N. Guarino, A. Oltramari, L. Schneider (2002). *WonderWeb Deliverable D17. The WonderWeb Library of Foundational Ontologies and the DOLCE Ontology*.

Masolo, C., Vieu, L., Bottazzi, E., Catenacci, C., Ferrario, R., Gangemi, A., Guarino, N. in D. Dubois, C. Welty, M.A. Williams (eds.), *Proceedings of the Ninth International Conference on the Principles of Knowledge Representation and Reasoning (KR2004)*, Whistler, Canada, June 2–5, 2004, pp. 267–277.

Narayanan, S., C. Baker, C. Fillmore, M. Petruck (2003). FrameNet Meets the Semantic Web: Lexical Semantics for the Web, Web Conference (ISWC 2003). Lecture Notes in Computer Science, 2003, Volume 2870/2003. Berlin, Heidelberg: Springer. 771–787.

Oltramari, A., A. Stellato (2008). Enriching Ontologies with Linguistic Content: An Evaluation Framework,*Ontolex*.

Peters, W., D. Tiscornia, M.T. Sagri (2007). The Structuring of Legal Knowledge in Lois. In *Artificial Intelligence and Law*. Legal knowledge extraction and searching & legal ontology applications, 15(2): 117–135.

Peters, W. (2009). Text Based Legal Ontology Enrichment. In N. Casellas, E. Francesconi, R. Hoekstra, S. Montemagni (Eds.) LOAIT 2009 IDT Series, Barcelona, 2009, 55–66.

Picca D., A. Gangemi, A. Gliozzo (2008). LMM: An OWL Metamodel to Represent Heterogeneous Lexical Resources. In *Proceedings of the International Conference on Language Resources and Evaluation (LREC)*, Marrakech, Morocco.

Ross, A. (1957 [1951]). Tû-Tû. *Harvard Law Review*, March 1957; 70(5): 812–825. Originally published in *Festskrift til Henry Ussing*. O. Borum, K. Ilium (Eds.) Kobenhavn Juristforbundet, 1951

Sartor, G. (2007). *Possesso e accettazione di concetti giuridici: un'analisi inferenziale*. In: *Analisi e diritto*, 67–89.

Sheffczyk, J., C.F. Baker, S. Narayanan (2007). Ontology-Based Reasoning About Lexical Resources.In*Proceedings of OntoLex 2006: Interfacing Ontologies and Lexical Resources for Semantic Web Technolo-gies, LREC-06*. Genova, Italy.

Searle, J.R. (1969). *Speech Acts: An Essay in the Philosophy of Language*. Cambridge University Press, Cambridge, MA.

Spinosa, P., M. Cherubini, G. Giardiello, S. Marchi, S. Montemagni, G. Venturi (2009). Legal Texts Consolidation Through NLP-Based Metada Extraction. In *Proceedings of ICAIL 2009*. ACM press, Barcelona.

Temmerman, R. (2009). Termontography and DOGMA for Knowledge Engineering within PROLIX. In R. Meersman, P. Herrero and T. Dillon (Eds.) *Proceedings of On the Move to Meaningful Internet Systems: OTM 2009*, Vilamoura, Portugal, November 1–6, Springer, Berlin, 534–543.

Tiscornia, D. (2006). The Lois Project: Lexical Ontologies for Legal Information Sharing. In *Proceedings of the V Legislative XML Workshop*, European University Institute, Fiesole, 14–16 June 2006.

Valente, A. (2005). Types and Roles of Legal Ontologies, in Law and the Semantic Web, LNCS, vol. 3369/2005, Springer, Berlin/Heidelberg, 2005, 65–76.

van Kralingen, R. (1993). A Conceptual Frame-Based Ontology for the Law. In *Proceedings of Jurix The Netherlands 1993*.

Venturi, G., A. Lenci, S. Montemagni, E.M. Vecchi, M.T. Sagri, D. Tiscornia (2009). Towards a FrameNet Resource for the Legal Domain. In N. Casellas, E. Francesconi, R. Hoekstra, S. Montemagni (Eds.) *LOAIT 2009*, IDT Series, Barcelona, 67–76.

Vossen, P. (Ed.) (1998). *EuroWordNet: A Multilingual Database with Lexical Semantic Networks*. Springer, Berlin/Heidelberg, 179.

Vossen, P., W. Peters, J. Gonzalo (1999). Towards a Universal Index of Meaning. In *Proceedings of ACL-99* Workshop USA: ACL.

Wyner, A.Z., R. Mochales-Palau, M.-F. Moens, D. Milward. (2010). Approaches to Text Mining Arguments from Legal Cases. In Francesconi E., Montemagni S., Peters W. and Tiscornia D. (Eds.) *Semantic Processing of Legal Texts*. Springer, Berlin/Heidelberg.

Wyner, A.Z., T.J.M. Bench Capon, K. Atkinson (2008). Three Senses of Argument. In P. Casanovas, G. Sartor, N. Casellas, R. Rubino (Eds.) *Computable Models of the Law*. Springer, LNCS, 2008, 146–162.

Chapter 10
A Legal Document Ontology: The Missing Layer in Legal Document Modelling

Monica Palmirani, Luca Cervone, and Fabio Vitali

10.1 Multi-layer Legal Document Modelling

CEN Metalex[1] is an open XML interchange standard for legal resources. It was developed with the awareness that plenty of national and local XML legal standards already exist or are being built inside of government, academic, private projects (Lupo et al. 2007; Vitali 2007). A lot of legal resources are on-line and in this moment all the European Members have a format for the on-line distribution of the Official Gazette resources (European Forum of Official Gazettes 2008a, b). So CEN Metalex seems to answer to the urgent request to normalize the abundance of local legal XML dialects. On the other hand a legal resource is a complex multi-layer informative architecture that includes several perspectives of analysis: (Fig. 10.1)

- text: part of the document officially approved by the authority with legal power;
- structure of the text: part of the document that states an organisation of the text;
- metadata: any information that was not approved by the authority in the deliberative act. The metadata can involve document description metadata (e.g. keyword), workflow (e.g. procedural steps in the bill), lifecycle of the document (e.g. history of the document over the time), document identification metadata (e.g. URL, URI, URN and annexes).
- ontology: any information about the reality in which the document act a role (e.g. for a judgement the juridical system concepts) or any concept called from the text that needs a modelling.
- legal knowledge representation: the part of the interpretation and modelling of the meaning of the text under legal perspective.

M. Palmirani (✉)
CIRSFID, University of Bologna, Bologna, Italy
e-mail: Monica.Palmirani@unibo.it

This contribution is a result of the Estrella IST-project IST-2004-027655.

[1] See: http://svn.metalex.eu/svn/MetaLexWS/documentation/2008proposal/2008proposal.pdf

G. Sartor et al. (eds.), *Approaches to Legal Ontologies*, Law, Governance
and Technology Series 1, DOI 10.1007/978-94-007-0120-5_10,
© Springer Science+Business Media B.V. 2011

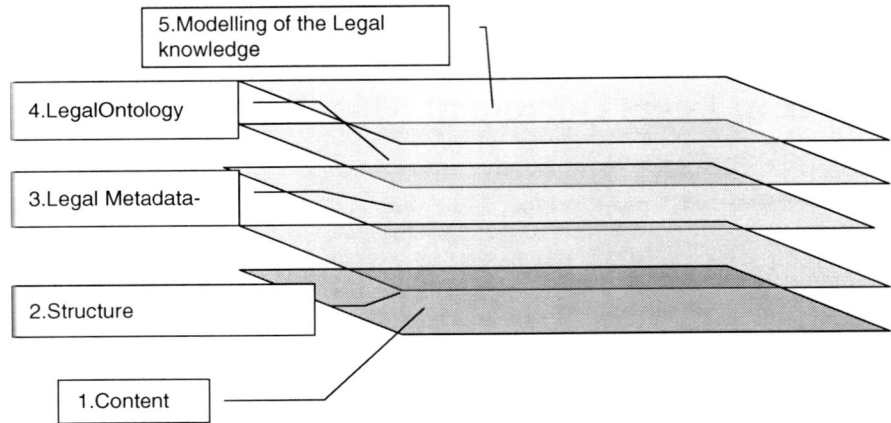

Fig. 10.1 Layers of representation in the legal document modelling

The complexity of the information included in a legal resource, the difficulty to interconnect all the layers in appropriate manner (granularity, cardinality of relationships, references, change over the time) and the need to harmonise heterogeneous sources convince us of the soundness to adopt a multi-layer architecture for legal cocument modeling. In this scenario CEN Metalex represents the layer 1st (text) and 2nd (structure) and in some way also the 3rd (metadata).

Nevertheless we need to put on the top of CEN Metalex a legal document ontology for permitting to all the other layer to referring to the part of the legal cocument not with the physical information (e.g. third block) but through semantic one (e.g. article 3). In the bibliographic field several XML standards (FRBR, Fremis, etc.) were adopted for modelling digital resources (e.g. book, manuscripts, music record, etc.), nevertheless they not include a semantic description of the legal main elements.

The purpose of this paper is to present LMIF—the Legal Metadata Interchange Framework—to fill this gap with the basic support of LIDO—the Legal Information Document Ontology. For demonstrating the LMIF effectiveness we start to analyze the CEN Metalex general principles, design approach and the characteristics. After we present LIDO that defines the ontology classes for modeling legal document structure semantically. The LIDO permits to assign to each neutral part cf CEN Metalex the appropriate legal significant using RDFa assertion in XML. For producing the RDFa assertion in an automatic way we use LMIF configuration that maps one time the native metadata meaning with the LIDO classes and produces to XSLT the information for including RDFa statement into the CEN Metalex file. In case the commitment is to not embed RDFa into CEN Metalex, an evolution of LMIF permits to foster directly the native metadata as originally thought.

10.2 CEN Metalex: Main Principles and Features

CEN Metalex is designed on several general principles as follows (Boer et al. 2008).

Reliance on existing standards. CEN Metalex is based on many web standards: XML, XML Schema, XML Namespaces, RDF, OWL, URIs, etc. It is also a Legal markup and takes in consideration the legal information resources organization. CEN Metalex implements its representation of the main legal document structure using architectural forms in XML. The attributes define the roles of the elements, and the element names are free to range in local vocabularies. This allows CEN Metalex to be neutral, general even if not generic.

Document Structure modeling and Pattern design. CEN Metalex should mostly concentrate the effort to preserve the structure of the original document in the conversion to XML. The attention is focused mostly on the content of the legal resources (document content) and on the metadata of the legal resources (document metadata). A strong subdivision between content, metadata and presentation is one pillars of the standard.

CEN Metalex is based on the strictly definition of data types (abstract, generic— simple and complex) and on the classes of elements (abstract and concrete). CEN Metalex is designed using 9 abstract element (*absBlock, absContainer, etc.*), 9 correspondent concrete elements, 11 abstract types (complex type) and 18 concrete types, 4 content model types (see the CEN/ISSS Workshop documentation for more details). Each element or content type belongs to one of the main 6 patterns: hierarchical containers (*hcontainers*); paragraphs (containers of text and inline elements); inline (no breaking of lines); milestones (empty elements in placeholder); metadata elements (values are specified as attributes or inside of Metadata containers—(*mcontainers*)—for collecting metadata elements).

General Descriptiveness. CEN Metalex preserves the original descriptiveness of the existing mark up in order to avoid in the normalization process to pass to an excessive generalization of the elements. For doing that a semantic and structural analysis of the original standard is necessary for understanding the meaning of each tag, attribute and its function in the description of the document. One other point of view it is to maintain all the naming of the original elements and attributes inside the converted document for allowing the reader to understand the result of the transformation. But this information is not enough for inferring the semantic meaning of the elements, especially in an heterogeneous document collection.

Metadata preservation. CEN Metalex is based on semantic RDFa statements for preserving the meaning of the original metadata but it is missing a real mapping between heterogeneous metadata models coming from different representations of the legal resources. CEN Metalex with RDFa statements can relate a particular metadata item to an ontology, thus making inferences possible on the assertion included in the document itself (it works mostly on literal and on the metadata value).

10.3 Supporting the CEN Metalex Model

Since CEN Metalex is a general interchange XML standard, it is not appropriate as a solution for marking up legal documents from scratch. So it is mostly used as intermediate document format for harmonizing heterogeneous document collections. For this reason CEN Metalex is supported by XSLT able to convert XML legal document already marked up in some national standard into CEN Metalex file.

For preserving during the conversion the meaningful of the metadata, we include RDFa assertions inside of the XML, for linking the structural part with the full ontology of classes, with clear distinction and no overlap of relations and literal values. For this reason it is not designed for capturing, with a direct descriptive tagging in the document, the semantic information of the structural parts, but the meaning of the textual components is surrogated through RDFa assertions. The RDFa works if a legal document ontology is well defined. So it is important to define a Legal Informatics Document Ontology able to fill the gap between the representation of the

This approach forces applications to extract from each document the assertions and to query on them. Our aim is to reinforce this mechanism and to improve the semantic annotation:

(a) to query the legal document through the ontology classes, using a meta-level and not through the literals embedded in the document;
(b) to produce the query using the original metadata naming embedded in the document and not the RDFa assertions that in some cases could be missed;
(c) to make reification queries possible at high level in order to discovery which national/local/native standards are using a given metadata item in the heterogeneous collection of documents (e.g. give me all the collection of document where is modeled the publication metadata).

To this end we introduce a middle layer called LMIF—Legal Metadata Interchange Framework- that can map each national standard metadata definition into the legal document ontology classes that are then used for retrieving the semantic information (one LMIF for each homogeneous collection of document).

In this way it is possible to define a minimal set of metadata, through LIDO, that allows the querying between heterogeneous legal documents based on different local or national standards and expressed in different languages. This mechanism (LIDO+LMIF) favors also the interoperability between different document databases (e.g. N-Lex[2] or Eur-Lex[3]).

This enrichment of the CEN Metalex potentiality is possible if an URIs naming convention is defined to identify the legal resources, even if they come from different applications, standards, and methodology. At the internal level, systematic ids need to be adopted to refer to parts and fragments.

---

[2]See http://eur-lex.europa.eu/n-lex/pays.html?lang=en

[3]See http://eur-lex.europa.eu/

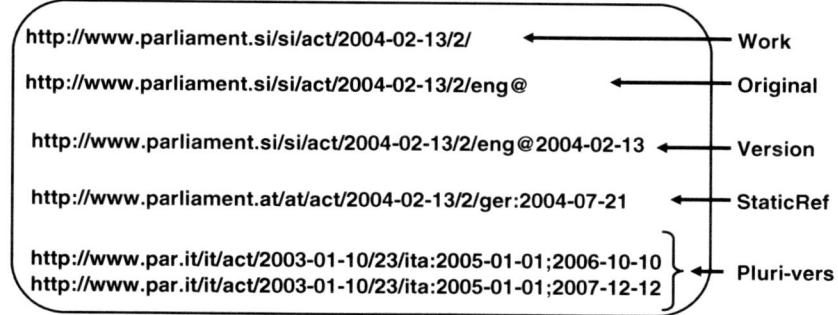

Fig. 10.2 Example of URI naming convention in CEN Metalex

Another important issue is to include a mechanism for representing the temporal model of the dynamicity of the legal document. It is expressed in the URIs naming convention and in the legal document organisation that permits versions, variants, plurality of versions, static and dynamic links are thus represented (Fig. 10.2).

10.4 LIDO—Legal Informatics Document Ontology

10.4.1 Definition of LIDO

If CEN Metalex is well oriented towards the structure of the document, it is missing a real legal document ontology to describe the legal meaning of the structural components in the text. So within a text marked up as a hierarchy container (*hcontainer*) it is not possible to distinguish between a chapter and an article because they use the same tag, the same properties, the same attributes and pattern. The same happens for each part of the legal document that includes legal axiological and ontological value, inalienable for the correct interpretation of the legal informatics resource as source of law. More and more the digitalization of the legal documents underestimates the semantic values and the legal validity. In order to maintain this important knowledge of the semantics of the parts in a legal document, it is fundamental to use a legal document ontology to represent it.

For this reason we have started to model a legal document ontology—LIDO—with the purpose to fill the gap in the state of the art in order to capture and model the legal axiological and ontological meaning of the structural parts of the legal document independently of the legal tradition, language, and standard used for the mark up.

LIDO is based on the FRBR ontology, takes inspiration from the CIDOC CRM and LKIF and from other important document ontologies created for bibliographic resources. On the basis of this consolidated state of the art we have taken in consideration the legal knowledge to fit in the document.

In our starting model focalised the attention on these first components:

a) The legal actions affecting the document and through the document (such as publication, delivery, etc.);
b) The legal temporal events (such as the date of commencement);
c) The structure of the legal resource (such as articles, etc.);
d) The semantic structure of the legal document organisation (preamble, preface, etc.).

Some examples of LIDO classes are described in the following specifying the definition, the axioms, the proprieties.

Legal temporal events

Class	Definition	Axioms	Property
Transposition_Event	Deadline within the member states must implement/ transpose the EU Directives into national Law.	It is > of the Delivery_Date It is > of the Commencement_Date	Transposition_Date
Modification_Event	Event when act the modification on the modified document	It is > of the Commencement_Date It is > of the Operational_Date	Source Destination Modification_Action Modification_Date Arguments
Commencement_Event	Event that starts the enter into force of the act	It is > of the Publication_Date	Commencement_Date
Operational_Event	Event that starts the efficacy of the act		Operational_Date
Delivery_Event	Event that deliveries the document		Delivery_Date Document_Number LegalDocType
Publication_Event		It is > of the Delivery_Date	Publication_Date Publication_Num Publication_Type Name_Publication

Structure of the Legal Resource

Class	Definition	Axioms
Higher_Division	Higher division of the legal resource	It is part_of Higher_Division
Basic_Unit	It is the basic normative element with a unique numbering in all the document. It is the basic of the normative citations.	It is part_of Higher_Division
Sub_Division	It is the basic normative element with a unique numbering in all the document. It is the basic of the normative citations.	It is part_of Basic_Element

10.4.2 The Reference Mechanism Between CEN MetaLex and LIDO

The reference mechanism for linking CEN Metalex to any external ontology is to use RDFa[4] assertion containing an RDF[5] statement.

The objective is to use the RDFa syntax to classify the structural part of the CEN Metalex text with the LIDO semantics added. The RDFa was chosen as syntax to allow embedding assertions directly in the document and for guaranteeing the self-containment of the semantic in-place into the XML structure and helping in this way web engines and spiders for using metadata to classify the document.

Furthermore RDFa was selected because it is possible, with an RDFa process, to extract in automatic way RDF statements also by reification.

On the other hand an important RDF construct can help this mechanism: the `rdf:type` predicate specifies a particular subject to be a member of the class in the object. Therefore the following statement says that the element `nir:pubblicazione` is an instance of the class `Act_of_Publication` (Table 10.1).

Table 10.1   Example of rdf:type usage

```
<rdf:Description rdf:about="nir:publicazione">
<rdf:type
rdf.resource="http://www.cirsfid.unibo.it/lido/lido.owl#Act_of_Publication">
</rdf:Description>
```

Example:

Using this predicate (rdf:type) we are able to exploit the RDFa syntax and permit an embedded annotation of the metadata within the XML structure, therefore we can use RDFa syntax for enriching the CEN Metalex with statements concerning the semantics of the structure.

RDFa uses the following syntax for making statements (Table 10.2)[6] :

Since in our case we need to connect the LIDO classes with their document values, we are using the above annotation approach respectively: for elements the second annotation (marked B) using the REL predicate; for the attributes the first annotation (marked A) with CONTENT.

The result inside of a CEN Metalex document using the embedded RDFa syntax is the following:

That means to say the following assertion:

1. the current document has a publication_act in the current metadata;
2. pubblicazione has a Type with value GU;

---

[4]http://www.w3.org/TR/xhtml-rdfa-primer/

[5]http://www.w3.org/TR/rdf-primer/

[6]http://www.w3.org/2006/07/SWD/RDFa/syntax/

Table 10.2 Example of RDFa syntax

A) ANNOTATION WITH A LITERAL

rdfa:about defines the subject. URI
rdfa:property defines the predicate. URI
rdfa:content defines the object as literal.

```
<rdf:about="" rdfa:property="lido:publication_date"
rdfa:content="19990517">
```

this statement says that the present document has a publication_date with content =
 19990517

B) ANNOTATION WITH A URI

rdfa:about defines the subject. URI
rdfa:rel defines the property where about is the subject.
 URI
rdfa:rev defines the property where about is the object
 (inverse property)
rdfa:href defines the object. URI

```
<rdf:about="" rdfa:rel="lido:publication_date"
rdfa:href="http://www.estrella.org/it/act/20041010/11/ita@/main.xml#span12">
```

this statement says that the present document's publication date is in the element with
 ID "span12"

---

3. pubblicazione has a number with value 113;
4. pubblicazione has Publication_date with value 19990517.

Finally using an RDFa processor (via XSLT) we obtain five RDF statements.

10.5 LMIF Level

10.5.1 LMIF Definition

The RDFa assertions are embedded within the CEN Metalex, therefore any semantic engine should be able to infer the semantic meaning of the local metadata element using the appropriate LIDO classes. Yet, this implies processing all the documents in a homogenous collection for detecting the correct semantic block inside each one of the XML documents. The engine devoted to process the semantic query, for this purpose, should infer all the mappings between the national metadata and the LIDO classes and in this approach the engine is not independent of the evolution of the XML standard or of LIDO itself.

Also during the conversion from national XML standard to CEN Metalex the RDFa annotation is no trivial task because the LIDO classes can change and vice versa also the metadata definition in the national standard could be modified. So an encoded solution, for instance embedded into an XSLT, is no longer a good solution.

A more reasonable approach is to externalise this mapping and use a vocabulary correspondence approach. So we define an LMIF (Legal Metadata Interchange Framework) layer that can make assertions on facts that are not explicitly present in the metadata items of the document but are inferred on the elements and the attributes of the local standard. LMIF is this a meta-level for making statements on the existing standard and making vocabulary independent the query as well as the semantic annotation inside of the CEN Metalex document.

This approach is clean and permits to the code of any engine or application to be unaware of the names of the LIDO classes or the native XML metadata items, but to rely on the LMIF definitions only.

As it is evident this approach has several advantages:

1. make assertions on the elements (tag) and attributes of a standard (reification);
2. maintain the semantic mapping outside of any application code;
3. separate in independent layers the levels of the standard design: CEN Metalex and LIDO can evolve independently;
4. produce a translator to access the RDFa sentences on the fly without requiring any the RDFa statement to be present, because it is possible to work on the LMIF mapping only;
5. provide better extensibility and maintainability;
6. map/integrate/compare different vocabularies coming from different local standards and make queries such as: return all the metadata items used in Europe for expressing the publication of the document.

LMIF fragment mapping the NIR[7] publication metadata into LIDO

10.5.2 LMIF Extension Syntax

Because LMIF was essentially RDF plain assertion, a new syntax XML was developed for expressing more complex metadata structure and relationships. The idea is to represent the mapping from national metadata into LIDO classes using a more expressive syntax that take in account the original structure of the modelled metadata.

In the case of the NIR element `nir:publication` we have the following nesting situation:

```
<pubblicazione tipo="GUUE" num="L 157" norm="20030626"/>
```

where the metadata publication is an element with three attributes. Following the RDF statement this means to break this tagging into at least four statements as

---

[7]NIR is NormeInRete Italian XML standard for making up legal document promoted by the CNIPA, Department of the Government. See for more details AIPA (2002).

Table 10.3 Example of RDFa statements into XML CEN Metalex

```
<mcontainer name="pubblicazione" id="metalex_idpubblicazione115252432"
xmlns:rdfa="http://www.w3.org/ns/rdfa/"; rdfa:about="" rdfa:rel="rdf:type"
rdfa:href="[lido:Act_of_Pubblication]" tipo="GU" num="113" norm="19990517">
    <meta id="metalex_idtipo115252488" name="pubblicazione-tipo"
    rdfa:about="#pubblicazione"
rdfa:property="[lido:Pubblication_Type]" rdfa:content="GU"/>
    <meta id="metalex_idnum115252592" name="pubblicazione-num"
    rdfa:about="#pubblicazione"
rdfa:property="[lido:Pubblication_Number]" rdfa:content="113"/>
    <meta id="metalex_idnorm115252672" name="pubblicazione-norm"
    rdfa:about="#pubblicazione"
rdfa:property="[lido:Pubblication_Date]" rdfa:content="19990517"/>
</mcontainer>
```

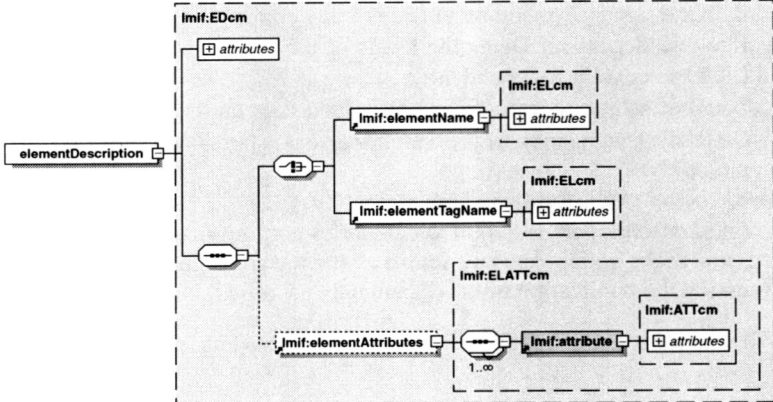

Fig. 10.3 elementDescription XML-schema tree

Table 10.4 RDF extraction form RDFa statements

```
<rdf:Description rdf:about="metalex_idpubblicazione115252432">
    <rdf:type rdf:resource="[lido:Act_of_Pubblication]"/>
</rdf:Description>
<rdf:Description rdf:about="metalex_idtipo115252488">
    <rdf:type rdf:resource="[lido:Pubblication_Type]"/>
</rdf:Description>
<rdf:Description rdf:about="metalex_idnum115252592">
    <rdf:type rdf:resource="[lido:Pubblication_Number]"/>
</rdf:Description>
<rdf:Description rdf:about="metalex_idnorm115252672">
    <rdf:type rdf:resource="[lido:Pubblication_Date]"/>
</rdf:Description>
```

showed in Table 10.3. But in this representation we can notice that we have missed the relationship that connects the main element and its attributes.

So we have designed an XML schema for improving the syntax expressiveness of LMIF with the intention to pass to OWL that promising to resolve also other complex situations.

ElementDescription element is introduced in LMIF for modelling element name, tag and its attributes in order to map more information on LIDO classes, properties and their relationships (Fig. 10.3 and Table 10.4).

In this way the previous definition shown in Table 10.5 is now represented in more expressive way as follows (Table 10.6):

Table 10.5 LMIF fragment related to the publication metadata

```
<?xml version="1.0" encoding="UTF-8"?>
<rdf:RDF xmlns:rdf="http://www.w3.org/1999/02/22-rdf-syntax-ns#"
     xmlns:rdfs="http://www.w3.org/2000/01/rdf-schema#"
     xmlns:nir="http://www.nir.it/2.0"
     xmlns:dsp="http://www.normeinrete.it/nir/disposizioni/2.0"
     xmlns:lido="http://www.cirsfid.unibo.it/lido/"
<rdf:Description rdf:about="nir:pubblicazione">
  <rdf:type rdf:resource="[lido:Act_of_Publication]" />
</rdf:Description>
<rdf:Description rdf:about="nir:pubblicazione-tipo">
  <rdf:type rdf:resource="[lido:Publication_Type]" />
</rdf:Description>
<rdf:Description rdf:about="nir:pubblicazione-num">
  <rdf:type rdf:resource="[lido:Publication_Number]" />
</rdf:Description>
<rdf:Description rdf:about="nir:pubblicazione-norm">
  <rdf:type rdf:resource="[lido:Publication_date]" rdf:datatype="xsd:date" />
</rdf:Description>
```

Table 10.6 LMIF new syntax

```
<rdf:Description rdf:about="nir:pubblicazione">
  <lmif:elementDesription type="required">
    <lmif:elementName value="nir:pubblicazione"
meaninng="[lido:Act_of_Publication]" vocabulary="http://www.cirsfid.unibo.it/lido/"/>
    <lmif:elementAttributes>
      <lmif:attribute name="nir:tipo" type="required"
meaninng="[lido:Publication_Type]" vocabulary=" http://www.cirsfid.unibo.it/lido/"" />
      <lmif:attribute name="nir:num" type="required"
meaninng="[lido:Publication_Number]" vocabulary=" http://www.cirsfid.unibo.it/lido/"" />
      <lmif:attribute name="nir:norm" type="required"
meaninng="[lido:Publication_Date]" vocabulary=" http://www.cirsfid.unibo.it/lido/"" />
    </lmif:elementAttributes>
  </lmif:elementDesription>
</rdf:Description>
```

10.6 Conclusions

The CEN Metalex is vocationally an interchange format and it is the best candidate to harmonize the plenty of obsolete legal XML standard not based on pattern, not designed using triple metadata assertion and with not clear division between content, metadata and presentation. For doing that some translators were developed as prototype inside of Estrella project (NIR, Metalex and Akoma Ntoso). But this conversion is not full if a legal document ontology is not used for linking the semantic part to the structure. We have proposed an embryonic legal document ontology—LIDO—that we intend to complete (partially is already available in OWL) and a mechanism for connecting LIDO to the XML structural part through RDFa annotation.

Moreover we have defined LMIF, a middle layer, that helps to make the mapping not only on the literal but associating the native metadata vocabulary with LIDO concepts. We discovered during the Estrella pilot cases that RDF syntax is not enough and an extension was made for capturing also the hierarchy and the nested metadata relationships.

During this second phase of the research we add also the possibility to access to the semantic without the RDFa statement but using directly the LMIF assertion.

The future work will concentrated on two tasks: (1) to improve the LIDO for making it a robust ontology fully inclusive of axioms useful for enhancing the engine retrieval[8] and the semantic query; (2) to improve the syntax of LMIF for permitting to express more and more complex native XML metadata structure. LMIF is able to normalize in triple RDF complex metadata structure for favouring a better exploitation from the web applications.

References

AIPA, Circolare AIPA/CR/40, Formato per la rappresentazione elettronica dei provvedimenti normativi tramite il linguaggio di marcatura XML, GU n. 102 del 3/5/2002.

Boer, A., W. Radboud, F. Vitali (2008). *MetaLex XML and the Legal Knowledge Interchange Format, in Computable Models of the Law*. Springer, Berlin Heidelberg.

European Forum of Official Gazettes (2008a). Report of the European Forum of Official Gazettes, 5th meeting Madrid, 25–26 September.

European Forum of Official Gazettes (2008b). Consolidation Interim Report of the Working Group, European Forum of Official Gazettes, 5th meeting Madrid, 25–26 September.

Lupo, C., F. Vitali, E. Francesconi, M. Palmirani, R. Winkels, E. de Maat, A. Boer, P. Mascellani (2007). General xml Format(s) for Legal Sources—Estrella European Project IST-2004-027655. Deliverable 3.1, Faculty of Law, University of Amsterdam, Amsterdam, The Netherlands.

Vitali, F. (2007). Akoma Ntoso Release Notes. http://www.akomantoso.org. Accessed 20 Januray 2009.

---

[8] See the paper presented in the Legislative XML workshop, Jurix 2008, *A native XML repository for heterogeneous legal resources: eXistimas*, Palmirani, Cervone.

Chapter 11
From Thesaurus Towards Ontologies in Large Legal Databases

Ángel Sancho Ferrer, Carlos Fernández Hernández, and José Manuel Mateo Rivero

11.1 Introduction

Legal information publishers are in the middle of a historical paradigm shift due to the shift in information technology support from paper to electronic. Not only is the change seen in delivery platforms or interface design, but also a huge increase in the number of documents to be managed, and a change in the technology to exploit "smart content".

These tools—that have worked for centuries—do not scale to new volumes of content, neither for the users that prefer full-text searching over navigating indexes nor for the investments by publishers to maintain and manually classify such a large number of documents.

While ontologies are a more sophisticated and promising modeling paradigm for automatic content processing, they have two limitations. First, today's user interfaces are focused on simplicity to enable the customer to provide simpler queries and thus inhibit exposing the full power of ontologies. Second, search engines at present remain unable to exploit knowledge using the full power of ontologies.

"Since the classic 'Handbook of Legal Information Retrieval' was published in 1984, improvement in legal information retrieval has not seen any major advancement. Quite to the contrary, information overload (...) has amplified the basic problems." (Mandala et al. 1998)

A first step to improve the efficiency of the search in legal databases is to understand what differentiates an expert's behavior from that of a novice, and to what level that expertise may be expressed in algorithms and data structures. One key observation is that experts are able to "build better queries," both for full-text and traditional paper taxonomical queries. Experts are more efficient because they have more knowledge on vocabulary, the content of collections and information tools. As expressed by Bunnell's Laws of Retrievability: "Everything is stored somewhere. The secret to retrieving things is simply finding out where they are stored".

Á.S. Ferrer (✉)
Research and Development Department, Wolters Kluwer Spain, Madrid, Spain
e-mail: asancho@wke.es

G. Sartor et al. (eds.), *Approaches to Legal Ontologies*, Law, Governance and Technology Series 1, DOI 10.1007/978-94-007-0120-5_11,
© Springer Science+Business Media B.V. 2011

So the question now is how to help users to formulate the "correct query" for that problem in that collection and retrieval engine. Or as expressed by John Brockman "in the last 50 years we have taught our Children answers to build knowledge; in the next 50 years we need to teach them to ask the right questions, since anyone can assume that all answers are just there" (Brockman 2002).

So the challenge is how and which methodology should be used to integrate the expert's knowledge into a search system. How can the search engine be made to work as a Conceptual Legal Search Engine, which makes a novice's query behave like an expert's query?

This paper is organized as follows: Section 11.2 details legal users' concrete needs, according to studies of their searching behavior. Section 11.3 explains why traditional knowledge classification systems (thesauri, taxonomies, table of contents) are not enough in large databases, and modern ontology solutions are still unmanageable in terms of performance in searches of millions documents. Section 11.4 describes technological developments, namely, the methodology of the legal dictionary used by the search engine and the benefits for the user of semantic processing. In Section 11.5, we briefly present other search developments. Section 11.6 describes future works and challenges. Finally, Section 11.7 presents the conclusions.

11.2 How Do Legal Professionals Search?

Information needs of judges and lawyers are more sophisticated than those of common web searchers:

- Their queries are more complex because legal problems involve not only finding an "object" (site, person, book, item) but describing a set of facts and legal consequences that cannot be expressed in only two or three words.
- Their results must be more precise, as the consequences of their analysis imply more responsibility. A "good result" is not enough. They must explore alternatives exhaustively and granularly.

When new search features are developed for legal professionals, it is almost compulsory to adapt them to the user's actual needs and behavior. Legal professionals are not technically oriented. Experience demonstrates that most of them will not make any extra effort to understand a search engine's internal logic. Therefore, the actual tendency is not to make the search forms more sophisticated but to anticipate the usual behaviors and mistakes. It is necessary to know how users search and what kind of problems they have when searching.

As explained in a previous paper, more than 80% of the queries actually made in a legal database are expressed as pure full-text searches (Sancho-Ferrer et al. 2008). Only a small percentage of queries use a thesaurus, tables of contents or metadata. In fact, this trend is increasing each year.

Users' more common complaints when doing legal research are: "there are too many results in the results list" or "depending on how I express the same idea of mine, the retrieved documents are different."

The search process is basically the same on paper and in electronic databases. It is a process of "trial and error" in which the user must do multiple queries until he finds the correct terms in a paper index or the query that retrieves good documents in a database. "Finding the correct search terms is a game of change, language approximation is minimal and even simple linguistic tools are missing" (Liebwald 2007).

11.2.1 Query Formulation for Paper Indexes

Sometimes we forget that this is also what happens in paper searches. The following description about legal research in printed material is illustrative (Elias and Livinkind 2005): "The first step in using the index and table of contents in any law book is to look up the key word in that index and table. If that's not successful because the word is not in the index or the index does not lead to relevant material in the book, the next step is to think of as many different phrasings and contexts of the word as possible. You simply will not know for sure whether or not a word will be fruitful until you try it".

For instance, let's think that your research question is whether "a drunk driving conviction results in the loss of a driver's license". The first step is to determine some key terms. One index classifies the issue under "intoxicating liquor, operating under the influence of", another one classifies it under "operating vehicle under influence of intoxicating liquor" and a third index classifies it under "driving under influence of drugs". These are three different starting letters of the alphabet to begin the exploration of different taxonomies.

11.2.2 Reformulation Strategies for Full-Text Search Engines

The way to formulate and reformulate queries in electronic tools to solve legal problems is different from those for paper tools, as the query does not only consist of trying a word in an index but of creating a natural language formulation. The kind of query reformulations we found can be classified in three groups:

- *Adding new terms.* The user begins with a very simple query, just with a few terms, that will retrieve a huge amount of documents and, for this reason, the user will have to add new terms to the query in order to reduce the number of results.

  Sometimes the user will add new terms that he has just read in the results list or sometimes will add terms that were already in his mind but were not included in the original query in an effort to avoid a very small result list.

  As a result of this, the new query retrieves fewer documents (Fig. 11.1.)
- *Deleting terms of the query.* Sometimes the user begins with a complex query with a lot of terms but he does not obtain good results. In those cases, the user will delete terms from the original query to simplify it.

  As a result of this new query, the user retrieves more documents (Fig. 11.2).

| Retenciones no declaradas |
| Retenciones a cuenta no declaradas |
| Retenciones a cuenta no declaradas en sociedades |

| Liquidación complementaria |
| Contabilidad liquidación complementaria |
| Impuesto Sociedades liquidación complementaria |

Fig. 11.1 Examples of query reformulation by adding terms

| Pensión compensatoria como rendimiento del trabajo |
| Consideración de la pensión compensatoria |
| Pensión compensatoria |

| Traslado de trabajador a otro centro |
| Traslado de trabajador |

Fig. 11.2 Examples of query reformulation by deleting terms

| Impuesto sociedades barricas |
| Impuesto sociedades toneles |

| Cotizaciones en el extranjero |
| Cotizaciones comunitarios |

Fig. 11.3 Examples of query reformulation by using alternative terms

- *Changing terms.* On occasions, after an unsuccessful query that fails to retrieve the necessary documents, the user will change the query terms with related or similar terms. The changed query will be as simple or as complex as the original one but with different terms.

  After changing terms, the user obtains different results (Fig. 11.3).

11.2.3 Expert's Behavior

An important point to frame the problem is understanding the differences between the queries formulated by experts and non-expert users.

Experts reformulate less because they construct a better query. But what is a better query and what kind of knowledge enables "creation of better queries"? Experts:

- know the legal domain, the categories to which reduce the problem;
- know the contents of the concrete database (the vocabulary used in those documents and concrete cases read so they can select terms of that specific case); and
- know the search tools to select (Boolean operators, thesaurus structure, tables of contents).

Experts select better "index terms" (from the thesaurus or from the specific collection) and follow better search strategies. For instance, while most users create a search such as "*leasing de un automóvil*", experts create a query like "*(leasing OR 'arrendamiento financiero'*) *NEAR (vehiculo OR coche OR automóvil)"*. They add synonyms, both from their knowledge of law and the documents, and construct a computer-oriented information request.

11.3 Information Tools

Certain knowledge-related concepts are dependent on the technology that supports auxiliary devices for the memory:

– The concept of "searching information" had no meaning in an oral culture.
– The need for "indexes", "metadata" or "thesaurus" appeared when the information on paper exceeded the quantity that could be explored by pure sequential search.
– The concepts of "natural language queries" or "relevance sorting of the results list" appeared only with the emergence of electronic databases.

As the Library of Alexandria grew in size, locating relevant material became increasingly difficult. The problem was how to help library patrons find an item when the repositories became too large for a sequential search. The poet Callimachus (ca 305–240 BC) solved the problem by compiling a catalogue called *The Pinakes*.

The solution was to create additional data, auxiliary information about the items: metadata, taxonomies, indexes, search engines and ontologies in that chronological order, so that they became the main types of tools to help tofind information.

11.3.1 Metadata

Metadata—data about data—are simply additional information about an object. They can be used (i) in an index, as categories to classify documents at indexing time by librarians or problems at search time by users; or (ii) in a sequential selection, namely, once in front of a list or on bookshelves (i.e. summary, title).

Another distinction can be made between objective and subjective metadata. Subjective metadata are more valuable, particularly metadata that describe the facts and consequences of a document, but they are also the most subtle and expensive to be created.

Moreover, metadata are the key piece that permits the creation of (i) indexes, that is to say, links to documents or pages; or (ii) taxonomies, namely, links to other terms. Metadata, when viewed from the index point of view are terms (a class, a hierarchy, a search space partitioning).

11.3.2 Indexes

An index aids the search by being a Search Space partitioning tool, defining a number of regions—that is, clusters or classes—to be used as navigation points.

It requires some structure, such as alphabetical order or other structure that can be navigated and, at each point, enables a clear decision for getting to the target:

- Indexes, catalogues (of books in a library), concordances (to pages in a book).
- Cluster of similar items and clustering is rather subjective to the test collection and the criteria used.

11.3.3 Controlled Vocabularies and Taxonomy Browsing

The next challenge is to control what terms can be used for indexing (classifications for the librarians) and searching (queries for users).In each type of metadata (index, facet), this can be limited by a plain closed list of terms that have been enumerated explicitly (controlled vocabularies) or more sophisticated views.

Taxonomies allow index terms (classes, subjects) to be arranged in a hierarchy. Thesaurus extend taxonomies and thus make them better able to describe the world by providing more relations between terms, such as "Broader Term (BT)", "Narrower Term (NT)", "Scope Note (SN)", "USE (another term is preferred instead of it)", "Top Term (TT)", "Related Term (RT)".

The use of a taxonomical list of terms (classification) is the most common way to access information, in the form of Tables of Content or Topical Indexes. In practice, most thesauri are just taxonomies or are exposed as that. Specialized taxonomies can be very useful for navigation in certain segments of legal activity because they express unique vocabulary in a limited number of highly focused nodes.

According to Foskett (1997) the main purposes of a thesaurus are basically:

1. To provide a standard vocabulary for indexing and searching—a controlled vocabulary
2. To assist the user in locating terms for proper query formulation (learning the domain).
3. To provide classified hierarchies that can broaden and narrow the current query request according to the user's needs (reformulating the query).

11.3.4 Thesaurus' Disadvantages

For the user:

- As the thesaurus tree becomes bigger, finding a concept in it becomes more difficult and requires more specialization and familiarity with the categories of the classification scheme.
- Due to its complexity, a thesaurus is more often "searched" instead of "browsed" in combination with full text search.
- It is harder to formulate complex queries because the thesaurus permits only hierarchical navigation whereas users want to enter "natural" search terms.

- In practice, some important nodes are over-developed and others under-developed, or some sections are not used (the first level can be too complex for a quick browsing operation and thus it must be searched).

For the Publisher:

- The modification of a thesaurus structure is difficult because this modification requires reclassification of documents. Document collections are dynamic and thesauri need regular maintenance.
- Analysis of documents delays time to market.
- Classification of documents is subjective, both for the analyst and the user.
- Thesauri are not useful for huge content collections.
- Users do not use them, as explained in Sancho Ferrer et al. (2008). Thesauri are losing their historical value in differentiating products and driving users' product choices.

11.3.5 Search Engines

This technology is less than 30 years old, but conceptually it is the same approach as "automatic creation of indexes". Full text is the "index terms": no restricted vocabulary, although it can be controlled by the use of text-transformation techniques. Metadata restrictions and taxonomy browsing are added filters.

A search engine uses a flat model of terms. Therefore, the search engine knows nothing about the relations between terms and about the different role that attributes and types of relations should play in weighting or substituting of terms.

11.3.6 Browse Versus Search

The Association for Computing Machinery's Special Interest Group on Information Retrieval provided the following description of the role of Faceted Search for a 2006 workshop:

"The web search world, since its very beginning, has offered two paradigms:

- Navigational search uses a hierarchy structure (taxonomy) to enable users to browse the information space by iteratively narrowing the scope of their quest in a predetermined order, as exemplified by Yahoo! Directory, DMOZ, etc.
- Direct search allows users to simply write their queries as a bag of words in a text box. This approach has been made enormously popular by Web search engines, such as Google and Yahoo! Search.

Over the last few years, the direct search paradigm has gained dominance and the navigational approach has become less popular. Recently a new approach has emerged that combines both paradigms, namely, faceted search.

Faceted search enables users to navigate a multi-dimensional information space by combining text search with a progressive narrowing of choices in each dimension. It has become the prevailing user interaction mechanism in e-commerce sites and is being extended to deal with semi-structured data, continuous dimensions, and folksonomies".[1]

In the early days of the Internet, the debate was "directory" versus "search." Yahoo's approach was quality: "how can technology give quality results?". The answer was hierarchy: Yahoo adopted a directory approach to navigation and subcategories blossomed underneath (end of 1994).

As surfers moved from a stance of exploration ("what's out there?") to expectation ("I want to find something that I know is out there"), search as a navigational metaphor began to make sense. In late 1995, Yahoo added search to its directory.

"The shift from exploration and discovery to the internet based search of today was inconceivable. Now, we go online expecting everything we want to find will be there". (Mandala et al. 1998)

11.3.7 Ontologies

Ontologies in a general definition are just "the specification of a conceptualization" (Gruber 1993). "A conceptualization is an abstract, simplified view of the world that we wish to represent for some purpose" (ibid.). The Semantic Web has popularized the need for this shared semantics in machine readable formats.

"The project of a common ontology which would be accepted by many different information communities in many different domains has thus far failed. Not all conceptualizations are equal" (Smith 2003).

From the point of view of search, ontologies can be seen as just another level of sophistication of the thesaurus, adding not only more relations but attributes and restrictions for each node.

As the search engine's "inverted index" philosophy does not have any knowledge about the relations between terms, the challenge is how to use all that modeled knowledge, both in the interfaces and in a search engine without introducing noise or performance problems (Casellas 2008).

11.4 Core Developments of the Semantic Search Engine

In the following pages, we are going to describe our work in designing and launching a search engine for a large legal database (Wolters Kluwer Spain's La Ley Digital) using natural language, semantic expansion, relevance-ranked results lists, dynamic summaries and suggested terms, based on Lucene search engine.

With this aim in mind, we must point out, from the very beginning, that the goal of building a Conceptual Legal Search Engine (Hafner 1998; Liebwald 2007) and the idea of using a lexical database like WordNet for improving information retrieval are about two decades old. However, we still do not know any successful commercial solution.

---

[1]http://www.sigir2006.org/

In our opinion, this is because "a fundamental weakness of current information retrieval methods is that the vocabulary that searchers use is often not the same as the one by which the information has been indexed" (Mandala 1998). Consequently, we think that conceptual retrieval systems may help to solve this weakness as they "will search not only for words explicitly articulated by the user, but also for terms conceptually implicit in such requests" (Susskind 2000).

The conclusions of the efforts when using a lexical database as WordNet for information retrieval are that recall increased, but simultaneously precision and performance decreased (Voorhees and Harman 2005). Therefore, our approach to make the search engine work at the level of concepts, thus increasing recall, precision and performance, has required that we develop both the technology and methodology from the ground.

11.4.1 Goals of User Experience Design

After analyzing different levels of functionality and the affordability of solving each technological challenge, we decided that our main goal would be to create a quick search that generates confidence in the system's knowledge. For these reasons, we chose to only generate synonyms and provide feedback about the semantic processing:

– *Compulsory synonyms*: our dictionary only includes strictest synonyms and does not allow users to check and uncheck all the expressions. A check boxed list of expressions scares users and slows down the search process because the user has to think about which expressions to include in the search (although the user does not know the impact).
– *Expressions shown*: we only display a selected range of synonyms to the user in the interface. Only the more representative expressions of the concepts are shown, as a full list could be too long and almost unreadable. The aim is to increase the user's confidence in the system because it has recognized the query and the related concepts (Fig. 11.4).

11.4.2 Terms, Words and Concepts

Search engines deal with "*terms*" (dictionary of symbols), while humans deal with "*concepts*" (ideas representation), although the information is expressed in natural language which is stored and communicated in "*words*" (written symbols). The mapping between "words" and "terms" is solved through text-transformation algorithms (tokenization, normalization of case and accents, stemmers, stop words), that are a one-to-one relation modified by deterministic rules. Nevertheless, the natural language mapping between words and concepts is not a one-to-one relation and is thus more complex because:

– The same concept can be expressed with different words (synonyms that produce silence cannot retrieve documents).

Fig. 11.4 Natural language processing and semantic expansion of the query: "leasing of a motor vehicle"

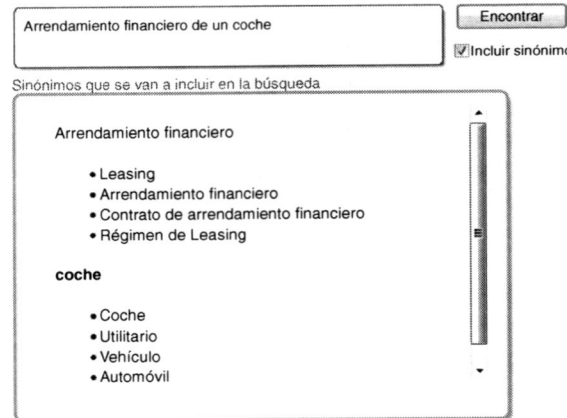

- The same word can refer to different concepts (polysemy, which creates noise by the ambiguity of retrieving bad documents).
- Several words together can have a specific meaning, different from each word individually (compound terms can create noise if not recognized as a literal expression).

In a first phase, we have decided to focus on a quick natural language query at the conceptual level. This means working on the strict synonym relation, and mapping simple and compound lexical expressions to concepts in the most transparent way to the user.

Semantic processing does not deal with ambiguous terms or other kinds of relations between concepts. However, the fact that the search engine is aware of concepts, not only isolated words, allows the following improvements:

- By including synonyms, a bigger number of potentially relevant documents are retrieved (*recall*).
- Through the recognition of compound terms, irrelevant documents are eliminated (*precision*).
- Conceptual indexing provides higher precision and retrieval speed (*performance*).
- These achievements collectively enable easy formulation of more complex queries (*natural language*).

11.4.3 Technological Developments

The goal is to make the search engine understand that a natural-language sequence of words like "loss of a driver's license for driving under the influence of alcohol" is using the same sequence of concepts despite the words used. For instance, this idea could be expressed as *"retirada del carnet de conducir por conducir en estado de embriaguez"* or as *"se le retiró el permiso de conducción porque conducía borracho"*. Although they do not have any word in common, the system should:

1. Identify that there are four concepts (some of these are multiword; stop words should be eliminated). For this query, there are about 70,000 different word combinations that the actual system recognizes as the same sequence of concepts.
2. Provide feedback through editorially created text about what has been understood, and the main synonyms that will be included in each concept.
3. Translate these codes into a query (term index) with relevance, highlighting, suggested terms and extracts.

The first step is to leverage the semantic knowledge. This structure (that we call "Knowledge Data Base") contains the lexical relations and is explained in Section 11.4.4. *An extended Synonym Ring-like database.* The second step is to integrate natural language with the search engine. Analytical technologies form the foundation for integrating semantic knowledge into a search engine, and this is where the natural language algorithm and dictionary introduces the text to the search engine. An inverted index structure is just a huge matrix of terms and documents: terms take the centre, so the mapping from the natural language symbols of the queries and the documents to a new coding of the basic symbol is the first step in changing the "understanding" of the search engine

There are two basic techniques to expand the semantics of the user's query.

1. Query cooking adds Boolean operators at query time (optional terms, phrasal terms, nested clauses, weightings). It is very flexible, but causes performance problems as collections grow along with the sophistication of semantic processing because more terms must be processed with Boolean operators. Query cooking also impacts highlighting and relevance scoring.
2. Injecting synonyms at index time solves these performance issues but requires developing specialized support technologies, such as analyzers and highlighters. These create several semantic levels of the same document and choose the abstraction specific query time processing.

Each of these techniques solves a part of the problem, but has limitations or side effects in:

– performance;
– relevance calculations;
– query parsing;
– highlighting;
– the mixed indexation of original and semantic views in the index;

- recognition of compound words (it is easy to go from one to multiple words but, for the reverse, two different analyzers must be used for the indexing and searching phases); and
- how to provide feedback for the user.

11.4.4 Index Time and Search Time Semantic Analyzers

The role of semantic analyzers is to transform the text of documents and queries into index terms. The classical tasks are tokenizing, normalizing, lemmatizing and removing stop words. Analyzers can enable other interesting transformations such as a soundex, fuzzy logic, geographical awareness, support for T9 keyboards and even color codifications (Gospodnetic and Hatcher 2005). Synonym-injection is an index process to add words not present in the document in the same position as the originally indexed word, so each word behaves equally at search time. This process has problems with compound expressions and highlighting.

For instance, the single concept of *"plan de opción de compra sobre acciones"*, a synonym expression of "stock options," should be indexed as multiple terms:

1. *Plan* (word)
2. *Opción* (word)
3. *Opción* (concept)
4. *Opción de compra* (concept)
5. *Opción de compra sobre acciones* (concept)
6. *Compra* (word)
7. *Compra* (concept)
8. *Sobre* (word)
9. *Acción* (word)
10. *Acción* (concept)
11. *Plan de opción de compra sobre acciones* (concept).

All eleven index terms of this example are different semantic views of one concept expressed in seven words. At search time, or when a human reads the text, there is only one concept. But during query formulation, any of those levels can be used to express the user's problem. For this reason, all of the inner semantics must be indexed, each one must retain some positional information and stop words must be removed. Some terms are just words without synonyms, while others are simple literal expressions to be treated as unitary symbols; and others are concepts with their own synonyms. The user can query at any of those levels, combined with other terms as well as at other levels of abstraction.

Processing complex queries and whole documents requires complex analysis, so efficient recursive routines are required. Two different analyzers must be created:

- The processing of documents at index time and at highlighting time.
- The processing of the query at search time and suggestion of terms from the result list to refine the query. This analyzer must be able to operate with and without

semantic processing, the query must provide an editorialized version of the most representative synonyms included and it must suggest the terms that have been tagged as useful for refining the query.

However, both analyzers working together are required for highlighting, one processing query terms and the other the document to tag.

The natural language algorithms pose two engineering challenges: (1) continuous matching against the semantic dictionary combined with detecting compound expressions requires controlled recursive processing; and (2) concepts can be contained in a broader concept that changes the meaning. In searching, the longest is what must be returned, and in indexing, all of them, but it is important to control when the buffer can be restarted safely.

The actual processing times in a single CPU are around 200 documents per second and 100,000 queries per second. This high performance is needed because the semantic analysis of texts happens in huge quantities and varieties in all parts of the search process (query, highlighting, term suggestion and indexation).

11.4.5 Data Structures and Authoring Methodology of the Semantic Dictionary

WordNet is the most extended and developed attempt to codify semantic and lexical information. However, the use of lexical ontologies such as WordNet has not been useful for us. Upon initial analysis, the approach appeared to meet our needs: a machine-readable lexical database that "is neither a traditional dictionary nor a thesaurus but combines features of both types of lexical reference resources. The building block of WordNet is a synonym set (synset) of all words that express a given concept." (Fellbaum 1998)

Our solution to map lexical expressions to concepts is a similar approach to the synsets or synonym ring, but soon the translation of that work was discarded as:

- The syntactical tagging does not help in most ambiguous search problems.
- The treatment of ambiguity creates noise, as a term belonging to two meanings will always expand to all the synonyms of all the senses.
- Other relations do not play a role in this phase of our system.
- The authoring methodologies are different (misspellings, text variations, when to create an expression or let the relevance play).
- More contents need to be developed.
- The integration with the search engine needed other structures.

To create the semantic dictionary, there are three different parts that need special data structures and author methodology:

- Indexation: information for the search engine, which is an exhaustive relation of lexical patterns, already processed by the analyzers.

– Search: information for the user, to be presented as feedback during query formulation, an editorialized selection of the main concepts.
– Suggested terms for refining queries presented in the results list—a selection of one of the lexical expressions as the most expressive of the concept, and a decision about whether this concept should be suggested for refining a query.

11.4.6 Criteria to Incorporate New Concepts and Expansion in the Dictionary

In this version of Wolters Kluwer Semantic Expansion, we are working only with pure synonyms and our experience is that we must be much more rigorous than we initially expected. Users will not complain about an expression that has not been created, but they will complain if a wrong expression is included and retrieves unexpected results.

In fact, synonyms are so natural to humans that most of the time users do not even notice the expansion ("yes, I've asked for 'leasing' and here there are documents about 'arrendamiento financiero', as I've typed in my query"). A common question is why we do not use a dictionary of synonyms. The reason is that they are more oriented to literature but, in fact, those are "similar or related terms", not exactly "interchangeable without changing the truth value of the proposition in which they are embedded".

The context can make "false synonyms", words that might act 90% of times as synonyms but in fact they are not, so there is the risk to bring the user something that is not strictly what he has requested. Consequently, more slow reading is needed to ask if the terms are:

– Are they pure synonyms? All of them equally interchangeable?
– Is there a risk of ambiguity?

There are very closely related terms that are not really synonyms (it is very usual in common language to use the part for the whole or a more abstract concept). Most of the time, they act as the same idea for a search, but maybe there is a concrete regulation or a sentence that determines different consequences because of small nuances. The only way to be sure is to read more documents (see below the Dynamic Summary, which is very useful for these internal tasks) and it is desirable to take a look at different document types to have multiple contexts (authors, judges and legislators).

As noted earlier, we do not create the ambiguous terms in this phase in order to avoid introducing noise. We let the relevance algorithms determine the correct meaning by a proximity with the other terms of the query. This has worked nicely, although more work in the future is needed as explained in Section 11.6.

11.4.7 *Compound Expressions*

There are lots of concepts expressed as a multiword expression that have a meaning different from the meaning of each individual word forming the compound (i.e. "value added tax", "stock options", "duty free shop"). Identifying these concepts (no double quotes) automatically avoids retrieving many documents that simply "have all the words" but are sent—through relevance ranking—to the bottom of the results list and are useless.

11.4.7.1 Typos

A non-obvious feature of this dictionary is that it becomes possible to identify and correct those typos that are necessary to retrieve documents. The traditional semantic approaches as WordNet do not solve typographical errors, as they are not a linguistic relationship. Nonetheless, this sort of errors can become essential for retrieval beyond what a "did you mean" feature can do.

For example, many legal documents talk about "*Vivenda*" instead of "*Vivienda*", but a "did you mean" functionality does not solve this problem. An indexation approach is needed; otherwise the documents containing the typos will not be retrieved. In fact, there are many documents that contain that typo and could constitute a large results list. If those documents are not retrieved, the user could think that there are not more documents. We have been surprised by the large number of typos in documents, some of them occur in the legislative text and cannot be modified by publishers. Typos are numerous in court decisions, but there are fewer occurrences in expert author's doctrinal content.

Our solution of handling typos semantically, at indexation time, eliminates the need for a "did you mean" solution. The semantic solution works regardless of how a word is queried or how it appears in a document.

11.4.7.2 Stop Words

Stop words typically do not contribute with meaning to the search and thus are removed from the query. Search engines typically consider articles and prepositions as being "empty." However, semantic expansion and expressions acknowledge the use stop words in creating compound expressions (sometimes called anti-phrasing) such as "a pesar de", "al hilo de", "teniendo en cuenta", etc.

Stop words are a concept of their own, just like the "zero" number was the last number to be "discovered", and once it receives this treatment, the algorithms fit logically.

11.4.7.3 Non-legal Terms

Additionally, a common misconception is that this is a "legal dictionary". A legal problem cannot just be represented with legal concepts because law deals with almost all things of common life (medical, financial, real state, etc.). Non legal concepts are, at least, 50% of the concepts used in real queries.

11.4.8 Term Suggestion Trough Local Content Analysis

The use of natural language and the automatic inclusion of synonyms in queries are the first part of creating a good query. A second step is creating more precise queries, reformulating them after reviewing the initial results set, e.g. adding words that provide better results. While the metadata-based faceted filtering exploits content attributes, it does not describe the problem more accurately.

The risk in refining queries is adding words:

– that produce zero results and
– with little meaning in the results set and that do not truly refine it and provide good documents.

The local content analysis methods use the semantic dictionary and a scoring by co-occurrence (also called unsupervised clustering or relevance feedback) (Liebwald 2007; Manning et al. 2008). These are new techniques that "leverage advanced statistics and may or may not provide acceptable results. These mathematically rooted techniques are still relatively new and rather unpredictable."[2]

It is common that the quality of the relevance algorithms development requires a cross-functional team of subject-matter experts who evaluate "when it works" and software engineers who identify "what could be changed". These statistical algorithms are integrating the former developments of semantic and dynamic document summary (beyond the scope of this paper):

– Semantics helps to select which terms to suggest as well as to extract the concepts from the documents.
– Dynamic Summaries help users to focus on the parts of documents that are more responsive to the query, which is done at high speed across large numbers of documents (Fig. 11.5).

11.4.9 Achievements and Benefits for Users

These achievements enable novice users to obtain similarly good results as expert users:

• *Semantic expansion*: by including synonyms in the query, users will not have to change terms of the initial query to add those synonyms as the system will do that for them. Confidence will be increased as the system generates more relevant synonyms than the ones the user would have in his mind. Finally, a more complex query can be formulated from the beginning because the system recognizes all those synonyms and their variations.

---

[2]http://www.ideaeng.com/pub/entsrch/2008/number_04/artile02.html#clustering

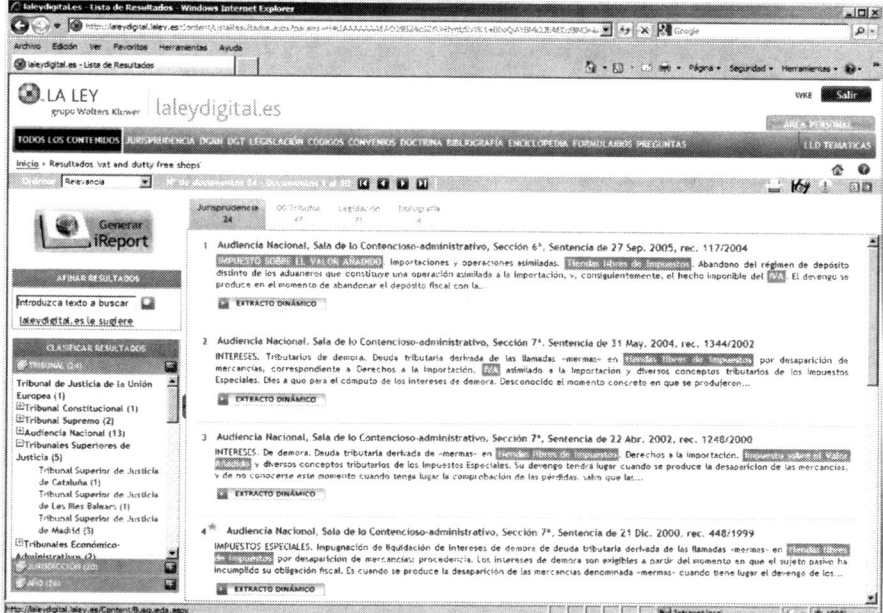

Fig. 11.5 Results page for the query "VAT in duty free shops"

- *Suggested concepts*: when users formulate very simple queries, they need some kind of assistant for obtaining more precise documents and avoid zero-hit results lists or irrelevant documents. To help users reformulate the query, we show the user a list of the most frequently occurring concepts in the documents retrieved so that he can easily add new terms to the query. Users benefit in two ways: they retrieve fewer documents but the documents that are retrieved are more relevant to the real problem they have to solve.

11.5 Other Search Functionalities Developed

Although this paper has focused on the semantic developments, it must be noted that they work together with other functionalities to leverage or complement the search experience. As explained before, the premises are:

– No query from two to four words reflects "a legal problem". There is always more information to add, to concretize the problem. Our markets need more precision such as eBay and Amazon.
– Experts create better queries because of their greater knowledge of the domain and the search technology.

But it is also important to note that:

– When working with databases lots of time is spent browsing and reading the documents.
– Users do not read beyond the first page of results.

In addition to the functionality explained above for improving query formulation (natural language, semantic expansion, suggested terms), there are new functionalities for the results list:

– New, improved relevance algorithms (Sancho Ferrer et al. 2008) that are specific to each document type and each product desired behavior. Scored relevance ranking is an important feature for query reformulation, as all the results that are beyond the second results page do not exist for the user. The user will thus reformulate the query even, if the best document could be in the results list. The suggested terms to refine the query are also obtained from the best documents.
– Faceted results. The historical approach of legal databases has been to expose as much metadata as possible in search forms to help the user precisely express his problem. The actual tendency is towards exposing the most frequently used metadata as post-search filters. It is the same information already present in pre-search metadata assistants. A related concept is universal search, without preselecting content sources and classifying the results by tabs, each one with its own metadata and term suggestions.
– Dynamic Summaries. Saves time in opening, scrolling and reading each document looking at "where and how this document is about my expressed query."

11.6 Future Research: How to Use Ontologies in a Search Engine?

The semantic expansion and suggested terms provide a new level in query reformulation through synonym substitution and the addition of terms. The next set of challenges deal with ambiguity and other relations between terms (hypernyms, hyponyms, meronims, Is-a, part-of/has-a), that need special treatment and that will add more quality in the future. Therefore, work with ontologies is required as they expand the terms expressed in a query term or in a document metadata in the following way:

• Suggesting alternative queries to be decided by users in the user interface.
• By the publisher's internal content enrichment, so instead of the simple controlled vocabulary for metadata or a thesaurus, they could use a whole range of elements of an ontology as index terms.
• By the search engine, as an autonomous Search Agent, capable of inferences and document selections without human intervention.

11.6.1 Interfaces and Internal Analysis Using an Ontology

Ontologies can be used to help users reformulate alternative queries in two ways:

– In the query: suggesting other terms or concepts to help his decisions. New user interfaces are needed for browsing ontologies.
– In the result list. Suggesting terms focused on a local content analyis, as it is done now but with more powerful schemas.

A related potential new task is the change in analysis work, using an ontology instead of a thesaurus as the model for classification, and enriching the nodes and attributes with expert knowledge for future exploitation by a search engine.

11.6.2 Characteristics of a Search Agent

A Search Agent is an autonomous software agent used for goal-oriented searching. It is more than a "reactive" results list calculator, which is what today's search engines are. Search agents are able to make ontological inferences to substitute query terms that a search engine can exploit.

The engine will be able to navigate through the terms as nodes of an ontology, to extract patterns of the set of indexed documents and raw content to suggest related terms and documents of the known collection, understanding the index as a representation of a sub-domain of knowledge enriched with external ontological structures of that domain. The main developments needed for this purpose are:

– The definition of the ontology structure to be managed by the search engine.
– The definition of an inference engine that can operate with a search engine and an ontology.
– Methodology to fill the ontology.
– A reliable Score Ranking. A score is not an absolute value, comparable between different queries, but only useful to compare a set of documents against a single query.
– Suitable performance, for all the whole new kinds of hidden calculations and explorations of the query terms and collection space.
– This also means challenges in usability: what to show before or after the query, how much can be done transparently, how much should be exposed to the interface and how much should be done automatically but with appropriate feedback.

The aim is to exploit the corpus of documents of an index as a "set of experiences" or knowledge in the same sense as an expert librarian could suggest "I remember having read something about something that could be also useful". As the search engine has "read" the contents, it can help users "to know what is there" in new ways beyond the traditional navigational use of the taxonomies.

So it will be necessary to combine statistical textual analysis and new algorithms in the search engine, turning the traditional scoring algorithms and the new term ontology into a tool for a search agent. There is a lot of potential knowledge in the index that when combined with external ontologies, and expert systems and decision-tree algorithms, can deliver new kinds of search improvements in traditional inverted index vector space models.

11.6.3 Other Improvements

The richer model to use at index and search time can deliver also other functionalities.

– Ambiguous terms. These should be solved in the indexation phase, only by the context and without a dialog with the user. It is simply not possible to mark the ambiguous terms manually in the documents.
– Personalized relevance, using metadata and user's profile. It is bout algorithms, not terms, but again it is a way to include in the query implicit information as the subject of interest or the geography. These special improvements can be achieved by the enrichment of documents, the connections with the users and the control of the algorithms.
– Recommendation of documents, using metadata and statistical analysis of documents, terms and users behavior.

11.7 Conclusions

The mission of professional information providers is the same: how to help to find suitable information for a problem. Users search because information means better decisions to solve a problem.

The new information support not only allows for new approaches but demands the creation of new kinds of content to take advantage of search technologies. We are in the middle of a change-of-scale problem, similar to what the Library of Alexandria faced. It means that we need to define new tools to manage those huge volumes of rolls, and what worked well up to 300,000 documents begins to be less efficient for 3,000,000 items.

Adding "knowledge" to the database makes it behave like an expert in law and searches. "Intelligence" should be no longer required from the user but from the tools we provide *working behind the scenes*. But this means more work: simplicity for the users means complexity for the publishers, investments in technology and moving from "smart content" to "smart search" have to take place.

The semantic indexation and natural language algorithms enable changing the way content is used by professionals and created by publishers, so the new search technologies oblige and allow new ways to approach the same cognitive problem of search (problem description and results selection).The new large repositories have created a change of scale that make subject-based taxonomy classification not suitable for the new availability of content.

Integration of thesaurus in a search engine is done only as a way to select a metadata and a clue for the relevance, but not used to reformulate queries or classify the results. Indexation is, from a cognitive perspective, the same as reading. The more knowledge the reader has, the better the understanding of what is being read. Nevertheless, the search problem remains the same:

- How documents should be enriched documents with auxiliary information to improve search? How to partition the search space? Which terms should be used to express useful information? When this information should be presented?
- How users should be taught to create good queries? How expert users' knowledge should be encoded in data structures and algorithms?

In the future, the librarian analysis will change to the new way of exploiting content enrichment and will have to adapt to the new information support technology. On the one hand, we are still solving the same cognitive problem for the user, which is the search of items, and on the other hand, publishers still have the same mission: creating auxiliary data and support for finding relevant content items. Nonetheless, the technology has changed the scale, the interfaces and the kinds of added value that can be included in large legal databases.

Acknowledgments We would like to thank John Barker, Director of Strategic Product Design in Wolters Kluwer's Global Platforms Organization, and Rosalina Diaz Valcárcel, Chief Execute Officer from Wolters Kluwer Spain, for their intellectual and professional support. We also want to underline the fact that most of these ideas were originated with Angel Bizcarrondo Ibáñez, from the Centro de Estudios Garrigues. Finally, we would like to acknowledge the interchange of ideas with Luis Pezzi, Manuel Cuadrado, Rene van Erk and Guy van Peel. This project has been funded by the Ministerio de Industria, Turismo y Comercio de España under the programs Profit (FIT-350100-2007-161) and Avanza I+D (TSI-020501-2008-80).

References

Brockman, J. (Ed.) (2002). *The Next Fifty Years: Science in the First Half of the Twenty-first Century*. Vintage Books, New York, NY.

Casellas, N. (2008). *Modelling Legal Knowledge Through Ontologies. OPJK: The Ontology of Professional Judicial Knowledge*. Ph.D. Thesis, Universitat Autònoma de Barcelona, Spain.

Elias, S., S. Levinkind (2005). *Legal Research. How to Find & Understand the Law*. 13th ed., Nolo Press, Berkeley, CA.

Fellbaum, C. (Ed.) (1998). *WordNet: An Electronic Lexical Database*. The MIT Press, Cambridge, MA.

Foskett, D.J. (1997). Thesaurus. In *Readings in Information Retrieval*. Morgan Kaufmann Publishers, Cambridge, MA.

Gospodnetic, O., E. Hatcher (2005). *Lucene in Action*. Manning Publications, Greenwich.

Gruber, T.R. (1993). A Translation Approach to Portable Ontology Specifications. *Knowledge Acquisitions*, 5(2): 199–221.

Hafner, C.D. (1980). Representation of Knowledge in a Legal Information Retrieval System. In *Proceedings of the 3rd annual ACM conference on Research and development in information retrieval*, Cambridge, England 139–153.

Liebwald, D. (2007). Semantic Spaces and Multilingualism in the Law: The Challenge of Legal Knowledge Management. In P. Casanovas, M.A. Biasiotti, E.F.M.T. Sagri (Eds.) *Proceedings of the Workshop on Legal Ontologies and Artificial Intelligence Techniques*, LOAIT-2007, at the International Conference on AI and Law (ICAIL'07) Stanford, 131–146.

Mandala, R., T. Takenobu, T. Hozumi (1998). *The Use of WordNet in Information Retrieval.* Coling/ACL Workshop, Montreal.

Manning, C.D., P. Raghavan, H. Schütze (2008). *Introduction to Information Retrieval.* Cambridge University Press, Cambridge, MA.

Sancho-Ferrer, A., J.M. Mateo-Rivero, A. Mesas-García (2008) Improvements in Recall and Precision in Wolters Kluwer Spain Legal Search Engine. In P. Casanovas et al. (Eds.) *Computable Models of the Law. Lanuages, Dialogues, Games, Ontologies.* LNAI 4884. Springer, Heidelberg, 130–145.

Smith, B. (2003). Ontology. In L. Floridi (Ed.) *Blackwell Guide to the Philosophy of Computing and Information.* Blackwell, Oxford, MA, 155–166.

Susskind, R. (2000). *Transforming the Law: Essays on Technology, Justice and the Legal Marketplace.* Oxford University Press, Oxford, MA.

Voorhees, E.M., D.K. Harman (2005). *TREC: Experiment and Evaluation in Information Retrieval.* The MIT Press, Cambridge, MA.

Chapter 12
The Computational Ontology Perspective: Design Patterns for Web Ontologies

Aldo Gangemi, Valentina Presutti, and Eva Blomqvist

12.1 Ontologies as Computational Artifacts

From a computational perspective, ontologies are artifacts that have a *structure*, a *function*, and a *lifecycle* (Gangemi et al. 2006; Gruber 2008). Structurally, ontologies consist in a vocabulary, which has linguistic features, and in a set of axioms, which have formal (logical, semantic) features. Functionally, ontologies "encode" a description of a world[1] for some purpose, e.g. the world of judgment procedures to be carried out, of normative systems to be maintained, of precedents to be collected and compared, etc. Therefore, ontologies must fit both a domain (e.g. *abusive discharge*) and a task (e.g. *collecting precedents*): this is implemented by representing the entities of the domain, by using the attributes and relations that are concerned by some purpose, e.g. social facts and agents as entities that are considered in an abusive discharge case, are dealt with by a judgment procedure, are involved in a norm conformity checking, etc. When representing those entities, the "limits" of an ontology are provided by the task that the ontology should help achieving, e.g. finding elements that are considered in different abusive discharge cases, matching case topics to legal professional competencies, time left, available funds, etc.

Finally, ontologies have a lifecycle: they are created, evaluated, fixed, and exploited just like any artifact. As an artifact, the *design* of an ontology is the core aspect.

In (Gangemi et al. 2006) ontology quality is modeled as dependent on good design. Three dimensions have been considered for quality assessment: *structure*, *content*, and *sustainability*. Structure can be measured objectively by considering various topological metrics on the ontology graph, or the formal consistency of the axioms. Sustainability can also be measured by matching the complexity of

A. Gangemi (✉)
Semantic Technology Lab, ISTC-CNR, Roma, Italy
e-mail: aldo.gangemi@istc.cnr.it

[1]That world can be the actual or current world, but it can also be a possible, counterfactual, impossible or desired world.

G. Sartor et al. (eds.), *Approaches to Legal Ontologies*, Law, Governance
and Technology Series 1, DOI 10.1007/978-94-007-0120-5_12,
© Springer Science+Business Media B.V. 2011

the ontology with the dynamics of the targeted world, and the resources and competences of the agency that has to maintain it. While important, however these dimensions are not enough to make an evaluation of an ontology for reusing or testing. Notably, *content* is the primary dimension of an ontology.

On the other hand, evaluating content compliance is not trivial. (Gangemi et al. 2006) singles out three evaluation sub-dimensions: *domain coverage, task coverage, and self explanation*. Domain and task coverage correspond to the intuitive fitness checks for artifacts that are mentioned above. An ontology for abusive discharge can be evaluated on its coverage of the relevant domain concepts, for example by means of matching the vocabulary of the ontology with a vocabulary extracted (manually or automatically) from e.g. a text corpus containing documents related to legal cases. But an ontology designer wants also an ontology that covers the relevant task(s) required by a project. In that case, we need to evaluate task coverage, which consists in characterizing the limits of an ontology project, typically by means of *competency questions*, e.g. *what type of firing parties have been sued by employees, and lost on their claims?*. If a designer is only interested in this kind of tasks, the ontology should contain enough content in order to answer a query like that one, in terms of vocabulary and axioms.

Ontologies can then span from a "domain-coverage-oriented" end (ontologies are in this case typically large and scarcely axiomatized), to an opposite "task-coverage-oriented" end (ontologies are in this case typically small-to-medium and quite richly axiomatized). Of course many ontologies fall in between the two ends of the scale.

The legal domain is very complex with respect to the typical social ontologies that currently dominate the semantic web, where computational ontologies have found a natural and pervasive use case. Legal knowledge builds on top of the physical and social worlds, actually creating a novel layer over the social world (Moore 2002).

Due to the autonomy (on one hand) and dependence (on the other hand) of the legal knowledge on both physical and social knowledge, legal reasoning tasks have evolved in a peculiar way, which include e.g. (cf. (Gangemi 2009)): *Requirement→Consequence* (if the factual knowledge is P, then the legal knowledge is Q), *Obligation→Right* (if A has an obligation towards B, then B has a right towards A), *Norm↔Case* (if a situation fulfils the conditions for violating a norm, it becomes a legal case), *CrimeScenario* (a crime is committed by a perpetrator and comes to the attention of authorities that pursue a criminal process), etc.

More than in regular tasks addressed by lightweight social ontologies, legal tasks denote the presence of *frames* (Fillmore 1968) that address the reasoning tasks mentioned. A frame is a unit of meaning that has cognitive reality. Cognitive agents use frames when interpreting their environment or other agents. Theories of meaning that attempt to assign specific concepts to words in general fail to take into account this important feature of cognitive agents. Words have meaning in context, and since a context is interpreted based on a frame, the context of word meaning is a frame. Frames have originated mainly in linguistics and cognitive science, and FrameNet (Baker et al. 1998) is still the most accurate resource for frames. In the legal domain, they have been studied in (Venturi et al. 2009).

Based on those and other considerations, e.g. modularity of knowledge, knowledge engineering has adopted the notion of frame directly (e.g. with (Minsky 1975)). or with names like "knowledge pattern" (Clark and Porter 1997) and "content ontology design pattern" (Gangemi 2005; Presutti and Gangemi 2008). While frames as units of meaning are not incompatible with the formal semantics currently in use for the semantic web e.g. with OWL (Mcguinness and van Harmelen 2004), they are not yet considered as the primary design objects for web ontologies and linked data (Bizer et al. 2009).

Web ontologies aim at formal consistency, or shared agreement of a vocabulary. Linked data collect huge amounts of facts to be used for querying interoperable data sources. For several domains, sparse facts and formally or pragmatically good ontologies are basically appropriate, even when their design is less than convincing cognitively speaking.

However, the complexity of some legal use cases (see Section 12.2) shows that sparse data or formally consistent models are not enough. They need a more accurate design, tailored to the task and cognitively plausible. Frames and knowledge patterns are a possible answer, as it is becoming clearer from realistic projects and experimentally (Blomqvist 2009; Blomqvist et al. 2010). A detailed defense of frames and knowledge patterns as the appropriate object of investigation in a pattern science for the Semantic Web is contained in (Gangemi and Presutti 2010).

In this chapter, we present a design-oriented view of computational ontologies: we concentrate on practical design issues and hybridization of methods and techniques (Section 12.2), referring to the *Ontology Design Patterns* (ODP) research programme (Section 12.3), and the eXtreme ontology Design (XD) methods (Section 12.4). Finally, we exemplify our perspective with a small legal use case (Section 12.5).

12.2 Ontologies and Applications

Ontology design is dependent in practice on (ontology) engineering applications, which involve the statement of functionalities and their implementation as techniques and tools. For a comprehensive framework of ontology design activities, and their relations to content, related data, formal languages, design patterns, social practices, organizations, teams, and functionalities, see (Gangemi and Presutti 2009b): it describes *codolight*, a network of ontologies for representing collaborative ontology design activities and data.[2](Adamou et al. 2010) is a tool that uses codolight for managing heterogeneous ontology engineering tools. In Section 12.4 we present some tools to support the methods for ontology design described in the following sections.

Before dealing with ontology design proper, we need to contextualize it within the broader ontology engineering techniques. Ontology engineering deals

---

[2]http://www.ontologydesignpatterns.org/cpont/codo/codolight.owl

with designing, managing, and exploiting ontologies within information systems. Ontologies are usually hybridized with other components in order to build semantic applications; e.g., when used jointly with:

- **query engines**, *querying* can be used to traverse the graph resulting from the encoding of the ontology, as well as to derive new assertions (e.g. with SPARQL (Pru 2008) Construct queries in case of RDF encoding of an ontology)
- **automated reasoners**, *consistency checking, implicit subsumption, instance and fact classification* can be performed to logically validate the axioms encoded in an ontology written in a formal language such as OWL (Mcguinness and van Harmelen 2004), as well as to infer new axioms that can be derived because of the logical axioms built in the formal semantics of the language
- **reengineering tools**, existing information resources such as relational databases, microformats, etc. can be transformed into semantic data, so extending the available knowledge spaces
- **matching tools**, ontologies can be linked together, enabling interconnected knowledge spaces (Euzenat and Shvaiko 2007)
- **computational lexicons, NLP tools**, and **machine-learning algorithms** (Basili et al. 2005; Coppola et al. 2009), *information extraction* and ontology learning from semi-structured and non-structured data make it emerge new legal knowledge to enrich or evolve legal ontologies (cf. (Gilardoni et al. 2005))
- **planning algorithms**, ontologies can assist or automatize *negotiation* or *execution* e.g. for *contracts, regulations, services*, etc. (García and Delgado 2005)
- **case-based reasoners**, ontologies can *formalize case abstractions* within more general frameworks, or can *classify cases* according to pre-designed descriptions (Forbus et al. 2002)
- **rule engines**, facts can be inferred e.g. for *causal responsibility assessment, conformity checking, conflict detection* and in general for *fact composition*(Gangemi et al. 2001, 2005).

Ontology engineering techniques are exploited in the context of "generic use cases" defined for a domain of application. In (Gangemi 2009), the main use cases for legal ontology-based applications are described, and related to the typical techniques employed for their implementation (Fig. 12.1). They are summarized here to better contextualize the computational ontology perspective in the legal domain:

- **Intersubjective agreement**: the task of getting consensus (or of discovering disagreement) about the intended meaning of a legal term, legal text unit, etc. This is inherent in any legal ontology project, but as a task *per se* is hardly pursued, since consensus reaching practices in Law are not carried out by adopting formal methods, and any formal representation has not been considered until now as a legal interpretation of a norm or regulation. For that reason, foundational ontologies in the legal domain are only appealing if they represent only partly axiomatized notions of e.g. *norms, legal facts*, etc., which are not specific of a given

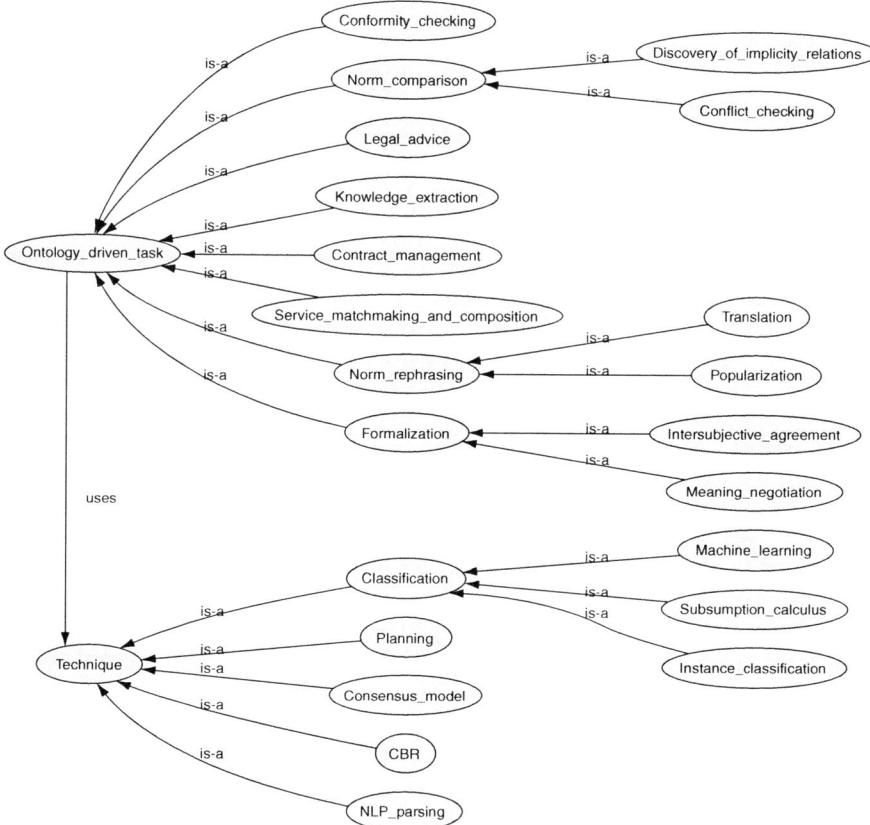

Fig. 12.1 A taxonomy of use cases for legal ontology-driven applications, and related techniques

legal system, and enable multiple, even conflicting specializations (cf. (Gangemi 2008) for a detailed discussion on how to formalize a domain-independent social or legal ontology involving norms).

- **Knowledge reengineering and extraction**: the process of extracting concepts, relations, named entities, and complex knowledge patterns from databases, documents, or corpora. This is a primary use case for legal knowledge engineering, due to the massive amount of unstructured or semi-structured legal information that constitute the sources for legal knowledge. In particular, methods based on the *linked data* principles (Bizer et al. 2009) can be used jointly with information extraction techniques, so generating large datasets of organizational and institutional knowledge, including legal data (cf. (Baldassarre et al. 2010) for a hybrid application in a public organization context).

- **Conformity checking**: the task aimed at verifying if a social situation (known in some way compliant with legal regulations) satisfies a legal description (norm, principle, regulation, etc.). In the generalized case, also situations already known to be legally relevant for some reason (e.g. a crime situation) can be checked for conformity against a further legal description (e.g. an appeal judgment procedure). This use case requires automated reasoning that goes beyond description logic classification engines, and e.g. needs rule engines, case-based reasoners (Forbus et al. 2002), and approximate inference engines to deal with open-textured concepts.

- **Representation**: a homogeneous language to represent both situations and the constraints from a legal description is highly desirable, otherwise a higher-order logic would be required to express constraints on constraints on constraints etc. on situations. The proposal in (Gangemi et al. 2005), briefly exemplified in Section 12.5, shows a viable approach to represent both constraints and instance data in a same, partitioned first-order domain of quantification.
- **Norm comparison**: the matchmaking between different norms. Norm comparison includes tasks such as: (i) *normative conflict checking* and handling between norms about a same situation type, (ii) *discovery of implicit relations* between a norm and other norms from a known corpus. Gangemi et al. (2005, 2001) show simple approaches to the classification of norm dynamics and conflicts within a finite set of norms after their first-order encoding.
- **Norm rephrasing**: expression of norms content in different terms, which can be either translations in a different natural language (Peters et al. 2007), or in a different form within a same natural language, e.g. for the purpose of popularization.
- **Contract management and execution**: a service assisting parties in the tasks of managing contract agreement and definition, and of following contract execution (García and Delgadoa 2005).

12.3 Ontology Design Patterns

Ontology Design Patterns (ODPs) are emerging as an important support for various ontology engineering tasks. Under the assumption that there exist classes of problems in ontology design that can be solved by applying common solutions (as experienced in software engineering), ODPs can support reusability on the design side. As described in (Gangemi and Presutti 2009a) ODPs can be of several types e.g. focusing on logical language constructs, architectural issues, naming, or efficient provision of reasoning services. In this paper we focus on Content ODPs (CPs). CPs are small (or cleverly modularized) ontologies with explicit documentation of design rationales, representing modeling best practices, and can be used as building blocks in ontology design (Presutti and Gangemi 2008). Gangemi (2009) contains examples of CPs for the legal domain.

As an example we describe a CP that is called *AgentRole*. It represents the relation between agents, e.g., people, and the roles they play, e.g., manager, meeting chair, father, and friend, as well as the disjointness of agents and roles. Figure 12.2

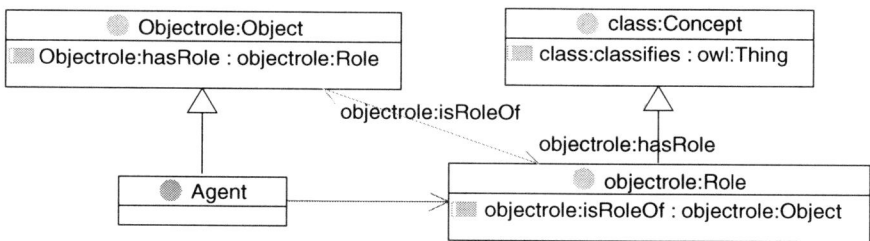

Fig. 12.2   The AgentRole Content ODP's graphical representation in UML

shows the UML diagram (produced by TopBraid Composer[3]) of the OWL version
of this CP. CPs are collected in different catalogues, such as the *ODP portal*.[4] In
addition to their diagrammatic representation, CPs are described using a number of
catalogue entry fields (c.f. software pattern templates), such as *name, intent, covered
requirements, consequences,* and *building block* (linking to an OWL realization of
the pattern).

Some legal examples will be presented in Section 12.5.

In Blomqvist et al. (2009) we presented the results of initial experiments on
CP reuse, showing that CPs are useful for constructing better and more (re)usable
ontologies. However, we also concluded that additional method and tool support
would be needed in order to truly benefit from CPs; common problems the participants experienced were to find the right CPs for their requirements, correctly
specialize and compose them, as well as discover possible mistakes in the solutions. In response to the results of the study in Blomqvist et al. (2009) we have
developed the XD Tools and a methodology (the eXtreme Design methodology—
XD) for CP-based ontology design (Presutti et al. 2009). The results of experiments
with such tools are reported in (Blomqvist et al. 2010), and show further improvements in team-based design practices, as summarized in the next section, which
introduces XD.

12.4 Extreme Ontology Design

With the name eXtreme Design (XD) we identify an *agile*[5] approach to ontology
engineering, a family of methods and tools, based on the application, exploitation,
and definition of ODPs for solving ontology development problems (Presutti et al.
2009).

---

[3]For notation details, see tool documentation: http://www.topquadrant.com/products/TB_
Composer.html

[4]http://www.ontologydesignpatterns.org

[5]We borrow the term *agile* from Software Engineering because XD is inspired by eXtreme
Programming and Software Factories as described in (Presutti et al. 2009).

12.4.1 XD Methodology for CP Reuse

We focus on XD for CP reuse in ontology design (hereafter referred to simply as 'XD'), which is currently the most elaborated part of the XD family. In XD a development project is characterized by two sets: (i) the problem space, composed of the actual modeling issues (local problems), e.g., to model roles played by people during certain time periods; (ii) the solution space, made up of reusable modeling solutions, e.g., a piece of an ontology that models time-indexed roles (a CP). Each CP, as well as the local problem, is related to ontology requirements expressed as *competency questions* (CQs) or sentences, but on different levels of generality. If a local problem can be described, partly or completely, in terms of the CQs of a CP, then that CP can be selected and reused for building the solution.

XD is test-driven and task-focused, resulting in highly modular ontologies where each module solves a small set of requirements. The main principles of XD include pair design, the intensive use of CPs, and collaboration; for details see (Presutti et al. 2009). The iterative workflow of XD contains 12 steps (Fig. 12.3), where the first four steps are concerned with project initiation, scoping, and requirements engineering (i.e. deriving the CQs from user stories), and the three final steps are concerned with the integration of modules into a final solution, hence, it is focused on the collaboration between the pairs. The evaluation of the collaborative part is

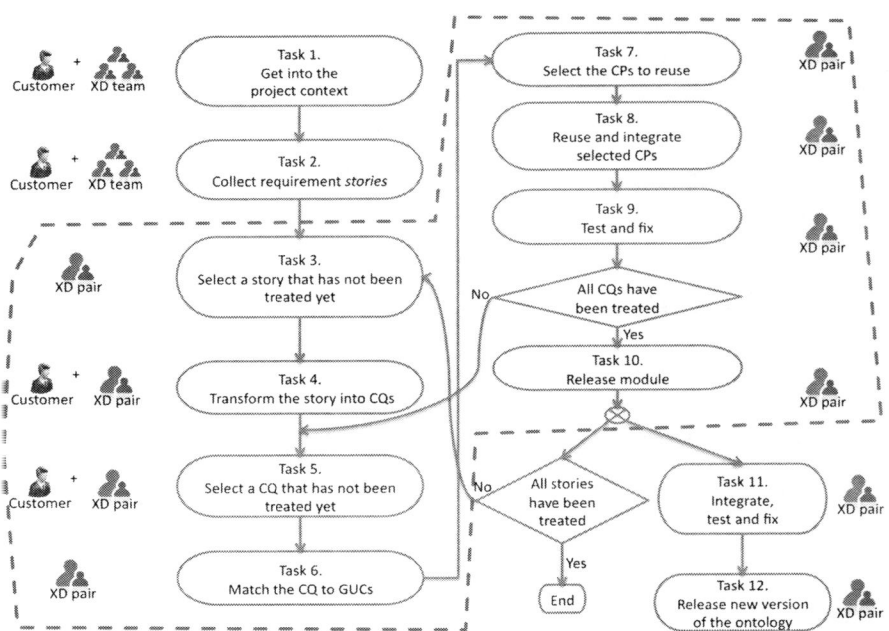

Fig. 12.3 XD workflow

ongoing work, hence we detail here the iteration by one design pair (creating and testing the modules), whereas the relevant steps include:

5. **Select a coherent set of CQs**. One or more of the CQs, i.e. a coherent set treating one modelling issue, are selected for a first development iteration.
6. **Match the CQs to CPs**. By matching the selected CQs to the requirements covered by CPs, candidate CPs for reuse are identified.
7. **Select CPs to use**. From the set of candidates the CPs that fit the local problem best, without unnecessary overhead, are selected.
8. **Reuse and integrate selected CPs**. Reusing CPs mean to import them into the ontology module to be built, specialize their classes and properties, and compose them, i.e., add properties or axioms that connect the CP specializations so that the module is able to answer the CQs.
9. **Test and fix**. The CQs are transformed into unit tests, e.g., SPARQL queries, and test instances are added. Tests are run, and any errors discovered are fixed, before selecting a new set of CQs for the next iteration.

12.4.2 XD Tools

The study presented in (Blomqvist et al. 2009) pointed at the need for tool support for ODP-based ontology design. The main needs identified by users were support for finding and selecting the right ODPs for their requirements, correctly specializing and composing them, and discovering possible mistakes in the resulting ontology. In order to address these requirements we have developed the eXtreme Design Tools (XD Tools),[6] a set of software components available as an Eclipse plugin, accessible through a *perspective* - eXtreme Design—compatible with Eclipse-based ontology design environments such as TopBraid Composer and the NeOn Toolkit.[7]

12.4.3 Main Functionalities of XD Tools

Currently, XD Tools is comprised of five main components supporting pattern-based design. The overall view of XD Tools GUI is depicted in Fig. 12.4. XD Tools' components are the following:

ODP Registry browser: Exposes sets of CPs to the user, in a tree-like view categorized by different aspects such as the domain of the CP (Fig. 12.4 bottom-left). In this way users can access a set of reusable CPs without having them locally stored. The default registry is provided by the ODP portal. The **ODP Details view** (Figure 12.4 bottom-right) shows all annotations of a selected CP. In this way CPs can be examined without downloading the

---

[6]http://stlab.istc.cnr.it/stlab/XDTools
[7]http://neon-toolkit.org

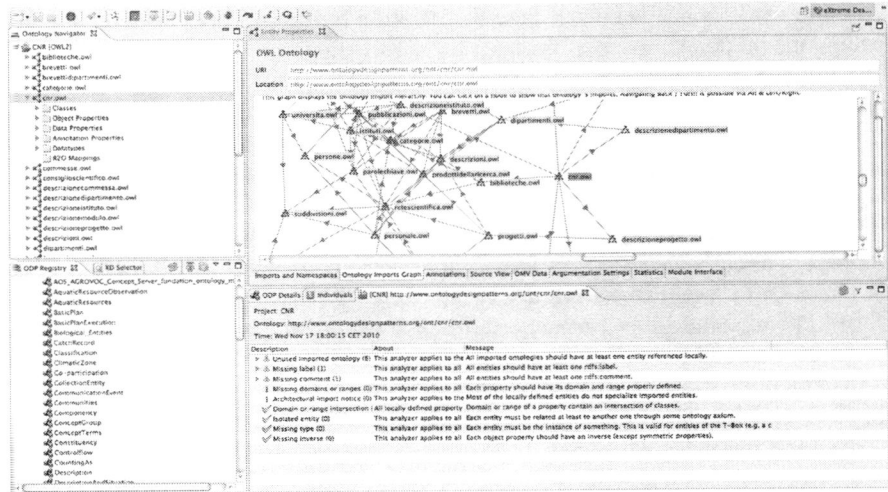

Fig. 12.4 XD tools GUI in the NeOn toolkit

OWL building block, or accessing an external website. By right clicking on a CP it can be downloaded through the "Get" command.

XD Selector: Proposes CPs, which can be reused, to the user. The task of matching the intent of a CP to the specific requirements can be challenging, especially if the CP catalogue is large. Since pattern selection is one of the most difficult tasks to automate, we have developed an extensible system that permits to plug in multiple services. Currently two services are available, i.e., search based on keyword indexing and latent semantic indexing, respectively. The suggested CPs can be downloaded through the "Get" command.

Specialization wizard: CP specialization, as the primary step of their reuse, concerns the specialization of ontology elements in the CP, through axioms such as subsumption. This can be challenging for an inexperienced user if it is done one element at a time, without guidance. From a user perspective, CP specialization has the following steps: (i) import the pattern into the working ontology, (ii) declare subClasses/subProperties for each of the (most specific) pattern elements needed, and (iii) add any additional axioms needed. The specialization wizard provided by XD Tools (Fig. 12.5(a)) guides the user through this process, with some steps being optional and some required. The wizard is activated by right clicking on a CP and selecting "Specialize".

XD Annotation dialog: Supports annotation of ontologies, based on customized annotation vocabularies. The annotation properties already provided by OWL/RDF and vocabularies such as OMV (Hartmann et al. 2005) and the CP annotation schema[8] are provided by default.[9]

---

[8]http://ontologydesignpatterns.org/schemas/cpannotationschema.owl

[9]Since CPs are small ontologies the properties can be used for ontologies in general.

XD Analyzer: Provides feedback to the user with respect to how "best practices" of ontology design have been followed. The XD Analyzer has a pluggable architecture, allowing to easily extend the set of heuristics expressing "best practices". Three levels of messages are produced; errors, warnings (identified "bad practices"), and suggestions (proposals for improvement). An error is, for instance, a missing type, i.e., all instances should have a specified class they are instances of. Examples of warnings are missing labels and comments, and isolated elements that are not referred to by other elements. Proposing to create an inverse for each object property that has no inverse so far is on the level of suggestions. An example view of the Analyzer is shown at the top of Fig. 12.4.

In addition, XD Tools provide several help functions, such as inline info boxes, help sections in the Eclipse help center, and cheat sheets.

12.4.4 Experimental Evidence for XD

Recent experiments (Blomqvist et al. 2010) on XD show the following improvements over the (already beneficial) usage of patterns without XD:

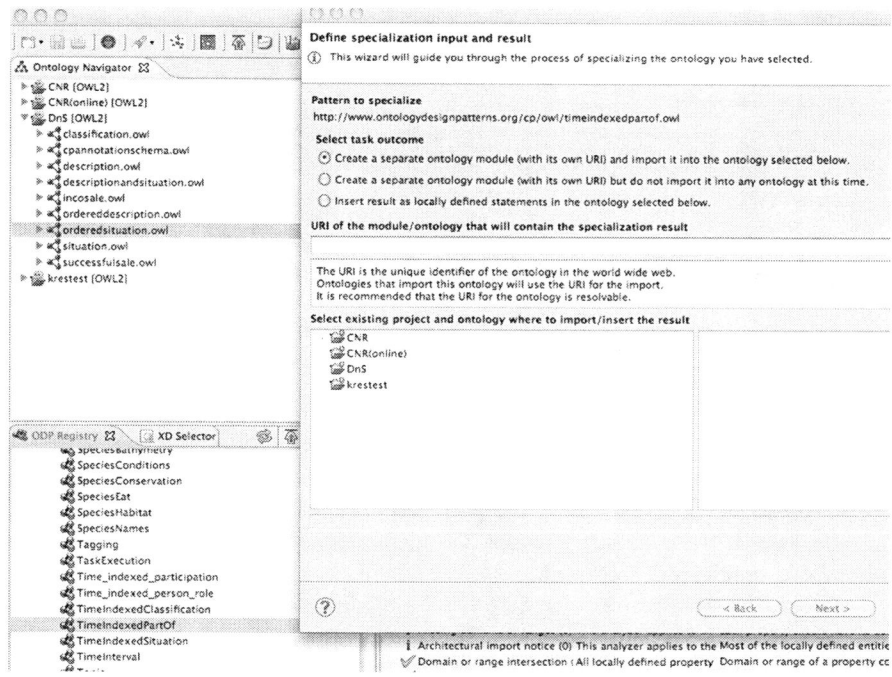

(a) Specialization wizard

Fig. 12.5 XD specialization wizard and annotation dialog

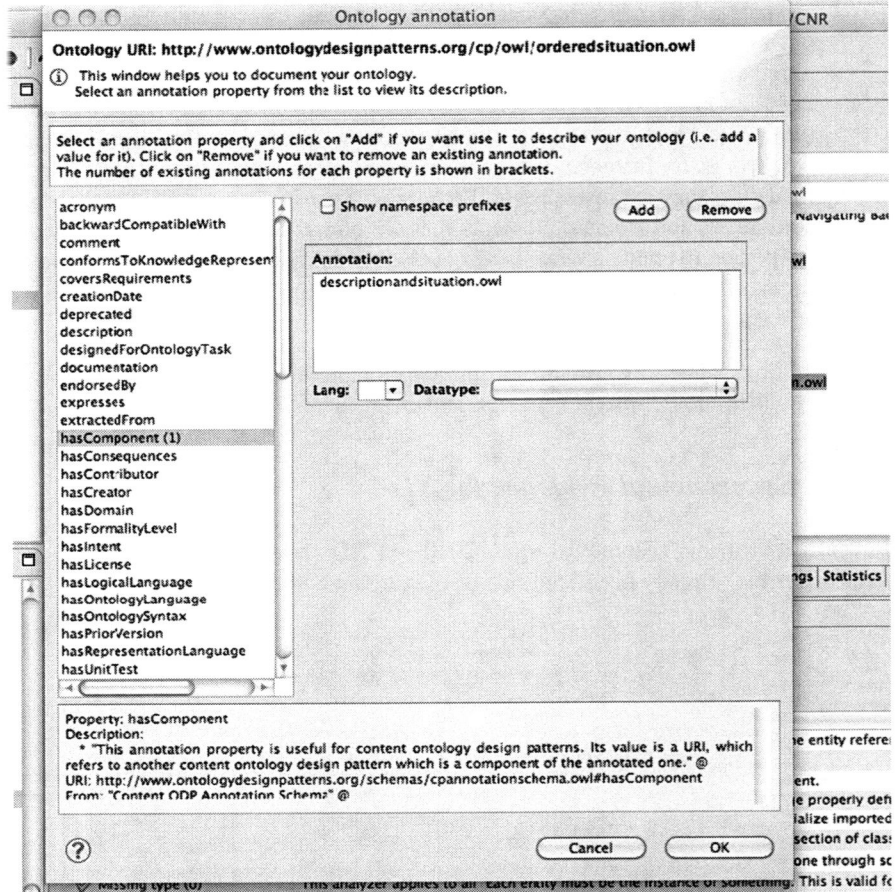

(b) XD annotation dialog

Fig. 12.5 (continued)

Usefulness of XD (1). That XD helped them to organize their work was proposed to the participants. Only 6% of the participant claimed they did not follow XD closely, hence, we conclude that the XD methodology is perceived as useful for organizing ontology design work.

'Natural' way to work with CPs (2). Methodologies are sometimes perceived as awkward and restrictive by users. However, participants felt comfortable with XD. From this we conclude that XD is descriptive and pragmatic.

Result quality (3). The terminological coverage of ontologies increased slightly (81% average across 3 different tasks), and the task coverage increased from 69 to 81%. The substantial increase seems to be in the task coverage.

Solving tasks faster (4). While still applying the same time limit to solve a problem, task and terminological coverage increased (although the increase in terminological coverage is limited).

Modelling 'mistakes' (5). The types of mistakes that are frequent are the same as in previous experiments, but with a decrease of the occurrence of the top-6 common errors of 15%. Two types of errors decrease significantly more than the others, i.e. the problems in representing n-ary relations (decrease by 64%) and missing datatype properties (decrease by 46%). We believe that the decrease can be attributed to the test-driven nature of XD. By requiring ontology engineers to test their model in a structured fashion, errors that can easily be discovered through unit tests.

We can confirm almost all of the results in (Blomqvist et al. 2009) when comparing to non-pattern-based design. However, terminological coverage kept stable in this setting while in the previous one it decreased. This can be easily explained by the new tool support, facilitating the reuse of CPs. The effects of the XD methodology can be seen mainly in the ontology quality, i.e., increased task coverage and particular previously frequent mistakes that drastically decreased. The frequent mistakes were all connected to missing parts, hence, we conclude that one main benefit of XD is its test-driven nature that forces the user to check every new module against the requirements. Additionally, we conclude that XD is perceived by users as a natural way of working with CPs.

XD Tools will be extended with more elaborate CP selection; we are currently working on methods for CQ-based CP selection rather than simple keyword search. Frame detection techniques (Coppola et al. 2009) seem to be key in the development of advanced CP selection.

12.5 A Legal XD Session

In this section, we will briefly exemplify the basics of XD-based ontology design with reference to the legal domain. Let's assume a team should develop an ontology for a semantic application that deals with abusive discharges, and has the following requirements, expressed in terms of competency questions (CQ) (Grüninger and Fox 1995) by an expert, e.g. a lawyer who is assessing the possibilities to take legal action against a company, on behalf of a customer:

1. who has sued someone for abusive discharge?
2. what parties have won in an abusive discharge cases?
3. what abuses are documented in abusive discharge cases?
4. what kind of parties have won in an abusive discharge cases?
5. what kind of abuses had more frequently the suing party win?

We concentrate only on the core steps here. The first core step (step 5 in Section 12.4.1), after eliciting the CQs from the expert (or extracting them from existing documentation), is to analyze the coherence of the steps: (1) to (3) are clearly the root CQs for gathering the basic knowledge: what cases, what parties won, and what abuses. (4) builds on top of (1) and (2), and (5) builds on top of (1) to (3). The designer will then try to match (step 6 in Section 12.4.1) the root CQs to existing CPs, and to select (step 7 in Section 12.4.1) the best-fitting ones. We document here only part of the process.

Matching can be made with the XD selection tool, but the legal coverage of ODP is still very small, and the current state of matching techniques for CPs only matches questions that are well documented in CPs.[10] In this case, a designer can design a new pattern, e.g. by matching the CQs to other repositories of frames that can be eventually reengineered as CPs. In order to highlight the relations between linguistic frames and CPs, we use here FrameNet (Baker et al. 1998).

For example, by using the *WordNet detour to FrameNet* tool (Burchardt et al. 2005),[11] it is possible to use WordNet relations to find closest matching frames even when the terminology is not already documented in FrameNet. The tool only starts from words, therefore we need to match frames incrementally. We detail the process for CQ1.

We firstly highlight the pivot words: *discharge, sue*. By firstly finding the near-synonyms of "discharge", we can find *dismissal*, which leads to the closest matching frame: *Firing*,[12] defined as: *An Employer ends an employment relationship with an Employee. There is often a Reason given for the action*. The elements of the Firing frame include *Employee, Employer, Reason, Position, Task, Place*, etc. For "sue", we use the similar *legal action*, and the detour tool returns the frame *Intentionally_act*,[13] which includes the elements: *Act, Agent, Event, Means, Explanation*, etc.

Once selected those two frames, step 8 requires us to reuse and integrate them. Since FrameNet is not a computational ontology, for reusing frames we employ its OWL version, called OntoFrameNet (Gangemi 2010). In OntoFrameNet, frames are encoded according to their original semantics: e.g. frames and frame elements are all individuals that have relations to lexemes, lexical units, etc. In semantic applications like the one we are designing an ontology for, the CQs require us to apply a *formal* semantics to concepts and relations (what cases, discharges, abuses, ...), therefore a refactoring is needed.[14] The typical refactoring pattern needed is described in (Coppola et al. 2009), and the results are depicted in Fig. 12.6 for the frame *Firing*.

After having *Firing* and *Intentionally_act* as CPs, we can use the XD specializer to specialize them; for example, by creating a new terminological skin to the Intentionally_act CP, as e.g. the *LegalAction* CP. We have so gathered an ontology that is rich enough to represent Employees that are discharged by Employers for some Reason, etc. Reasons, e.g. the Employee had reported suspicions of fraudulent

---

[0]There is ongoing work on implementing a broader matching tool.

[1]http://www.coli.uni-saarland.de/albu/cgi-bin/FN-Detour.cgi

[2]http://framenet.icsi.berkeley.edu/index.php?option=com_wrapper&Itemid=118&frame=Firing

[3]http://framenet.icsi.berkeley.edu/index.php?option=com_wrapper&Itemid=118&frame=ntentionally_act

[4]Not all semantic applications need such a refactoring, e.g. annotations and lightweight querying can use OntoFrameNet in its basic form.

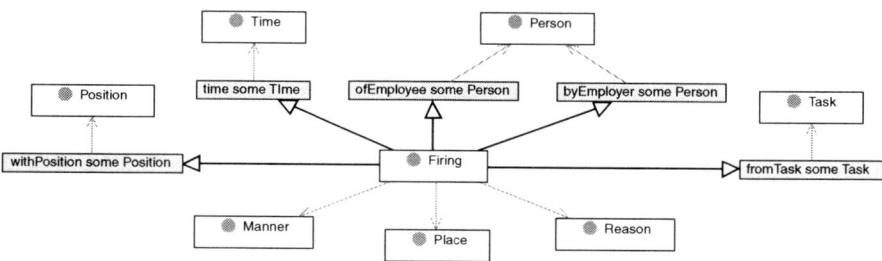

Fig. 12.6 The Firing frame in OWL, after its refactoring as a regular content ontology design pattern.

activity of the Employer to the police, for an abusive discharge can then be linked to the LegalAction CP as Explanations for taking action against the employer.[15]

This has been a sketchy reconstruction of the procedure, which also resulted longer because of the need to search for additional CPs. OntoFrameNet frames are going to be uploaded on the ODP portal: once there, the described procedure will be available directly from the XD selector.

There are more steps that can be carried out: testing and fixing (step 9), swapping requirements between pairs in a team, integration made by a separate pair, further integration with CPs selected or reengineered for the other CQs, etc.

12.6 Conclusions

We have presented a design-oriented view of computational ontologies. After referring to the typical methodological and technological environments of semantic applications in the legal domain, we have introduced ontology design patterns as the "ontology way" on linguistically and cognitively motivated frames as units of meaning. The eXtreme ontology Design methodology for using ontology design patterns has been sketched, and exemplified in a small legal use case.

Regarding other perspectives taken in this book, our view of computational ontologies is rather neutral. Philosophically speaking, whether a direct reference or a constructivist assumption is taken on ontology, it does not affect the design of computational ontologies: those assumptions just add more or less strong constraints on what kind of things should be represented. From the point of view of legal theory, whatever fundamental concepts are chosen will impact on the way legal frames are conceptualized and then reused for ontology design. Ultimately, it is only the matching between requirements (however they are conceived or declared) and solutions that counts for pattern-based design. Finally, issues related to the kind of representation and reasoning language should be used for legal

---

[15]A simple ontology that shows the result of XD for CQ1 can be downloaded from http://www.ontologydesignpatterns.org/cp/owl/legal/abusivedischarge.owl

ontologies: crisp, fuzzy, appropriate for open textured concepts, rule- or description-logic-based, etc. only partly affect pattern-based design: if requirements reveal the need for e.g. probabilistic versions of OWL, the solutions have to take into account also the extra-expressivity needed, but the methodology is not changed by that.

Acknowledgements This research was partly funded by the European Commission through projects NeOn (FP6 IST-2005-027595) and IKS (FP7 ICT-2007-3/No. 231527).

References

Adamou, A., V. Presutti, A. Gangemi (2010). Kali-ma: A Semantic Guide to Browsing and Accessing Functionalities in Plugin-Based Tools. In P. Cimi-ano, S. Pinto (Eds.) *Proceedings of the Conference on Knowledge Engineering and Knowledge Management (EKAW2010).* Springer, Galway, Ireland.

Baker, C.F., C.J. Fillmore, J.B. Lowe (1998). The Berkeley FrameNet project. In *Proceedings of the 17th International Conference on Computational Linguistics,* vol. 1. Association for Computational Linguistics, Montreal, Quebec, Canada, 86–90.

Baldassarre, C., E. Daga, A. Gangemi, A. Gliozzo, A. Salvati, G. Troiani (2010). Semantic Scout: Making Sense of Organizational Knowledge. In P. Cimiano, S. Pinto (Eds.) *Proceedings of the Conference on Knowledge Engineering and Knowledge Management (EKAW2010).* Springer, Galway, Ireland.

Basili, R., M. Pennacchiotti, F.M. Zanzotto (2005, February). Language Learning and Ontology Engineering: An Integrated Model for the Semantic Web. In B. Magnini (Ed.) *2nd Meaning Workshop* organized in Trento, Italy.

Bizer, C., T. Heath, T. Berners-Lee (2009). Linked Data – The Story So Far. *International Journal on Semantic Web and Information Systems,* 5(3):1–22.

Blomqvist, E. (2009). *Semi-Automatic Ontology Construction Based on Patterns.* Ph.D. thesis, Linkoping University, Department of Computer and Information Science at the Institute of Technology.

Blomqvist, E., A. Gangemi, V. Presutti (2009). Experiments on Pattern-Based Ontology Design. In *K-CAP 2009.* ACM, New York, NY.

Blomqvist, E., V. Presutti, A. Gangemi, E. Daga (2010). Experimenting with eXtreme Design. In P. Cimiano, S. Pinto (Eds.) *Proceedings of the Conference on Knowledge Engineering and Knowledge Management (EKAW2010),* Springer, Galway, Ireland.

Burchardt, A., K. Erk, A. Frank (2005). A Wordnet Detour to Framenet. In *Proceedings of the GLDV 2005 Workshop GermaNet II,* Bonn.

Clark, P., B. Porter (1997). Building Concept Representations from Reusable Components. In *Proceedings of AAAI'97.* AAAI press, Menlo Park, CA, 369–376.

Coppola, B., A. Gangemi, A.M. Gliozzo, D. Picca, V. Presutti (2009, June). Frame Detection Over the Semantic Web. In *6th Annual European Semantic Web Conference Heraklion, Greece (ESWC2009),* 126–142.

Euzenat, J., P. Shvaiko (2007). *Ontology Matching.* Springer, Heidelberg, DE.

Fillmore, C.J. (1968). The Case for Case. In E. Bach, R.T. Harms (Eds.) *Universals in Linguistic Theory.* Holt, Rinehart, and Winston, New York, NY, 1–210.

Forbus, K.D., T. Mostek, R. Ferguson (2002). An Analogy Ontology for Integrating Analogical Processing and First-Principles Reasoning. In *IAAI'02: Proceedings of the 14th conference on Innovative applications of artificial intelligence.* AAAI Press, Menlo Park, CA, 878–885.

Gangemi, A. (2005). Ontology Design Patterns for Semantic Web Content. In *The Semantic Web ISWC 2005,* LNCS, vol. 3729. Springer, Berlin.

Gangemi, A. (2008). Norms and Plans as Unification Criteria for Social Collectives. *Journal of Autonomous Agents and Multi-Agent Systems,* 16(3): 70–112.

Gangemi, A. (2009). *Introducing Pattern-Based Design for Legal Ontologies*. IOS Press, Amsterdam.

Gangemi, A. (2010). *What's in a Schema?* Cambridge University Press, Cambridge.

Gangemi, A., C. Catenacci, M. Ciaramita, J. Lehmann (2006). Modelling Ontology Evaluation and Validation. In *Proceedings of ESWC 2006*, 140–154. Budva, Montenegro.

Gangemi, A., D.M. Pisanelli, G. Steve (2001). A Formal Ontology Framework to Represent Norm Dynamics. In *Proceedings of the Second International Workshop on Legal Ontologies (LEGONT)*. Amsterdam, Netherlands.

Gangemi, A., V. Presutti (2009a). Ontology Design Patterns. In S. Staab, R. Studer (Eds.) *Handbook on Ontologies*, 2nd ed., International Handbooks on Information Systems. Springer, Berlin.

Gangemi, A., V. Presutti (2009b). The Collaborative Ontology Design Ontology (v2), Deliverable D2.1.2 of the NeOn project.

Gangemi, A., V. Presutti (2010). Towards a Pattern Science for the Semantic Web. In *Semantic Web Journal* 0: 1–7.

Gangemi, A., M.T. Sagri, D. Tiscornia (2005). *Legal Ontologies and the Semantic Web*, Chapter A Constructive Framework for Legal Ontologies. Springer, Berlin.

Garcia, R., J. Delgado (2005). An Ontological Approach for the Management of Rights Data Dictionaries. In *Proceeding of the 2005 Conference on Legal Knowledge and Information Systems*. IOS Press, Amsterdam, The Netherlands, 137–146.

Gilardoni, L., C. Biasuzzi, M. Ferraro, R. Fonti, P. Slavazza (2005). Lkms – A Legal Knowledge Management System Exploiting Semantic Web Technologies. In *International Semantic Web Conference*, Galway, Ireland 872–886.

Gruber, T. (2008). Ontology (Computer Science) – Definition in Encyclopedia of Database Systems.

Gruninger, M., M. Fox (1995). Methodology for the Design and Evaluation of Ontologies. In *Proceedings of IJCAI'95, Workshop on Basic Onto-Logical Issues in Knowledge Sharing, April 13, 1995*, Montreal.

Hartmann, J., Y. Sure, P. Haase, R. Palma, M. del Carmen Suarez-Figueroa (2005). OMV – Ontology Metadata Vocabulary. In C. Welty (Ed.) *Ontology Patterns for the Semantic Web Workshop*, Galway, Ireland.

Mcguinness, D.L., F. van Harmelen (2004, February). OWL Web Ontology Language Overview. W3C recommendation, W3C.

Minsky, M. (1975). A Framework for Representing Knowledge. In P. Winston (Ed.) *The Psychology of Computer Vision*. McGraw-Hill, New York, NY, 108–133.

Moore, M.S. (2002). Legal Reality: A Naturalist Approach to Legal Ontology. *Law and Philosophy*, 21: 619–705.

Peters, W., M.-T. Sagri, D. Tiscornia (2007). The Structuring of Legal Knowledge in Lois. *Artificial Intelligence and Law*, 15(2): 117–135.

Presutti, V., E. Daga, A. Gangemi, E. Blomqvist (2009, November). eXtreme Design with Content Ontology Design Patterns. In *Proceedings of the Workshop on Ontology Patterns (WOP 2009), collocated with ISWC-2009*, vol. 516. CEUR Workshop Proceedings.

Presutti, V., A. Gangemi (2008). Content Ontology Design Patterns as Practical Building Blocks for Web Ontologies. In *Proceedings of ER2008*, Barcelona, Spain.

Pru (2008, January). SPARQL Query Language for RDF. Technical report, World Wide Web Consortium.

Venturi, G., T. Agnoloni, S. Montemagni, M.T. Sagri, D. Tiscornia (2009). Towards a Framenet Resource for the Legal Domain. In P. Casanovas, U. Pagallo, G. Ajani, G. Sartor (Eds.) *Proceedings 3rd Workshop on Legal Ontologies and Artificial Intelligence Techniques joint with 2nd Workshop on Semantic Processing of Legal Text (LOAIT 2009)*, Barcelona, Spain 2: 67–76.

Chapter 13
A Learning Approach for Knowledge Acquisition in the Legal Domain

Enrico Francesconi

13.1 Introduction

Knowledge modelling represents a structural pre-condition for implementing the Semantic Web concept as well as intelligent systems dealing with legal information. In the last few years many efforts have been made for implementing legal ontologies and a vast literature exists in this domain (see (Breuker et al. 2009) for a state-of-the-art review). One of the main problem in this field, addressed in literature, is represented by a trade-off existing between *consensus* and *authoritativeness* in legal knowledge representation.

Consensus is an issue faced in knowledge representation in general, as underlined by several authors (Gangemi et al. 2002, Guarino 1997), since ontological conceptualization has to be shared between stakeholders (Studer et al. 1998). Several approaches have been undertaken to reach consensus in legal knowledge representation: for example the *common-sense terms* approach (Hoekstra et al. 2009) based on common sense understanding of the terminology identifying concepts, as well as the *folksonomy* approach[1] based on social and collaborative activities of concepts selection and categorization (Gruber 2006).

Knowledge representation in the legal domain, however, shows peculiarities due to the importance of having authoritative systems based on legal rules for legal assessment and reasoning, concerning the problem of determining whether a case is allowed or disallowed given a body of legal norms (Breuker et al. 2008; Capon and Visser 1997). Authoritative issues are also important for advanced search engines, based on semantic annotation of legal documents, able to retrieve not just documents but also the contained norms (Biagioli and Turchi 2005). In these systems users are interested in *rules* on a specific domain (relations between norms, support

---

E. Francesconi (✉)

ITTIG-CNR, Institute of Legal Information Theory and Techniques, Italian National Research Council, Florence, Italy

e-mail: francesconi@ittig.cnr.it

[1] Folksonomies (or social tagging mechanisms) have been widely implemented in knowledge sharing environments; the idea was first adopted by the social bookmarking site del.icio.us (2004) http://delicious.com

G. Sartor et al. (eds.), *Approaches to Legal Ontologies*, Law, Governance and Technology Series 1, DOI 10.1007/978-94-007-0120-5_13,
© Springer Science+Business Media B.V. 2011

to legal reasoning), as a consequence they look for *authoritativeness* in knowledge representation.

Both common-sense terms and folksonomy approaches are well suited to reach *consensus* on domain concepts, however, when applied to the description of *legal rules*, the gap between consensus and authoritativeness is usually emphasized. For example, by the common-sense terms approach, social and communicative words typical of the legal domain can be provided (Breuker and Hoekstra 2004a): in this approach experts may provide description of rules on entities as well as translating them into technical terminology (Hoekstra et al. 2009), but this activity might reduce *consensus*. Similarly, in the folksonomy approach stakeholders may provide description of rules regulating entities, which might be lacking in *authoritativeness*.

Another way, discussed in literature (Euzenat and Shvaiko 2007; Francesconi et al. 2008), to provide consensus in knowledge modelling is to find conceptual equivalences through ontology mapping techniques; however, such techniques do not provide any additional contribution to the authoritativeness in knowledge representation.

Nowadays a very active research area in ontology development is represented by knowledge acquisition from texts (Buitelaar et al. 2005,Cimiano 2006), since electronic texts still represent the most widely used communication medium on the Web. This approach can play an important role in legal knowledge modelling, in particular in *legal rules* modelling, since written text is the most widely used way of communicating legal matters (Lame 2005; Saias and Quaresma 2005; Walter and Pinkal 2006). Knowledge acquisition techniques, usually supported by machine learning and natural language processing, can be used for implementing taxonomies or suggesting concepts for upper level ontologies, mainly hand-crafted by domain experts, as well as for identifying and representing *legal rules*. Such techniques represent a more neutral approach for identifying relevant concepts for knowledge modelling, thus contributing to reach consensus.

In this paper a learning approach supporting the acquisition of legal rules contained in legislative documents is presented: it is based on a semantic model for legislation and implemented by using knowledge extraction techniques over legislative texts. This methodology is targeted to provide a contribution to bridge the gap between consensus and authoritativeness in implementing systems based on legal rules: *consensus* can be better reached by limiting human intervention in legal rules description, which are extracted from *authoritative* texts as the legislative ones.

This paper is organised as follows: in Section 13.2 an approach to legal rules modelling and acquisition is presented, in Section 13.3 a semantic model for legislative texts is introduced, in Section 13.4 a knowledge acquisition methodology is shown and tested, finally in Section 13.5 some conclusions, discussing the benefits of the described learning approach, are reported.

13.2 A Learning Approach for the Acquisition of Legal Rules

The proposed approach for legal knowledge acquisition is based on learning techniques targeted to extract *legal rules* from text corpora. Legal rules are essentially "speech acts" (Searle 1969) expressed in legislative texts regulating *entities* of a domain: their nature therefore justifies an approach targeted to the analysis of such texts.

Therefore, the proposed knowledge acquisition framework is based on a twofold approach:

1. Knowledge modelling: definition of a semantic model for legislative texts able to describe legal rules;
2. Knowledge acquisition: instantiation of legal rules through the analysis of legislative texts, being driven by the defined semantic model.

This approach traces a framework which combines a top–down and a bottom–up strategy: a top–down strategy provides a model for legal rules, while a bottom-up strategy identifies rules instances as expressed in legislative texts.

The bottom-up knowledge acquisition strategy in particular can be carried out manually or automatically. The manual bottom–up strategy consists, basically, in an analytic effort in which all the possible semantic distinctions among the textual components of a legislative text are identified. On the other hand the automatic (or semi-automatic) bottom–up strategy consists in carrying out the previous activities being supported by tools able to classify Rules, according to a defined model, and to identify the involved Entities. In this paper this second strategy is presented.

13.3 Knowledge Modelling

The proposed approach is based on knowledge modelling, which is oriented to interopreability and reusability. It is conceived according to two main principles: (1) Knowledge representation by Semantic Web standards; (2) Separation betweeen types of knowledge.

The first aspect is aimed at reaching interoperability among knowledge-based applications, exploiting the expressiveness and reusability of the RDF/OWL semantic Web standards. The second aspect, on the other hand, aims to guarantee reusability of the knowledge resources.

The need of identifying and separating different types of knowledge has been widely addressed in literature (Casellas 2008). For example (Breuker and Hoekstra 2004b) criticised a common tendency to indiscriminately mix domain knowledge and knowledge on the process for which it is used, addressing it as *epistemological promiscuity*. Similarly (Bylander and Chandrasekaran 1987), (Chandrasekaran 1986) and (van Heijst 1995) pointed out that usually knowledge representation is affected by the nature of the problem and by the applied inference strategy; this key-point is also referred by (Bylander and Chandrasekaran 1987) as *interaction problem*: it is related to a discussion regarding whether knowledge about the domain and knowledge about reasoning on the domain should be represented independently. In this respect (Clancey 1981) pointed out that the separation of both types of knowledge is a desirable feature, since it paves the way to knowledge sharing and reuse.

The knowledge model proposed in this work reflects these orientations and it is organized into the following components:

1. Domain Independent Legal Knowledge (DILK)
2. Domain Knowledge (DK)

DILK is a semantic model able to provide classification of Rules expressed in legislative texts, while DK is any terminological or conceptual knowledge base (thesaurus, ontology, semantic network) able to provide information and relationships among the Entities of a regulated domain. The combination of a DILK model with one or more DKs is able to describe, from a semantic point of view, Rules instances and related domain Entities expressed in legislative texts. For this reason we call the proposed methodology to legal knowledge modelling the *DILK-DK* approach.

13.3.1 DILK

DILK is conceived as a model for legal Rules, independently from the domain they apply to. In literature several models (classification) of legal rules have been proposed, from the traditional Hohfeldian theory of legal concepts (Hohfeld 1913), (Hohfeld 1917), until more recent legal philosophy theories due to Rawls (1955), Hart (1961), Ross (1968), Bentham and Hart (1970, 1st ed. 1872), Kelsen (1991).

In this respect a particular attention is worth to be given to the work of Biagioli (Biagioli 1991), (Biagioli 1997). In the 1990s Biagioli tried to combine the work of legal philosophers on rules classification with the Searlian theory of rules perceived as "speech acts". Following the Raz's lesson (Raz 1977), which considers the entire body of laws and regulations as a set of *provisions* carried by speech acts, namely sentences endowed with meaning, Biagioli underlined two views or *profiles* according to which a legislative text can be perceived:

- a structural or *formal profile*, representing the traditional legislator habit of organizing legal texts in chapters, articles, paragraphs, etc.;
- a semantic or *functional profile*, considering legislative texts as composed by *provisions*, namely fragments of regulation (Biagioli 1997) expressed by speech acts.

Therefore a specific classification of legislative provisions was carried out by analyzing legislative texts from a semantic point of view, and grouping provisions into two main families: *Rules* (introducing and defining entities or expressing deontic concepts) and *Rules on Rules* (different kinds of amendments).

Rules are provisions which aim at regulating the reality considered by the including act. Adopting a typical law theory distinction, well expressed by Rawls, they consist in:

- *constitutive rules*: mainly rules on entities of the regulated reality. They consist in rules introducing entities ("rules of the game" (Ricciardi 1997)) and rules which assign a juridical profile to the entities ("empowering norms" or "rules in the game" (Ricciardi 1997));
- *regulative rules*: they discipline actions ("rules on actions") or the substantial and procedural defaults ("remedies").

On the other hand, Rules on Rules are provision types in which we can distinguish:

- *content amendments*: they modify literally the content of a norm, or their meaning without literal changes;
- *temporal amendments*: they modify the times of a norm (come-into-force and efficacy time);
- *extension amendments*: they extend or reduce the cases on which the norm operates.

In Biagioli's model each provision type has specific arguments describing the roles of the entities which a provision type applies to (for example *Bearer* is argument of a *Duty* provision).

Provision types and related *Arguments* represent a semantic model for legislative texts (Biagioli 1997). They can be considered as a sort of metadata scheme able to describe analytically the content of a legislative text.

For example, the following fragment of the Italian privacy law:

A controller intending to process personal data falling within the scope of application of this act shall have to notify the "Garante" thereof, . . .

besides being considered as a part of the physical structure of a legislative text (a *paragraph*), can also be viewed as a component of the logical structure of it (a *provision*). In particular, it can be qualified as a *provision* of type *Duty*, whose arguments are:

Bearer:	"Controller"
Object:	"Process personal data"
Action:	"Notification"
Counterpart:	"Garante".

The specific textual anchorage of the Biagioli's model represents, in our point of view, its main strenght. Since the DILK-DK approach aims at representing Rules instances as expressed in legislative texts, we consider the Biagioli's model, limited to the group of Rules, as a possible implementation of the *Domain Independent Legal Knowledge* (DILK). Rules on Rules affect indirectly the way how the reality is regulated, since they amend Rules in different respects (literally, temporarily, extensionally): therefore such provisions type should be taken into account as far as they change Rules.

13.3.2 DK

In legislative texts *Entities* regulated by provisions are expressed by lexical units, however no additional information on such entities are provided. This information can be provided by a *Domain Knowledge* (DK) giving conceptualization of entities expressed by language-dependent lexical units.[2] Information on such entities at language-independent level, as well as their lexical manifestations in different languages can be described by a DK.

A possible DK architecture has been proposed within the DALOS project[3] according to two layers of abstraction:

- an *Ontological layer*: conceptual modelling at language-independent level;
- a *Lexical layer*: language-dependent lexical manifestations of the concepts at the Ontological layer.

More details on the DALOS DK architecture, as well as a possible implementation of it for the domain of consumer protection, can be found in (Agnoloni et al. 2009).

13.4 Knowledge Acquisition

Knowledge acquisition within the DILK-DK framework consists of two main steps:

1. DILK instantiation
2. DK construction

13.4.1 DILK Instantiation

The DILK instantiation phase is a bottom-up strategy of legislative text paragraphs classification into *provision types*, as well as specific lexical units identification, assigning them roles in terms of *provision arguments*. The automatic bottom–up strategy, here proposed, consists in using tools able to support the human activity of classifying provisions and extracting their arguments.

Three main steps can be foreseen:

- Collection of legislative texts and conversion into an XML format (Bacci et al. 2009)

---

[2]"Typically regulations are not given in an empty environment; instead they make use of terminology and concepts which are relevant to the organisation and/or the aspect they seek to regulate. Thus, to be able to capture the meaning of regulations, one needs to encode not only the regulations themselves, but also the underlying ontological knowledge. This knowledge usually includes the terminology used, its basic structure, and integrity constraints that need to be satisfied." Grigoris Antoniou, David Billington, Guido Governatori, and Michael J. Maher, "On the modeling and analysis of regulations", in *Proceedings of the Australian Conference Information Systems*, pages 20–29, 1999.

[3]http://www.dalosproject.eu

- Automatic classification of legislative text paragraphs into provisions (Biagioli et al. 2005; Francesconi and Passerini 2007)
- Automatic argument extraction (Biagioli et al. 2005).

Legislative documents are firstly collected and transformed into a jurisdiction-dependent XML standard (NormeInRete in Italy, Metalex in the Netherlands, etc.). For the Italian legislation a module called xmLegesMarker of the xmLeges[4] software family, has been developed (Bacci et al. 2009): it is able to transform legacy contents into XML so to identify the formal structure of legislative documents.

13.4.1.1 Automatic Classification of Provisions

For the automatic classification of legislative text paragraphs into provision types, a tool called xmLegesClassifier, of the xmLeges family, has been developed. xmLegesClassifier has been implemented using a Multiclass Support Vector Machine (MSVM) approach, as the one reporting the best results in preliminary experiments with respect to other machine learning techniques (Francesconi and Passerini 2007). With respect to (Francesconi and Passerini 2007), in this work MSVM is specifically used to classify Rules. Documents are represented by vectors of weighted terms and some preprocessing operations are performed on pure words to increase their statistical qualities:

- Stemming on words in order to reduce them to their morphological root
- Stopwords elimination
- Digit and non alphanumeric characters represented using a special character

Moreover *feature selection* techniques are applied to reduce the number of terms to be considered, thus actually restricting the vocabulary to be employed (see e.g. (Sebastiani 2002, Yang and Pedersen 1997)). We tried two simple methods:

- An unsupervised *min frequency* threshold over the number of times a term has been found in the entire training set, targeted to eliminate terms with poor statistics.
- A supervised threshold over the Information Gain (Quinlan 1986) of terms, which measures how much a term discriminates between documents belonging to different classes. Being D the set of training documents, the Information Gain of term w is computed as:

$$ig(w) = H(D) - \frac{|D_w|}{|D|}H(D_w) - \frac{|D_{\bar{w}}|}{|D|}H(D_{\bar{w}})$$

where H is a function computing the entropy of a labelled set ($H(D) = \sum_{i=1}^{|C|} -p_i \, log_2(p_i)$), being p_i the portion of D belonging to the *ith* class, D_w is the set of training documents containing the term w, and $D_{\bar{w}}$ is the set of training documents not containing w.

---

[4]http://www.xmleges.org

Entropy in information theory measures the amount of bits necessary to encode the class of a generic element from a labelled set, and thus depends on the dispersion of labels within the set.

Information Gain measures the decrease of entropy obtained by dividing the training set basing on the presence/absence of the term, thus preferring terms which produce subsets with more uniform labels. Basically it measures the discriminative power of a term, with respect to different classes; in other words it measures the effectiveness of an attribute in classifying the training data. In fact, given a term w and a set of data, labelled as positive (S_+) and negative (S_-) examples, the optimal case for the information gain value of w is represented by the situation in which all the documents containing w belong to a single specific class, say S_+, and all the documents which do not contain w belong to S_-, (in our case the entropies of the two sets of documents $H(D_w)$ and $H(D_{\bar{w}})$ would be 0 and the information gain $ig(w)$ maximum $(ig(w) = H(D))$). This method basically allows to select terms with the highest discriminatory power among a set of classes.

Once basic terms have been defined, a vocabulary of terms T can be created from the set of training documents D, containing all the terms which occur at least once in the set. A single document d will be represented as a vector of weights $w_1, \ldots, w_{|T|}$, where the weight w_i represents the amount of information which the ith term of the vocabulary carries out with respect to the semantics of d. We tried different types of weights, with increasing degree of complexity:

- a *binary* weight $\delta(w,d)$ indicating the presence/absence of the term within the document;
- a *term-frequency* weight tf(w,d) indicating the number of times the term occurs within the document, which should be a measure of its representativeness of the document content;
- a combination of *information gain* and *term-frequency* $(ig(w, d) \times tf(w, d))$;
- a *tf-idf* weight which indicates the degree of specificity of the term with respect to the document. Term Frequency Inverse Document Frequency (Buckley and Salton 1988) is computed as

$$tfidf(w, d) = tf(w, d) \times log(|D_w|^{-1})$$

where $|D_w|$ is the fraction of training documents containing at least once the term w. The rationale behind this measure is that term frequency is balanced by *inverse document frequency*, which penalizes terms occurring in many different documents as being less discriminative.

A wide range of experiments was conducted over a dataset made of 258 examples (text fragments containing Rules), collected by legal experts, distributed among 6 classes representing as many types of provisions (Table. 13.1).

Table 13.1 Dataset of provision types

Class labels	Provision types	Number of documents
c_0	Definition	10
c_1	Liability	39
c_2	Prohibition	13
c_3	Duty	59
c_4	Permission	15
c_5	Penalty	122

After terms preprocessing, we tried a number of combinations of the document representation and feature selection strategies previously described. We employed a *leave-one-out* (loo) procedure for measuring performances of the different strategies and algorithms. For a dataset of n documents $D = \{d_1, \ldots, dn\}$, it consists of performing n runs of the learning algorithm, where for each run i the algorithm is trained on $D \backslash d_i$ and tested on the single left out document d_i. The loo accuracy is computed as the fraction of correct tests over the entire number of tests. Table 13.2 reports loo accuracy and train accuracy, which is computed as the average train accuracy over the loo runs, of the Multiclass Support Vector Machine algorithm for the different document representation and feature selection strategies. The first three columns (apart from the index one) represent possible preprocessing operations. The fourth column indicates the term weighting scheme employed (binary (δ), term frequency (*tf*), infogain $\times$ term frequency (*ig$\times$tf*), term frequency-inverse document frequency (*tf–idf*)). The two following columns are for feature selection strategies: the unsupervised *min frequency* and the supervised *max infogain*, which

Table 13.2 Detailed results of MSVM algorithm for different document representation and feature selection strategies.

#	repl. digit	repl. alnum	Use stem	Weight scheme	Min freq sel.	Max IG sel.	Loo acc (%)	Train acc (%)
0	no	no	no	δ	2	500	89.53	100
1	yes	no	no	δ	2	500	88.76	100
2	yes	yes	no	δ	2	500	88.76	100
3	yes	yes	yes	tf	2	500	91.09	100
4	yes	yes	yes	tf-idf	2	500	89.15	100
5	yes	yes	yes	ig	2	500	89.15	100
6	yes	yes	yes	ig × tf	2	500	89.15	100
7	yes	yes	yes	δ	2	250	89.92	100
8	yes	yes	yes	δ	2	100	82.55	100
9	yes	yes	yes	δ	2	50	82.17	96.12
10	yes	yes	yes	δ	2	1000	90.31	100
11	yes	yes	yes	δ	0	500	92.24	100
12	yes	yes	yes	δ	2	500	92.64	100
13	yes	yes	yes	δ	5	500	92.24	100
14	yes	yes	yes	δ	10	500	89.92	100

Table 13.3 Confusion matrix for the best MSVM classifier

Classes	c_0	c_1	c_2	c_3	c_4	c_5
c_0	122	0	0	0	0	0
c_1	1	9	4	0	1	0
c_2	0	3	55	0	1	0
c_3	2	0	1	6	1	0
c_4	1	1	3	0	8	0
c_5	0	0	0	0	0	39

actually indicates the number of terms to keep, after being ordered by Information Gain. Finally, the last two columns contain loo and train accuracies.

Replacing digits or non alphanumeric characters does not improve performances, while the use of stemming actually helps clustering together terms with common semantics. The simpler binary weight scheme appears to work better then term frequency, probably for the small size, in terms of number of words, of the provisions in our training set; this fact makes statistics on the number of occurences of a term less reliable. Only slight improvements can be obtained by performing feature selection with Information Gain, thus confirming how SVM algorithms are able to effectively handle quite large feature spaces.

Finally, Table 13.3 shows the confusion matrix for the best classifier, the MSVM indexed 12, reporting details of predictions for individual classes. Rows indicate true classes, while columns indicate predicted ones. Note that most errors are committed for classes with fewer documents, for which poorer statistics could be learned.

13.4.1.2 Automatic Provision Arguments Extraction

A tool called xmLegesExtractor (Biagioli et al. 2005) of the xmLeges family has been implemented for the automatic detection of provision arguments.

The purpose of xmLegesExtractor[5] is to select relevant text fragments (lexical units) corresponding to specific semantic roles that are relevant for the different types of provisions. xmLegesExtractor is realized as a suite of Natural Language Processing tools for the automatic analysis of Italian texts (see Bartolini et al. 2004a, b, 2002), specialized to cope with the specific stylistic conventions of the legal parlance. A first prototype takes in input single legislative texts paragraphs in raw text, coupled with the categorization provided by the xmLegesClassifier, and identifies lexical units corresponding to provision arguments.

The approach follows a two–stage strategy. The first stage consists in a syntactic pre–processing which takes in input a text paragraph, tokenized and normalized for dates, abbreviations and multi–word expressions; the normalized text is then morphologically analyzed and lemmatized, using an Italian lexicon specialized for the analysis of legal language; finally, the text is POS-tagged and shallow parsed into non–recursive constituents called "chunks". A chunked sentence, however,

---

[5]xmLegesExtractor has been developed in collaboration with the Institute of Computational Linguistics (ILC-CNR) in Pisa (Italy)

does not give information about the nature and scope of inter–chunk dependencies. These dependencies, whenever relevant for semantic annotation, are identified at the ensuing processing stage.

The second stage consists in a semantic annotation phase, basically in the identification of all the lexical units acting as arguments relevant to a specific provision type. It takes in input a chunked representation of legal text paragraphs and identifies semantically relevant structures by applying a specific provision type oriented grammar, locating relevant patterns of chunks which represent entities with specific semantic roles within a provision type instance Fig. 13.1.

Some experiments testing the reliability of xmLegesExtractor have been carried out on a dataset of 209 provisions.

The aim of this evaluation is to assess, for each provision type, the system reliability in identifying all the relevant semantic roles foreseen by the model. For each class of provisions in the dataset, the total number of semantic roles to be identified are collected in a gold standard dataset; this value was then compared with the number of semantic roles correctly identified by the system and the total number of answers given by the system. Some results are reported in Table. 13.4: here, Precision is scored as the number of correct answers returned by system over

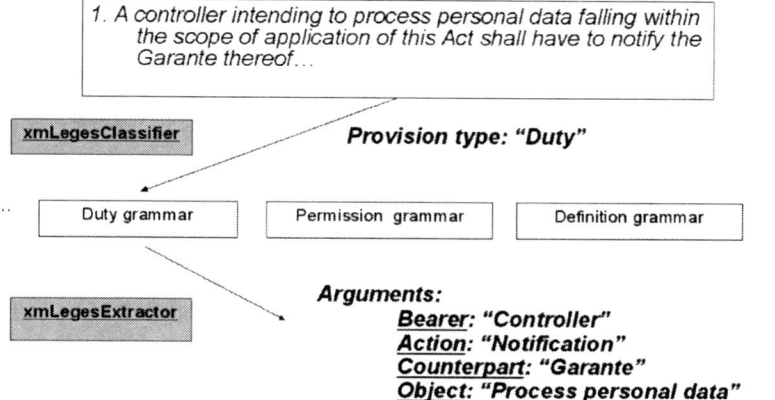

Fig. 13.1 The combination of xmLegesClassifier output and the grammar approach used by xmLegesExtractor

Table 13.4   xmLegesextractor experiments

Class labels	Provision type	Dataset	Precision	Recall
c_2	Prohibition	13	85.71%	92.30%
c_3	Duty	59	69.23%	30.50%
c_4	Permission	15	78.95%	100.00%
c_5	Penalty	122	85.83%	89.34%
	Total	209	82.80%	73.68%

the total number of answers returned, while Recall is the ratio of correct answers returned by system over the number of expected answers.

13.4.2 DK Construction

Lexical units and their roles within a provision identified by xmLegesExtrac-or represent language-dependent lexicalizations of provision arguments. More nformation on the identified entities, as well as their relations within a specific domain, can be obtained by mapping lexical units to concepts in existing Domain Knowledges (DKs), if any. On the other hand such information can be consider as a ground to construct domain knowledges (in terms of thesauri or domain ontologies).

Actually the construction of DKs is not a specific task of *legal* ontologists, but of ontologists *tout court*, since a Domain Knowledge has to contain information on entities of the domain independently form a legal perspective. This is an important aspect to underline, in order to design a knowledge architecture whose components can be reused.

A DILK-DK learning approach only suggests language-dependent lexical units for DKs, which can be implemented by projecting lexical units on a large text corpora of a specific domain, inferring conceptualizations by term clustering, as well as using statistics on recurrent patterns for discovering term relationships. This issue is out of the paper scope; a vast literature exists on this topic, therefore the interested reader can refer to (Buitelaar and Cimiano 2008).

13.5 Conclusions

A knowledge modelling approach for the legal domain, called DILK-DK approach, has been presented. It aims to keep distinct domain knowledge from its legal perspective. Moreover an automatic approach based on machine learning and NLP techniques to support bottom–up knowledge acquisition from legislative texts within the DILK-DK framework has been shown.

The proposed learning approach for legal knowledge acquisition can provide several benefits:

- it contributes to implement taxonomies or suggest concepts for hand-crafted ontologies (Walter and Pinkal 2009; Lenci et al. 2009)
- it contributes to bridge the gap between authoritativeness and consensus for legal rules representation, since it is able to extract rules directly form legislative texts, which are authoritative sources (by definition), nevertheless promoting consensus, since rules are automatically extracted from legal sources, limiting human interaction.

References

Agnoloni, T., L. Bacci, E. Francesconi, W. Peters, S. Montemagni, G. Venturi (2009). A Two-Level Knowledge Approach to Support Multilingual Legislative Drafting. In J. Breuker, P. Casanovas, M. Klein, E. Francesconi (Eds.) *Law, Ontologies and the Semantic Web*, vol. 188 of *Frontiers in Artificial Intelligence and Applications*. IOS Press, Amsterdam, 177–198.

Bacci, L., P. Spinosa, C. Marchetti, R. Battistoni (2009). Automatic Mark-Up of Legislative Documents and Its Application to Parallel Text Generation. In N. Casellas, E. Francesconi, R. Hoekstra, S. Montemagni (Eds.) *Proceedings of the 3rd Workshop on Legal Ontologies and Artificial Intelligence Techniques joint with 2nd Workshop on Semantic Processing of Legal Texts*. Huygens Editorial, Barcelona, 45–54.

Bartolini, R., A. Lenci, S. Montemagni, V. Pirrelli (2002). The Lexicon-Grammar Balance in Robust Parsing of Italian. In *Proceedings of 3rd International Conference on Language Resources and Evaluation*. Las Palmas, Canary Islands, Spain.

Bartolini, R., A. Lenci, S. Montemagni, V. Pirrelli, C. Soria (2004a). Automatic Classification and Analysis of Provisions in Italian Legal Texts: A Case Study. In *Proceedings of the Second International Workshop on Regulatory Ontologies*. Larnaca, Cyprus.

Bartolini, R., A. Lenci, S. Montemagni, C. Soria (2004b). Semantic Mark-Up of Legal Texts Through Nlp-Based Metadata-Oriented Techniques. In *Proceedings of 4rd International Conference on Language Resources and Evaluation*. Lisbon, Portugal

Bentham, J., H.L.A. Hart (1970). *Of Laws in General*. Athlone, London, (1st ed. 1872).

Biagioli, C. (1991). Definitional Elements of a Language For Representation of Statutory. *Rechtstheorie*, 11: 317–336.

Biagioli, C. (1997). Towards a Legal Rules Functional Micro-Ontology. In *Proceedings of workshop LEGONT '97*. Melbourne, Australia.

Biagioli, C., F. Turchi. (2005). Model and Ontology Based Conceptual Searching in Legislative Xml Collections. In *Proceedings of the Workshop on Legal Ontologies and Artificial Intelligence Techniques*, Bologna, Italy, 83–89.

Biagioli, C., E. Francesconi, A. Passerini, S. Montemagni, C. Soria (2005). Automatic Semantics Extraction in Law Documents. In *Proceedings of International Conference on Artificial Intelligence and Law*, Bologna, Italy, 133–139.

Breuker, J., R. Hoekstra (2004a). Core Concepts Of Law: Taking Common-Sense Seriously. In *Proceedings of Formal Ontologies in Information Systems*. Torino, Italy.

Breuker, J., R. Hoekstra (2004b). Epistemology and Ontology In Core Ontologies: Folaw and Iricore, Two Core Ontologies For Law. In *Proceedings of EKAW Workshop on Core ontologies*. CEUR. Whittlebury Hall, Northamptonshire, UK.

Breuker, J., S. van de Ven, A. El Ali, M. Bron, S. Klarman, U. Milosevic, L. Wortel, A. Forhecz (2008). Developing Harness. ESTRELLA Deliverable 4.6/3b, European Commission.

Breuker, J., P. Casanovas, M. Klein, E. Francesconi (Eds.) (2009). *Law, Ontologies and the Semantic Web. Channelling the Legal Information Flood*, vol. 188 of *Frontiers in Artificial Intelligence and Applications*. IOS Press, Amsterdam.

Buckley, C., G. Salton (1988). Term-Weighting Approaches in Automatic Text Retrieval. *Information Processing and Management*, 24(5): 513–523.

Buitelaar, P., P. Cimiano (Eds.) (2008). *Ontology Learning and Population: Bridging the Gap Between Text and Knowledge*, vol. 167 of *Frontiers in Artificial Intelligence and Applications*. IOS Press, Amsterdam.

Buitelaar, P., P. Cimiano, B. Magnini (2005). Ontology Learning From Text: An Overview. In Buitelaar et al. (Eds.) *Ontology Learning from Text: Methods, Evaluation and Applications*, vol. 123 of *Frontiers in Artificial Intelligence and Applications*. IOS Press, Amsterdam, 3–12.

Bylander, T., B. Chandrasekaran (1987). Generic Tasks for Knowledge-Based Reasoning: The "Right" Level Of Abstraction For Knowledge Acquisition. *International Journal of Man-Machine Studies*, 26(2): 231–243.

Bench Capon, T.J.M., P.R.S. Visser (1997). Ontologies in Legal Information Systems; The Need For Explicit Specifications of Domain Conceptualizations. In *Proceedings of the 6th International Conference on Artificial Intelligence and Law*. ACM Press, New York, NY, 132–141.

Casellas, N. (2008). *Modelling Legal Knowledge through Ontologies. OPJK: The Ontology of Professional Judicial Knowledge*. Ph.D. thesis, Institute of Law and Technology, Autonomous University of Barcelona.

Chandrasekaran, B. (1986). Generic Tasks in Knowledge-Based Reasoning: High-Level Building Blocks for Expert System Design. *IEEE Expert*, 1(3): 23–30.

Cimiano, P. (2006). Ontology Learning and Population From Text. In *Algorithms, Evaluation and Applications*. Springer, Berlin.

Clancey, W.J. (1981). The Epistemology of a Rule-Based Expert System: A Framework for Explanation. Technical Report STAN-CS-81-896, Stanford University, Department of Computer Science.

Euzenat, J., P. Shvaiko (2007). *Ontology Matching*. Springer, Berlin.

Francesconi, E., A. Passerini (2007). Automatic Classification of Provisions in Legislative Texts. *International Journal on Artificial Intelligence and Law*, 15(1): 1–17.

Francesconi, E., S. Faro, E. Marinai (2008). Thesauri Alignment for Eu Egovernment Services: A Methodological Framework. In *Proceedings of the JURIX 2008 Conference*. IOS Press, Amsterdam, 73–77.

Gangemi, A., N. Guarino, C. Masolo, A. Oltramari, L. Schneider (2002). Sweetening Ontologies With Dolce. In A. Gangemi, N. Guarino, C. Masolo, A. Oltramari, L. Schneider (Eds.) *Proceedings of the 13th International Conference on Knowledge Engineering and Knowledge Management (EKAW02)*, LNCS, vol. 2473. Springer, Sigüenza, Spain.

Gruber, T. (2006). Where the Social Web Meets the Semantic Web (Keynote Abstract). In I.F. Cruz, S. Decker, D. Allemang, C. Preist, D. Schwabe, P. Mika, M. Uschold, L. Aroyo (Eds.) *The Semantic Web – ISWC 2006, Proceedings of the 5th International Semantic Web Conference*, LNCS, vol. 4273. Springer, Berlin, 994.

Guarino, N. (1997). Semantic Matching: Formal Ontological Distinctions For Information Organization, Extraction, and Integration. In M.T. Pazienza (Ed.) *Information Extraction: A Multidisciplinary Approach to an Emerging Information Technology*, LNCS, vol. 1299. Springer, Berlin, 139–170.

Hart, H. (1961). *The Concept of Law*. Clarendon Law Series. Oxford University Press, Oxford.

Hoekstra, R., J. Breuker, M. Bello, A. Boer (2009). Lkif Core: Principled Ontology Development for the Legal Domain. In J. Breuker, P. Casanovas, M. Klein, E. Francesconi (Eds.) *Legal Ontologies and the Semantic Web*. IOS Press, Amsterdam.

Hohfeld, W.N. (1913). Some Fundamental Legal Conceptions as Applied in Judicial Reasoning. I. *Yale Law Journal*, 23: 16–59.

Hohfeld, W.N. (1917). Some Fundamental Legal Conceptions as Applied in Judicial Reasoning. II. *Yale Law Journal*, 26: 710–770.

Kelsen, H. (1991). *General Theory of Norms*. Clarendon Press, Oxford.

Lame, G. (2005). Using Nlp Techniques to Identify Legal Ontology Components: Concepts and Relations. *Lecture Notes in Computer Science*, 3369: 169–184.

Lenci, A., S. Montemagni, V. Pirrelli, G. Venturi (2009). Ontology Learning from Italian Legal Texts. In J. Breuker, P. Casanovas, M. Klein, E. Francesconi (Eds.) *Law, Ontologies and the Semantic Web*, vol. 188 of *Frontiers in Artificial Intelligence and Applications*. IOS Press, Amsterdam, 7594.

Quinlan, J.R. (1986). Inductive Learning of Decision Trees. *Machine Learning*, 1: 81–106.

Rawls, J. (1955). Two Concepts of Rule. *Philosophical Review*, 64: 3–31.

Raz, J. (1977). *Il Concetto di Sistema Giuridico*. Il Mulino, Bologna.

Ricciardi, M. (1997). Constitutive Rules and Institutions. In *Meeting of the Irish Philosophical Club and the Royal Institute of Philosophy*, Ballymanscanlon.

Ross, A. (1968). *Directives and Norms*. Routledge, London.

Saias, J., P. Quaresma (2005). A Methodology to Create Legal Ontologies in a Logic Programming Based Web Information Retrieval System. *Lecture Notes in Computer Science*, 3369: 185–200.

Searle, J.R. (1969). *Speech Acts: An Essay in the Philosophy of Language*. Cambridge University Press, Cambridge, MA.

Sebastiani, F. (2002). Machine Learning in Automated Text Categorization. *ACM Computing Surveys*, 34(1): 1–47. URL http://faure.iei.pi.cnr.it/fabrizio/Publications/ACMCS02.pdf.

Studer, R., V. R. Benjamins, D. Fensel (1998). Knowledge Engineering: Principle and Methods. *Data Knowledge Engineering*, 25(1–2): 161–197.

van Heijst, G. (1995). *The Role of Ontologies in Knowledge Engineering*. Ph.D. thesis, Social Science Informatics, University of Amsterdam.

Walter, S., M. Pinkal (2006). Automatic Extraction of Definitions From German Court Decisions. In *Proceedings of the COLING-2006 Workshop on Information Extraction Beyond The Document*, Sidney, 20–28.

Walter, S., M. Pinkal (2009). Definitions in Court Decisions – Automatic Extraction and Ontology Acquisition. In J. Breuker, P. Casanovas, M. Klein, E. Francesconi (Eds.) *Law, Ontologies and the Semantic Web*, vol. 188 of *Frontiers in Artificial Intelligence and Applications*. IOS Press, Amsterdam, 95–113.

Yang, Y., J.O. Pedersen (1997). A Comparative Study on Feature Selection in Text Categorization. In *Proceedings of the Fourteenth International Conference on Machine Learning*. Morgan Kaufmann Publishers Inc., San Mateo, CA, 412–420.

Chapter 14
Towards an Ontological Foundation for Services Science: The Legal Perspective

Roberta Ferrario, Nicola Guarino, and Meritxell Fernández-Barrera

14.1 Introduction and State of the Art

Despite the ubiquity of the notion of service and the recent proposals for a unified *Services Science* (Chesbrough and Spohrer 2006), multiple inconsistencies between definitions of service from different disciplines (and even within the same discipline) still exist (Alter 2008; Baida 2006). In particular, despite the general goal of this science is—arguably—to allow people and computers to smoothly interact with services in the real life, many modelling approaches (especially those focusing on *Web* services) seem to focus mainly on the aspects related to *data and control flow*, considering services as *black boxes* whose main characteristic is to interoperate in a well-specified way (see, for instance, Janssen and Wagenaar 2003; Papazoglou and Georgakopoulos 2003; Traverso and Pistore 2004; Vetere and Lenzerini 2005). This black box model has certainly its own advantages, but, according to a recent paper by Petrie and Bussler (2008), apparently it seems to work well only within *service parks*, where run-time interoperability is technically feasible because services are very constrained. As the authors put it, "some interoperability among service parks might emerge, but it could take a long time".

Focusing on services as business processes, on the other hand, has its own problems. Overall, the limits of the two approaches (Web services vs. business processes) are well described in a recent note by Katia Sycara (2007), who observed that, on the one hand,

> current Web services proposals don't enable the semantic representation of business relations, contracts, or business rules in a machine-understandable way,

while, on the other hand,

> current business-process languages [...] are at a low abstraction level and don't provide formal business semantics". In conclusion, "a need exists to model informal business requirements in ways that make it feasible to translate them into precise business-service specifications, including operational interfaces and rules for procedures,

R. Ferrario (✉)
Laboratory for Applied Ontology, ISTC-CNR, Trento, Italy
e-mail: ferrario@loa-cnr.it

G. Sartor et al. (eds.), *Approaches to Legal Ontologies*, Law, Governance
and Technology Series 1, DOI 10.1007/978-94-007-0120-5_14,
© Springer Science+Business Media B.V. 2011

timing, integrity, and quality. Such modelling must be driven from the top down, directly from business requirements [. . .]. The modelling would provide a functionality that's entirely understandable from a business perspective; it would depend on business context, goals, and operational standards, but shouldn't depend on the technology used to implement them. The models would provide business value directly relating to business purposes and could be understood and used without knowledge of underlying IT artefacts.

This is exactly the perspective we are adopting in this paper, which calls for a broad, interdisciplinary effort such as that envisioned by services science (Chesbrough and Spohrer 2006). Under this perspective, we are convinced that a proper, general ontological foundation for the notion of service is a fundamental requirement for such endeavour. This is the long term goal of our work.

The present paper has two main purposes: first of all, we want to explore the foundations of a new ontology of services aiming at establishing a common, unifying framework for representing services according to different views, based on a vision that considers services as complex systems of commitments and activities, involving real people, organizations, and actual circumstances. In other words, we believe it is crucial to take into account the whole *service system* (Alter 2008) that interacts with Web services through complex chains involving people and computers, which however have always *people* at their ends. That's why in this paper—while trying to be general enough to account for any kind of service—we mostly emphasize the role of *social* and *business-oriented* services, adopting a *global view* which, in a sense, goes against the strict separation between the external and the internal view advocated by semantic Web services standards such as WSMO (Fensel and Bussler 2002; Roman et al. 2005).

The second goal of the paper is that of understanding how *responsibility* is distributed among different agents playing different roles in the whole service system. In order to do so, it is necessary to perform a comprehensive analysis of the notions connected to responsibility, including the juridical implications, which become particularly important in cases where services do not meet the customers' expectations.

A first reason for a global, *transparent box* approach to service modelling comes from the observation that the *terminology* needed to properly expose, retrieve and interact with a service, and especially that needed to understand and negotiate Service Level Agreements (SLAs), unavoidably requires a common understanding of the general service process structure, and the related activities involving the value exchange process between the producer and the customer (see Weigand et al. 2009; Terlouw and Albani). Of course, in some cases service producers may have very good reasons for not exposing their internal workflow details, but the point is that, in general, SLAs *may* refer to some details concerning the *way* the service is implemented, whose nature is not specified in advance. So, since the boundaries between the external and the internal service description cannot be defined in advance for all kinds of service, a global approach seems to be the only viable alternative for a foundational ontology of services.

A further reason for a global approach focused on responsibilities lies in the fact that, in many cases, it is important to account for the way a service-based architecture impacts the organizational structure (indeed, service process re-engineering typically impacts organizational re-engineering). In this case, it is crucial to model in the proper way the links between services, people and organizations, where responsibilities play a crucial role.

For sure, modelling services according to this global view is not an easy task, however. The notion of service is so subtle and ambiguous that many researchers simply have given up adopting a clear definition, relying on a variety of intuitive notions mainly coming from practical considerations, which lack unfortunately a coherent framework. In other words, we are still facing the general question: *what is a service?* Is there a single notion behind this term? And if there are multiple aspects, how are they related? How is the internal view of services as *business processes* related to the external view of services as exposed (aggregates of) functionalities?

In this paper we shall address these questions by introducing a novel, general approach to service modelling founded on the basic principles of ontological analysis, centred on the notion of *service commitment* as a temporal state resulting from an agent's promise to guarantee the execution of certain actions in the interest of potential beneficiaries in correspondence of certain triggering events. In this view, services are modelled by means of a layered set of interrelated temporal activities, each one with its own participants and spatiotemporal location. Under this respect this approach shares many similarities, in its main inspirations, with Alter's work on service systems (2008), as well as O'Sullivan's work on non-functional requirements for services (2006), and Baida et al. work on the service value chain (2001). This proposal is meant to be a first concrete step towards a unified, rigorous and principled ontology. The analysis of the service system's structure and of the responsibilities distribution across this structure is necessary in order to build a model which is as faithful as possible to the social, business and legal perspectives.

The legal perspective, which is the main focus of this paper, is especially important in a world where international economic and political interaction requires communication between different legal systems, and ensuring mutual understanding becomes a strategic goal for guaranteeing conflict prevention and resolution. Indeed, the lack of unified conceptualizations in legal discourse can flaw the whole communication process, giving place to legal uncertainty, diverging interpretations of legal relations and—consequently—impasse situations that can only be solved through costly judicial procedures. Since the notion of service is a central one both for private and public law, the development of a foundational ontology of services plays an important role in the construction of a conceptual language for legal analysis. This paper aims therefore at providing a framework for the design of an abstract service model potentially applicable to different legal systems, where the notions of responsibility, liability and delegation are structured together, thus enabling the analytic description of services together with their juridical implications. Such detailed description, based on general legal notions such as duty, right and obligation, offers a formal framework useful to assess real life interactions and draw conclusions on the responsibility and liability of different actors. This is especially relevant nowadays where the puzzling complexity of contractual relations makes the task of liability a location particularly intricate.

14.2 The Proposed Approach

14.2.1 The Basic Idea

If we start from the simple question "what is a service?", it is immediately very evident that there is a huge confusion, not only in the layman's common sense, but also in the way the term is used in the literature. Sometimes the term "service" is used to indicate an *action* (actually performed by somebody), or a generic *type of action* (including in this category data manipulation procedures such as those typically described as Web services), or perhaps the *capability* to perform some action; other times it refers to the *result* of such action, which is typically a *change* affecting an object or a person, or just the (subjective) *value*, or utility of such change; moreover, in certain settings (like Public Administrations) the term often denotes an *organization* acting (or in charge of acting) in a certain way in the interest of somebody.

In our opinion, all these notions are somehow connected, and contribute to better specify the notion of service, but none of them can be properly identified with what we believe people are commonly referring to when asking for a service. More or less "official" definitions occurring in the ICT literature do not help much (some relevant exceptions are Alter 2008; O'Sullivan 2006; Baida et al. 2001; Dumas et al. 2003).

To see how these various definitions are related, let us start with some simple questions, focusing on very general public services such as fire-and-rescue, snow removal, children care, etc. What do we *pay for*, when we fund such services with our taxes? What does it mean that, for instance, in a municipality there are such services, at a certain time? Is anybody extinguishing a fire or removing some snow *at that time*? No, certainly not necessarily. We can legitimately say that *here and now* both a fire-and-rescue service and a snow removal service are *present*, even though there are no lit fires, nor is it snowing. It suffices to say that there is someone (firemen, snow removal operators) who is *prepared* to perform precise actions in case something happens (fire, snow). So our core notion of service is based on the following statement:

> A service is present at a time t and location l iff, at time t, an agent is explicitly committed to guarantee the execution of some type of action at location l, on the occurrence of a certain triggering event, in the interest of another agent and upon prior agreement, in a certain way.

So, in a sense, at the core of any service there is a *commitment* situation in which someone (the service *provider*) guarantees the execution of some kind of *action(s)*[1]

---

[1] Alternatively, instead of focusing on *actions* to be executed, one can decide to treat commitment as directed towards *conditions* to be achieved, as it happens in Chesbrough and Spohrer (2006).

in the interest of somebody who agrees (the *service customer*), at a certain cost and in a certain way. This action is executed by the a *service producer*, who may coincide with the service provider, may be somebody else *delegated* by the service provider, or even coincide with the service customer (e.g. in rental services, where the action of using the rented good is actually performed by the service customer).

From the ontological point of view, this commitment situation is a static temporal entity, i.e. a *static event* in the sense of the DOLCE ontology[2] (Masolo et al. 2003), which involves the participation of a single agent, the *provider*. This commitment state typically starts at the time of the commitment act, and its duration is determined by the commitment's act itself,[3] which typically specifies some constraints concerning the way the commitment will be fulfilled.

As we shall argue in the rest of the paper, service commitment needs to be distinguished from *service content*, which concerns the kind of action(s) the provider commits to guarantee, and *service process*, which is a set of business processes implementing the service commitment (see Fig. 14.1). In turn, we distinguish service commitment from *service availability*, which involves a service process running at a certain time and location: this allows us to account for malfunctioning periods or working pauses, where the commitment still holds but the service is not available.Following Castelfranchi (2003); Jennings (1993); Verdicchio and Colombetti (2003); and Singh (1997), the commitment act can be seen as a *speech act* that most of the times is codified in a *document*, i.e. in an institutional object that can assume many different forms: a contract, an official declaration or deliberation, a service level agreement,[4] etc.

In institutional settings, the *provider*, the agent who commits, is typically a Public Administration. On the other hand, the service *producer*, who actually executes the action(s) guaranteed by the provider, may not necessarily coincide with the provider, and can be either a PA or another kind of (private) organization, delegated by the provider; in some exceptional cases even an individual agent. The same holds for

---

In this case, the commitment's content can be expressed by a proposition. In the perspective of services, this difference amounts to focusing on the actions that must be executed in order to reach a certain desired state or directly on the achievement of such desired state. We could in fact leave this choice open, as the two alternatives seem both very reasonable: sometimes the customer is just interested in some particular state to hold, disregarding how it has been reached, other times the commitment concerns the action to be performed, even independently of the actual achievement of a specific result. In any case, we believe the latter case is more frequent and thus representing a commitment with respect to actions is more in line with our analysis.

[2]Although the term "event" has often a dynamic connotation, we use such term in the more general sense of *entity which occurs in time* (also called *perdurant* in the DOLCE ontology). In this understanding, states and processes are considered as special event kinds.

[3]We assume that the commitment act (the *speech act*) is instantaneous, and occurs at a time which does not necessarily coincide with the beginning of the availability state.

[4]In the actual practice, the term "service level agreement" typically refers to the negotiation that the producer conducts with the user; here we are using the locution in a coarser sense, which includes also the provider-producer and provider-user agreements, as well as, possibly, those between the provider and the community to which services are provided.

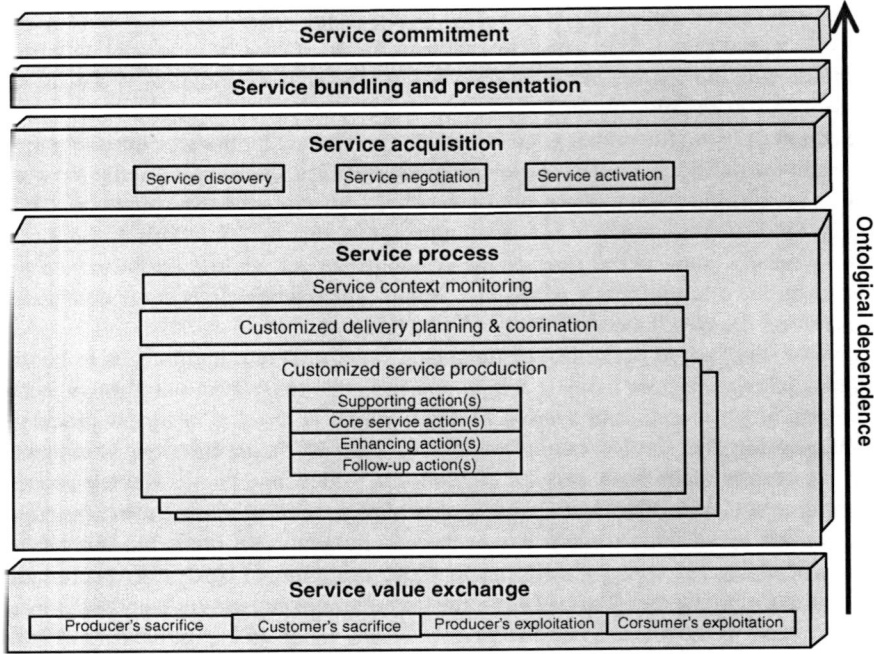

Fig. 14.1 The layered structure of service activities

:he *service customer*, who can in turn be a PA, an organization, or an individual
agent, the latter being much more common than in the previous case.[5]

The last element present in the definition is the *triggering event*; two kinds of
triggering events can be singled out. The first one, more trivial, is a simple request
made directly by the customer (like a parent in need who requires children care); in
this case the *service invocation* coincides with the triggering event. The second one
is the occurrence of a particular event kind, like the lighting of a fire in a wood, or a
difficult situation observed by a social assistant, that triggers the action.[6] Of course,
since the occurrence of the triggering event is not known in advance, the action time
is in general much shorter than the availability time, so a service may be available
at a certain time even if none of its foreseen actions do actually occur.

It is worth stressing an original feature of our definition, namely the inclusion
of the triggering event. Traditionally, approaches on services are goal oriented; take
for instance the definition from Cauvet and Guzelian (2008): "A service delivers

---

[5]In some cases, like in rental services, the service customer may coincide with the service producer.
We do not discuss this case here, however.

[6]To be more precise, it is the *observation* of such event that triggers the action. It is worth noting
that, for this reason, many services include among their supporting activities an explicit monitoring
activity, which can be executed by the producer itself or delegated to another agent.

a process to achieve a certain goal by using resources". Note however that actually the goals may in some cases be just implicit, or even different if you compare the producer's perspective with the customer's perspective. In such cases, specifying the service also in terms of the triggering event and the action to be performed in correspondence of such event seems to be less ambiguous. The service's goal doesn't disappear in our approach, and indeed it is present in what has been called the service content, but the triggering event allows to justify the passage from service availability to service invocation. Moreover, note that a triggered action may not necessarily succeed. What the provider guarantees may in some cases be only the action's performance, not its result. This changes also the mechanisms for the evaluation of service quality, which must distinguish between actions/processes and resulting states.

14.2.2 Services and Goods

To better understand the nature of our proposal—that services are temporal entities (events) based on *commitments*—let us briefly discuss the difference between services and goods. According to the World Trade Organization, services are a sort of intangible goods, so that a service might be defined as anything you can buy, but "you can't drop on your foot". Yet, Ted Hill (1977) insists on the fact that services are not a special kind of goods, because goods and services belong to quite different ontological categories: goods are both *transactable* and *transferable*, while services are transactable, but not transferable. In Hill's own words, "a surgical operation is not some kind of immaterial drug": when you buy the drug you become an *owner* of it, in the sense that you can decide about its behaviour (i.e., assuming it in your body), while when you pay for the surgical operation you are not actually becoming the owner of it.[7] In support to this argument, we argue that the ontological reason why services are not transferable is exactly because they are events: you cannot *own* an event, since if owning implies being in control of temporal behaviour, then, strictly speaking (at the token level), the temporal behaviour of an event is already determined, and changing it would result in a different event. So events are not transferable simply because they are not "ownable". Since services are events, they are not transferable as well.

So, in conclusion, it seems legitimate to assume that goods are *objects* (endurants, in DOLCE's terms), while services are *events* (perdurants). One may observe however that our economy is full of examples of transactions involving services, where the service seems to pass from hand to hand: certainly somebody may buy Amazon, for instance: our point is that in this case the transaction involves the Amazon *company*, not Amazon's *service*: there is a change of ownership concerning the service producer, but not the service itself, which remains the same (as long as the Amazon company doesn't change its legal identity, and its service content—the actions it offers—remains the same).

---

[7]An interesting analysis of the notion of ownership can be found in McCarty (2002).

14.2.2.1 Transferability of Services as Transferability of a Right

We have seen that a service, being an event, is not transferable. However, certainly we can transfer a right *to a service*. In the context of services, a right to a service implies a deontic position, in the sense that someone has a right if there exists a certain corresponding duty. A right of *A* of receiving a service would correspond then to the duty of *B* to provide the service, namely, to the duty of participating (as the main agent) in the *commitment event* that is at the basis of every service. A right can be reified, that is, considered as an object, and this is actually a common move in the legal domain.[8] And a right can be *owned*, in the sense that somebody can decide how to affect its "behaviour" (e.g., deciding *when* the right is claimed).

What is the conclusion of this conceptual analysis with regard to the notion of service? That even if a service is not directly transferable, since it is an event, *rights to services* are transferable: the object of the transmission is in this case the right, and the service is the event which the right refers to. In other words, having the right to a service is the same as being able to legitimately claim the performance of a certain service (set of actions) by some other party. And what can be transferred, from a legal perspective, is precisely this legal position that enables someone to legitimately claim the performance of a service.

A similar analysis can be applied to the notion of "good". In this case however the ownership (intended as the capability to influence the temporal behaviour) concerns the good itself, and not just the right to use it. In other words, we can own a good *in addition to* owning the right to exploit it, while for services the only thing we can own is the right to exploit them. Note that, although in many cases ownership transfer for goods implies a physical transfer (change in physical location), this is not always so, as in the case of real estates.

14.2.2.2 Transferability of Services as Transfer of a Duty

From the provider's point of view, a service transfer might be understood as well as the *transmission of the duty to provide the service content*. However, we should distinguish between *total* transfers of this duty from an agent to another (including all related responsibilities towards the service customer), and *partial* transfers (i.e., *delegations*), which maintain some responsibilities on the side of the delegating agent. The latter case is typical of public services, whose content is to be guaranteed by the state. Indeed, the public entity can *transfer a part of the duties* that compose its obligation to a private entity—namely, the obligation to actually *produce* the services in specific circumstances—but not its general duty and it will therefore keep part of the responsibility. Let us imagine health services. Health service can be a public service in the sense that the State has the responsibility of guaranteeing it. The State can, however, agree with a private party (private medical company) that whenever

---

[8]Rights were already clearly distinguished in Gaius' classification of the law as objects: "Res incorporales: things which cannot be touched, such as those consisting in rights, e.g. an inheritance, a usufruct, obligations".

citizens need health assistance, the private party will provide it. The responsibility over the service remains in the State, since it cannot completely delegate this duty.[9] However, the particular duty of satisfying concrete needs arising from specific situations (e.g. concrete medical care needs derived from the situation in which someone breaks his leg) is assigned to the private entity to which the service is entrusted. The duties related to health services are thus split between the state (the *provider*) and a private actor (the *producer*). A similar situation occurs in the case of subcontracting, by which the general contractor delegates to the subcontractor the performance of a specific task, keeping nonetheless responsibility towards the client.

On the contrary, a *total* transfer of duty can happen in the private sector, where we can distinguish two cases, depending on whether the duty comes from a *generic* commitment towards potential customers, or from a specific commitment concerning an *actual* customer, under specific circumstances. In the first case, it is common to talk of business transfers. This means that, if a business provides a private service with no special limitations on its transfer (and assuming that the service buyer fulfils all the necessary legal requirements), the full responsibility is simply transmitted to the acquiring party (let us imagine for instance the previously mentioned transfer of Amazon, or the transfer of a restaurant, or a hairdressing salon). In the second case, the transmission of a particular service, that is, of the concrete obligation to provide a service to a party, will be possible if this does not substantially alter the quality of the service contracted by the party or, if otherwise, the latter provides consent (let us imagine for instance that we reserve a room in a hotel and when we get there the hotel is full and they send us to another hotel within the same group).

As a conclusion, let us insist that, despite the cases above can be described as service transfers in the everyday jargon, properly speaking, according to our definition, the transfer does not involve the service itself, but rather certain *normative positions* (duties or obligations) that refer to it. Moreover, we maintain that, while an internal delegation process concerning the actual *production* of service content certainly does not alter the identity of a service under our definition, a *total* transfer of duty implies the existence (or the creation) of *another* service, different from the original one. If the owner of Amazon changes, while Amazon maintains its legal status and its service content remains the same, then the service remains the same, because the provider is still the same. On the contrary, if the provider changes (e.g., because the company dissolves after being bought by another), then the service changes, although the service content may remain the same. Suppose that for instance there are two companies, A and B, providing exactly the same service content (possibly at different prices). According to our definition, we say that there are two distinct services. If now A buys B (that is, the *company* B, with all its duties and rights, is transferred to A) the result is that the service provided by B disappears, and only one of the previous services survives.

---

[9] And this would therefore imply that complaints can still be directed to the State in case the service provided by the private company does not work well.

14.2.3 The Basic Ontological Structure of Services

Let us continue our analysis with another question: what's happening when a service is *produced*? As we have seen, a service may be concretely available even if it is not actually delivered, or maybe will be never delivered: we keep paying the firemen even if no fires occur. So, in our approach, a service has to be distinguished from its actual *delivery* to a particular customer. Indeed, typically the same service guarantees multiple deliveries. By the way, to avoid confusions, we propose an important terminological distinction: strictly speaking, it is not *the service* which is delivered, but its *content*, i.e., the actions intended to be performed in the interest of the customer. So a service implies first of all a concrete commitment (from the side of a *provider*) to guarantee the production of a certain content, consisting in actions of a certain kind executed in a certain way. Altogether, the various actions that ultimately lead to service content production (performed by the service *producer* on behalf of the provider) constitute the *service process*. We shall say that a service process *implements* a service commitment. The concrete delivery to a particular customer presupposes however a *service acquisition* activity engaged by the latter, which typically negotiates a *service offer* resulting from *service bundling and presentation* activities on the producer's side. Finally, to complete the picture, we have to take into account the activities related to the value exchange chain, which include the service exploitation from the customer's (*customer's exploitation*), the sacrifice needed to access to the service (*customer's sacrifice*), as well as the corresponding activities from the producer's side.

So, as illustrated in Fig. 14.1, a service is conceived as a complex event, with five main proper parts: service commitment, service presentation, service acquisition, service process, and service value exchange. In the following, we shall discuss these notions in more detail, with the aim to establish the basis for an ontology of services able to account both for *service descriptions* from an external point of view (typical of Web services and Service Oriented Architectures) and for *service processes* from an internal, business modelling point of view.

First of all, let us remark that all the blocks described in Fig. 14.1 are *events* (*perdurants*, in DOLCE's terminology). This means that they can be characterized, roughly, by their *temporal location* and by their *participants*, linked to the event by means of what are usually called *thematic relations*: agent, patient, theme, instrument. . . Specifying a service (or a service kind) amounts to constraining these events by imposing suitable restrictions on their temporal locations and thematic relations. So, for instance, non-functional requirements such as those discussed in O'Sullivan (2006) are represented as attributes of specific service components, each involving a particular aspect (participant/thematic relation) of a particular service event. The resulting analysis, which we cannot discuss in detail for reasons of space, looks very similar to Alter's *service responsibility tables* (2008), where the rows correspond to service components (events), and the columns to specific aspects to be considered (thematic relations). We give therefore a clean ontological foundation to a business-oriented proposal. Moreover, specifying the agents involved in each event allows for a fine-grained account of the *organizational impact* of a certain service.

Note that, although the relationships between these various events (for instance, whether or not they involve the same agents) may vary according to the nature of the service specified, there exists a systematic ordering relationship between them, so that a service has a *layered structure*. This ordering relationship is not so much a temporal precedence (indeed most of these events are temporally overlapping), but rather an (existential) *ontological dependence* relationship: in order for an event at a certain layer to occur, some event at the higher level has to occur. Ultimately, all the events belonging to the service process presuppose some acquisition event, which in turn presupposes the service commitment.

At this point it is important to notice the central role played by actions and events in this account for the description of services; this is in contrast with the major trend, which is to describe services in terms of pre-conditions and post-conditions, like in WSMO, where processes are represented as transitions between states (Roman et al. 2005). Under a different perspective, the two approaches could also work in conjunction.

There are several reasons why in our opinion it is important to explicitly represent events; first of all, though for the front-office in most cases it is enough to know which is the starting state and which the desired one, for the back-office it is important that the whole process be transparent (to know who does what and when), especially when a failure is at stake. But malfunctioning is not the only reason: without events one does not have sufficient expressiveness to distinguish two different commitments with the same content but different deadlines. Even if one sees these deadlines as non functional properties, it is hard to use them, say, for expressing a SLA without a clear semantics.

Again, in Parasuraman et al. (1985) a list of service quality's determinants is given, in which at least a couple of these determinants are strongly space-time dependent: responsiveness, connected with timeliness of service and access, defined by (among others) three items: "waiting time to receive a service [...]; convenient hours of operation; convenient location of service facility."

By using only pre- and post-conditions other subtle but important differences are lost. Take for example these two scenarios: 1. an unemployed woman who becomes pregnant and 2. a pregnant woman who becomes unemployed. In our account, the two scenarios can be distinguished by the fact that in 1 the pregnancy is the triggering event, while in 2 it is the unemployment. This difference may result in the activation of different services (for instance, a financial aid in 1 and a help in searching a new job in 2, or a legal enquiry on the employer if there's a suspicion of unfairness). In a pre- post-conditions framework both scenarios have the same pre-conditions and thus should activate the same services. Notably, the literature in economics has since long recognized that comparing the outcomes of services is not enough in order to evaluate their quality. See for instance (Parasuraman et al. 1985) (similar distinctions appear in Sasser et al. 1978; Gronroos 1978, Lehtinen and Lehtinen 1982):

> Quality evaluations are not made solely on the outcome of a service; they also involve evaluations of the *process* of service delivery.

Let us now consider the various events constituting the service process internal structure. In Fig. 14.1, the containment relationship between the various blocks represents the parthood relationship. The core constituent of a service process is a set of basic activities (each called *customized service production*[10]), centred on the delivery of service content to a *single customer*. In addition to the *core service action(s)* depending on the service nature, a customized service production may include *enhancing actions* intended to increase the service value or differentiate it from those of competitors (Hill 1977) as well as *supporting actions* needed to enable the core service consumption and *follow-up* actions intended to monitor the core action's results. In addition to customized delivery activities, the service process includes various back-office activities concerning *customized delivery planning and coordination*, plus an activity we have labelled as *service context monitoring*—which seems to be neglected by most current approaches—which involves the various actions necessary to detect the event that triggers service production, which can be an external situation or a customer's request: without an explicit modelling of such activity, there would be no way to account for delays or improper management of triggering events.

As a presupposition to service production, typically some *service acquisition* activities are required from the side of the customer.[11] These include *service discovery*, which is the event where the service provider (or producer) and the service customer first meet together; *service negotiation*, which involves an agreement between the two parties, and *service invocation*, which refers to the event where the customer agrees to the service (not necessarily implying immediate production).

On the other hand, the service production results in a complex chain of transfers of value, which are represented in Fig. 14.1 as the event Service value exchange. With a simplification, this is decomposed in *Producer's cost, Customer's cost, Producer's revenue* and *Customer's revenue*.

While in the case of the producer, most of the times (both for cost and for revenue) the value has to be intended in terms of money, in the customer's case things are more complicated. For instance, especially for services in the social domain, the customer's cost can be seen as an action whose results go somehow against some of the recipient's desires, but which the customer is still willing to perform, like the *service sacrifice* mentioned in Roman et al. (2005). Also the customer's revenue sometimes is not expressible in monetary terms, but only as some wellness state. Moreover, even though there's always an ultimate recipient of a service, we could also have indirect recipients, like the community that pays with its taxes for the service and benefits in terms of enhancement of its social conditions.

In conclusion, we can say that a service is characterized in a *prescriptive* way (*commitment level*), while a service process in a *descriptive way* (*implementation*

---

[10]In the context of public services, a single event of customized service production is often called an *intervention*.

[11]Even in the case of free, public services, it is difficult to imagine a case where the customer is not required to actually discover the service, or make a minimal sacrifice to exploit it.

level). The commitment level is where the "rules of the game" are established: what types of action compose the service, what types of agents are entitled to execute those actions, what types of agents may qualify as recipients, what types of events can become triggering situations. It is also the level where legal responsibility is at stake. In fact, from the point of view of the service offering, it is not important who in particular executes certain actions, but rather that a certain kind of action is executed in a certain way, by an agent who displays certain features and has some competences. The agent who is responsible that the required conditions are met is usually an organization, such as for instance a public administration. Such responsibility is usually distributed and assigned according to some structural constraints, i.e. by devising a structure of roles and sub-organizations. The ontological analysis of organizations is thus a topic tightly connected to the ontological analysis of services.

When we come to the actual service process, the various *kinds* mentioned at the commitment level need to be instantiated in concrete *tokens*. Individual agents are those who realize the core actions of service production, whose recipients are, ultimately, concrete agents (citizens); also the triggering situation is the occurrence of a precise (instance of) event. The service production level is thus characterized at the *descriptive* level, the one the data that are recorded and transferred belong to.

Finally, let us mention the issue of spatio-temporal location of services. In very general terms, one could say that in most cases when somebody makes available a service, this availability spans over a spatio-temporal region which includes the spatio-temporal region in which the core service actions will (possibly) be executed; in rare cases, the two can coincide. For some special services, the analysis can be further complicated by the fact that the service may be delivered in a place and at a time and received in another place at another time. We won't enter into these details at present, but the issue needs to be investigated.

14.3 Responsibility, Right, Duty, Obligation

14.3.1 Connections Between the Main Notions

Before exploring in more detail the juridical implications of services in terms of the layered structure of interrelated events described above, let us focus in this subsection on the notion of responsibility, which is quite central in the study of services, analysing it under many respects, including its significance from a juridical point of view and its connection with the related notions of right, duty and obligation.

For a start, a definition of responsibility that can be found on a common business dictionary[12] is the following: "Duty or obligation to satisfactorily perform or complete a task (assigned by someone, or created by one's own promise or circumstances) that one must fulfil, and which has a consequent penalty for failure."

---

[12]http://www.businessdictionary.com/

As we can see, this definition includes both the possible sources and the common consequences of responsibility. As possible sources it mentions both an exogenous assignment (as in the case of delegation, that we will see in a while) and a promise coming from the same agent who's taking the responsibility (as in the case of commitment). Note that, if there is an exogenous assignment, the corresponding commitment is not necessary: for instance, a government may be responsible for the population's health without actually committing to it. In any case, the consequence of having (undertaken) a responsibility is to become the bearer of an obligation that, if not fulfilled, would bring about a sanction (which is the last element of the definition above).

When responsibilities are institutionally established and codified in a contract (such as a Service Level Agreement), then a relationship originates between the service provider and the service customer, such that then each customer's rights is connected to a correspondent obligation for the service provider; very often this obligation is accompanied by a possible sanction, in case the obligation is not fulfilled.

The right of the customer to have the service fulfilled, and the belief that the agent will be sanctioned in case it is not, engenders an expectation in the customer that the service will be delivered.

If we look at it from a juridical perspective, *responsibility* refers to the situation of being accountable to someone for something. There exist many types of responsibility depending on the kind of normative order that makes one accountable: social responsibility if the normative order is the social order, moral responsibility if the normative order is a particular moral system and legal responsibility if the order is a legal system, among others. The core meaning of the notion of responsibility involves therefore the existence of a certain kind of normative order that should be observed.

In the legal domain, a difference is made between the general notion of social responsibility and a stricter notion of *liability*, which refers to the elements that are generally required for incurring legal blame because of the violation of a social responsibility, and, in private law, for being compelled to comply with a court order to pay damages or compensate in some other way the damage done (Lucy 2007). Criminal liability entails punishment, which frequently takes the form of imprisonment. This way, legal responsibility (liability) can be seen as the concept that enables to blame someone for unlawful action. Once the responsible subject is declared liable, actions can be taken to compel him or her to compensate the harm done or to punish him or her.

Legal liability requires the existence of an agent, whose conduct is considered legally relevant; a patient, affected by that conduct; the conduct or action; and the wrong or harm, understood as the effects on the patient. Agent and patient do not necessarily have to be concrete physical persons; in private law both agents are private parties, in public law the harm is in general terms not merely caused to an individual party, but to the community or to the general interest (this is one of the criteria for distinguishing private law and criminal law).

Note that, as observed above, legal responsibility (liability) inherently requires *a pre-existing normative order against which to judge the agent's conduct.* This normative order can be translated into particular *normative positions* (rights and duties). These normative positions define the liability-responsibility relation and permit to allocate specific roles to the agents involved. A landmark contribution to the notion of duty and right is (Hohfeld 1913), where an analysis of fundamental juridical notions is presented. In this work "duty" and "right" are considered correlative concepts that can be represented through the following scheme: *"[. . .] if X has a right against Y that he shall stay off the former's land, the correlative (and equivalent) is that Y is under a duty toward X to stay off the place."* (Hohfeld 1913). If X's duty (or obligation) is not fulfilled, then there will possibly be legal responsibility and liability.

Taking into account this general framework and according to the model of services presented above, in the context of services provision we can envisage different sources for legal responsibility (liability):

- breach of contract (of obligation) [*contractual responsibility*]
- specific damages resulting from the breach of contract [*contractual responsibility*]
- specific damages resulting form the wrongful performance of service: civil and criminal responsibility [*extra contractual responsibility*].

These different types of legal responsibility (liability) are connected to the breach of different kinds of duties or obligations. Let us imagine a public service, namely, health care. We can distinguish different duties in this regard:

1. the duty of providing particular health care services (doctor assistance, medical tests, diagnosis, treatment,. . .) at particular moments and to particular individuals. It is therefore a contractual obligation or duty.
2. the duty of performing the actions directed to provide health care services according to general diligence (standards of conduct in the medical field determined by the community of medical professionals and their practices) and according to certain conditions explicitly established in a certain context. These latter conditions can be established by the regulation (in a particular country) for health service providers. It could be regarded therefore as an extra-contractual obligation or duty.

If duty 1 is not fulfilled, this can be seen as a breach of contract (obligation) and as specific damages resulting from the breach of contract; whereas if duty 2 is not fulfilled, this could be regarded as damages resulting form the wrongful performance of the service: civil and criminal responsibility.

The previous scheme can be applied to the framework of public services. The cases presented can be understood in terms of abnormal function of the public service, according to Principle I of the Council of Europe Recommendation

R (84) 15 of the Committee of Ministers to Members States relating to public liability:

> Reparation should be ensured for damage caused by an act due to a failure of a public authority to conduct itself in a way which can reasonably be expected from it in law in relation to the injured person. Such a failure is presumed in case of transgression of an established legal rule.

However, state liability is not excluded in case the function of the service is normal, if it is considered unfair that the citizen bears the damage. This is stated in principle II.1:

> Even if the conditions stated in Principle I are not met, reparation should be ensured if it would be manifestly unjust to allow the injured person alone to bear the damage, having regard to the following circumstances: the act is in the general interest, only one person or a limited number of persons have suffered the damage and the act was exceptional or the damage was an exceptional result of the act.

The transferability of these different responsibilities varies. Responsibility travels along with the corresponding normative position, that is, with the specific duty. If the duty is transmitted to a private party, the corresponding liability is as well transmitted. Nevertheless, the more abstract statutory duty consisting in the obligation to guaranteeing the existence of a structure or organisation that provides a particular service is not transferable. This duty is established by laws, quite often constitutional texts, which determine that the state is responsible of guaranteeing certain public services to which citizens have a right. This is why some peculiarities exist in the regime of public responsibility. For instance, the establishment of strict liability, which affects not only the state, but as well the private bodies that are providing the service on the basis of a license (Beladiez 1997); or, even if the service (duty 1, duty 2) has been transferred to a private entity, complaints might have to be directed to the state (this was once the case in Spanish regulation (Pérez 1999)). The state could be held liable as well, for instance, in case the statutory certification bodies had not performed well their task and had granted permission to operate to a private medical centre that did not fulfil the minimal conditions and some concrete injury had been caused to a patient. It could be held responsible as well in case the damage was due to a compulsory clause imposed by the state in the public contract granting permission to the private entity to provide the service.

14.3.2 Patterns of Responsibilities, Obligations and Rights Across Service Structures

The starting point of our analysis is the event of service commitment, in which a service provider commits with someone (a community, or an authority) that a certain service content will be produced for the benefit of a designated kind of customer.

In the literature a distinction is traced between implicit and explicit (or "explicitly represented", in Singh's terms) commitment, that goes back to the more traditional approaches, like that of Becker (1960), who distinguishes between commitment by default and commitment by conscious decision. In institutional settings the commitment is usually codified in a document, like a contract (and gives rise to contractual responsibility); this contract creates new juridical entities: it creates an obligation for the provider; this may be a direct obligation to perform certain kinds of actions or it can consist in seeing to it that such kinds of actions are performed by someone else. In this latter case the contract envisions also a delegation action. When a provider delegates the execution of a service to a producer, the action creates an obligation on the side of the producer (of executing the service) and a right from the side of the provider (of having the service executed, so as to be able to fulfil its previously determined obligations towards the community or authority whom the commitment was addressed to). Delegation relations may be seen as responsibility transfers between agents. As noted in the previous subsection, if the duty of executing the action is transferred (delegated), also the responsibility of that action is transferred; nonetheless, the obligation of guaranteeing that the service is executed (which pertains the public authority that plays the role of provider) is not transferable. It is interesting to notice that in (1997) Singh explicitly lists delegation among the operations that can be executed on commitments. He also highlights the fact that when a commitment is delegated, agents shift their roles: he says that the role of debtor is shifted, that is to say that the commitment passes from the provider to the producer, who has now the responsibility with respect to the execution of the service actions. We are aware of the fact that this description is a simplified one, as the responsibility can sometimes be shared in varying proportions.

In (Falcone and Castelfranchi 2001) a classification of different types of delegation relations based on three dimensions is traced. In particular, along the first dimension, based on the nature of interaction, the authors distinguish between weak, mild and strong delegation: in weak delegation there is no agreement, no requests and no intended influence, so that the one who delegates just exploits the actions of the other; in mild delegation there is still no agreement and no request, but the desired behaviour is in some way induced; finally, in strong delegation there is an explicit agreement on which the delegation is founded. It is obviously this latter type of delegation that is at stake between service provider and producer, as the delegation in this case comes into being just with the signature of a contract or some other formal agreement.

Another dimension that is of interest for this discussion is the one based on the degree of task specification, that distinguishes between open, close and intermediate delegation, depending on whether the object of delegation is more or less specified, in a spectrum ranging from open delegation with minimal specification to close delegation with complete specification, with various degrees classifiable as intermediate delegation.

The degree of specification of the delegation depends on what is written in the delegation agreement or contract, similarly to the case of the service commitment contract, where the commitment's content can be more or less specified concerning the way the core actions are executed.

Disregarding who is in charge of executing the service actions, the commitment also creates a right on the side of the customer.

Even though, as we just mentioned, in most cases public institutions make their commitment public through a contract or a deliberation, it happens very often that, while the assumption of the commitment on the side of a public entity is explicit, its acceptance by the beneficiaries is only implicit and given "by default" by their belonging to a particular social community. This default acceptance assumption ensures that the beneficiary can claim the execution of a certain service even without having signed any contract or having negotiated anything with anybody on this respect.

The chain of rights and obligations generated by the commitment event also imposes various kinds of constraints on the other events composing the service. For example, during the activities of service bundling and presentation, the service producer is constrained in that it cannot promise anything that is excluded by the contract signed at the time of the commitment event. Also, what is advertised in the presentation must not be anything that cannot then be executed. The fact that the service is presented in a certain way may also give additional rights to the customer, like the right to have it executed in the way in which it has been presented (not always, sometimes if the contract doesn't explicitly commit to execute the service as it is advertised in the presentation phase, it may be that the customer does not acquire such right, but at least the producer becomes liable of being sanctioned for what it has promised and then not fulfilled. In this case maybe the customer can be refunded, thus acquiring another, different, right).

Also the service negotiation phase is very important from a juridical standpoint, since when a new contract with a specific customer is signed it has to comply with what established in the general commitment contract, but it can add details to that. This customized contract makes the producer's obligations more precise (possibly adding new obligations) and creates specific rights for individual customers (differently from the commitment, where rights were attributed to classes of customers).

The service process is the phase in which what has been promised in the commitment and in the negotiation phases is realized. According to the level of detail of the contracts resulting from these two phases, the various actions of the service process can be executed in a more or less pre-defined and specific way.

It is important to notice that the service process also includes a service context monitoring activity. The way this monitoring is performed is also regulated; usually, this regulation is primarily given in the commitment, where the provider also commits on monitoring, but can decide whether to execute such monitoring directly or to delegate it to someone else. This delegation can be directed either to the producer of the service, or to a different entity, that is then only in charge of the monitoring. In case it is delegated to the producer, this can further delegate it to some other entity.

The commitment towards monitoring (be it direct commitment or a commitment acquired via delegation) and the consequent rights and obligations that it brings with it, underline the importance of the triggering event in the structure of the service. If the entity in charge of monitoring fails to detect the presence of the triggering event, the service process cannot be initiated. In this case it is not the service producer that has to be deemed responsible for the failure of the service process, since this was not initiated due to the lack of the "start signal" given by the detection of the triggering event.

Finally, after having verified that in the service process phase all that was promised in the previous phases has been properly realized, a right of receiving some income on the side of the producer arises in the service value exchange phase. Consequently, for the provider (or the community in public services' cases), an obligation of providing such income to the producer is created. The amount of such exchanges is usually fixed in the negotiation phase. If the contract also specifies some constraints in the customer's costs (for instance, the fact that a service has to be produced in a restricted timeslot) and these are not met, a new negotiation phase can take place.

14.4 A Revised Version of Alter's Responsibility Tables

An author who also deems the concept of responsibility as central for service science is Steven Alter, who, in a recent article (Alter 2008) has presented a conceptual instrument that he calls "service responsibility tables" (SRT); these are aimed at facilitating a better understanding of services primarily based on the responsibilities assigned to each role; moreover, Alter suggests to add as many columns as necessary in order to address different aspects of analysis. In practice, Alter isolates two orthogonal components of services: the constituting actions and, for each of these actions, the responsibilities of the involved stakeholders; he thus describes *how* such stakeholders participate to the various events. These *modes* of participation individuate the *role* the participants play in the various events constituting the service.

Even though the topics suggested by Alter are heterogeneous and sometimes confusing, we are interested in his idea of representing the events composing a service and the role participants have in these events and in using the tables to represent the distribution of responsibilities across the events composing the complex structure of the service system.

In order to represent all this, we take inspiration from a notion introduced in linguistics to account for the internal structure of events: so-called *thematic relations* (or *thematic roles*), expressing the nature of the relationship between an event and its participants. Adding thematic relations to those linking an event to its own qualities (such as temporal and spatial location) we have a full set of attributes at our disposal, among which the following ones appear to be as especially relevant for our purposes:

- Agent (the active role, the one who acts in the event)
- Theme/Patient (the one who undergoes the event; the patient changes its state, the theme does not)
- Goal (what the event is directed towards—typically a desired state of affairs)
- Recipient/Beneficiary (the one who receives the effects of the event)
- Instrument (something that is used in the performance of the event)

- Location (where the event takes place)
- Time/duration (when the event takes place, or how long it lasts)

As a result, in the service responsibility table we have the main composing events n the rows (service commitment, service acquisition, service process, service value exchange. . .) and the thematic relations in the columns.

In order to give an idea of the approach, we take an example and we represent it using the tables. The example is directly taken from Hill (1977) and it is about a guy who goes to the mechanic's garage to have his car repaired. The aim of Table 1 is that of representing in an explicit way the fundamental constraints that need to be specified in an actual service description. This can bring many advantages both in the comprehension of the service's features and in the many different evaluations of service quality that can be made under various viewpoints, among which the legal one, that is particularly relevant in this context.

The table describes the events in which a generic car repair service is articulated. The values we put in the various cells allow us to express the relevant constraints that distinguish this service from others.

We start with service commitment. During the commitment event, that chronologically comes first and is the one that all the other events depend on, the garage's owner commits with a Public Administration (for instance the Chamber of Commerce) with a subscription act and his commitment consists in guaranteeing that someone (the mechanic) will execute a certain type of job (illustrated in the job description, on which he commits) according to the local rules. This commitment is valid in the whole Province (for instance) and starting from that very moment on.

After the commitment, we have the service acquisition, which in turn is composed by three different events: discovery, negotiation and activation. During discovery the customer looks for a garage (that is then the *theme* of his search) with the goal of having his car repaired. Note that not all the cells in this line are filled, meaning that, for instance, the instrument used for the discovery activity is not specified. Should we describe a service based (exclusively) on a certain mediator for the discovery process, the name of such mediator would be specified in the "Instrument" cell.

After the service is discovered, the negotiation between customer and mechanic starts; the goal is (probably) an agreement and the negotiation is on the service customization (in other words, how the service type in the job description is tailored to the customer's needs). At that point the mechanic activates the service, i.e., the related scheduling and organization activities. The last two events usually take place in the garage and the whole service acquisition event is performed after the commitment has been taken and before the occurrence of the actual repair.

The actual service process (as can be noted from Fig. 14.1) is a very complex one, consisting of a lot of interconnected activities; here, for simplicity reasons, we choose to represent only the service's core actions.

In the service process event, the mechanic, with his tools and in his garage, performs some actions on the car aimed at having it repaired; this in the interest of the customer.

Finally, there is an articulated service value exchange event, which is constituted by a bunch of activities corresponding to what counts as a "sacrifice" or an "exploitation" from the producer's and customer's points of view. This is a complex topic, that deserves a more thorough examination, because both the components of cost and those of revenue can be many and different evaluations can be conducted with different purposes. Simplifying a lot, here we can say that the mechanic counts as a sacrifice his working hours with the goal of being paid, while the customer counts as a sacrifice the money he pays, the time to go to the garage, the time the car is unavailable and so on with the goal of having the car repaired; the mechanic earns money, while the customer's revenue consists in having his car available again.

There are some remarks that can be made; first of all, from the knowledge representation point of view, one thing that can be easily observed is that some values must be the same across multiple cells; for instance, the mechanic plays a role of agent in service process, while he plays the role of patient in service acquisition. This might be a problem, as most languages ordinarily used to talk about services (like those based on description logics) are not expressive enough to account for co-reference between variables.

Another remark—a methodological one—is that these tables can be further refined, for example by decomposing the service process event in its internal layers.

Even though the example is quite elementary, it is already possible to see how much additional information the table can convey. The table can also help visualizing the responsibility relations specific to definite events that can be deduced by looking at how the thematic roles in the event are filled. For instance, it is easy to infer from the table that the garage's owner is responsible of the availability of the car repair service, as it is described in the job description according to what it is written in the subscription act signed with the Chamber of Commerce. Similarly, the mechanic is responsible of executing the repair as it has been agreed with the customer in the negotiation phase. As we already noted, the chain of delegation and the transfer of responsibilities are issues that are particularly relevant in the domain of services and the table (with the due refinements) could be a useful tool to visualize all this in a clearer way.

14.5 Concluding Remarks and Future Issues

In this paper we have proposed a novel framework aimed at constituting a common ontological foundation for services science. Let us briefly discuss what the main contributions of this approach are, and what future research directions we are considering.

1. *Revisitation of the difference between internal and external service views.* We have seen that the black box model of services based on external behaviour is too limited, and that a higher expressivity is necessary both to describe services

in terms of their internal structure and to properly characterize SLAs and non-functional attributes.

2. *Improvement of the classic definition of services coming from economics.* We have seen that Hill's definition based on change is not general enough, since, for instance, it does not allow to consider services which do not necessarily produce a change, such as fire control.

3. *Focus on core actions instead of pre- and post-conditions.* We have seen how pre- and post-conditions cannot by themselves capture important aspects of services, related to the way the service process is performed.

4. *Activity-based service representation.* We have seen how to describe a service in terms of a layered structure of related activities (events, in the most general sense of this term). The separation of the various activities described in Fig. 14.1 allows us to properly account for non-functional properties, which instead of generically belonging to the service as a whole are attributes that characterize specific activities. In this way, it is possible to determine what aspect of a given service implementation is responsible for a certain service property. In particular, spatio-temporal attributes can be easily taken into account.

5. *Comprehensive business-oriented approach.* We have introduced a clear distinction between service commitment, service process, and service content, taking also into account important issues affecting service quality and evaluation, such as bundling and presentation activities, acquisition activities, and actions related to the service value chain.

6. *Conceptual analysis of the patterns of responsibilities across services.* We have conducted an analysis that takes into account the legal perspective, which is central with respect to service level agreements.

7. *Common framework to describe service according to different views,* in terms of more or less general constraints among the various service activities, providing an ontological foundation to the technique of *responsibility tables* introduced by Alter.

Given the preliminary nature of the present paper, many are the directions in which the analysis can be extended and enriched.

For sure, in order to be effective, this exploratory work needs to result in a formal model, that will constitute an ontology of services that, as a component of a modular social ontology, should be in the end connected with an ontology of organizations.

Acknowledgments This work is carried out under the scope of the activities of the LEGO lab (www.lego-lab.it), a joint e-government initiative located in Trento, as well as the TOCAI.IT project, funded by the Italian Ministry of Research (Tecnologie Orientate alla Conoscenza per Aggregazioni di Imprese su InterneT) and the project "CSS—Cartella Socio-Sanitaria" founded by the Autonomous Province of Trento. The initial ideas at the basis of this project have emerged from a fruitful collaboration with "Servizio Politiche Sociali e Abitative" of the Autonomous Province of Trento concerning the revision of a catalog of social services, to be shared among different Public Administrations. The first author is funded by a PostDoc grant from the Autonomous Province of Trento.

References

Alter, S. (2008). Service System Fundamentals: Work System, Value Chain, and Life Cycle. *IBM Systems Journal*, 2008; 47(1): 71–85.

Baida, Z., J. Gordijn, H. Akkermans (2001). *Service Ontology*. Free University, Amsterdam.

Baida, Z. (2006). *Software-Aided Service Bundling—Intelligent Methods & Tools for Graphical Service Modeling*. Vrije Universiteit, Amsterdam.

Becker, H. (1960). Notes on the Concept of Commitment. *American Journal of Sociology*, LXVI: 32–40.

Beladiez Rojo, M. (1997). *Responsabilidad e imputación de danos por el funcionamiento de los servicios públicos*. Tecnos, Madrid.

Castelfranchi, C. (2003). Grounding We-Intention in Individual Social Attitudes: On Social Commitment Again. In M. Sintonen, K. Miller (Eds.) *Realism in Action—Essays in the Philosophy of Social Sciences*. Dordrecht. Kluwer, 195–212.

Cauvet, C., G. Guzelian (2008). Business Process Modeling: A Service-Oriented Approach. In *HICSS '08, 41st Annual Hawaii International Conference on System Sciences*. IEEE Computer Society.

Chesbrough, H., J. Spohrer (2006). A Research Manifesto for Services Science. *Communications of the ACM*, 49(7): 35–40.

Dumas, M., et al. (2003) Towards a Semantic Framework for Service Description. In *Data Semantics 9: Semantic Issues in E-Commerce*. Kluwer, Hong Kong, 239.

Falcone, R., C. Castelfranchi (2001). The Human in the Loop of a Delegated Agent: The Theory of Adjustable Social Autonomy. *IEEE Transactions on Systems, Man, and Cybernetics, Part A*, 31(5): 406–418.

Fensel, D., C. Bussler (2002). The Web Service Modeling Framework WSMF. *Electronic Commerce Research and Applications*, 1: 113–137.

Gronroos, C. (1978). A Service-Oriented Approach to Marketing of Services. *European Journal of Marketing*, 12(8): 588–601.

Hill, T.P. (1977). On Goods and Services. *Review of Income and Wealth*, 23(4): 315–338.

Hohfeld, W.N. (1913). Some Fundamental Legal Conceptions as Applied in Judicial Reasoning. *The Yale Law Journal*, 23(1): 16–59.

Janssen, M., R. Wagenaar (2003). From Legacy to Modularity: A Roadmap Towards Modular Architectures Using Web Services Technology. In R. Traunmüller (Ed.) *Electronic Government*. Berlin, Heidelberg: Springer 95–100.

Jennings, N.R. (1993). Commitment and Conventions: The Foundation of Coordination in Multi-Agent Systems. *The Knowledge Engineering Review*, 8(3): 223–250.

Lehtinen, U., J.R. Lehtinen (1982). *Service Quality: A Study of Quality Dimensions*. Service Management Institute, Helsinki.

Lucy, W. (2007). *Philosophy of Private Law*. Oxford University Press, Oxford.

Masolo, C., et al. (2003). The WonderWeb Library of Fundational Ontologies and the DOLCE ontology. WonderWeb Deliverable D18, Final Report (vr. 1.0. 31-12-2003).

McCarty, L.T. (2002). Ownership: A Case Study in the Representation of Legal Concepts. *Artificial Intellingence and Law*, 10(1–3): 135–161.

O'Sullivan, J. (2006). Towards a Precise Understanding of Service Properties. In *Faculty of Information Technology*. Queensland University of Technology, 232.

Papazoglou, M.P., D. Georgakopoulos (2003). Service-Oriented Computing. *Communications of the ACM*, 46(10): 25–28.

Parasuraman, A., V.A. Zeithaml, L.L. Berry (1985). A Conceptual Model of Service Quality and Its Implications for Future Rersearch. *Journal of Marketing*, 49(4): 41–50.

Pérez Moreno, A. (1999). Responsabilidad en la gestión indirecta de obras y servicios públicos. In J.L. Martínez, A. Calonge (Eds.) *La responsabilidad patrimonial de los poderes públicos*. Marcial Pons, Madrid, Barcelona, 399–418.

Petrie, C., C. Bussler (2008). The Myth of Open Web Services: The Rise of the Service Parks. *IEEE Internet Computing*, 12(3): 94–96.

Roman, D., et al. (2005). Web Service Modeling Ontology. *Applied Ontology*, 1(1): 77–106.

Sasser, W.E.J., R.P. Olsen, D.D. Wyckoff (1978). *Management of Service Operations: Text and Cases*. Allyn & Bacon, Boston, MA.

Singh, M.P. (1997). An Ontology for Commitments in Multiagent Systems: Toward a Unification of Normative Concepts. *Artificial Intelligence and Law*, 7: 97–113.

Sycara, K. (2007). Unthethering Semantic Web Services. In D. Martin, J. Domingue (Eds.) *Semantic Web Services*, Part 2, D. IEEE Intelligent Systems, 11–13.

Terlouw, L., A. Albani, An Enterprise Ontology-Based Approach to Service Specification. *IEEE Transactions on Services Computing*, to appear.

Traverso, P., M. Pistore (2004). Automated Composition of Semantic Web Services into Executable Processes. In *International Semantic Web Conference* (ISWC'04). Hiroshima, Japan.

Verdicchio, M., M. Colombetti (2003). A Logical Model of Social Commitment for Agent Communication. In *AAMAS 2003*. Elsevier. Melbourne, Australia.

Vetere, G., M. Lenzerini (2005). Models for Semantic Interoperaility in Service-Oriented Architectures. *IBM Systems Journal*, 44(4): 887–903.

Weigand, H., et al. (2009). Value-Based Service Modeling and Design: Toward a Unified View of Services. In P. van Eck, J. Gordijn, R. Wieringa (Eds.) *Advanced Information Systems Engineering*. Springer, Berlin, 410–424.

Chapter 15
Legal Multimedia Ontologies and Semantic Annotation for Search and Retrieval

Jorge González-Conejero

15.1 Introduction

Nowadays, legal professionals are used to consuming an important part of their time searching, retrieving, and managing legal information. However, the recent explosion of multimedia legal contents has resulted in rising costs and requires more management capacities than ever before. Improving the functionalities for search, retrieval, and management of multimedia legal documents is paramount to fully unlock the potential of those contents for legal practice and to develop specific management solutions for different profiles of legal users (Brickell and Langer 2009).

Multimedia files carry a meaning which can be very versatile. For a human, the meaning of the message is immediate, but for a computer that is far from true. This discrepancy is commonly referred to as the *semantic gap* (Smeulders et al. 2000). In addition, the extraction of high-level concepts from multimedia is more difficult than from text. In multimedia field, high-level concepts are generated from low-level features captured from files, and the result of methods that capture different properties from the video or image, for instance, pattern recognition algorithms. It is also difficult to evaluate the similarity of the different concepts extracted from the multimedia content and place it in a multimedia ontology. The main idea is to automatically segment images, video sequences and key frames into areas corresponding to salient semantic objects (*e.g.* cars, road, people, etc.). Semantic multimedia annotation is the process of automatically detecting the presence of a concept in an image or video stream. In the literature, there are several works that address the multimedia annotation based on their meaning for different fields. In (Ballan et al. 2010) an approach for automatic annotation and retrieval of video content is presented, based on ontologies, rule learning with first order logic and semantic concept classifiers. An automatic video retrieval method based on high-level concept detectors is presented in (Snoek et al. 2007), defining a set of machine learned concept detectors

J. González-Conejero (✉)
UAB Institute of Law and Technology, Autonomous University of Barcelona, Barcelona, Spain
e-mail: jorge.gonzalez.conejero@uab.es

G. Sartor et al. (eds.), *Approaches to Legal Ontologies*, Law, Governance
and Technology Series 1, DOI 10.1007/978-94-007-0120-5_15,
© Springer Science+Business Media B.V. 2011

enriched with semantic descriptions. In (Zha et al. 2007) a more general and comprehensive ontology to annotate video contents is described. Usually, an ontology consists of a lexicon, properties and relations. In this work, LSCOM (Snoek et al. 2006) is used to construct the lexicon and describe concept property as the weights of different modalities which are obtained manually or by data-driven approach, and model two types of concept relations. The work (Gonzàlez et al. 2008) presents a Cognitive Vision System which explains the human behavior of monitored scenes using natural language texts. Here, the trajectories of human agents are obtained to generate textual interpretations of their motion, also inferring the conceptual relationship of each agent. The human behavior model is based on Situation Graph Trees.

Most of the current research focuses on event recognition and classification based on the extraction of low-level features. However, these approaches are mostly limited to a very small number of different event types, e.g. detecting a moving person, recognizing specific objects, etc. Usually, ontologies are used to enrich the query performed by the final user/application to extract concepts, and then to match them in the annotated multimedia file. Recently, ontologies have been effectively used to perform semantic annotation and retrieval of multimedia content. In the case of video annotation the terms of the ontologies are associated to the individual elements of the video either manually or automatically, exploiting the results of the advancements in pattern recognition and image/video analysis. In this case, combinations of multimedia features are extracted from the media and linked to the terms of the ontology. To support effective retrieval of video data, capturing the different patterns of a concept, we need extended ontologies, that allow the integration of low-level expressive power of visual data with the structured high level semantic knowledge expressed in textual form. Concepts and categories defined in a traditional ontology are not rich enough to fully describe or discriminate the diversity of the possible visual events. The possibility of extending linguistic ontologies with multimedia ontologies has been suggested in (Jaimes et al. 2003).

Nevertheless, to the best of our knowledge, there are no available systems within the judicial domain to automatically index, tag or annotate audiovisual files taking into account the requirements from judicial procedures. The annotation process for multimedia files produced by the judicial domain has several important benefits for legal professionals. One of the most important features is that it facilitates the search, improving the legal frameworks and applications focused on, for instance, e-learning (Xin 2009) and e-discovery (Baron and Thompson 2007).

The aim of this work is: (1) discuss the suitability of annotating and indexing legal multimedia contents through a legal multimedia ontology; and (2) analyze the problems that arise when the extracted concepts from multimedia contents are placed in a multimedia ontology. The paper is organized as follows: in Section 15.2 a brief summary of classical ontologies is reported; Section 15.3 reviews the languages used to implement ontologies, their properties, the related work in this field and a discussion of the suitability of multimedia ontologies in the legal domain and the problems that arise when a multimedia ontology is generated directly from the concepts extracted from a multimedia file; finally, Section 15.4 summarizes the work.

15.2 Ontologies

Gruber defined an ontology as a formal, explicit specification of a shared conceptualization (Gruber 1993). It is an abstract model of some phenomenon in the world that identifies the relevant concepts of that phenomenon. The four concepts present in a general ontology are: (1) "conceptualization" which refers to an abstract model of some phenomenon in the world, which identifies the relevant concepts used; (2) "explicit" which means that the type of concepts used and constrains on their use are explicitly defined; (3) "formal" which refers to the fact that the ontology should be machine readable; and (4) "shared" which reflects the notion that an ontology captures consensual knowledge.

Ontologies have been proposed to solve the problems that arise from using different terminologies to refer to the same concept, or using the same term to refer to different concepts (Guarino 1998). They consist of definitional aspects such as high-level schemas and assertional aspects, entities and attributes, interrelationships between entities, and domain vocabulary, all connected in a semantic manner. They have been generally associated with logical inferencing and recently have begun to be applied to the Semantic Web (Berners-Lee et al. 2001). Ontologies provide specific tools to organize and provide a useful description of heterogeneus content. For humans, ontologies enable better access to information and promote shared understanding. For computers, ontologies facilitate comprehension of information and more extensive processing. Figure 15.1 depicts an example of an ontology from the Neurona Project. This project is developed at the Institute of Law and Technology (IDT) and it is focused on the Spanish Data Privacy Act.

15.3 Multimedia Ontologies

Ontologies have applications in many areas including natural language translation, medicine, standarization of product knowledge, electronic commerce, and geographic information systems, among others. There is a natural increase on demands to store, organize, and query videos with the advances in digital technologies. Although linguistic terms are appropiate to distinguish event and object categories, they are inadequate when they must describe specific patterns of events or multimedia entities. High level concepts expressed through linguistic terms and pattern specifications represented through visual or auditory concepts should both be organized into a new extended ontologies that couple linguistic terms with visual/audio information. These new extended or multimedia enriched ontologies are known as *multimedia ontologies*. A multimedia ontology, broadly speaking, specifies the knowledge of the world through multimedia documents in a structured way. An

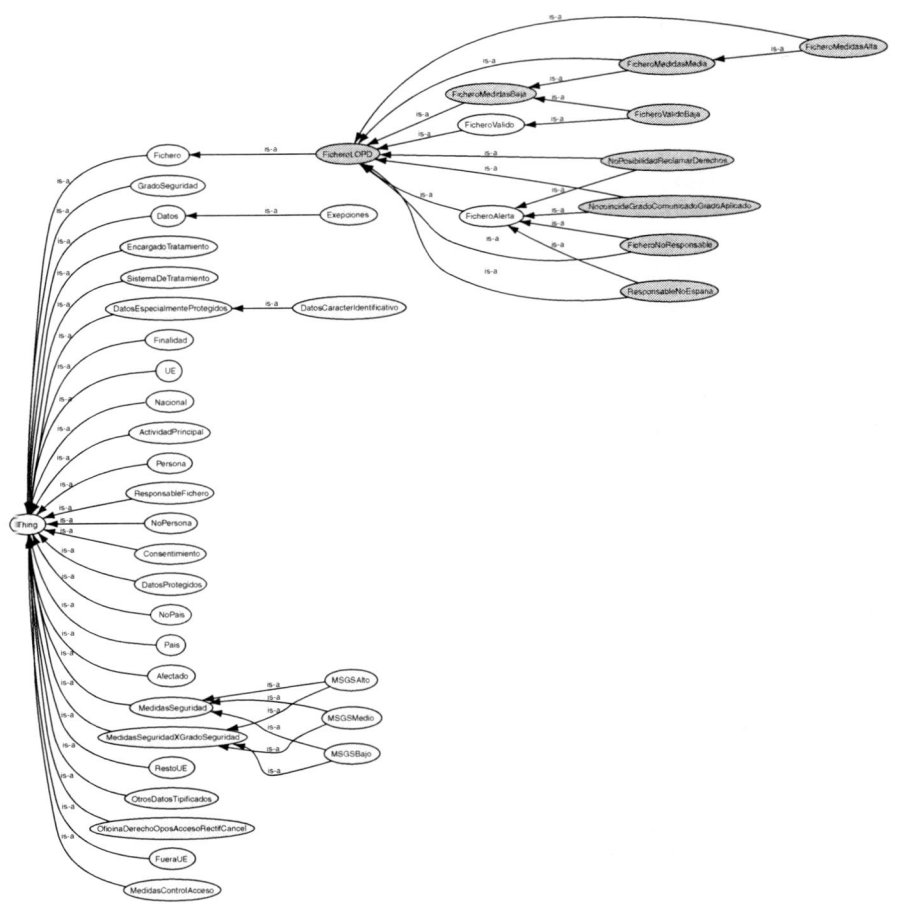

Fig. 15.1 Ontology from the neurona project

ontology is a formal, explicit specification of a domain. Typically, an ontology consists of concepts, concept properties and relationships between concepts. In a typical
multimedia ontology concepts might be represented by multimedia entities (images,
graphics, video, audio, etc.) or terms.

The literature presents several examples for the multimedia ontology field.
Figure 15.2 depicts a brief scheme for a general multimedia ontology (Dong and
Li 2006) where three different types of classes are present: multimedia entities, non
multimedia entities and descriptor entities. Multimedia entities are further classified
into image, video and audio. Non-multimedia entities include agent, place, time
and instrument, and descriptor entities include visual descriptors, audio descriptors,
structure descriptors and semantic descriptors. Figure 15.3 shows an example of one
video segment property within the ontology developed in (Dong and Li 2006). Here,

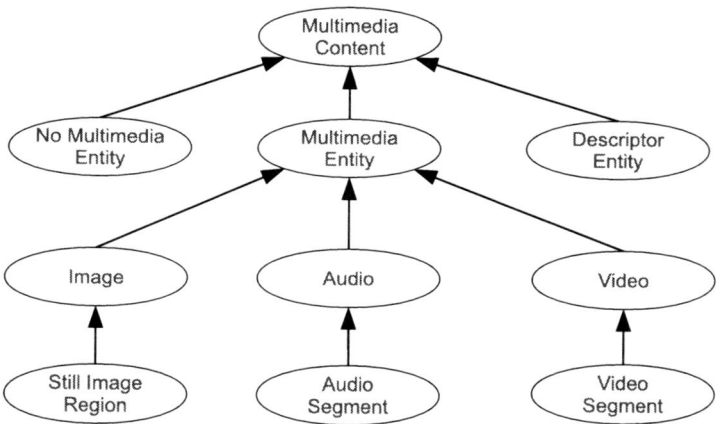

Fig. 15.2 Multimedia ontology scheme (Dong and Li 2006)

Fig. 15.3 Video segment
property in a multimedia
ontology (Dong and Li 2006)

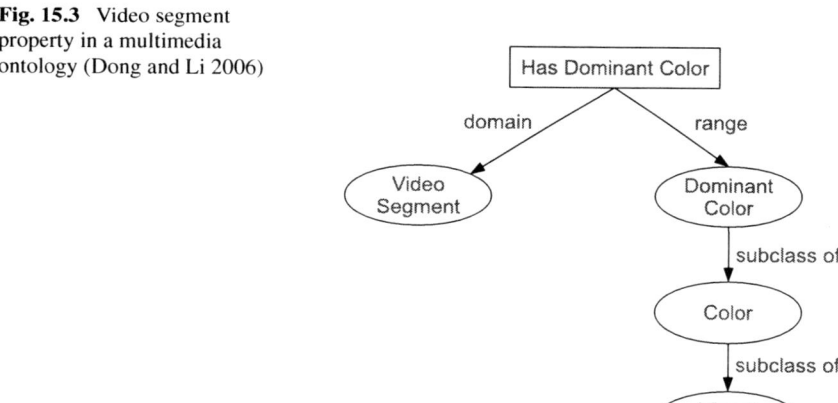

"Has Dominant Color" is a video segment property. This property correlates "Video Segment" class, a multimedia entity, with "Dominant Color" class, a descriptor entity. "Dominant Color" is a subclass of "Color" class and "Color" is a subclass of "Visual Descriptor". By following this subclass chain, "Video Segment" class is further related to "Color" class and "Visual Descriptor" class, both of them are descriptor entities. Properties can also be viewed as links between individuals from domain and individuals from range.

15.3.1 Languages

There are several ontology languages in the literature (like OWL or WSMO family) available with different expressiveness and reasoning capabilities. The main criteria for the selection of an ontology language are its knowledge representation mechanism and the inferencing reasoning support needed by an application. The high complexity of multimedia modeling requires a representation language with high semantic expressiveness. OWL combines the required expressiveness for multimedia ontologies and the compliance to W3C standards. Consequently, it is the most appropiate language for multimedia knowledge representation. On the other hand, there are languages that are specifically devised for multimedia applications that are able to integrate the conceptual and media spaces. In (Ghosh et al. 2007), M-OWL is presented as an extension of the OWL and supports the explicit definition of media properties for the concepts. In (Chang et al. 1995) TAO-XML language paradigm is defined for representing multimedia objects based on: (1) hypergraph that specifies the component objects and their structural relations; and (2) a knowledge structure which describes the enviroment and the actions of the object.

15.3.2 Properties

The two main advantadges of multimedia ontologies are: (1) the possibility to associate automatically occurences of events or entities to higher level concepts by checking their proximity to visual concepts that are hierarchically linked to higher level semantics; and (2) the unification in the same ontology of both specific domain concepts and their multimedia low and mid level descriptions allowing the development of more user friendly interfaces for contend-based browsing and retrieval.

These advantadges model the domain of multimedia data, specially the visualizations in still images and videos in terms of low-level features and media structure descriptions. Low-level features are machine-oriented and can be automatically extracted, for instance MPEG-7, whereas high-level semantic concepts require manual annotation of the medium or are restricted to a specific domain.

MPEG-7 standard is formally known as Multimedia Content Description Interface. While the prior standards focus on coding representation of audio and visual content, MPEG-7 focuses on description of multimedia content. MPEG-7 complements the existing MPEG standards suite and aims to be applicable to many existing formats, which include non-MPEG format and non-compressed formats as well. Table 15.1 summarizes the most important parts of the MPEG-7 standard suitable to manage legal multimedia files. In the literature there are several works that describe the different parts of the MPEG-7 standard, see for instance (Avaro and Salembier 2001; Hunter, 2001; Sikora, 2001).

Table 15.1 Brief description of the 5 parts of the MPEG-7 standard suitable to manage legal multimedia contents

• **Part 1 Systems**: specifies system level functionalities, such as preparation of MPEG-7 descriptions for transport/storage, synchronization of content descriptions, and development of conformance decoders
• **Part 2 Description Definition Language**: is a derived by extension of XML schema to address other requirements specific to MPEG-7
• **Part 3 Visual**: specifies features such as color, texture, shape and motion. Other elements required are structure, viewpoint, localization, and temporal
• **Part 4 Audio**: addresses different classes of audio
• **Part 5 Multimedia Description Schemes**: specifies a high-level framework that allows generic description of all kinds of multimedia

Multimedia ontologies can be of two types:

- **Media-specific ontologies** (domain independent): they have taxonomies of different media types and describes properties of different media.
- **Content-specific ontologies** (domain ontology): they describe the subject of the resource, such as the setting or participants. Since these ontologies are not specific to the media, they could be reused by other documents that deal with the same domain.

The most common applications of a multimedia ontology are either content visualization, content indexing, knowledge sharing, learning and reasoning. Focused on one or more of the following purposes: annotation, analysis, retrieval (context-based retrieval), reasoning, personalized filtering and meta-modeling (ontologies used to model multimedia processes and procedures).

15.3.3 Related Work

In the literature, there are several works that address the multimedia ontology issue. As we stated before, the possibility of extending linguistic ontologies with multimedia ontologies has been suggested in (Jaimes et al. 2003) to support video understanding. Here, authors suggest the use of modal keywords, that is, keywords that represent perceptual concepts in several categories such as visual, aural, etc. In (Mezaris et al. 2004) a hierarchy of ontologies has been defined for the representation of the results of video segmentation. Concepts are mapped in keywords and are mapped in an object ontology, a shot ontology and a semantic ontology. In (Vembu et al. 2006) a sport event ontology is proposed to overcome the limitation in describing semantics of videos using MPEG-7. Multimedia Ontology Manager (MOM) (Bertini et al. 2006) is a complete system, which has been developed according to the priciples and concepts of pictorially enriched ontologies. It facilitates the performing of automatic annotations and creates extended text comentaries of video sequences. An approach to semantic video object detection is presented in (Dasiopoulou et al. 2005). Here, semantic concepts are defined in RDF(S) ontology together with qualitative attributes, low-level features, object spatial relations and multimedia processing methods.

The annotation of sports videos is an important issue and researchers have been dedicating importants efforts in this field. In (Bertini et al. 2007), a solution for the implementation of multimedia ontologies for the soccer video annotation is shown. Visual prototypes are added as specialization concepts defined in a classical ontology. In addition, the more general concepts are put in correspondence with the more general visual features of the video like color and texture, while the more specific concepts of the domain are put in correspondence with domain specific visual features. A semi-automatic annotation of soccer videos from text is presented in (Alan et al. 2008). The annotated videos are stored in MPEG-7 format in an object-oriented database. The main idea is to align the extracted metadata with the corresponding video segments, allowing users to query videos according to their semantic meaning.

Traditionally, annotations of multimedia documents have been focused on two different directions: the first approach consist of low-level descriptors as dominant color ; the second approach is oriented to the content dimension and corresponding annotations as person or vehicle. A software environment to bridge between the two directions is M-OntoMat-Annotizer (Petridis et al. 2006) that allows for linking low-level MPEG-7 visual descriptions to conventional Semantic Web Ontologies and annotations. The constructed ontologies include prototypical instances of high-level domain concepts together with a formal specification of corresponding visual descriptors. It allows the formalization of the interrelationships of high and low level multimedia concept descriptions allowing new multimedia content analysis, reasoning and retrieval. In (Dong and Li 2006), a multimedia ontology based on MPEG-7 multimedia description tools is presented. Here, the authors propose an strategy to integrate multiple domain ontologies and design a term extraction procedure to automatically extract domain specific ontological terms from textual resources of multimedia data.

15.3.4 Legal Multimedia Ontologies and Semantic Concepts Extraction

In the legal domain, the annotation, index and tag of the multimedia contents have become and important issue. In Spain, the Civil Procedure Act of January 7th, 2000 (1/2000) introduces the video recording of oral hearings. Consequently, Spanish civil courts are currently producing a massive number of multimedia files that have substituted the written transcripts and have become part of the judicial file, together with suits, indictments, injunctions, judgments and pieces of evidence. Lawyers, prosecutors and judges need to access these contents when preparing similar cases or when appealing to superior courts. Furthermore, the 1/2000 Civil Procedure Act does not include a protocol establishing how to obtain audiovisual records. In addition, the procedures to store, classify and retrieve audiovisual records may vary even from court to court, with no common database available to store the audiovisual records.

Usually, multimedia documents require a cognition stage where codified elements that contribute to their understanding are recognized. Data inside multimedia usually is represented in a implicit way making difficult even for machines or humans to represent it from a low level of description. In the e-sentencias project (Casanovas et al. 2009), authors make an important effort to develop a framework that allows: (1) playing on-line judicial videos stored in a centralized database; and (2) semantic-based annotation of the legal multimedia contents. The aim was to classify legal videos from oral hearings in function of their typology. From the experience, we reported that ontologies are a powerful tool where represent important elements for classification and their relationship. A set of expert lawyers defined the set of elements, events and their relationships that characterized the process of video typology classification. In spite of that, we found that most of the key elements were defined by experts in a high-level of description, for instance, either when someone says some word or when someone is talking. In order to be able to define higher level elements from multimedia data, system must rely into computer cognitive approaches like some machine learning methods. As an example, even if a legal procedure is represented by an ontology, a diarization process was carried out using the audio signal to define when someone in the courtroom is talking. Building an ontology that is able to work with higher level data within the multimedia files could be done by adding elements able to combine the results and uncertainly of concrete pattern recognition methods. On the other hand, in (González-Conejero et al. 2010) the management of these multimedia contents including their semantic annotation is discussed. In this work, a centralized scheme is proposed and the management of the files provided by the judicial domain is carried out by two international standards as MPEG-7 and JPEG2000.

Other works, (Gracia et al. 2010a, b), manage multimedia contents where emotional speech analysis is performed for mediation and court environments and speech diarization is used for the annotation of legal multimedia contents, respectively. There are several semantically rich patterns useful for both navigation and analysis defined on multimedia. In some multimedia like broadcast news, recorder meetings and oral hearings structure of the events can be highly characterized by the sequence and identity of the speakers taking part. Usually multimedia is divided into segments or shots that contain coherent units from the point of view of structure, for example in the video analysis shots are a group of similar consecutive images. In terms of sound analysis, signal is divided into segments each containing a unique sound source, sources are defined by a set of meaningful categories like: speech, music and silence/background. A diarization process is a computational method for label speech segments in terms of the identity of the speaker taking part. Process usually involves both, estimating the number of speakers appearing in the data and also assigning to speakers their own speech segments. State of the art techniques involved in the process include a three step process: (1) break speech segments into turns: sub-segments where probably only one speaker is taking; part (2) cluster turns until reach a statistically plausible number of speakers; and (3) assign speaker identity to each turn belonging to same speaker cluster. As hearings are primarily characterized for being mostly a moderated environment where each participant has specific turns to take part. Diarization on recorder hearings provide: (1) a graphical representation which contains semantical meaning related to the speaker's specific roles; (2) the representation of the oral hearing structure regarding the order and the duration of the interventions. For example the questioning performed by a lawyer to a witness could be easily identified by searching a set of interrelated interventions.

Speech analysis also can provide a set of emotional tags on speech segments. Emotions are embedded inside human speech and they are reflected on it by certain signal patterns. This speech patterns are reflected in both spectral properties: loudness, pitch, etc. and temporal evolution: short term perturbations characteristic of arousal, lower duration of syllables, etc. Emotional analysis on speech can be approached by using a machine learning classification scheme, where a classifier or a combination of classifiers is used for learn acoustic characteristics of certain emotions. An emotional speech database is required in order to extract features and train the classifier. Given a novel utterance speech is segmented into structural (phonetically-related) units. Features are extracted from each segment and the classifier scheme provides a probability or distanced of the segment features to a certain learned emotion.

Nevertheless, in these works no multimedia ontologies are used. It is clear that to capture all the semantic concepts that the diarization and emotional speech recognition mentioned above manage is a complex issue. In other words, to apply multimedia ontologies directly to the extraction of multiemdia concepts detection is to bridge the semantic gap. A fundamental requirement is to be able to capture the multimedia's semantic content in such a way that corresponds to the human view of multiemdia semantics. Different methods for generic concept detection have been extensively studied, but the question of how to exploit the structure of a multimedia ontology and existing inter-concept relations has not received similar attention. In (Koskela et al. 2007) a measuring concept similarity in multimedia ontologies based on a clustering method is discussed.

15.4 Conclusions

Legal professionals consume most of their time searching and retrieving legal information. Furthermore, the explosion of legal multimedia contents in the judicial domain produces an enormous quantity of these files that have to be stored in a way that facilitates the search process. E-discovery and e-learning are fields that also need to store the information in a structured manner to improve the search and retrieving applications. This work is aimed to study the application of multimedia ontologies to the legal multimedia contents taking advantage of the combination of multimedia elements, terms present in classical ontologies and the flexible representation of knowledge that classical ontologies provide. However, to place the semantic information extracted from a multimedia file into a multimedia ontology is a drawback that arise due to the semantic gap.

Language used to implement the ontology is also an important issue. There are several approaches as the OWL or WSMO family. The OWL combines the expresiveness for multimedia ontologies and the compliance to the W3C, making it suitable to represent legal multimedia ontologies. On the other hand, there are languages that are specifically devised to manage this kind of ontologies with multimedia content.

Traditionally, ontologies have been associated with logical inferencing, although, recent research efforts have begun to be applied to the Semantic Web. Legal ontologies are domain ontologies, that is, specific ontologies and represent a specific knowledge. Nevertheless, the implantation of audiovisual material in the judicial domain and the limitation that arise when classical ontologies deal with multimedia contents suggest that multimedia ontologies are suitable to improve the representation of knowledge in this field improving the search and retrieval applications. Most of the proposals in multimedia ontologies rely in the MPEG-7 standard and its visual descriptions. In addition, the MPEG-7 is composed by 10 parts which 5 of these parts are suitable to manage legal multimedia files, providing a flexible fashion to manage these kind of files.

Finally, we can conclude that the management of legal multimedia files through the MPEG-7 standard and multimedia ontologies can improve the storage requirements and the semantics/metadata management produced by the annotation process. The state-of-the-art summarized in this work is fully applicable to the legal domain. However, the particularities of the judicial procedures—for instance, the closed structure of oral hearings—have to been taken into account to improve the concept and event detection. Nevertheless, it is clear that the application of multimedia ontologies into fields like diarization, or emotion speech recognition have several drawbacks due to the semantic gap. That is, to place the high-level concepts extracted from multimedia files in these fields into a multimedia ontology is a complex issue because of machines are not able to understand the implicit meaning within the multimedia contents.

Acknowledgments This work has been partially supported by the Spanish Government (Ministerio de Ciencia e Innovación and Ministerio de Industria, Turismo y Comercio) under Grants TSI-020501-2008-131 and CSO2008-05536.

References

Alan, O., S. Akpinar, O. Sabuncu, N. Cicekli, F. Alpaslan (2008). Ontological Video Annotation and Querying System for Soccer Games. In *International Symposium on Computer and Information Sciences*, Istambul, Turkey, 1–6.

Avaro, O., P. Salembier (2001). MPEG-7 Systems: Overview. *IEEE Transactions on Circuits and Systems for Video Technology*, 11(6): 760–764.

Ballan, L., M. Bertini, A. Del Bimbo, G. Serra (2010). Video Annotation and Retrieval Using Ontologies and Rule Learning. *IEEE Multimedia*, in press.

Baron, J.R., P. Thompson (2007). The Search Problem Posed by Large Heterogeneous Data Sets in Litigation: Possible Future Approaches to Research. In *International Conference on Artificial Intelligence and Law*. ACM, Barcelona, 141–147.

Berners-Lee, T., J. Hendler, O. Lassila (2001). The Semantic Web. *Scientific American*, 284(5): 34–43.

Bertini, M., A.D. Bimbo, C. Torniai (2007). Soccer Video Annotation Using Ontologies Extended with Visual Prototypes. In *International Workshop Content-Based Multimedia Indexing*, Bordeaux, France, 212–218.

Bertini, M., A.D. Bimbo, C. Torniai, R. Cucchiara, C. Grana (2006). MOM: Multimedia Ontology Manager. A Framework for Automatic Annotation and Semantic Retrieval of Video Sequences. In *International Multimedia Conference. Proceedings of the 14th annual ACM international conference on Multimedia*, 787–788.

Brickell, J.L., A.M. Langer (2009). Adapting to the Data Explosion: Ensuring Justice For All. In *IEEE International Conference on Systems, Man and Cibernet-ics Society*. IEEE, 86–90.

Casanovas, P., X. Binefa, C. Gracia, E. Teodoro, N. Galera, M. Blazquez, M. Poblet, J. Carrabina, M. Monton, C. Montero, J. Serrano, J.M. Lopez-Cobo (2009). *Law, Ontologies and the Semantic Web: Channeling the Legal Information Flood*, vol. 188 of *Frontiers in Artificial Intelligence and Applications*, Chapter The e-Sentencias Prototype: A Procedural Ontology for Legal Multimedia Applications. IOS Press, Amsterdam, Netherlands, 199–219.

Chang, H., S. Chang, T. Hou, A. Hsu (1995). The Management and the Applications of Tele-Action Objects. *ACM Journal of Multimedia Systems*, 3(5–6): 204–216.

Dasiopoulou, S., V. Mezaris, I. Kompatsiaris, V. Papastathis, M. Strintzis (2005). Knowledge-Assisted Semantic Video Objectdetection. *IEEE Transactions on Circuits andSystems for Video Technology*, 15(10): 1210–1224.

Dong, A., H. Li (2006). Multi-Ontology Based Multimedia Annotation for Domain-Specific Information Retrieval. In *IEEE International Conference on Sensor Networks, Ubiquitous, and Trustworthy Computing*, 158–165.

Ghosh, H., S. Chaudhury, K. Kashyap, B. Maiti (2007). *Ontologies. A Handbook of Principles, Concepts and Applications in Information Systems*, vol. 14 of *Information Systems*. Springer, US, 265–296.

Gonzalez, J., D. Rowe, J. Varona, F.X. Roca (2008). Understanding Dynamic Scenes Based on Human Sequence Evaluation. *Image and Vision Computing*, 27(10):1433–1444.

Gonzalez-Conejero, J., E. Teodoro, N. Galera (2010). *Intelligent Multimedia: Managing Creative Works in a Digital World*, vol. 8 of *Legal Information and Communication Technologies*, Chapter Legal Multimedia Management and Semantic Annotation for Improved Search and Retrieval. EPAP, 395–408.

Gracia, C., X. Binefa, M. Poblet (2010). *Intelligent Multimedia: Managing Creative Works in a Digital World*, vol. 8 of *Legal Information and Communication Technologies*, Chapter Emotional Speech Analysis in Mediation and Court Environments. EPAP, 364–378.

Gracia, C., X. Binefa, E. Teodoro, N. Galera (2010). *Intelligent Multimedia: Managing Creative Works in a Digital World*, vol. 8 of *Legal Information and Communication Technologies*, chapter Diarization for the Annotation of Legal Videos. EPAP, 379–393.

Gruber, T.A. (1993). A Translation Approach to Portable Ontology Specifications. *Knowledge Acquisition*, 5(2): 199–220.

Guarino, N. (1998). *Formal Ontology in Information Systems*, Chapter Formal Ontology and Information Systems. IOS Press, Amsterdam, Netherlands, 3–15.

Hunter, J. (2001). An Overview of the MPEG-7 Description Definition Language (DDL). *IEEE Transactions on Circuits and Systems for Video Technology*, 11(6): 765–772.

Jaimes, A., B. Tseng, J. Smith (2003). Modal Keywords, Ontologies, and Reasoning for Video Understanding. In *International Conference on Image and Video Retrieval (CIVR 2003)*.

Koskela, M., A.F. Smeaton, J. Laaksonen (2007). Measuring Concept Similarities in Multimedia Ontologies: Analysis and Evaluations. *IEEE Transactions on Multimedia*, 9(5): 912–922.

Mezaris, V., I. Kompatsiaris, N. Boulgouris, M. Strintzis (2004). Real-Time Compressed-Domain Spatiotemporal Segmentation and Ontologies for Video Indexing and Retrieval. *IEEE Transactions on Circuits and Systems for Video Technology*, 14(5): 606–621.

Petridis, K., D. Anastasopoulos, C. Saathoff, C. Timmermann, I. Kompatsiaris, S. Staab (2006). M-OntoMat-Annotizer: Image Annotation. Linking Ontologies and Multimedia Low-Level Features. In *Engineered Applications ofSe-mantic Web Session (SWEA) at the 10th International Conference on Knowledge-Based and Intelligent Information and Engineering Systems (KES 2006)*, Bournemouth, UK, 633–640.

Sikora, T. (2001). The MPEG-7 Visual Standard for Content Description – An Overview. *IEEE Transactions on Circuits and Systems for Video Technology*, 11(6): 696–702.

A. Smeulders, M. Worring, S. Santini, A. Gupta, R. Jain (2000). Content-Based Image Retrieval at the End of the Early Years. *IEEE Transactions on Pattern Analysis and Machine Intelligence*, 22(12): 1349–1380.

Snoek, C.G., B. Huurnink, L. Hollink, M. de Rijke, G. Schreiber, M. Worring (2007). Adding Semantics to Detectors for Video Retrieval. *IEEE Transactions on Multimedia*, 9(5): 975–986.

Snoek, C.G., M. Worring, J. van Gemert, J. Geusebroek, A. Smeulders (2006). The Challenge Problem for Automated Detection of 101 Semantic Concepts in Multimedia. In *MULTIMEDIA '06: Proceedings of the 14th annual ACM international conference on Multimedia*, New York, NY, 421–430.

Vembu, S., M. Kiesel, M. Sintek, S. Bauman (2006). Towards Bridging the Semantic Gap in the Multimedia Annotation and Retrieval. In *First International Workshop on Semantic Web Annotations for Multimedia (SWAMM)*, Edinburgh, Scotland, UK.

Xin, C. (2009). E-Learning Applications and Challenges. In *International Conference on Future Information Technology and Management Engineering*. IEEE, Sanya, China, 580–583.

Zha, Z.-J., T. Mei, Z. Wang, X.-S. Hua (2007). Building a Comprehensive Ontology to Refine Video Concept Detection. In *Proceedings of the International Workshop On Multimedia Information Retrieval*, Augsburg, Bavaria, Germany, 227–236.

Author Index

G. Sartor et al. (eds.) *Approaches to Legal Ontologies*, Law, Governance
and Technology Series 1, DOI 10.1007/978-94-007-0120-5,
© Springer Science+Business Media B.V. 2011

Concepts Index

Lightning Source UK Ltd.
Milton Keynes UK
06 January 2011

165235UK00001B/27/P